Public
Budgeting and
Management

Public Budgeting and Management

Alan Walter Steiss
Virginia Polytechnic Institute
and State University

Lexington Books
D.C. Heath and Company
Lexington, Massachusetts
Toronto   London

213340

Third printing September 1975

Published simultaneously in Canada.

Printed in the United States of America.

International Standard Book Number: 0–669–82149–7

Library of Congress Catalog Card Number: 77–186340

Table of Contents

CONTENTS   ix

List of Figures

List of Tables

Preface

Strategic planning and urban management, budget analysis, and the scheduling and control of public activities require significant long-term professional training. It is important, however, that all students of urban affairs gain a fuller understanding and appreciation of these basic components of the budgetary and public management process. The primary objective of this book is to provide such an understanding.

Governments, like private organizations and individuals, are constrained by a scarcity of resources. No matter how much money it can command, no government can avoid the need for compromise among objectives—both present and future. The allocation, timing, and staging of resources to carry out public programs are basic to long-range policy objectives of government. Government policies can be determined most effectively if a rational choice is made among alternative courses of action, with full knowledge of the implications of each alternative. To achieve such knowledge, quantitative and qualitative management information must be collected, organized, analyzed, and communicated in a systematic manner in order to cast light on the consequences of spending limited public resources in various directions.

The first six chapters deal with the field of public management. Public management, as defined here, involves the application of management science techniques to the field of public administration. In these six chapters, an examination is made of: the appropriate scope for the emerging field of public management, the potential applications of systems techniques in public decision-making, concepts of public administration and policy formation, authority relations, and the importance of communication in public decision-making. The first part of the book concludes with a suggested model for public decision-making.

Chapters 7 through 12 deal with the process of public budgeting. In this second part, the techniques of management science are discussed in the context of public resource allocation. An elaboration of the systemic planning approach is offered and an examination is made of the use of cost-effectiveness analysis in public decision-making. This discussion concludes with an examination of the politics of public budgeting.

The author would like to acknowledge the contributions of several colleagues in the preparation of the following chapters: Chapter 7, Roy F. Kenzie; Chapter 8, Leo Jakobson; and Chapter 12, Jean S. March and George William Cox; and to Eric Snyder for the preparation of the illustrations.

1 Systems Techniques in Public Management

Effective public management is increasingly becoming a most complex and difficult task. Not only is the margin for error between success and failure shrinking, but matters that require management often appear to be unmanageable. Managing the many separate but interrelated activities of a public program is often more complicated than performing the activities themselves. Increasing demands for timely decisions, rapid technological change, shorter effective lifespans of governmental programs, and an overall faster tempo in urban society combine to make management responsibilities in the public sector more demanding and more intractable.

Public Management — What Is It?

Effective management involves the direction, coordination, and control of resources to achieve some purpose or objective. Management is frequently referred to as "the art of getting things done." It is a dynamic art, involving a blending and directing of human and physical resources available in a system of administration. The basic objective of effective management is to bring into focus and give consistency to action programs in the achievement of some required goal.

The concept of management evokes many images. Making a profit in a corporation, winning a battle, passing an examination, or preparing a budget, all require management. While these examples represent four rather diverse activities, management can be generalized to cover these and all other similar tasks that might be identified.

Although many concrete examples of the tasks of management in the public sector can be given, in truth there is no good definition of public management. Or perhaps it should be said that, while there are good short definitions, there are no good short explanations. The immediate effect of all one-sentence or one-paragraph definitions of public management tends to be mental paralysis rather than enlightenment and stimulation. This is because any serious definition of a complex activity — as against an epigrammatical definition, however witty — inevitably contains several abstract words or phrases which can be explained only by reference to other abstract words and phrases. In the process, the reality and importance of "it" — the activity being defined — becomes clouded and lost.

1

With this warning in mind, an attempt may be made to define public management in terms of the procedural tasks with which it must be concerned:

1. Establishment of overall strategic goals and objectives and selection of objectives of a particular public enterprise
2. Determination of requirements to meet these objectives and the establishment of necessary operations or activities to carry out the strategic plan, including a selection of the best sequence for performance of these operations (the operations plan)
3. Determination of available resources (men, money, machines, materials, and time) needed for the public program as a whole, and the judicious allocation of these resources according to the operations plan (the operations schedule)
4. Control of the entire process from point of decision or commitment to completion by reacting to deviations between predicted and actual progress in order to insure that the public program will be kept to its schedule

The functions of public management are best performed as a balance between objective method and subjective ability. The effectiveness of public management is measured by the results (performance or output) achieved and particularly by the response time required to make necessary adjustments when things go wrong.

This operational definition of public management consciously attempts to circumvent the long-standing controversy over the so-called *policy-administration dichotomy*.[a] The "separation of functions" doctrine is abandoned in this definition on the grounds that it is an unrealistic and unnecessary distinction in modern government. Both the functions of the policy-maker and the policy administrator are encompassed by the concept of public management as outlined above.[b]

---

[a]Under this doctrine, the processes of government are divided into two basic parts: (1) deciding what should be done (the function and definition of politics); and (2) carrying out the decision (the role and definition of public administration). Since this doctrine had a most significant influence on the development of the field of public administration, a further examination of the concept will be presented in a subsequent section.

[b]The concepts of organization and management may require further explication at this point. Organization is structure; management is functioning. Each is dependent upon and inconceivable without the other. Organization and management are merely convenient categories of analysis – two different ways of viewing the same phenomena. One is static and seeks formal patterns; the other is dynamic and follows movement. Organization may be defined as the structure of authoritative and habitual personal interrelations in a management system. Management is action intended to achieve rational cooperation in an organizational system.

Decision-Making as a Function of Public Management

Decision-making is one of the most pervasive functions of public management. If an agency is to carry out its mandate, decisions must be made and action programs arising from these decisions must be implemented effectively. Rational decision-making, however, is dependent upon effective analysis of the problems confronting the agency and a long-range planning framework through which goals and objectives can be identified and policies and programs can be systematically evaluated.

To make effective decisions, pertinent and timely information must be available to public management. Decision-makers in the public sector are constantly deluged by a vast sea of data. Often these data are disorganized and irrelevant to the problem at hand. Needed facts, even when presented, frequently are impossible to extract. Therefore, at the heart of effective public management is the need to develop a well-organized, on-going *management information system*.

Before any decision is reached, certain specific questions should be raised; among these are the following:

1. What are the alternative courses of action, if any?
2. What is the cost (and benefits) associated with each alternative?
3. What are the risks?
4. What uncertainties surround the problem situation?
5. When must the decision be made?
6. What will be the consequences if the decision is delayed?

In managing public programs — both large and small — failure to have answers to these and other basic questions can be costly or even disastrous.

In recent years, the field of management science has provided managers and administrators with vastly improved techniques for goal identification, problem analysis, and decision-making. Management scientists have noted that decision-making can be considered in many ways. Some decisions — particularly those concerning tactical considerations — can be made with some degree of certainty as to the outcome of subsequent actions. However, there are a great number of situations in which the decision-maker must deal with an uncertain future, and his decisions also involve a certain amount of risk.[c] In general, it is the responsibility of management to reduce uncertainty and to bring risk

---

[c]Although the terms are often used interchangeably, there is a significant distinction between "uncertainty" and "risk." This distinction will be discussed more fully in a subsequent section.

within certain tolerable limits and thereby to improve the rational basis upon which to make public decisions.

Public Management and Planning

As the program demands of government continue to increase in both size and complexity, ways must be found to develop better program plans, to allocate more effectively the available resources to program activities, and to control more closely all aspects of public programs in the face of rising uncertainty as to the future.[d] Quite obviously, planning is a vital function of public management. To date, however, traditional concepts of public planning frequently have been an appendage to, rather than a vital part of, the processes public management.

In attempting to identify the appropriate role of planning in public management, a distinction must be made between *strategic planning* and *operations planning*. Strategic planning involves the selection of overall goals and objectives and the development of strategies (including policies and guidelines) for achieving those objectives. Operations planning is concerned with tactics of performance and the use of resources to achieve the overall objectives which are integral parts of strategic plans. Operations planning is concerned primarily with the programming, scheduling, and control of various individual program activities. Effective and efficient operations planning *always* means the difference between "on time" and "late." Effective and comprehensive strategic planning *can* mean the difference between success and failure in the delivery of vital public services.

Many practitioners in the field of public administration espouse a planning posture. Frequently, however, their approach is limited to a form of operations planning. While a critical aspect of the public management process, operations planning without strategic planning can do little to reduce the uncertainty that surrounds many of the activities of government. As a consequence, public programs may be carried out more efficiently, but the more important issue of their effectiveness — their ability to achieve long-range and comprehensive objectives — will be left unresolved.

The Application of Management Science
Techniques in the Public Sector: A Caution

Various techniques have been developed in the field of management science for dealing with risk and uncertainty; some of the more significant of these

---

[d]Public management operates through programs and projects. In certain operations, there is a continuous cycle of activities or process over which management must exercise control. In other situations the program may be a one-time job. Both types of operations, however, can be classified as programs. The first can be considered continuous and the second static. A static project or program, basically, is one which has a definable beginning and a definable end.

techniques will be discussed later. Linear and mathematical (nonlinear) programming, quadratic and differential equations, the theory of games, probability theory, search theory, data derivation and deduction, stochastic processes, matrix algebra, symbolic logic, simulation, cost-benefit analysis, information theory and the like — these are some of the esoteric terms for the new techniques in decision-making.

A caution must be advanced at the outset, however, against a notion too often assumed these days to be a reality, namely, that much of public decision-making is going to become automated. Some authors would have us believe that these techniques of management science eventually will take over, "solving" the critical problems and "making" the actual decisions. One writer even speaks of "instant planning" (i.e., the point at which enough hard data can be stored in a computer to make long-range planning decisions on a "real-time" basis) as a realizable objective in the near future. The techniques of management science do not relieve the decision-maker of the responsibility for making decisions. Their application merely provides him with better information upon which to base his judgment; with greater rationality upon which to apply intuitive choice. Some of the analytical techniques of management science, such as linear programming, probability theory, cost-benefit analysis, and simulation, are of proven value; others, such as quadratic programming, operational gaming, and search theory, have potential value; still others, like formal game theory, appear to have little or no practical application to most public decision situations. In general, these techniques are of the greatest value where the effects of a large number of controlled variables must be considered, where the number of relevant uncontrollable variables is small, where relevant causes and effects are factual in nature and can be stated and measured numerically or symbolically, and where there are reasons to believe that past relationships will continue to hold in the future.

The major limitations of such methods are significant, however; among these are the following: (1) factors of a value nature in decision-making, of necessity, must frequently be excluded because they cannot be described or measured objectively — judgments must be tempered with considerations of qualitative factors even after all the quantitative tests are made; (2) specialists often must work with assumptions that may not be valid, such as the assumption that critical relationships identified in the past will hold in the future; (3) automated data processing equipment is often necessary because the utilization of some mathematical formulae would be seriously limited if economical computation techniques were not available; (4) since qualitative factors cannot be made part of the formula, these techniques often cannot identify the "best" alternative to a given decision situation; and finally, (5) these techniques cannot implement decisions. To amplify this last point: only the most naive, inexperienced administrator would assume that properly made decisions, as a rule, will be carried out properly. Therefore, there is a constant need to provide techniques for evaluating performance and mechanisms to check on the fulfillment of decisions and the adherence to overall strategic planning objectives.

Thus, until the intangible and unmeasurable elements that necessarily affect decision-making can be quantified, many of the techniques of management science will have only limited application in certain areas of decision-making. Even the experts insist that the final decisions can rest only with management and will continue to be made by human beings.

It remains the purpose of this book to examine the concepts and techniques of management science and to relate their application to the art and science of effective public management in a dynamic, changing society. Emphasis will be placed on the processes and methods for ensuring incisive action in the processes of public management and budgeting.

Systems Techniques in Public Decision-Making

Broadly speaking, any orderly analytic study designed to help a decision-maker identify a preferred course of action from among possible alternatives might be called a systems analysis. Systems analysis, as a formal problem-solving approach, had its origins in the defense sector during and following World War II. Systems analysis represents an approach to, or way of looking at, complex problems of choice (decision-making) under uncertainty. As such, it should have extensive application and utility in the field of public management.

Such an extension of the techniques of systems analysis to the public sector is long overdue. While systems analysis has received widespread application in the "hard" sciences and in the military sector, it has barely entered the domain of the social sciences. In planning, education, welfare and health, and other nonmilitary activities, as Olaf Helmer has remarked in his perceptive essay:

. . . we are faced with an abundance of challenges: how to keep peace, how to alleviate the hardships of social change, how to provide food and comfort for the in-affluent, how to improve the social institutions and the values of the affluent, how to cope with revolutionary innovations, and so on.[1]

Growing Interest in Public Applications of Systems Analysis

It was perhaps inevitable that pressures would emerge from all levels of government to apply a "systems" approach in an effort to resolve the problems confronting government. In the United States and Great Britain, especially, the call has gone out for more scientific approaches to the planning and administration of governmental programs — from Congressmen and members of

Parliament to small-town mayors; from Cabinet members to community welfare workers; from labor leaders to professors.

Actually, systematic analysis of routine operations is widespread throughout the civil government as well as in commerce, industry, and the military. In these applications, analysis takes its most mathematical form and, in a certain sense, its most fruitful role. Such problems typically involve an attempt to increase the efficiency of a man-machine system in a situation where it is clear what "more efficient" means. Analysis often can be reduced to the application of a well-understood mathematical discipline, such as linear programming or queuing theory, to a generic "model." By a specification of its parameters, the model can be made to fit a wide variety of operations. An "optimum" solution is then obtained by means of a systematic computational routine. Analysis of this type is usually called operations research rather than systems analysis.

There are many other decisions or problems, civilian as well as military, where computational techniques can help only with subproblems. Such problems will normally involve more than the efficient allocation of resources among alternative uses. They are not "solvable" in the same sense as efficiency problems in which some "payoff" function can be maximized in a clear expression of what one is trying to accomplish. Under these more complex situations, the objectives or goals of the action to be taken must be determined first. Decision problems associated with program budgeting are mainly of this type — where the difficulty lies in deciding what ought to be done as well as in how to do it, where it is not clear what "more efficient" means, and where many of the factors in the problem elude quantification. Final program recommendations thus must remain, in part, a matter of faith and judgment.

Definition of a System

An obvious first step in exploring the wider-spread application of systems techniques in the field of public management is to spell out more fully the terms to be used. Hall and Hagen provide the following definition of a *system*: " . . . a set of objects together with relationships between the objects and between their attributes."[2] Further, they define *objects* as the parts or components of the system and *attributes* as the properties of objects, and point out that the *relationships* to which they refer are those that "tie the system together."

In general, then, a system may be defined as any entity, real or conceptual, which is composed of interrelated or linked parts. These parts can consist of activities and events as well as objects and concepts. Interrelationships are a key aspect of the systems concept.

The concepts outlined above constitute a widely held definition of a system; yet, they are so broad as to include virtually any interdependent set of activities or things. A computer is a system, composed of a processor, data-receiving and data-emission elements, control elements, and a memory. An automobile engine is a system which uses several resource inputs such as air, gasoline, oil, and electricity; has a structure of pistons, valves, sparkplugs, a crankshaft, and so forth; and has certain measurable performance outputs. A community is a system, composed of interacting units designed to meet basic human needs.

These somewhat diverse examples of systems have several characteristics in common. Each has a *structural configuration* (an arrangement of component parts), and each performs certain *functions*. Each system operates in a larger *environment* (or as a subsystem of some larger system) and requires certain *inputs* from this environment.[e] A system can be thought of as moving through various states, following some definable *process* or set of procedures (the dynamic aspects of a system). Each of the systems cited produces a set of *outputs* (which are related, in turn, to the functional aspects of the system). These outputs have a *feedback* effect on the system as a whole by providing new inputs on subsequent cycles and by suggesting necessary modification in structure and process to improve performance. While many disciplines choose to focus on one particular aspect of a system as a vehicle for analysis, a complete understanding of a given system can be derived only by taking cognizance of all these aspects.

Several other systems characteristics are important to an understanding of the conceptual development of systems theory. The *boundaries* of a system often may be defined somewhat arbitrarily depending on the interests of the person studying a particular system. Outside these boundaries is the larger environment in which the system operates and with which the open system interacts. Large, complex systems tend to have an *equilibrium position* or *position of stability* to which a system tends to return after it has been disturbed.[f] As Litterer observes: "This return is usually a result of compensating actions on the part of the system. Hence it can appear that the system is attempting or seeking to return to this point or, as it is sometimes expressed, the organization or system is seeking this goal."[3]

Closed systems characteristically "run down," in that energy differences among the system elements disappear until some common level is reached. This is the characteristic known as *entropy*. In a living organism, for example,

---

[e]This concept must be understood within the context of *open* and *closed* systems. A system is closed, according to von Bertalanffy, "... if no material enters or leaves it." A system is open "... if there is import and export and, therefore, change of the components." ("The Theory of Open Systems in Physics and Biology," in *Systems Thinking*, edited by F. E. Emery (Baltimore, 1969), p. 70.)

[f]In systems terms, a *disturbance* is viewed as simply that event which initiates change within a system. A disturbance may be positive or negative (functional or dysfunctional), and it may be internally induced or may come about as a result of some external force acting on the system.

maximum entropy would be the condition of death. Open systems experience entropy; however, they may possess the ability to overcome it. This ability of open systems to overcome entropy centers on the concept of *equifinality*. Whereas in a closed system, the initial state determines absolutely the final condition, in open systems an initial state can have several possible final states and a final state can have several different initial states. This concept reinforces the notion of *teleos*, or goal-directedness, in open systems. By seeking certain goals, an open system can achieve greater organization and thereby counter the tendency toward maximum entropy.

This defense against entropy in open systems is achieved, in part, through the process of *regulation*. This property is evidenced by the fact that the parts or properties of systems can be changed to bring performance of the system toward some point of stability (i.e., to achieve certain goals). Three types of regulation may be identified:

1. Adjustment: in which the whole is reestablished from the original parts
2. Control: where certain predetermined "standards" are defined, and the system's performance is measured against these standards — usually through a process of feedback — and appropriate modifications are made
3. Learning: after several disturbances and use of control mechanisms to regain stability or equilibrium, a system may change its internal characteristics so that it can anticipate similar future disturbances and handle them more effectively

Definition of the Urban System

The term "urban system" has been used by various authors to refer to the physical aspects, institutions, activities, and values which exist within an urban area. These factors can be defined in the context of the systems characteristics outlined above. While a city can be considered a system at the broadest level, it is composed in turn, of a number of component subsystems, such as the political-governmental, economic, social, physical-environmental, and behavioral subsystems. These subsystems, in turn, also are made up of subsystems (or sub-subsystems). The political subsystem, for example, includes such components as political parties, elected administrators, public managers, the mass media, courts, legislative bodies, civic associations, and special interest groups. These systems and subsystems exhibit the properties of general systems described previously and are usually open systems.

The conceptualization of various aspects of urban systems may be aided in their application to the processes of public management by substituting more familiar terminology for some of the concepts outlined thus far. For example, *inputs* may be thought of in terms of "resources," "goals," "values," or "intentions." The *conversion process*, whereby inputs are transformed into outputs, may be seen to involve the processes of "decision-making," "planning," and "program implementation." *Outputs* may be viewed as "products," "decisions," "performance," or "achievement of objectives." *Feedback* involves the processes of "management," "control," and "regulation."

In general, systems theory does not seek to examine individual components of a system at some given point in time. The theory, rather, takes a holistic point of view, concerned with the interrelations and functioning of a total system over time. This is not a simple approach to large, complex, open systems such as an urban system. As Litterer has pointed out:

. . . viewing organizations as open systems leaves the organization open to many disturbances, demands, and difficulties, previously assumed away. It brings to the fore a most crucial question: how are the various elements of the organization controlled and coordinated to produce the means of satisfying the needs and goals of the many who have claims on the organization? [4]

Definition of Analysis

"Analysis" is a more familiar term, meaning roughly the act of investigation or examination. In its generic sense, analysis is derived from the Greek verb of the same spelling meaning "to separate anything into its component parts or elements." In a rigorous sense, an analysis consists of breaking down the whole into its parts in order to find out their nature, proportion, function, and relationship. In chemistry, for example, compounds or mixtures are broken down into their constituent substances in order to determine their composition (qualitative analysis) and proportion (quantitative analysis). In mathematics, problems are broken down into equations and the relations among the variables are examined, e.g., through differential calculus.

Analytical techniques applied through a systems approach, therefore, involve the conjunction of the two concepts and their operational definitions. These techniques involve the separation of a system into its component parts (subsystems) in order to examine their relationships to one another and to the system as a whole.

The Essence of the Systems Method

Application of a systems approach involves a comparison of alternative courses of action in terms of their costs and effectiveness in attaining a specific objective. Usually this comparison attempts to designate the alternative that will minimize costs, subject to some fixed performance requirement (for example, to reduce unemployment to less than 2 percent in two years, or add a certain number of miles to the interstate highway system); or, conversely, it attempts to maximize some physical measure of performance subject to a budget constraint. Such evaluations are called cost-effectiveness analyses, or, alternatively, cost-utility and cost-benefit analysis. Since these analytical techniques often receive the lion's share of attention, the entire study is also frequently called a cost-effectiveness analysis. But this label puts too much emphasis on just one aspect of the decision process. In analyses designed to furnish broad policy advice, other facets of the problem of greater significance than the comparison of alternatives are: (1) the specification of sensible objectives, (2) the determination of a satisfactory way to measure performance, (3) the influence of considerations that cannot be quantified, and (4) the design of better alternatives.

Model Construction: A Framework for Choice

The virtue of a systems approach is that it permits the judgment and intuition of experts in relevant fields to be combined systematically and efficiently. The essence of the method is to construct and operate within a "model," a simplified abstraction of the real situation appropriate to the question. Such a model may take such varied forms as a computer simulation, an operational game, or even a purely verbal "scenario." The model introduces a precise structure and a terminology that serve primarily as an effective means of communication, enabling the participants in the study to exercise their judgment and intuition in a concrete context and in proper relation to others. Moreover, through feedback from the model (the results of computation, the counter-moves in the game, or the critique of the scenario) experts have a chance to revise early judgments and thus arrive at a clearer understanding of the problem and its context, and perhaps of their subject matter. As Charles Hitch has observed, systems techniques ". . . should be looked upon not as the antithesis of judgment but as a framework which permits the judgment of experts in numerous subfields to be utilized — to yield results which transcend any individual judgment."[5]

Asking the Right Questions

In the practical application of systems techniques to problems of the real world, two more essential elements are worth noting. The first is the need to address the right problem in the first place. The second is the need to interpret the results of analysis in terms of real-world decisions or other problems and issues.

As Peter Drucker has suggested, the most common source of error in management decisions arises from an emphasis on finding the *right answer* rather than on asking the *right question*.[6] As Drucker has observed:

. . . the important and difficult job is never to find the right answer, it is to find the right question. For there are few things as useless — if not as dangerous — as the right answer to the wrong question.[7]

Thus, Anatol Rapoport asserts that the first step in solving a problem is to state it.

The statement usually involves a description of an existing state and a desirable state of affairs where the factors involved in the discrepancy are explicitly pointed out. The success with which any problem is solved depends to a great extent on the clarity with which it is stated. In fact, the solution of the problem is, in a sense, a clarification (or concretization) of the objectives.[8]

Vague statements of the situation lead to vague methods, where success is doubtful or, at best, erratic. The more a given situation is extensionalized, the better the classification of the problem, and the greater the promise of a successful solution.

If the problem cannot be stated specifically, preferably in one interrogative sentence which includes one or more goals, then the analysis of the problematic situation has not been adequate or of sufficient depth. Emotional behavior, or the frequent tendency of human beings to seek the path of least resistance, may result in a superficial analysis, followed by a statement of the "apparent" problem instead of the "real" problem. An excellent solution to an apparent problem, of course, will not work in practice, because it is the solution to a problem that does not exist in fact. A short-circuiting of this state in the analysis process actually may result in more time being spent later to get at the real problem when it becomes painfully evident that further analysis is required.

Interpreting the Results of Analyses

Even the best applications of systems techniques have their limitations. Improper applications can be worse than useless. It is all too easy for the analyst to begin to believe his own assumptions, even if drawn out of thin air, and to attach undue significance to the results of his analysis, especially if it involves some sophisticated mathematics and a lot of hard work. Some clients are too easily impressed by analyses, especially if the results come out of electronic computers and are agreeable or plausible and impressively presented.

To be sure, there are some hard-nosed skeptics, but not enough of them. Moreover, some people are skeptical for the wrong reasons; for example, because the results of the analysis are displeasing and not because of questionable features of the analysis process.

In view of these considerations, therefore, it is most important, if not vital, that the results of analysis be interpreted and tested continuously in terms of the real-world problems. This is a responsibility of both the analyst and the client.

The Process of Analysis

In the majority of their applications, systems techniques are concerned with problem-solving; that is, given a problem with certain determinants and desired end results, the process of analysis can be employed to seek a resolution of the problem. The desired end results are analogous to the state of increased order and organization. If the system under study is assumed to be *closed*, then it would not be feasible to introduce modifications in order to achieve the desired end results — the system would eventually achieve some state of equilibrium based on the initial determinants. However, since processes of open systems are capable of being reversed, the problem may have a "better" solution than the "inevitable" one suggested by the initial determinants. The task of the systems analyst, then, becomes one of determining the parameters within which action is feasible, developing alternatives which conform to these parameters, and testing alternatives to discover which provides the most desirable solution.

There are five basic elements in a systems analysis, and each is present and should always be explicitly identified.

The objective (or objectives).   Systems techniques are applied primarily to help choose a policy or course of action. The first and most important task of the analyst is to discover what the decision-maker's objectives are (or should be) and then how to measure the extent to which these objectives are in fact attained by various choices. This done, strategies, policies, or possible actions can be examined, compared, and recommended on the basis of how well they accomplish these objectives.

The alternatives.   The alternatives are the means by which it is hoped the objectives can be attained. They may be policies, strategies, specific actions, or instrumentalities. They need not be obvious substitutes for each other or perform the same specific functions. Thus, education, antipoverty measures, police protection, and slum clearance all may be alternatives in combating juvenile delinquency.

The costs.   The choice of a particular alternative for accomplishing the objectives implies that certain specific resources can no longer be used for other purposes. These are the costs. For a future time period, most costs can be measured in money terms, but their true measure is in terms of the opportunities they preclude. Thus, if the goal is to lower traffic fatalities, the irritation and delay caused to motorists by schemes that lower automobile speed in a particular location must be considered costs, for such irritations and delay may cause more speeding elsewhere.

The model (or models).   A model is a simplified, stylized representation of the real world that abstracts cause-and-effect relationships essential to the question under study. In any analysis of choice, the role of the model (or models, for it may be a problem in a single formulation) is to estimate for each alternative the costs that would be incurred and the extent to which the objectives should be attained.

A criterion.   A criterion is a rule or standard by which to rank the alternatives in order of desirability. It provides a means for weighting cost against effectiveness.

The fundamental importance of the model can best be seen in its relation to the other elements of analysis. The advantage of employing a model lies in forcing the analyst to make explicit what elements of the situation are taken into consideration and in imposing the discipline of clarifying the concepts being used. The model thus serves the important purpose of establishing unambiguous intersubjective communication about the subject matter at hand.

The process of analysis takes place in three overlapping stages:

The Formulation Stage.   Issues are clarified, the extent of the inquiry is limited, and the elements are identified.

The Search Stage.   Information is gathered and alternatives generated.

The Evaluation Stage.   Various alternatives are examined by means of models, which reveal the consequences or outcomes that can be expected to follow from each alternative; that is, what the costs are and the extent to which the objectives are attained; a criterion can then be applied to weigh the costs against performance and thus the alternatives can be arranged in some order of preference.

Given a particular problem, the application of systems techniques would involve the following procedures:

A. The Formulation Stage
    1. Definition and classification of the problem situation;
       (a) Specification of the nature of the problem, i.e., whether it is generic or unique

      (b) Identification of participants in the decision-making process

      (c) Identification of apparent determinants or initial conditions governing the problem situation

      (d) Determination of decision-makers' objectives

      (e) Statement of desired end-results to be achieved

2. Identification of parameters, boundary conditions, or constraints which determine the range of possible solutions

3. Analysis of processes or operations involved in the achievement of an optimal solution

4. Projection of determinants to ascertain the likely directions that the problem will take in the future and possible consequences if the problem is allowed to go unsolved

5. Definition of the measure of efficiency to be used relative to each objective to be obtained (goals) and selection of a common measure (standard) of efficiency

B. The Search Stage

6. Formulation of alternative courses of action designed to reach the desired end-results

7. Construction of a model to include the variables of the system than are subject to control and those variables not subject to control

8. Search for a "best" or optimal solution (by testing the various alternatives against the model) so as to determine the "control variables" that maximize the system's effectiveness

C. The Evaluation Stage

9. Selection of an optimal solution to the problem and initiation of action programs to bring about this solution

      (a) Testing of the solution to determine its effectiveness in predicting changes in the system

      (b) Development of controls for a given solution by establishing procedures for detecting significant changes and specifications as to the modifications to be made in the solution if such changes occur

      (c) Implementation of the selected solution by establishing recommended decision rules and action programs and procedures

10. Interpretation of above steps in light of the expectations of the system and the output feedback

The crucial step in these procedures lies in the evaluation of differentials of cost and effectiveness associated with each of the alternatives. The interpretation of this evaluation provides the basis for the recommendation of a particular alternative or set of alternatives.

Unfortunately, things seldom are this tidy; too often the objectives are

multiple, conflicting, and obscure; alternatives are not adequate to attain
the objectives; the measures of effectiveness do not really measure the extent
to which the objectives are attained; the predictions from the model are full
of uncertainties; and other criteria that look almost as plausible as the one chosen
may lead to a different order of preference.

When this happens, another approach must be taken. A single attempt or
pass at a problem is seldom enough. The key to successful analysis is a continuous cycle of formulating the problem, selecting objectives, designing
alternatives, collecting data, building models, weighing cost against performance,
testing for sensitivity, questioning assumptions and data, reexamining objectives,
opening new alternatives, building better models, and so on, until satisfaction
is obtained (or until time and money force a cutoff).

In brief, system techniques attempt to look at the entire problem in its
proper context. Characteristically, application will involve a systematic investigation of the decision-makers' objectives and of the relevant criteria; a comparison
– quantitative insofar as possible – of the cost, effectiveness, risk, uncertainty,
and timing associated with each alternative policy or strategy for achieving
the objectives; and an attempt to design better alternatives and to select other
goals if those examined are found wanting.

The Role of Analysis in Decision-Making

It should be noted that there is really nothing new about the procedures
just outlined. They have been used, more or less successfully, by managers
in government and industry for many centuries. The need for considering cost
relative to performance must have occurred to the earliest planners and administrators. Systems analysis, thus, is not a catchword to suggest that something
totally new is being done; at most, what is being done is being done better.
What may be novel in the approach is that this sort of analysis is an attempt to
look at the entire problem systematically with emphasis on explicitness,
quantification, and the recognition of uncertainty. Also novel are the schemes
or models used to explore the consequences of various choices and to eliminate
inferior action in situations where the relationships cannot be represented
adequately by a quantitative model.

Two Positions Regarding the Role of Analysis

It might be said that there are two extreme positions regarding the role
of analysis in the decision-making process. On the one hand, it might be argued
that the long-range decision problems under consideration by public management
are just too complex to be handled by the current state of the analytical art.

Decisions must be made purely on the basis of intuition, judgment, and experience. This is the *zero analysis* position.

At the other extreme, there are those who tend to think that all problems should be tackled in a purely analytical (usually meaning quantitative) fashion, with an eye to essentially "making" the decision. Such a view implies explicit calculations of costs and benefits for all the alternatives under consideration. At times, this may be possible for very narrowly defined, low-level suboptimization problems; but even here the application is questionable.

More generally, in dealing with major problems of choice, if the analyst approaches the analytical task in an inflexible, "hard core" frame of mind, he is likely to be in for trouble. For example, he soon may give up in complete frustration; he may wind up with such a simplified model that the resulting calculations are meaningless; or the result might be that his conclusions are presented two years after the critical time of decision and are therefore useless to the decision-maker.

In most cases, the relevant range of analysis is between the two extremes cited above. In such a context, there is a wide scope of analytical effort that can be useful. Furthermore, even when only relatively incomplete sets of quantitative calculations of cost and utility or effectiveness can be made (probably the general situation), much can be done to assist the decision-maker. In sum, the analytical process should be directed toward assisting the decision-maker in such a way that his intuition and judgment are better than they would have been without the results of the analysis. On occasion, only a small sharpening of judgment may have a high payoff.

Dealing With Ambiguity in the Results of Analysis

Applications of systems techniques seldom if ever yield unambiguous solutions to problems — solutions which can be accepted without further consideration. The difficulty, of course, stems from the fact that analytical results typically hinge on some ambiguous factors. Properly applied, systems methods will not suppress this ambiguity. Rather, the analysis will present complete enumeration of the results of various alternative assumptions about the ambiguous factors. A bad analysis may suppress the ambiguity — deliberately or inadvertently — and may present what purports to be the right answer. This solution will not survive careful scrutiny, however. Unfortunately, it sometimes does survive the inadequate scrutiny it often receives.

As a result of irreducible ambiguities, the application of systems techniques is frequently limited to a narrowing of alternatives and does not completely solve the problems of the public manager or decision-maker. The analyst may only present a relatively small listing of "better" system solutions from which the decision-maker can choose. If properly conducted, the analysis may reveal a relatively small list of what appear to be the more important measures of system costs and benefits (or effectiveness). The analysts may even go so far as to recommend a particular choice based on their own judgment and/or scale of values. Of course, when an analyst does this, he goes beyond his role as a technician.

Another important use of systems techniques is as a disciplinary and educational device. The explicit approach involved in the application of systems techniques calls for a spelling-out — and preferably exposing to full view — of the various elements of the analysis. This provides a framework which can increase the likelihood that the right questions will be asked and the right considerations will be taken into account.

This process can be highly educational to both the client and the analyst. It provides a greater range of objective information and thereby improves the bases of judgment. Moreover, it can and often does lead to a consideration of elements of problem situations which might not otherwise have been thought of, including new or different decision criteria and new or different alternative systems.

In many cases, the principal payoff of good analysis is not in indicating the preferred solution or solutions from among a predetermined set of alternatives. Rather, it is in the suggestion of promising additional systems to be considered and tested, leading to the development of better systems than were dictated by the constraints or "givens" of the original problem. The added systems may involve known solutions which, for some reason, were overlooked initially or prematurely ruled out of consideration. Or they may be newly invented systems, devised to remedy the major deficiencies in other alternatives — deficiencies brought to light by the analysis. The application of systems techniques, of course, does not provide the public manager with any magic formula for determining which alternative should be considered, much less a foolproof method for inventing new systems. Nevertheless, one of the principal benefits that can accrue to public management from the application of these techniques can be the stimulation of improved systems design.

The Structuring of Problems as an Aid to Decision-Making

Contrary to what some of the more enthusiastic advocates of quantitative analysis may assert, it is this author's view that systems techniques can play a modest, though very significant, role in the overall public decision-making process. In practically no case should it be assumed that the results of the analysis will "make" the decision. The really critical problems are just too difficult, and there are too many intangibles (e.g., political, psychological, and sociological constraints which cannot be fully quantified) which cannot be taken into account in the analytical process.

In that rare circumstance where a fairly complete set of calculations of costs and benefits is possible and a resulting conclusion about a preferred alternative is reached, it just may be that the conclusion itself is not the most useful thing to the decision-maker. In the first place, the analysis usually cannot take everything into account, particularly the more nebulous, non-quantitative considerations. These considerations the decision-maker himself must allow for. But more importantly, most high-level decision-makers are very busy men, who do not have time to structure a particular problem, to think up relevant alternatives (especially the more subtle ones), to trace out the key interactions among variables in the problems, and so on. These services should and can be provided by the analyst. And it is precisely this sort of contribution that may be most useful to the decision-maker. The fact that the analysis reaches a firm conclusion about a preferred alternative, in many instances, may be of secondary importance.

Concern for Man Himself

Albert Einstein, in Robert Lynd's book, *Knowledge For What?* warns that ". . . concern for man himself and his fate must always form the chief interest of all technical endeavors. . . ."[9] Rational public decision-making, using a systems approach, must be cognizant of the importance of human values, goals, and desires in the process of analysis. Decisions based on value-sensitive methodologies will mean a brighter future for the urban system. The techniques of public management applied to arrive at rational decisions must contain within their analytical structures a "concern for man himself."

A Reexamination of the Concept of Costs and Benefits in the Public Sector

Traditional uses of systems techniques have been in the areas of weaponry research and development and in the space program. The techniques have been strongly oriented toward weighing costs against benefits for various scientific and physical problems within the constraints of a specific budget. As Bernard Rudwick has observed: "The process of system evaluation basically compares each system alternative against an objective and determines the values of a system based on information found by asking six key questions."[10] These six questions relate to: (1) the system objective; (2) the operational availability of a proposed alternative system; (3) the operational configuration of the system; (4) the cost of implementation; (5) the effectiveness of the proposed system in meeting the objective; and (6) the risks and uncertainties involved in obtaining the stated performance on schedule and at the estimated cost.

While in the McNamara-Hitch era of DOD the decision-making process

regarding weapons procurement was streamlined to some extent, it must
be remembered that during this time many weapons systems did exhibit
tremendous cost overruns. Many writers have suggested that these "failures"
bode ill for a systems methodology applied to public decision-making. Such
critics often overlook the fact that it was not the techniques of analysis
that "failed." Rather, it was the inability of decision-makers to handle the value
questions involved in identifying systems objectives (question 1) and in
establishing tolerable levels of risk and uncertainty (question 6).

The transfer of systems techniques from managerial to public problems in
the urban environment raises questions that are even more difficult to answer.
The urban systems analyst must consider the roles of decision-makers, the
measures of systems performance, the seemingly limitless effects of alternatives,
and the debates of values that constantly arise in an urbanized society. In
applying systems techniques to urban problems, the analyst must contend with
a multitude of goals, a complex set of participants, and the risks and uncertainties
of managing a politicized urban society. As Cyril Herrmann has pointed out:

Industrial research methods cannot be superimposed directly on it [the city]. . . .
A space program . . . has a limited and tightly controlled number of decision
makers, while a city has as many as there are residents. Furthermore, a space
program has only one specific goal, whereas a city has many . . . and often finds
them in conflict with one another.[11]

A wholesale transfer of traditional systems techniques to an urban environment is destined to fall short of meeting the needs of analysis in view of the
various complex components of the urban system. The many competing and
conflicting subsystems of urban life require more than an analysis of costs
weighed against benefits. Although traditional systems techniques may be useful
in analyzing such urban problem areas as waste and water pollution, transportation systems and physical construction needs, public investment decisions,
and the like, even these more physical points of analysis interact at all levels
with human values. Whereas the Defense Department may be thought of,
theoretically, as a closed system regulated by a fixed budget, the urban system
is an open system "regulated" by the vagaries of politics. Applying a self-
constraining technique to a system replete with human-value consideration will
not produce rational value-free decisions for urban managers to consider.

The Optimization of Many Subsystems

To transfer the techniques of systems analysis to social conditions in urban
society, certain salient points must be considered. As the traditional techniques
attempt to optimize alternatives and arrive at a "best possible" solution, the

analysis of the urban condition necessitates the optimization of many subsystems, each important to the total system under examination and each laden with value question-requiring answers. The techniques of systems analysis permit the selection of that alternative which involves the lowest total cost at the highest ratio of user benefits to total costs. Minimizing costs has become the most important goal in many quarters. This emphasis stems from the limitations of our current techniques — an inability to quantify more fundamental measures of systems effectiveness. The transfer of systems techniques to the urban environ-ment cannot be accomplished successfully unless heretofore scientific techniques can be oriented towards a recognition that human values are as much an interacting component of the urban system as economic considerations, fiscal constraints of budgeting, and factors of physical development. As Henry Maier, the mayor of Milwaukee, has suggested: ". . . we have no completely adequate social science knowledge that will let us 'solve' — in any quick and definitive way — the various social, economic, and physical problems of American."[12]

Three Significant Differences

To bridge the gap between the scientific and value-oriented techniques of urban analysis, the difference inherent in each approach must be understood. First, most systems techniques consider problem-solving something to be applied to immediate problems, whereas methods appropriate to the processes of public management, while problem- and solution-oriented, must consider problems that will exist in the future as well as problems that require long-term remedial solutions. Second, the method of evaluating alternatives in systems approaches focuses on measurable costs and benefits, whereas in the processes of public management alternatives must be evaluated by subjective considerations such as political compromise, careful "guesstimations," and even "gut feelings." A third significant difference lies in the area of measurability and quantification. Systems methodologies rely on quantification as a structural process; the wholesale transfer of this process, however, cannot be made to the urban condi-tion. Simon Ramo speaks of a final, important limitation of the systems approach: "It is the handling of the 'unknown' factors . . . weighing the impor-tance of human reactions, for example, or guessing political influences, or generally dealing with technological issues that lend themselves little to measurement and quantification."[13]

The Need for "Hybrid" Techniques

A synthesis of the scientific method and the processes of public management is the bridge or "hybrid" that, when carefully applied to the analysis of urban problems, will result in decision-making that is rational and sensitive to science as well as to value judgments. One approach towards the integration of the scientific method with human elements for rational decision-making is set forth in *Systemic Planning: Theory and Application*.[14] The theory of systemic planning addresses the conflict between the desire to use management tools for decision-making and the loss of the human element that often results from the application of these tools. The objective of systemic planning is to offset the tendency to allow technical developments to obscure more intangible concerns. It seeks to integrate the rigorous techniques and methods of contemporary systems approaches with judgmental and qualitative planning practices. Within the structural process of analysis, systemic planning seeks to reduce the significant differences between systems techniques and traditional methods of public planning and administration. Two salient points of compromise directly affect the decision-makers: (1) a blending of identification and clarification of problems, not solely on the basis of current or immediate problems, but also in anticipation of future problems; and (2) a balance of costs and effectiveness, where certain identifiable objectives — social as well as budgetary — are matched against alternative costs — present as well as future costs.

In an urban system — regulated by the political subsystem — any attempt to quantify human values through decision-rendering mechanisms would ensure that such analyses would cease to be a science. They would act as a misguided tool of the political regulators.

The application of a value-sensitive methodology, on the other hand, would ensure that the decision-makers considered not only traditional goals, objectives, and means, but also the impact of public decisions on the basic values of the polity.[g] An awareness of the value system that supports society must be a factor in the setting of public goals and in the framework of analysis applied in selecting means to achieve these goals. Policies and legislation, if included in the goal design, must have a built-in responsiveness to human values. Just as the methodology of analysis within the urban system must reflect social values, so too must this reflection carry over to the implementation of public policies and programs.

Public management may be envisioned as the antithesis of nihilism. Thus, public management must be responsible for developing the broadest and highest aspirations to give meaning and purpose to the day-to-day activities of a community. The "concern for man himself" must pervade all levels of the public management process — from the identification of problems and issues to the selection and implementation of public plans and programs.

---

[g]Sensitivity to human considerations entails a recognition that the goals of society are not merely physical and social "desired end states" or ideal conditions. They include the customs and cultural institutions that the human system holds sacred. Planning for society should not be considered simply planning for an aggregate of vested interests.

2 The Nature of Decision-Making

While studies of decision-making enjoy great currency in many disciplines, it is difficult to gather these diverse contributions into a single frame of reference. The collective formulations of various fields of study are unavoidably colored by disciplinary preconceptions and intellectual biases. The problem is further compounded by the fact that, when dealing with the decision-making process, many writers prefer to use other terms, such as "policy," "judgment," or "choice," without making a clear distinction as to similarities and differences implicit in these terms.

Some Basic Definitions

Since *decision, decision-making, policy,* and *policy formulation* are terms with which this discussion will be primarily concerned, it seems appropriate to set forth some basic definitions as a precedent to any further exploration of the public decision-making process and the role of public management in this process.

Decision

Etymologically, "to decide" means "to cut off," "to terminate," coming from the Latin *decidere*, through the French *decider*. In its present usage, it suggests the coming to a conclusion; "a settling or terminating, as of a controversy, by giving judgment on the matter." A decision ". . . presupposes previous consideration of a matter causing doubt, wavering, debate, or controversy and implies the arriving at a more or less logical conclusion that brings doubt, debate, etc., to an end."

A number of disciplines have assumed the task of defining the term "decision." The sociologist R. M. MacIver has suggested that:

A preliminary to conscious activity is a decision between alternatives – to do this or to do that, to do or not to do. In the process of decision-making the individual assesses a situation in the light of these alternatives. A choice between values congenial to the larger value-system of the individual is somehow reached.[1]

Bruno Leoni, the political economist, suggests that a decision can be conceived as the final act of a sometimes long and complicated process of choices.[2] These choices may involve goals, values, factors of uncertainty, complex strategies, and so on. Similarly, Edwin Stene, a political scientist and public administrator, asserts that "Decision is the conscious consideration and conclusion regarding a course of action."[3] Robert Tannenbaum, in discussing the role of the manager in business organizations, states "Decision-making involves a conscious choice or selection of one behavior alternative from among a group of two or more behavior alternatives."[4]

Choice

These various definitions raise the question of whether "decision" and "choice" are synonymous in normal usage. Herbert Simon, in his definition of decision, suggests that the two words may be used interchangeably to refer to a process whereby the numerous alternative actions possible are narrowed down to the one that is acted upon.[5] Leoni, on the other hand, suggests that although these two terms are often used interchangeably, they are not, in fact, synonymous. He asserts that it is possible to decide something without choosing, as in the case when an individual "has no choice."[6] Deciding without choosing, according to Leoni, may refer merely to a psychological attitude at the moment of decision; the individual making the decision may not be conscious of any preliminary comparison of alternatives.

Rational and Nonrational Decisions

Decisions come in all shapes and sizes. They are often judged to be "rational" or "irrational" depending on the particular perspective or viewpoint of the individual making the judgment. Public decisions frequently may not appear "rational" as rational economic decisions are generally defined. Many writers have therefore concluded that the criteria of rational decision processes often cannot be applied in public decision situations.

A decision is generally defined as rational or nonrational according to some set of rules defining what actions are reasonable or consistent with a given set of premises. In this connection, it is possible to identify four basic categories of nonrational decisions.

1. Illogical decision — when an innovator confuses a possible and a necessary consequence of his action
2. Blind decision — when certain consequences important to the decision are not considered

3.   Rash decision — when a decision is made after an incomplete or hasty
     review of the discernible alternatives
4.   Ignorant action — when there are mistakes about the facts or available
     relevant facts are omitted from consideration

Accepting these distinctions, it may be suggested that "nonrational"
decisions *cannot* be considered completely devoid of consistency; they are,
indeed, perfectly consistent with their premises. Therefore, what may be judged
nonrational or irrational action by an observer may be totally "rational" to
the actor, given his set of premises.

Thus a principal objective of public management should be to assist the
decision-maker in making more rational decisions, i.e., to circumvent the shortcomings brought about by the forms of nonrational action listed above.

Habitual Response

A number of writers have used the term "decision" without any implication
of a requisite conscious or deliberate process. In this view, "decision" simply
refers to the fact that a "selection" has been made of one course of action over
another, even though this selection may simply consist of established reflex
actions, as for example when a typist strikes a particular key on the typewriter.

Other writers, particularly in psychology, have taken great pains to distinguish decision from such habitual responses.[a] George Katona, exemplifying
this point of view, makes the following distinctions:

Genuine decisions . . . require the perception of a new situation and the solution
of the problem raised by it; they lead to responding to a situation in a new way.
In contrast, habitual behavior is rather common. We do what we did before
in a similar situation . . . . The main point is that the psychological process
involved is different from that in genuine decision. Routine behavior, or using
rules of thumb, are suitable terms to describe the second form of behavior.[7]

Chester Barnard provides a fairly succinct summary of the view held by
many management scholars and practitioners of the distinction between
decision and habitual response.

The acts of individuals may be distinguished in principle as those which are the
result of deliberation, calculation, thought, and those which are unconscious,
automatic, responsive, the results of internal or external conditions present or

---

[a]As will be discussed in further detail in a subsequent section, other writers have made
the further distinction between "innovative decisions" and "programmed decisions," the
latter closely paralleling routine behavior in Katona's terms

past. In general, whatever processes precede the first class of acts culminate
in what may be termed "decision."[8]

Barnard's definition suggests that human behavior results from either
conscious or unconscious processes; and that when these processes are conscious,
they culminate in decisions. The second, unconscious, or perhaps more appropriately, automatic, responses, may be called "habit." Many writers emphasize
this distinction between conscious and unconscious action, between the volun-
tary and the involuntary response, although a few maintain that if an individual
follows one course of action, he forgoes other possible courses of action,
and thereby makes a "decision."

Criteria for Selection

Explicit or implicit in the definition of a decision is the central notion that
a decision involves the *selection* of one alternative from among two or more
possible courses of action. In this sense, even taking the position that no decision
will be made is a "decision" in that it represents a selection from among the
available alternatives.
This central idea of selection leads to a number of implications.

1. If a decision is a selection of one from among several alternatives, then there
   must be a reason for making a selection. The selection process must involve
   some sort of strategy of evaluation which focuses on the objective or
   objectives in mind. Thus, there is the implication that decision-making
   should be purposive behavior, i.e., guided by goals or objectives.
2. Since decision-making is or should be goal-oriented, a choice among
   alternatives typically is a choice among means to achieve some end or ends.
   Relatively few of the decisions which an individual makes are related
   directly to his value structure — these decisions are based primarily on the
   varying backgrounds and accumulated experiences of the individuals
   concerned. Therefore, decisions among ends are largely subjective decisions,
   that is, measured by one's personal standards rather than by objective
   standards.
3. To the extent that a value system is shared by a group of individuals (an
   organization, community, nation, or society), it is possible to devise some
   objective means of testing all other decisions which relate directly or
   indirectly to this value framework. In terms of a means-ends hierarchy,
   intermediate goals are decisions made in the belief that they will serve as the
   means to the achievement of one or more ultimate goals. Since a decision
   among means is relevant to some goals, there is an objective basis in this

type of decision for determining whether a choice is an appropriate or sound decision (are the alternative means selected conducive to the achievement of the selected goal?).[b]

4. The selection of one from among several alternatives implies further that there is a process of evaluation or a strategy which accumulates with experience; that is to say, current decisions are tempered or colored by past decisions as well as by an overall value system. This also suggests that the outcome of decisions, over time, can contribute to the modification of the value system or, at least, intermediate goals in the means-ends hierarchy.

5. Finally, implicit in the notion of selection among alternatives is the fact that the evaluative process culminates in a "judgment;" that is, reasons for and against each of the alternatives are sought and appraised, and ultimately a final judgment is made.

Judgment and Decision

If these interpretations are accepted as valid, then the term "decision" must be taken to mean a judgment among ends or among means to achieve some ends. However, the term "judgment" is somewhat ambiguous, and if it is to have any value as an essential part of the definition of decision, it too must be more clearly defined.

In common usage, "judgment" has come to mean any action, which, after certain deliberations, pronounces the differences or agreement of two elements of thought.[c] Since judgment is an assertive, intellectual act, truly habitual responses must be ruled out as decisions. The door must be left open, however, for a process of selection involving a judgment from among alternatives which have become routinized or habituated. In subsequent discussion, such responses will be called "programmed decisions." With this qualification, "decision" may be formally defined as *an intellectual assertion (either affirmative or negative) among alternative ends, or among alternative means to achieve some ends.*

---

[b] In this connection, one very important function that any organization performs is to provide individuals with goals. To these organizational goals, an individual may attach his own framework or value system. With ends, goals, or objectives largely defined for him in an organizational context, decisions are largely among means.

[c] In the terminology of logic, judgments are a class of categorical propositions, in that they contain subject and predicate terms joined by copulas (which always take a form of the verb "to be") and often modified by "quantifiers" (which indicate the extent to which members of the subject term are referred). Judgments must not be confused with all propositions, however. While all propositions are expressed in subject-predicate form, not every proposition expresses a judgment. Propositions which express a wish, a question, or an exclamation do not reflect judgments, for example, because they are not assertive statements.

Economic Decision Theory — An Overview[d]

Rather sharp distinctions have been made in the literature of decision theory between business and public organizations. Particularly striking is the contrast between the more fully developed theories of business decisions — the economic theory of price and administrative theory — and analyses of public bureaucracies found in recent sociological and political theory. The contrast rests, rather explicitly, on two fundamental differences: (1) the treatment of goals; and (2) the treatment of expected returns and costs.

Theories of business behavior assume that organizational goals are given: organizations attempt to maximize profits. These theories assume that the goal is operational: business enterprises know when they are (and when they are not) fulfilling this goal and what courses of action will satisfy the goal. More recently, various students of business decision-making have begun to question these basic assumptions, and in this questioning, have begun to cast some doubts on the apparent distinctions drawn between the goals of public and private organizations.

However, it is in the treatment of expected returns and expected costs in the classical description of business behavior that the major "distinctions" between the public and private sectors seem to arise. It is this area, therefore, that must receive principal consideration if the basic theoretical premises of economic decision theory are to be adapted to the operations of public organizations.

Underlying Premises of Expected Costs and Returns

Theories of business decision-making generally assume that estimates of costs and returns are made in some form by individual firms. It is further assumed that investment behavior of the firms depends heavily on such estimates. For example, the standard theory of price treats investment and internal resource allocations as hyper-simple problems of maximization. The firm invests in each alternative available to the extent that the marginal returns from such investments will equal the opportunity cost. Except insofar as sunk costs are involved, the firm makes little distinction between internal and external investments; that is, all marginal returns are equal to the best alternative return available. Under these conditions, "efficiency" — the ratio of obtained to potential return — is equal to one.

---

[d]To a large extent, theoretical formulations concerning the processes of decision-making, both in the public and private sectors, are derived from economic theory. This important area of conceptual development will be taken up in greater detail in a later section. At this point, however, certain basic premises are significant to an understanding of the nature of decision-making in general terms.

Implicit in such theories is the assumption that private organizations continuously scan all alternatives and continuously adjust their investment portfolios to changes in the pattern of available alternatives. These theories assume that firms have accurate information on the costs to be incurred and the returns to be received from each alternative. Thus, decisions are made on the basis of this information. As noted below, these assumptions have been attacked by both economists and organization theorists.

Attempts to revise standard theories of economic decision-making have been designed primarily to modify these basic assumptions through (1) the introduction of probability distributions, and (2) the substitution of expected profit (or utility) for the form of profit (or utility) specified in the original formulations. Under this approach, the modern entrepreneur is assumed to know (with certainty) the probability distributions of outcomes from all available alternatives. Therefore, he can compute the expected value of any particular alternative and equate expected marginal return with expected opportunity cost.

At the same time, the assumption of infinite search has been replaced by a theory of search that recognizes certain costs of searching for an adequate solution. This modification makes the allocation of resources for securing information one of the investment decisions to be made.[9] The modern businessman does not scan all alternatives nor does he have all of the necessary information concerning all alternatives. He invests in information only so long as the marginal expected return gained from the information exceeds expected opportunity costs.

Exceptions Taken to Classic Assumptions

There is general consensus that these theories, and specifically the economic versions of them, have been rather valuable in both normative and empirical analyses of aggregate economic behavior. Since this has been the major traditional interest of economic analysis, many economic theorists have found no pressing reasons for reexamining the assumptions of these standard theories.

On the other hand, economists and others interested in the behavior of individual organizations have not been entirely satisfied with the classic assumptions or their modifications. These assumptions have been subject to criticism on two major grounds. As normative theory, they have been challenged for accepting too readily the Bernoullian concept of expected utility. Alternative formulations, arising primarily from considerations introduced by von Neumann and Morgenstern in their *Theory of Games*, seem to have some preference among these critics. In terms of their empirical applications, four major objections have been raised to the more or less "pure" theory of expectations.

First, classic theories assume continuous competition among all alternatives for all resources. As Coase has pointed out, the perfectly competitive market for internal resources is a major implicit assumption of the standard theory of the firm.[10] Such a description of organizational behavior, however, is distinctly different from that implicit in many treatments of other forms of organizations. For example, public administration models seem to emphasize local adaptation to specific problems. These models stress problem-solving at the expense of long-range planning, in direct contradiction to the concept of a perfectly competitive market for internal resources.

Second, basic economic decision theory makes the search activity (and thus information) simply one of the several claimants for available resources, to be evaluated in terms of calculable costs and expected returns. Simon and others have questioned this treatment of search behavior.[11] These authors place considerable emphasis on dissatisfaction as a stimulant to search, on the "conspicuousness" of alternatives as factors in decision considerations, on external effects on the generation of information, and on the sequential characteristics of alternative evaluation. Thus, Simon posits the model of "satisficing man" as an alternative to the classic economic model of "maximizing man."

A third criticism, closely related to those just noted, relates to the substantial computation activity required on the part of the organization. Shackle and others have argued that classic economic theory exaggerates both the computational ability and, more importantly, the usual computational precision of human beings.[12]

Finally, standard economic theories treat expectations as exogenous variables; they are given, not explained. However, such an eminently logical extention of certainty theory to the treatment of uncertainty ignores a major psychological aspect of uncertain situations, namely, the interaction of expectations and desires. Quite aside from such interaction, taking expectations as a *given* in a theory of economic decision-making seems akin to taking the outcomes of all individual games as a *given* in a theory of football championships.

These critical exceptions to classic economic decision theory must form an important input to the development of a decision model for public organizations. The concept of "satisficing," as formulated by Simon, provides a concise summary of these exceptions. Much of the literature of public decision-making, furthermore, has been built on this basic concept.

The Concept of "Satisfice"

The concept of "satisfice" was first suggested by Simon in *Models of Man* and later more fully developed in *Organizations* with James March.[13] According to Simon, most theorists until recently accepted the model of "maximizing" (economic) man. Maximizing man is assumed to have all the alternatives that he needs before him and is able to rank them with reference to the desirability of their consequences. His ranking ability rests on his possession of a "utility function," which can be equated to his value system or goals.

Satisficing (administrative) man, on the other hand, is moved by various stimuli to search for alternatives. When he finds an alternative that is "good enough" (i.e., one that suffices), he intelligently avoids spending time, energy, and resources on further search (i.e., he is satisfied).

Wildavsky has applied this concept to the public budget-making process by suggesting that agencies simplify their calculations by lowering their sights; instead of trying to maximize their position, budget officials are content to "satisfice." In so doing, Wildavsky contends, public officials ". . . leave the area of intrinsic merits because it does not help them make decisions and turn instead to other criteria which may not be 'rationale' but which do help them."[14] Thus, Wildavsky is suggesting that in the main these decisions are not made with reference to a basic set of goals.

Since the elementary components of the problem-solving process (the search and screening phases), as Simon has described them, are characterized by a great deal of "randomness," many have interpreted Simon's satisficing model as being without goal identification. According to these interpretations, satisficing man reconciles himself to the fact that his choices are bound to be made intuitively and on extrinsic rather than intrinsic bases, since most of the consequences of any choice are incomparable on any operational scale of values.

In many respects, the above is a misinterpretation of Simon's conceptual framework. Although in his discussion of satisficing Simon tends to be relatively indifferent to high-level goal-determination processes, he makes it clear that one can call an alternative "satisfactory" only if it meets some set of standards established prior to its selection. Such standards, however, must be equated with goals. If they are not themselves ultimate goals, they must be evaluated on the basis of their relation to some set of ultimate goals.[e] The process involved in balancing ideals, estimates of feasibility, and probable costs of further search is generally far more subtle than the interpretations of Simon's theories would suggest. Thus, the phrase "successive approximations" would seem appropriate in this regard. This concept, used frequently by Chester Barnard, and currently applied in quantitative decision procedures through the technique of stepwise maximization, assumes an operational goal or set of goals toward which "approximations" are made.

Individualistic and Group Decisions

Up to this point in the discussion, the perspective of decisions has been largely an individualistic one. Such a frame of reference is inherent in a great many of the writings on decision theory. There is frequently an awareness, at

---

[e]The notion of formulating standards of adequacy at the outset of the search process is closely related to the concept of "means-ends chains" introduced by Simon in his examination of administrative behavior. This concept will be explained further in a later section.

least implicitly, that decisions of one individual will affect others, and moreover, that the decisions of individuals are not only competitive (when individuals are "out for themselves") but also cooperative.[f] The majority of writers, however, draw their concepts of decisions from market choice theories, as outlined above.

Some authors have attempted to deal with cooperative or "group" decisions by developing special systems which enable different individuals to arrive at essentially the same inferences and, therefore, essentially the same decision. These systems are based on the premise that some set of standard procedures, if applied independently to the same set of data, will yield a consensus in the form of a group decision. For the most part, however, these systems are still unproven for group decisions in the real world and remain in a highly theoretical stage.

Very few mechanisms for group decisions have been devised outside of voting procedures, or *majority rule* and *verbal bargaining*. As Bross has observed, majority rule works only when decisions are relatively nontechnical, and when the group loyalty is strong enough so that those voting in the minority are willing to stay with the group and accept the majority decision.[15] Verbal bargaining (which may operate in conjunction with majority rule procedures), on the other hand, is subject to serious limitations, many of which arise from inadequacies in normal language. Thus a group may assume that a consensus has been reached, but because of semantic difficulties actual agreement on the main point of discussion may not have been achieved.

The concept of group decision-making is important to the analysis of organizational processes and, in particular, the area of public decision-making. Public decisions are seldom the result of a single individual's choice. Even in those cases where the responsibility for a decision is clearly that of an individual, judgment generally is made *in view of* the impact on others in the system. Further, the decision of a "whole group" may or may not be the same decision that each individual in the group would have made if he were in a position to decide for the group. Group decisions lack clear unanimity and therefore are not identical with each single individual decision within the group.

This raises a number of important points in connection with decision-making theories based on economic considerations, i.e., market choice theories. The first difference between the processes of economic decision-making and group decision-making relates to the level of knowledge possessed by individuals concerning the possible results of alternative decisions. It is not realistic to presume that in both situations the level of knowledge is the same. The decision-maker in the marketplace can be assumed to have greater knowledge of the alternatives because of (1) the greater continuity of market choice, and (2) the

---

[f]In game theory, for example, provision is made in the so-called zero-sum n-person game for individuals to cooperate with one another in "coalitions." This departs from the normal competitive decision-making situation upon which much of the basic theory is formulated.

difference in the amount of knowledge required to compare alternatives in the two cases. Many group decisions are "one-shot" situations, and as a result the group has little experience on which to base its deliberations. Further, group decisions, particularly in the public sector, involve a number of "unknowns" for which there is little precedent. More importantly, however, is the fact that in market choice, the decision-maker is often the entity for which the selection of alternatives is made as well as the selecting entity. In group decision-making, on the other hand, where selection is made through majority rule, an individual may be the acting or selecting entity, but the collectivity (the group) is the entity for which the decision is made. Even if an individual in the group decision situation knows everything about the consequences of each possible collective decision, he can never predict with certainty which of the alternatives presented will be selected by the majority.[16]

A second fundamental difference between individual economic decisions and group decisions, suggested by Buchanan and others, is that the individual in the market situation tends to act as if all the social variables were determined outside of his behavior. The individual in the group decision situation, on the other hand, is more conscious of the influence his selection or vote might have in determining the final collective action. This awareness will often result in a somewhat different "scale of preference:" in the market situation, the individual will strive to satisfy his own tastes, while in the group situation, he will refer to the values of the group as well as his own values.

A third difference stems from the fact that in group decision-making the responsibility for making any particular selection among the available alternatives is necessarily divided; it is a "collective" decision. Therefore, under the protection of shared responsibility, the individual may select an alternative which he might not otherwise choose if he were to bear the responsibility for the decision alone. By the same token, the privilege to participate in a group decision situation is a franchise. Whether or not it is exercised by a given individual, a decision will still result.

A fourth and perhaps most important distinction is that alternatives of market choice normally are in conflict only to the extent that the law of diminishing returns is operative.[17] If an individual desires more of a particular commodity or service, the market normally requires only that he take less of some other commodity or service, given a fixed or limited set of resources. In contrast, alternatives in a voting situation are mutually exclusive; that is, the selection of one alternative precludes the selection of another, as far as the individuals belonging to the group are concerned. This situation arises from the fact that many alternatives in group decision-making do not allow "composite solutions." To be sure, group decisions made through verbal bargaining can result in compromises, and in fact this is the purpose of such bargaining. However, in situations when the alternatives are "put to the vote," the resulting individual choices are of the "all or none" variety.[18]

An important consequence, illustrated in the writings of von Mises, is that in the marketplace the "dollar vote" is never overruled; the individual is never placed in the position of being a member of a dissenting minority, at least as far as the existing or potential alternatives of the market are concerned. As has been suggested, in the majority rule situation, the individual may be compelled to accept a result which is contrary to his expressed preference.

From this may be derived an important characteristic of a major sector of public decision in a democracy. Many public decisions are reached through a process of majority rule, either by direct public vote or by a vote of duly elected representatives of the public. It may be suggested that such decisions imply some form of *coercion*. The voter who is in the minority at first makes his choice, but eventually must accept a decision which he had rejected; his decision-making process has been overthrown.[19] The only alternative open to him is to leave the group.

These qualifications of economic decision theory, as applied to group situations, have an important bearing on the present work. Rather than defining group decision in terms of consensus or agreement among a number of individuals, as is the approach of the more typical adaptations of economic decision theory to group situations, in the context of this discussion group decisions will be understood to involve an element of coercion for those "voting" in the minority.

What Is Policy?

While there is a growing literature on "policies" and the processes of policy formulation,[g] as with the term "decision", relatively few of these writings have clearly defined what is meant by the terms. For example, Charles Lindblom has discussed at length the questions of policy formulation and decision-making without clearly delimiting either of these terms except by example or by a description of a process.[20]

Differing Interpretations as to the "Level" of Policy

Some writers have suggested that the term policy should be reserved for statements of intention and direction of a relatively high order. In the words of Harold Lasswell:

------

[g]The term "policy" seems to be a typically English concept. There is no direct corresponding word in French (the words *politique, diplomatie,* and *ligne de conduite* are frequently used in translations), Italian (the word *politica* means "tactful or diplomatic"), German, or Spanish. Bruno Leoni relates a story about a Russian commander in Berlin immediately following the Second World War who became extremely alarmed when invited by the American and English commanders to cooperate in a common "policy." He had no instructions from Moscow and was fearful of becoming involved in some sort of political agreement that would not be approved by his superiors. (Leoni, *op. cit.*, p. 94.)

The word "policy" is commonly used to designate the most important choices made either in organized or in private life . . . . Hence, "policy" is free of many of the undesirable connotations clustered about the word political, which is often believed to imply "partisanship" or "corruption."[21]

The basic emphasis of the policy approach, therefore, is upon the fundamental problems of man in society, rather than upon the topical issues of the moment.[22]

Policy has also been defined in more behavioristic terms. Jacob and Flink, in a recent study concerned with an identification and analysis of the values which influence "public policy decision making," define policy as: ". . . an integrated program of actions which an actor (or group of actors) is accustomed or intends to undertake in response to a given problem or situation with which he is confronted."[23]

Frequently linked with the concepts of decisions and policies are such generically defined terms as "values" and "goals." Kaplan has suggested, for example, that rational decision-making is largely a matter of acting so as to secure some set of values.

Whatever theories are formulated to schematize rational choice, some set of values must play a part in the analysis. The preferred terms are "utilities" and "social welfare functions," but the labels themselves solve no problems. There is first the task of determining what values are in fact being pursued, to be entered in the payoff matrix.[24]

Some scholars emphasize in their definition of values the fact of choice or preference of the individual for a given object or situation over others. Robert C. Angell, for example, defines values as ". . . lasting preferences for the way in which one's social world is structured and operated."[25] Lasswell defines values as ". . . 'a category of preferred events,' such as peace rather than war, high level of production and employment rather than mass unemployment, democracy rather than despotism, and congenial and productive personalities rather than destructive ones."[26] Lasswell also equates values with "needs" or "goals."[27] Jacob and Flink, on the other hand, suggest that values are ". . . normative propositions held by individual human beings of what human beings ought to desire, e.g., the desirable."[28]

A Hierarchical Relationship

It would appear that, as with many concepts in the social sciences, there are no universally accepted definitions of these important terms which are a part of the public manager's vocabulary. Perhaps, as Clyde Kluckhold has observed,

"No definition can hope to incorporate or synthesize all aspects of each concept established in the various fields of learning and yet remain serviceable."[29]

Acknowledging these limitations, it may be suggested that the terms "value," "goal," "policy," and "decision" can be related in a hierarchical manner. For the purposes of further discussion in the present work, these terms are defined as follows:

1. Value — an element of a shared symbolic system (referred to as a value system), acquired through social learning, which serves as a guide for the selection from among perceived alternatives of orientation
2. Goals — an articulation of values, formulated in the light of identified issues and problems, toward the attainment of which policies and decisions are directed
3. Policy — (a) a broad guide to present and future decisions, selected in the light of given conditions from a number of alternative courses of action; (b) the actual decision or set of decisions designed to carry out the chosen course of actions, and (c) a projected program consisting of desired objectives (goals) and the means of achieving them
4. Decision — an intellectual assertion (judgment) as to appropriate ends, or appropriate means to achieve some ends, arrived at after careful consideration and deliberation of alternatives, and conditioned by an articulated policy or set of policies

Problem-Solving Versus Decision-Making

As has been pointed out, one of the most troublesome obstacles to the development of a fuller understanding of patterns of decision-making stems from the generic use of the term "decision." Clearly all decisions are not of the same magnitude. In some instances, decision-making may be a relatively simple task, and decisions may be made as a matter of routine; indeed, the decision-maker may not even realize that he is making them. In other cases, however, decision-making may call for the most demanding exercise of judgment, reasoning, and imagination.

In the first instance, a decision is merely the device that activates some precast response — a response that literally is held in readiness for the advent of a decision-demanding situation. A habituated pattern of behavior is evoked and channels the flow of activities toward some given commitment. In the more complex cases, however, a decision becomes a means of outlining a commonly acceptable response where none existed before. Such situations arise because unfamiliar demands result in a lack of agreement as to relevant pattern of response to achieve a particular goal, or there is disagreement as to the goals themselves. Such decision situations require innovation rather than a precast response.[h]

It is unfortunate that the terms "problem-solving" and "decision-making" are so frequently used interchangeably.[i] The process of problem-solving, that is, the process of providing the right answers in relatively clear-cut decision situations, could serve as a useful distinction in discussing patterns of decision-making. A good deal of the discussion of decision-making tends to center on problem-solving situations, thereby providing a somewhat distorted picture of the decision-making process.

Most decisions that can be made using problem-solving techniques are relatively routine, tactical decisions. If both the conditions of the situation and the requirements that must be satisfied are known, problem-solving is the only thing necessary. In such cases, the task is merely one of choosing from among a few obvious alternatives; the decision criterion is usually one of economy. Thus an alternative is selected which will accomplish the desired objective with the least effort and disturbance to established patterns of activity.

While many tactical decisions may be relatively complicated and important, they are invariably unidimensional. The situation is a "given" and the requirements are evident. The only problem is to find the most economical adaptation of known resources.

The more important decisions, the decisions with far-reaching implications, are generally decisions of *strategy* in that they involve (1) either finding out what the situation is, or changing it; or (2) either finding out what the available resources are, or what they should be. In the public sector, this class of decisions includes all those dealing with community goals and objectives and the means of achieving them. Decisions affecting the level of productivity or output of a private organization fall into this category, since they are always aimed at changing the total organizational situation. Also included are all decisions regarding major capital expenditures both in the public and private sectors. Strategic decisions — whatever their magnitude, complexity, or importance — should never be made through a strict problem-solving approach.

---

[h]Simon's distinction between programmed (routine) and nonprogrammed problem-solving embodies the same perspective presented in this and subsequent discussions of routine, adaptive, and innovative responses to decision situations. See: *The New Science of Management Decision-Making* (New York, 1960).

[i]Braybrooke and Lindblom (*op. cit.*, p. 249) state, for example, that: "The kind of problem we are talking about when we use the term 'problem-solving' is, of course, the kind of problem that calls for a decision or a policy . . . We normally use the terms 'problem solving,' 'policy-making,' 'decision-making,' and 'policy analysis' synonymously." Thus it may be suggested that difficulties associated with Braybrooke and Lindblom's critical discussion of "synoptic" problem-solving, in part, arise from the context in which they use these terms.

The Professional and Problem-Solving

Several writers have suggested that, at best, public administrators and planners can only hope for a fuller opportunity to engage in problem-solving.[30] Self-imposed limitations on participation in the politics of decision-making may contribute, in part, to this relatively narrow role for professionals in government as much as the unreceptiveness of decision-makers. The concept of problem-solving, as defined here, is somewhat contrary to the more comprehensive approach advocated by many professionals in government. Assuming that the previously cited authors are correct in their observations, this ambivalence toward problem-solving will undoubtedly result in considerable frustration for the professional working in the public sector.

It may well be, however, that the relegation of professionals to problem-solving situations stems from their focus on providing "right answers" rather than on the more difficult task of posing the right questions. John Friedmann has suggested that, given the contemporary characteristics of development, the character of economic decision-making, and the high degree of interdependency among communities and regions, the public planner can only perform "adaptive planning."[31] Friedmann defines adaptive planning as an attempt to relieve temporary crises in housing, education, local transportation, municipal water supply, outdoor recreation, and so forth which may be caused by exogenous factors. In short, adaptive planning is closely akin to problem-solving. But adaptive planning treats the symptoms without looking into the underlying causes which give rise to these problems.

In drawing generalizations from a study of the Piedmont area of North Carolina, Parker and Daland suggest that there are four characteristic stances taken by planning directors in their dealings with decision-making situations.

The first avoids any semblance of controversy and involves purely factual studies on noncontroversial subjects. The second, and more common, involves factual studies of controversial subjects and the giving of opinions on facets of the problem when formally requested by official bodies. The third involves specification of alternative solutions, or plans, indicating the pros and cons of each. In the final approach the planning director commits himself to a specific plan he deems superior to all others and attempts to commit others to the same plan.[32]

To a large extent, these categories can be extended to encompass the activities of all professionals in government.

The first two approaches clearly fall within the realm of problem-solving. There may be an innate necessity to build public programs from relatively short-range, problem-solving activities. If the processes of public management are to be effective contributors to public decision-making, however, the professionals must look beyond problem-solving situations. Public management must play a more innovative role in the decision-making process. Every professional in the public sector is an innovator to the extent that he creates ideas in the course of his technical activities. However, the process of conveying these ideas to those points in the leadership structure of the community where they will be acted upon and emerge as public decisions, is the sense in which the term "innovation" is used here.

Adaptive and Innovative Decisions

What are some of the implications of professionals becoming decision-innovators? Much attention in decision theory has focused on a selection process involving fairly well-defined alternatives. The more complex activities required in the initiation of tasks or in "creative problem-solving," where alternative solutions are not immediately available, have seldom been studied and are little understood. Only tentative suggestions can be offered as to the professional's role in innovative decision-making.

In their more recent research and writings, Simon, March, and their colleagues have given attention to the question of how new ideas and new tasks are introduced into the decision-making process.[j] Simon and March make the following distinction between "programmed" and "nonprogrammed" problem-solving:

Programmed activity generally involves a great deal of problem-solving of a rather routine and reproductive sort. That is to say, only under unusual circumstances is the detail of a program so stereotyped that it is stored in the memory as a series of specific instructions. On the contrary, in most situations the execution of a program involves a considerable amount of reconstruction of the program details, but without requiring extensive and difficult searches or computations. Contrariwise, the unprogrammed activity in innovation generally requires a great deal of "productive" problem-solving.[33]

---

[j]James March and Herbert Simon examine in detail the nature of innovative activity and, in particular, the processes by which new programs of decision and action are discovered, and put into effect. One of their conclusions is that both the rate and type of innovation depend on the location of individuals in the communication structure of the organization. The man who recognizes a problem or the need for a program innovation and introduces it into the organization's communication system exercises important influence in the decision-making process. The person who is in a position to perform a "broker function," i.e., to filter and select from the flow of innovative communication, also shares considerably in this influence (Simon and March, *op. cit.*, pp. 187–188). The notion that each position in an organization's communication network provides its incumbent with certain types and amounts of potential influence and authority in the decision-making process is an important element in the present conceptual development. These points will be discussed further in a subsequent section.

Adaptive Decisions — Adjustments Within
Established Expectations

In view of the foregoing discussion of routine problem-solving (programmed) activities as situations involving tactical rather than strategic decisions, it would seem appropriate to insert a third category in the programmed-nonprogrammed continuum to account for those decisions which begin with programmed responses but require considerable amounts of "reconstruction of the program details." Such decision activities might be called *adaptive decision-making.*

Adaptive decisions provide a means of modifying established patterns of response and thereby reestablishing a flow of productive activity on a more or less stable basis. Adaptive decisions seek to alleviate built-up pressures by removing the immediate sources of demand or by providing a satisfactory alternative solution to that which is sought.[k] Since such adaptations may not get at the root causes of the problem, they are often only temporary solutions. As pressures continue to mount, adaptive decisions may no longer suffice, and, in some situations, may even contribute to the stress on the decision system.

Since accommodation is relatively less painful and less disruptive to the status quo than innovation, most patterns of activity that come to be dysfunctional to an organization are translated into adaptive rather than innovative decisions. Adaptive decisions lead to certain revisions in expectations, whereas innovative decisions may lead to new or substitute expectations. The term "expectations" is used in this sense to denote the indigenous criteria against which those persons affected by a particular decision gauge its efficacy. The principal test of the efficacy of new patterns produced by a decision is their compliance with the minimal expectations sanctioned by the social system i.e., an organization, group, community, or even society.[l]

When these expectations have been more or less met, the fine adjustments that lead to routinization of responses are initiated, and the revised pattern is gradually "programmed" as a legitimized pattern of response. However, as has been suggested, adaptive decisions may include some ill-conceived steps or unanticipated side effects which, in turn, produce new and unfamiliar stresses

---

[k]The notion of adaptive decisions meeting an immediate situation by providing a "satisfactory" solution is closely related to the concept of "satisficing," as formulated by Simon.

[l]Jay Jackson has formulated an interesting model in this connection, building on Barnard's concept of a "zone of indifference" (i.e., the region in which a person of given status expectations will accept without question the decisions of his superiors). Jackson postulates a "Return Potential Model," consisting of two orthogonal dimensions, one representing social behavior, i.e., the act of an Actor, and the other dimension representing the "expectations" of Others.[34] It is possible to draw a curve through this space which represents the expectations and therefore, the potential sanctions of all the Others in a social system for an Actor's behavior in a given situation. From this formulation, it may be suggested that consensus — although originally a matter of individual expectations — comes to represent a normative agreement as to what is acceptable.

while effectively dissipating those that initially evoked the need for adjustment. In such cases, further adaptive decisions may be required to produce more satisfactory patterns.

The structure of a system, however, is malleable only up to a point. Adaptive adjustments must be devised within limits. When the suggested accommodations call for changes exceeding these limits (when a regulator can no longer bring the system back to a steady state or point of equilibrium), a major problem emerges. This might be called the "policy problem," in that such a situation requires innovative decisions to bring about a major modification in the ends as well as the means.

In one sense, an innovative decision differs from the adaptive variety principally in the rate at which change comes about. A series of adaptive decisions may eventually introduce as substantial a change in the structure of the system as would come about from an innovative decision. The two modes differ in intent, however, for the innovative decision is a deliberate attempt to deal with an intolerable situation through a frontal attack rather than through oblique, incremental operations.

This is not to deny the value of incremental decisions. In fact, several students of administration have held that the highest art of decision-making is to successfully determine when to induce change in innocent increments and when to use the bold stroke of innovation. Situations requiring innovative decisions, however, involve issues that run to the roots of a system, issues so central and compelling that they cannot be disposed of either obliquely or incrementally.

Innovative Decisions – Accommodation Through New Expectations

The innovative decision arises either from a desire to reconcile some internal or external pressures incompatible with a central element of the system's character or from a desire to deflect such a demand sufficiently to preserve the status quo. Regardless of the motivation for innovation, the process is about the same. Once the innovation has been activated, an overt appraisal of the organization's identifiable goals and objectives generally follows in an effort to place the innovation in the proper perspective of the whole organization. As William Gore has suggested, the process of making these concerns overt is exceedingly difficult. The process of appraisal often brings to the surface the conflicting motives distributed among several otherwise discontinuous roles within the community structure. Since a community is an aggregate of people not organically linked with each other but collaborating through a social system (a system which they have inherited and continually remake), individual goals frequently diverge and become inconsistent with the overall goals and aspirations of the community. So long as the goals of the community remain unstated, i.e., are not explicitly held up to the light for examination, these inconsistencies, while dysfunctional to the total system, may go unnoticed. However, when innovation is introduced and community goals must be made explicit, such conflicts become evident and must be dealt with if the system is to remain stable. As Gore states the proposition:

Many personalities make it possible to pursue mutually exclusive goals simultaneously *until circumstances arise that throw the clash of purposes in divergent activities against each other, precipitating the tension latent in the undertaking from the beginning.* [35]

Simon and March also suggest that "tension" or "stress" plays an important role in innovative action. However, their formulations differ somewhat from those of Gore: ". . . innovation will be most rapid and vigorous when the 'stress' on the organization is neither too high nor too low." According to this hypothesis, if achievement too easily exceeds aspirations (a condition of low stress), apathy results; if aspirations are very much above achievement (high stress), frustrations or desperation result. According to Simon and March:

In the first case, there is no motivation for innovation; in the second case, neurotic reactions interfere with effective innovation. Optimal "stress" results when the *carrot* is just a little way ahead of the donkey — when aspirations exceed achievement by a small amount.[36]

Simon and March offer other postulates which suggest that the rate of innovation is likely to increase when (1) existing procedures are unsatisfactory to meet changes in the environment; (2) performance is below some established standards; (3) there is a gradual upward movement of aspirations; and (4) opportunities are accidentally encountered.

Thus, while Gore views "tension" as an undesirable but unavoidable byproduct of innovative decisions, March and Simon consider some stress necessary to motivate innovation. Setting aside the semantic differences in these formulations, it would seem evident that both positions are valid. That is to say, the stress of demands placed on a system can trigger the decision-making process; such stress comes from external sources. If the decision responses are either routine or adaptive, relatively little adjustment is necessary and the system continues to function as before. If, however, major innovative decisions are required, internal stress or tensions may be generated within the system. This stress, in turn, may give rise to further adaptive decisions in order to return the system to a more even condition (steady state).

Adaptive and Innovative Processes in
Public Decisions

The failure of many studies of community decision-making to recognize
the various possible patterns of decision responses (a result of their generic use of
the term "decision" has produced a somewhat distorted picture of public
decision-making. Many decisions made within the structure of government never
reach the stage of a "public issue," because over time programmed decision
mechanisms have been developed to deal with a large number of decision-
demanding situations. Other potential issues are circumvented (at least temporarily) by adaptive decisions. Innovative decisions frequently generate public
controversy since these require a reexamination of ends (goals) as well as
the formulation of means to resolve decision-demanding situations.

Innovative decisions are governed by a process somewhat akin to the
systems concept of the Law of Requisite Variety. As was said previously
in connection with the outline of systems terminology, a system seeks to
develop regulators to ward off disturbances and maintain the system in a steady
state or at a point of equilibrium. The ability of the regulators to counter
disturbances is governed by the range of responses available to the regulatory
mechanisms. A regulator must have as many possible responses (as great a
variety) as there are potential or real disturbances. This is the Law of Requisite
Variety; stated more picturesquely, *only variety (of the regulator) can destroy
variety (of the disturbances).* [37]

Applying this concept to the public decision-making process, it may be
asserted that the range of innovation possible in decision-demanding situations is
contingent upon the capacity of the regulatory devices available to government.
This capacity, in turn, is often dependent on the technical personnel within
government and the freedom with which these professionals are permitted to
operate within the decision-making process.

Finally, public decisions seldom have the finality suggested by many
studies. Both innovative and adaptive decisions frequently generate further
adaptive or routine decisions which are not made in full view of this public and
which significantly may alter the original public decision.

3 Who Makes Public Policies and Decisions?

It may be argued that it is impossible to anticipate fully the range of decision situations that might arise in the future. However, while the content of all future public decisions cannot be predicted with any accuracy — nor the most effective manner in which they should be made — the subject matter of many decisions should have a high degree of predictability. Well over 80 percent of the decision situations that face public managers require programmatic or, at best, adaptive decisions. Further, such decision situations usually fall within a relatively small number of categories.

Since there is seldom adequate analysis of decision situations, however, a significantly large percentage of these decisions "go looking for a home," that is, there is a notable time lag between recognition of the need for a decision and the determination of an "appropriate" level at which the decision can be made. Further, when such decisions are made, most of them are made at a much higher level of public management than necessary.

The Policy-Administration Dichotomy

To place authority and responsibility for various kinds of decisions requires first that decision situations be classified according to kind and character. Such standard classifications as "policy decisions" and "operating decisions" are meaningless for all practical purposes. These arbitrary classifications also give rise to endless debates of a highly abstruse nature.

Lasswell has suggested that while policy decisions are generally associated with top-level administrators, they are frequently prescribed or influenced by other groups or individuals outside the top policy-making circle.[1] Jacob and Flink also discuss the role of major and minor prescribing groups in the formulation of policy decisions: ". . . in a governmental agency, a policy making board may be the major prescribing group for the executive roles. But in each of his operations the top official of the agency customarily deals with subordinates who form a minor prescribing group for aspects of the role that may never be considered by the policy making board as a prescribing group."[2]

Various other writers also have suggested that major policy decisions are not always made in the upper echelons of an organization but are "backed into" through the accumulation of a number of lesser decisions. Lepawsky, for example, asserts that "Administrators at all levels of responsibility are being constantly thrown into the area of decision-making, and their decisions inevitably add up to major policies in the subsequent course of events."[3]

There is, however, a cadre of writers who maintain a more traditional stance on the "separation of functions" between policy-makers and policy-administrators. Focusing their attention at the point where decisions are legitimized (i.e., at the top levels of decision-making and policy formulation), these writers conclude that public decisions are made through an incremental process, involving continuous compromise and adjustment. These studies tend to ignore the role of the administrator and other professionals in government. Much of the coordination and comprehensiveness which these writers find lacking in the public decision system must be provided at this level in the process.

The Separation-of-Functions Doctrine

These comments raise some fundamental questions about the traditional "separation of functions" between policy-makers and policy-administrators. In order to better understand the role of management in the public decision-making process, it may be useful to trace the development of this separation-of-functions doctrine, which has been a standard item in the public administrator's repertoire for several decades.

Efforts to make a clearer distinction between the policy-maker and the administrator can be traced back as far as the writings of Thomas Paine.[a] The more contemporary formulations, however, were introduced into academic political science by Frank Goodnow and Woodrow Wilson in the first clear break with the a priori rationalism of late nineteenth-century political science. Wilson, writing in 1887, suggested that all government was divided into "politics" and "administration" and assigned to certain units of government the function of policy-making and control, while reserving for others the expert task of executing these policies. This led Goodnow to reject the descriptive validity of separation of powers. The activities of government, he maintained, could not be accurately classified under the traditional triad; rather, there were in all governments two primary or ultimate functions — politics, or "the expression of the will of the state," and administration, or "the execution of that will."[4] In making this distinction, however, Goodnow was not attempting to make concrete divisions in terms of branches of government or equating a given operation with a given agency. Instead, he was differentiating behavior. Goodnow stated quite clearly that while the operations or functions performed

---

[a]Paine, in *Rights of Man*, objected to the classical separation of powers as an effective principle of government. His classification rested in what is now called politics and administration. In government, Paine suggested, there are two primary functions — legislating, or enacting law, and executing, or administering law. He classified the judicial function as executive.

by government could be conceptualized (differentiated) in terms of policy and administration, the authorities (concrete agencies) entrusted with such operations could not be completely separated.

The conceptual character of Goodnow's distinction was quickly lost, however, as other writers began to contribute to the literature of the emerging field of public administration. W. F. Willoughby, for example, attempted to give an even more distinct status to administration by not only marking it off from policy-making, but by setting it up as a fourth branch of government.[5] Soon the emphasis of public administrators shifted to concrete agencies which were assumed to carry out administrative functions, as opposed to policy-making bodies such as the legislature.

By the early twenties, when the first textbooks in the field of public administration began to appear, many basic doctrines had gained considerable clarity and acceptance. These early textbook-writers sought to collect, systematize, and defend these doctrines. In many cases, the basic factual categories and data relating to public administration were then built upon these doctrines. Having gained the status of authoritative textbook presentation and having been given an aura of science, the doctrine — and even the factual categories — tended to be accepted as firm and lasting truths. A synthesis and a crystallization had occurred.[6]

While the synthesis was a significant achievement, the hardening of doctrine into dogma — the crystallization — was unfortunate. For a period of more than a decade, from the mid-twenties until the late thirties, students of public administration were generally content with the conceptual structure that had been erected.

The separation-of-functions doctrine served early students of public administration rather well. It enabled them to distinguish and to emphasize that part of government in which they were most interested, i.e., the execution of decisions. It justified a new emphasis on the proper professional or "scientific" training for administrative work. More important, it lent support to the notion that, if administration is a function distinct from politics, then politicians should not be permitted to meddle or interfere with administration.[b]

Other Basic Doctrines of Public Administration

A second firm doctrine of public administration during this early period was that administration could be made into a science or, at the very least,

---

[b]Many earlier writers in the field of public administration before World War I were as much interested in a program of political reform as in administrative improvements. These two objectives were conceived to be closely related and were sought through the same programs. After the war, however, students of administration tended to become more specialized — more intent on administrative change — leaving programs of political reforms to others. They declared their independence of politics — a word and realm of low prestige during this period.

lend itself to study in a manner similar to that of the phenomena of physical science. This concept in turn led to the suggestion that the scientific study of administration would make possible the discovery of principles which were more or less analogous to the laws of physical science. Such an orientation reflected the interest of public administrators in the earlier movement associated principally with Frederick W. Taylor — the scientific management movement. Just as Taylor had "discovered the best way" to operate activities in the private sector through the application of a "proper methodology," students of public administration sought parallel principles in the public sector.

Two of the keystones in this expanding framework of administrative guidelines were the parallel concepts of the "division of labor" and the "principle of specialization." These concepts were given a prominent place in Gulick's classic essay, "The Theory of Organization."[7] Inherent in these concepts is the strategy of putting large numbers of people to work on relatively small tasks by subdividing large collective objectives. It was assumed by many, as a reflection of the writings of Durkheim and others in the emerging field of sociology, that this approach was a part of our heritage and that wherever organization was to be found, these principles were in operation.

Another important doctrine of early public administration was that "economy and efficiency" served as the central, if not the sole, goal of administration. Getting "fair, just and good" men into public office is not sufficient; what is important, to this doctrine, is that government be conducted in an economical and efficient manner. These objectives, in turn, could be achieved only through scientific study and the discovery and application of the proper principles of administration.[8]

POSDCORB: A Summary of Basic Doctrine

In the twenties and thirties, administrative process first gained a position coordinate with structure-oriented constructs of the formative period of public administration. During this time, the technology of administration could best be understood in terms of the staff functions of government, i.e., personnel, budgeting, planning, management analysis, and public information.

In the mid-thirties, Luther Gulick, in a noted essay in the *Papers on the Science of Administration*, set forth the concept of POSDCORB as a memory-aiding device to recall the functions of the executive in administration: Planning, Organizing, Staffing, Directing, Coordinating, Reporting, and Budgeting.

The fact that *planning* came first in Gulick's formulation was probably an accident of phonetics. Operations planning, however, was a very prominent concept in the scientific management movement and was therefore carried over and amplified in administrative thinking and writing during the thirties. This amplification was brought about, in part, as a reaction to laissez-faire economic policies, which many thought brought on or heightened the effects of the Depression. Thus, concepts of economic planning joined earlier formulations of operations planning as basic responsibilities of the administrator.[c]

Gulick's treatment of organizing further developed the themes of division of labor and specialization of function. To these basic concepts were added a further elaboration of the differences between line and staff activities (*staffing*), the *directive functions* of the executive and administrator, and the need for and means of *coordination*. Of particular interest in these formulations is a discussion of the advantages and disadvantages of emphasizing (1) purpose, (2) process, (3) people or things, and (4) place in constructing or modifying an organization. Gulick's essay presents essentially what might be termed "organization-chart" theory — theory which is characterized by strong emphasis on logical, rational, prescribed relations between persons or functions.[9]

Of the various POSDCORB categories, *reporting* was the least developed conceptually (as measured by contemporary interest in the role of communications in organization and decision-making theory). Reporting in this context meant the communication of information up and down the chain of command (the established, formal hierarchy) and outward from the organization to those to whom the organization was responsible.

The emphasis in *budgeting* during this period was on the central control of spending (the performance budget was still ten years away). The budget was viewed as a safeguard against political abuse of public funds. However, the initial stages of a management orientation to budgeting, in which an emphasis was placed on the efficient performance of work and prescribed activities, were evident in the writings of Gulick and others.

In summary, the philosophy of early public administration was that: (1) proper analysis of governmental functions divides administration from politics; (2) the sphere of administration is one to which scientific analysis can and should be applied; (3) the application of scientific methods of inquiry leads to the discovery of principles and techniques of organization and administration; and (4) these principles, in turn, determine the way in which governmental functions can be administered most economically and efficiently.

A Shift in Emphasis and the Human Relations Approach

With the coming of the Roosevelt administration, the line between administration and policy began to be readjusted. This was the era of Merriam, Brownlow, Emmerich, White, Pfiffner, and others who contributed to the

---

[c]Physical land-use planning was carried out by other agencies within the structure of local and state government.

further development of a formal conception of public administration. Their
writings were distilled from the experience of several generations of administrators into a cogent representation of the structure and processes of organization.[d]

During this same era, an additional dimension of organization emerged
as a result of the efforts of the Harvard Business School and the research
of Roethlisberger and Dickson in their focal study of "human relations" in the
early twenties.[10] The proponents of this new point of view maintained
that organizations must be conceived of and operated as more than mere "pieces
of societal machinery"; organizations are manned by people and these people
must be treated as human beings, not as cogs of a machine. Thus the human
relations school paved the way for a growing concern with the social dimension
of organizations.

Sociologists and social psychologists, following the lead of Max Weber,
turned their attention to bureaucratic organizations. From their observations,
they found a good deal more than hierarchies of authority and command
and formally ascribed activities. An organization, said the social psychologists,
has several faces.[e] The formal arrangement — embodied in the rational system of
action and represented by formal organization charts — constitutes only one
of these faces, but one especially appropriate for presentation to the external
world. Social realities of the inner workings of any organization, however,
frequently run contrary to the ideal of a smooth-operating, well-lubricated
machine. Therefore, organizations tend to turn their other face from those
outside their membership. Typically, this involves a discreet amount of
self-deception about internal problems, so that the inner face may be hidden
even from those within the organization.[f]

The attention of those interested in administration as a form of group
process shifted to leadership in the late forties and from leadership to communication, to the dynamics of motivation, to reward and penalty systems, and
more recently, to group decision-making. Contributors in this area include Robert
Bales, Bernard Bass, Howard Baumgartel, and Edith Bennett, among others.

By the end of the Second World War, partly in recognition of the growing

------

[d]The label "classical theory," which March and Simon use to characterize writings of
this era, indicates its position in the study of public administration today. It remains the
foundation and the legitimatizing rationale of those who practice administration, and as long
as these accepted ideas can be reinterpreted in the context of current problems, traditional
theory will have a useful place.

[e]This point will be discussed further in connection with the concepts of influence and
authority in organizations.

[f]Victor Thompson's book, *Modern Organization* (New York: Alfred Knopf, 1962), is
perhaps the most extensive work to date on the "defense mechanisms" adopted by organizations to shore up the legitimacy of role definitions and consequently, the legitimacy of the
formal aspects of organizations. Thompson identifies three such defense mechanisms: (1)
ideology — systems of ideas and beliefs supportive of hierarchical positions; (2) dramaturgy —
the means by which persons in hierarchical positions seek to control the impressions of others
about the nature of these positions and their accompanying roles; and (3) bureaupathy —
the rigid and ritualistic performance of role as an attempted escape from insecurity.

interest in the informal structure of organizations, a more flexible definition
of the relationship between policy and administration had emerged. Perhaps one
of the outstanding statements of this emphasis was presented by Paul Appleby,
who had served as Undersecretary of Agriculture and Assistant Director
of the Budget during the forties under the Roosevelt Administration.

Administration is, within rather wide limits, the application of policy generally
formulated in law. Successively the application is made more specific by
policy formulations applied to particular publics, made still more specific by
application to smaller publics, and finally to individual cases. Conversely, it
is the formulation and application of policy in particular cases made more and
more general at successively higher levels representative of successively larger
publics, until at the highest executive level, the President, is representative of the
whole American public. Administration is in very large measure these two
processes carried on simultaneously.[11]

It may be said that legislative bodies make very general policy, and that administrators make policy by applying the general policy at successively less abstract
levels.[12]

The rigid, even dogmatic, separation of politics and administration has been
almost wholly abandoned, at least in a conceptual sense. It has become proper
to regard administration as a process diffused by or permeated with politics —
both the contest for power (whether or not it is a party contest) and the making
of policy. As Norton Long has observed:

However attractive an administration receiving its values from political policy-
makers may be, it has one fatal flaw. It does not accord with the facts of
administrative life. Nor is it likely to. In fact, it is highly dubious even as an
ideal. Though the quest for science, mathematical precision and certainty has an
undeniable psychological appeal, it runs the risk of becoming a fastidious
piece of ivory-tower escapism.[13]

Thus, Sayre has suggested that a reappraisal of the separability of politics and
administration has been undertaken in most orthodox textbooks in the field
of public administration. Sayre contends that a consensus seems to have
developed around the following themes: (1) public administration is a major
political process; (2) organization theory is a problem of political strategy; and
(3) public administration is ultimately a political theory.[14] To these
observations may be added the suggestion of Martin Landau that this reappraisal
has come about because the terms "policy" and "administration" were employed
not as concepts but as names of institutions.

In concretizing the concept of administration, equating it with a given branch or
agency of government, a dichotomy was formed that was inevitably to be
repudiated . . . . Had careful consideration been given to the analytic character

of these concepts in the first place, had they not been confused with "real types," the sharp swing which has occurred would probably not have been necessary.[15]

A "New" Emphasis on Decision-Making

In the late forties, some writers began to suggest that the whole process is one of *decision-making*, regardless of its policy or administrative nature. Alvin Brown, writing in 1945, in the tradition of Gulick, Urwick, and Mooney, stated that ". . . if planning is the highest of the three phases of administration . . . decision may be said to be the highest act of administration."[16]

It is Herbert A. Simon, however, who must receive credit for casting the concept of decision-making in a starring role. Noting that Chester Barnard and Edwin Stene both pointed the way in the thirties, Simon asserts that decision-making is the pivotal act of administration. Few books in administrative theory have aroused as much controversy as Simon's *Administrative Behavior*, published in 1947.[g] The crux of the objections raised concerning Simon's formulations is that, by separating fact and value in decision-making, Simon produced ". . . a new and subtle version of the earlier formulation of the separation of policy and administration."[17]

The Doctrine of Logical Positivism

Simon introduced to the literature of administrative theory the doctrine of *logical positivism*. Asserting a close connection with modern physical science, logical positivism abhors metaphysics, dismisses ethics, emphasizes empiricism, and places a high premium on rigorous, logical analysis. A sharp distinction is made in logical positivism between questions of fact ("is" questions) and questions of value ("ought" questions). Basic to Simon's formulation is the concept that the realm of value is the realm of preference, of morals or ethics, and therefore cannot be empircally verified.[18]

In the logical-positivist view suggested by Simon, the administrative process is (or can be) an applied science, in which knowledge of emprical

---

[g]A second edition was published in 1957. Except for the addition of an introduction, the text is unchanged. However, in this introduction Simon includes a number of new conceptions, such as the "model of satisficing," which substantially alter the rationale of his original formulations. This led reviewers such as Edward C. Banfield ("The Decision-Making Schema," *Public Administration Review*, Vol. 17 (Autumn, 1957), pp. 278–285) to speak of "straining and the pretense," and to conclude that it "was a better book ten years ago than it is now." Banfield suggests that Simon destroyed the "rationale of the old conceptual scheme without offering any new one and without, apparently, being aware of what he has done." p. 284).

regularities is used to achieve whatever goals or values are given by the political system. The administrative process is inevitably a question of value and fact. Thus, in logical-positivist terms, the critics are correct in their assertions of the pervasiveness of politics or policy in the administrative process. However, their criticisms go too far, and in so doing, miss an important logical — and methodological — distinction between questions of fact and questions of value.

This orientation provided Simon with an effective instrument for reasserting and defending the doctrines of public administration which had characterized the earlier period of the twenties and the thirties. His conceptual and methodological frameworks are completely different, however. In Simon's scheme, a decisions is defined as a conclusion drawn from a set of premises. These premises are of two kinds:

1. factual premises — subject to empirical testing in order to ascertain their validity; and
2. value premises — imperatives which are not subject to testing since they are concerned with what "ought to be " rather than with what "is."

Simon's purpose in stressing this distinction is to make clear the "different criteria of 'correctness' that must be applied to the ethical and factual elements in a decision."[19] Here Simon is suggesting that the rules of scientific procedure, particularly the rule of observation, cannot warrant value judgments. Value judgments are analytic propositions (i.e., their denial constitutes a self-contradiction). Since they are analytic, such judgments cannot be part of the body of empirical science constituting the basis for factual (synthetic) statements.[h]

Simon employs this distinction to clarify policy and administration by asserting that organizations are based on not one but two modes of division of labor and specialization. In addition to the recognized type of horizontal specialization — division of labor according to a particular task — there is a form of vertical specialization in which the division of labor is based on authority rather than work. Thus Simon concludes that the higher the rank of an individual, the more his job consists of decision-making and the fewer the actual performances he will be called on to carry out. Decision-making, in turn, is divided in such a way that the higher-in-rank establish broad policy lines, while lower-echelon positions administer policy by breaking it down into more detailed and specific decisions. Thus, decisions are made at several levels within an organiza-

---

[h]If value judgments are to be deemed "correct," it must be because they are in accord with some set of axiological rules. "Oughts" are defined in terms of such rules, and therefore, they are not deducible from the "is." Different criteria of correctness must be applied in each case.

tion; however, policy-making is concentrated at the top, policy specification
is carried out by the middle echelon, and the actual work performance is
carried out by the lower ranks.

The important point to be derived from this construct is that the hierarchical structure of any organization permits all decisions, except those defining
ultimate objectives, to rest on factual rather than on value premises, that is,
to be decisions concerning means rather than ends.[i] Therefore, once the overall
objectives are established, the hierarchical structure serves as a framework
for means-ends chains — specifying for each member of the hierarchy the ends
of his task, and thus confining his duties to the selection of the best means
for achieving those ends. In other words, each member of the hierarchy has his
value premises supplied by his superiors and his search for alternative means
narrowed by procedural regulations.

Simon's formulations do not differ conceptually from those of his critics
who argue that policy-making and administration must be viewed as a continuum;
that policy-making does not occur at a single point in an organization, but at
many levels, and further, that these points shift as time, circumstances, and
political behavior demand. Simon was not attempting to defy reality in
his formulations of the division of decision-making responsibilities. Rather, he
attempted to distinguish various and essential components of those responsibilities. In this respect, Simon's objectives again parallel those of Goodnow;
Simon has attempted to differentiate operations or functions and not concrete
agencies. He has isolated certain characteristics of the decision process, for
purposes of analysis only, in an effort to develop a set of concepts that will
permit empirically valid descriptions of administrative situations. Insofar as
decisions lead to a selection of final goals, they may be treated as "value
judgments" — the value component predominates; insofar as decisions implement
those goals, they may be treated as "factual judgments" — the factual component
predominates.

Planning and the Policy-Administration Dichotomy

As has been pointed out, public administration models tend to emphasize
problem-solving rather than long-range planning. As a consequence, for several
decades the processes of public planning and the practices of public administration have been somewhat at odds. These conceptual differences have arisen
despite the fact that the fields have common origins.

---

[i]Simon suggests that rational decision-making may be viewed as consisting of means-
ends chains, i.e., given certain ends, appropriate means are selected for their attainment; but
once reached, the ends become the means for the attainment of further ends. Properly conceived, economy and efficiency are measures of comparative effectiveness of means in
achieving ends — any ends. As such, these concepts from earlier administrative theory have
an essential role in the applied science of administration as formulated by Simon.

Planning, like public administration, emerged as a recognized governmental function in the early twentieth century, when many local governments were still characterized by boss-rule, backroom politics, corruption, and inefficiency. To insulate the planning function from undue political influence, early theorists sought to establish an independent body of citizens who would have long tenure and would be beyond the reach of "politics." This was the ideal which the 1928 Standard City Planning Enabling Act, written by a nine-man committee of leaders of the planning movement, tried to approximate.

The members of the commission should feel secure in their tenure of office as long as they perform their functions faithfully and retain the confidence of the community. Conceivably, however, a situation might arise where a mayor might wish to remove members of the commission because they had recommended something that was not in harmony with his political desires. The members of the commission should be protected from such a situation by specifying removal for cause only and requiring the mayor to file a statement for his reasons.

The authors of the 1928 Standard City Planning Enabling Act, especially Alfred Bettman and Edward M. Bassett, believed in the concept of the independent city planning commission. It was Bassett's view, for example, that the master plan "should be kept within the four walls of the city planning commission."

The 1928 Act had great influence on city planning legislation throughout the country. The independent planning commission concept predominated up to World War II, and is still held by many members of the planning profession. It had its strongest advocate in the writings of Rexford Tugwell, whose view of planning as a "fourth power," in addition to the executive, legislative, and judicial powers, influenced the thinking of many planners during the thirties and forties.

They heyday of the independent city planning commission came to an end in the late forties, however, when permanent professional staffs began to be established in the larger cities. As planning budgets were increased and the relative influence of the planning commission began to grow, further controls over the independent commission were asserted by the appointing authorities — the city council or the mayor.

One of the significant contributions to this shift was Robert Walker's study of thirty-seven city planning commissions, published in 1941.[20] Walker offered substantial evidence to show that independent commissions had relatively little influence on community development. He proposed a second concept of the role of public planning, in which the planning director would serve as a staff aid to the chief executive and the planning commission would serve in an advisory role to the planning director. While Walker's proposal placed the public planner in the role of a political activist and confidant to the chief executive, interpreters of the staff-aide concept viewed the planner primarily as a technical expert. To further remove the planning function from the political arena and to give assurance that planning was in accord with the democratic process, further emphasis was placed on the advisory nature of planning. A planner makes recommendations as to course of action, but the final determination of policies and courses of action must lie with those officials in government who can be held accountable for their decisions, i.e., the legislative and executive officials directly responsible to the citizens of the community.

The concept of the planner as an advisor on matters of policy, rather than as an innovator, remains a fundamental precept in the ethos of a majority of planning practitioners. As John Dyckman has observed:

Neither scientist nor political-mover, the city planner is still no ornamental appendage of government. His forte is command over a commodity which, though rough and home-made, is still not accessible to most citizens. That commodity is a view of the future; not the future of a single enterprise, but of a whole complex system like the urban community. The planner is thus a purveyor of vital advice.[21]

The Myth of Apolitical Action

The planning profession has been criticized by persons from inside and outside its ranks for its deliberate aloofness from the political process. Henry Churchill, a staunch supporter of the principle of decision by the majority, has suggested that planners perform technical rather than professional functions since they merely offer alternatives to the persons who are the real decision-makers. If planners wish to become professional, Churchill concludes, they must seek both power and responsibility for making decisions affecting urban development.

More recently, Francine Rabinovitz has suggested that: ". . . only if the profession's image includes the picture of the planner as rightfully a political actor will the planner attain both professional rewards and the completion of concrete programs."[22] This would seem to imply that the planning profession is still struggling in the darkness created by the shadow of the separation-of-functions doctrine of the twenties and thirties. Thus Rabinovitz concludes that until planning casts off this "myth of apolitical action," it is doomed to be "an occupation in the process of attempting to be professionalized" — "a function in search of an identity."

Rabinovitz advances the hypothesis that the norms of the planning profession provide little induced motivation to choose a more politicized role and, in fact, provide disincentives to do so. The suggestion is also made that the personality of the average planner inhibits him from becoming more of a political activist. While there is little evidence to support this somewhat social-psychological hypothesis, Rabinovitz is not alone in her "personality" thesis. Dyckman, for example, has observed that ". . . there has been a very sharp distinction between the practice of city planning whose evangelism is, after all, distinctively middle-class, civic-club salvation and the politics of American city government, which is dominated by working-class realists with a low regard for missionaries."[23]

The Relationship Between Planning and Policy-Making

While planners have been reluctant to expand the definition of their role to include greater political involvement, others have suggested that, try as he may, the planner cannot avoid political involvement if he is to carry out effectively his professional responsibilities. As Norton Long has observed:

Plans are policies and policies, in a democracy at any rate, spell politics. The question is not whether planning will reflect politics but whose politics will it reflect. What values and whose values will planners seek to implement?[24]

The politics of planners in the past, Long observes, has been ". . . the politics of a do-gooding elite, of middle-class respectability, of newspaper support, and of a widespread acceptance that planners have a special wisdom akin to that of Platonic philosopher kings."[25] However, Long adds, if the products of planning labors are to be more than mere "civic New Year's resolutions," planners, like public administrators, must become involved in the political process.

When the greasy, grimy hands of politics are laid on planning because it means votes, the subject and its practitioners have come of age. This means planning has come to matter. The fearful would do well to join Ophelia in a nunnery.[26]

The intrinsic relationship between planning and the making of policy has also been asserted by C. Easton Rothwell.

Planning suggests a systematic attempt to shape the future. When such planning becomes a prelude to action, it is policy-making. For policy, broadly speaking, is a body of principles to guide action. The application of policy is a calculated choice — a decision to pursue specific goals by doing specified things. The formulation and execution of policy usually consist of four steps: (1) a clarification of goals, (2) an exhaustive evaluation of the situation to be met, (3) the selection of a course of action by weighing the probable consequences of various alternatives, and (4) the determination of optimum means for carrying out the action decided upon. Since the situation to be met is normally not static but involves a complex of moving forces, policy and action are, in effect, a design to

shape the future by exerting influence upon trends that flow from the past
into the present.[27]

There is some evidence to suggest that the public planner has begun to
adopt this broader definition of planning as an integral part of the policy
formulation process. In a survey by Rabinovitz and Pottinger, some 200 planning
directors were asked to define the role of their agency in its relations with the
policy-making bodies of the community.[28] Seventy-one percent of the
respondents stated that they purposely integrated policy advice and value
judgments with their technical recommendations, while only four and a half
percent saw their role as strictly a technical one. The remaining group (24.4
percent) stated that some "unavoidable" policy judgments were found in their
technical recommendations.

It would appear that planning practitioners, like public administrators, are
faced with the dilemma of seeking to influence public policy without getting
involved politically — of retaining the prestige of technical expertise while
hoping to affect the course of practical political affairs. This somewhat
schizophrenic attitude is in part a product of education and training and the
traditions that have grown up as these professions have struggled for their
identity. It may be suggested that the planning profession is now at the point
reached by public administration in the late forties: facing a growing awareness
that it must become involved in more than the mere execution of decisions
handed down by policy-making bodies, but unable to determine exactly the
degree of involvement in the political process necessary to make planning a more
effective voice in public decision-making. As James Lee has observed, planning
and planning administration, while intimately related, are not the same
thing.[29]

Models of Community Decision-Making

To this point in the discussion, the public decision-making process has been
examined apart from the broader environment in which these decisions take
place — the community. Public decisions are seldom made without some
consideration of their impact on the community. Therefore, it would seem
appropriate to expand the scope of discussion in order to examine the contributions of various studies of the community decision process.

Peter Rossi has defined a *community decision* as: ". . . a choice among
alternative modes of action whose goals are the change or maintenance of
community-wide institutions or facilities and which is made by an authoritative
person or group within the community institutions."[30] To the average
citizen, however, it may often appear that community decisions emerge from
two sources: (1) a somewhat arbitrary product of impulse and caprice on the
part of decision-makers who are unable to reconcile effectively the diverse

viewpoints of the community; and (2) the expressed choice of a relatively small
group of "influentials" operating behind the scenes.

Support for the "Common Man" Definition

For the most part, studies of community decision-making — ranging from
the "power structure" model suggested by Floyd Hunter to the "pluralistic"
model introduced by Robert Dahl and his colleagues — tend to support this
"common man" definition of the public decision-making process. Mann and
others have suggested, however, that it is possible to think of these two models as
extremes on a continuum, with large diversified metropolitan areas tending to
concentrate at the diffused-influence extreme (the pluralistic model) and smaller,
specialized communities exemplifying the concentrated-power model.[31]
As John Dewey has observed, there is a common confusion in human thinking
between a true contradiction which embraces all possibilities, and a contrast
which lists only two out of a number of possibilities. Much of the apparent
controversy in the social sciences over the two basic models of community
decision-making can be attributed to this problem, as well as to mere interdisciplinary squabbling.

When much of the sound and fury is set aside, it would seem that these two
models are in substantial agreement on a number of points, in terms of underlying assumptions, methodology, and findings. Therefore, the following discussion will not delve deeply into the controversy generated by these studies but
will instead concentrate on the points of agreement. Before undertaking this
discussion, however, it will be useful to examine briefly some of the earlier
community studies which have provided a foundation for these models.

The Early Studies of Community Control Systems

Anthropologists have used the community as a basic unit of analysis for
many years and have produced a rich library of community studies. The
anthropological style of investigation was first applied to an American community in the early twenties, when the Lynds undertook their study of Muncie,
Indiana. The Lynds' study, *Middletown*, and their later study, *Middletown in
Transition*, represent an important innovation in the methodological approach
used to describe and analyze American society.

The Lynds' studies of Muncie concluded that business interests and in
particular the Ball family dominated the city in many ways. The machinery of
justice was influenced by the rich or by corporations, the mass media censored
news that was adverse to the business class, approval for civic improvements
had to be secured from the leading business interests in the city, and so forth.

Many writers have challenged the findings of the Lynds on the basis of the facts that: (1) the examples presented in the two studies showed that the elite did not always rule merely in its own interests, because similar values were "distributed to different groups within classes, to lower classes, and to groups cutting across class boundaries," and (2) the Lynds were largely committed to an antibusiness, leftist viewpoint.[32] Nevertheless, the Middletown studies were such an achievement that they exerted a very powerful infleunce over the thinking of other people.

Shortly after the publication of *Middletown in Transition*, W. Lloyd Warner went to Newburyport, Massachusetts to conduct his study, published as *Yankee City*. Warner's account was more than an anthropological study of a tribal community. The class structure, labor, the corporation, the ethnic groups, and so on which he found there did not lend themselves to ethnographic study. However, Warner was able to build on this methodology to produce a fundamental approach to modern community analysis.

As Polsby has observed, Warner never confronted the question of power directly, except in one chapter where he attempted to show that the greater the importance of a city official, the higher his social status. Warner assumed a coalition between "adjacent" classes, since the "high control officers" were composed primarily of upper- and upper-middle-class persons.

Two other studies of this early period were August Hollingshead's *Elmtown's Youth*, a study of Morris, Illinois, and Warner's study, *Democracy in Jonesville*. Both of these studies supported the notion of upper-class control and social and economic power affecting every aspect of community life.

The Basic Models of Community Decision-Making

The next major innovation in the study of community control systems was begun in 1946, when Floyd Hunter, a social worker who was fired from his job in Atlanta, set out to find the reasons for his dismissal. In the process, he formulated the reputational approach to community analysis.

According to Hunter's power-structure model, a relatively small number of people in effect decide what the community will do. Although these decisions are legitimized by authoritative persons (i.e., elected officials), the "decision-makers" are not politicians but the big industrialists and businessmen of the community. Moreover, this small group of economic influentials operating behind the scenes is monolithic or at least highly cohesive. According to the power-structure model, the power of the elite is pervasive and unidimensional — it operates everywhere and on every question that the community decides.[j]

---

[j]This model generally fits what many planners and public administrators have come to believe from years of frustration in trying to achieve better implementation of their programs and plans. It implies that the professional in government is probably wasting his time in trying to establish close working relationships with elected officials. Instead he should plant his ideas for community action someplace closer to the top of the power pyramid.

Hunter's methods of determining the "power elite" of Regional City (Atlanta) are fairly well known, involving such conventional behavioral science research techniques as the interview, the panel, the interaction analysis. Hunter used a panel of judges to rank the most influential or "powerful" members of the community and from a list of 175 rated by his panel, selected forty as the principal subject of his book. Hunter then singled out ten "top leaders" from the list of forty by asking questions such as: "If a project were before the community that required decision by a group of leaders — leaders that nearly everyone would accept — which ten on the list of forty would you choose?"[33] Hunter thus began with the assumption of a leadership elite; since he had no clear criterion for top leadership, he relied on reputation as a principal indicator of influence. Greer has suggested that this approach will yield evidence of a power structure even if one does not exist, since people are anxious to identify leadership roles if approached in this manner.

Hunter's approach had considerable influence on community analysis during the forties and early fifties, principally on those studies conducted by sociologists. It was not long, however, before political scientists began to react. They said, in effect, that power is something that can be known only by its effects. To study the effects of power, it is necessary to study complex situations in which someone wins and someone loses and something happens that is different from what would have been had there not been this process.

Dahl, Polsby, and others of the pluralistic school of community decision theory are in accord with power-structure theories to the extent that they recognize the existence of power inequalities in a community. Pluralists assert, however, that these inequalities are "dispersed" rather than concentrated and cumulative. From their studies, they conclude that a community is really governed by a number of segments of power or influence and that no one segment is influential in all questions or public issues. The initial assumptions underlying studies of community decisions, the pluralists maintain, should be that communities are polyarchic rather than hierarchical; that power is diffused rather than concentrated behind the scenes.

Dahl, in his study of New Haven, [34] focuses his attention on actions of individuals in the present, confining the discussion to issues that are in the public arena at a given point in time. He selects three issue-areas — party nominations, urban redevelopment, and public education — as a "fair sample" of the important major decisions made in the community. From an intensive study of these issues, Dahl concludes that there is a minimal overlap in leader participation and power is therefore diffused and pluralistically based.[k]

Others have reached somewhat similar conclusions. Sayre and Kaufman, studying governmental processes in New York City, found a diffused pattern that could be best described in terms of a number of smaller pyramids rather than as a single large one.[35] Banfield's studies of Chicago, [36] concentrating

---

[k]Much of the criticism of Dahl's approach has centered on the choice of issue-areas, so widely different as to practically guarantee the finding of minimal overlap in participation.

on the forces influencing political leaders, suggest that the "influentials" are usually not big industrialists and businessmen but spokesmen of civic associations at a lower level.[1]

Norton Long's view of community decision-making as an "ecology of games" can be seen as an interesting variation on the basic pluralistic model.[37] Long concludes that there are many types of games being "played" in a city, i.e., a political game, a banking game, a social game, a newspaper game, and so forth. These games are integrated by "bridging" persons; that is, persons who participate in more than one game. These bridging persons or intermediaries not only serve as "scorekeepers," but also transmit information among the games. Long concludes that there is no one group which holds the set of games together, no one who has an overall interest and concern for the total community. Thus, decisions are not made by an economic or social elite, or by pluralistic groups; they are made by default.

William Wheaton has provided a synthesis of the diffused influence model:

In most cities there is no monolithic structure of power, pyramidal in shape, with a few influentials at the top making basic decisions for both the private and the public sectors of the economy. Rather there is a multiplicity of lesser concentrations of power, relatively independent of each other, competing for influence at times and in certain subject matter areas, cooperating at other times and in other subject matter areas, occasionally engaged in outright conflict and often used by political leaders to reconcile tensions and conflicts within the community. Political institutions should be viewed as a part of this system of power and influence, which is in constant flux.[38]

Points of Similarity Among These Approaches

As has been pointed out, much of the apparent controversy over the two basic models of community decision-making can be attributed to mere interdisciplinary squabbling. This controversy has shown the differences between the two approaches but has failed to indicate the various areas in which the two models are in substantial agreement.

Both approaches treat "decisions" as a generic term. Relatively little attention is given by Hunter, *et. al.* or Dahl and his colleagues to the notion that there are levels of decisions in the sense that this concept has been formulated by Simon and others in organization theory. Both approaches assert that public decision-making at any given time occurs within a relatively narrow "agenda of alternatives." This leads to the conclusion that most decisions affecting

---

[1]Banfield's conclusion that an "elite" could if it wished ". . . exercise a great, and probably a decisive, influence . . . " on public decisions confuses somewhat the controversy between the two models.

the community are made by individuals or groups without any public involvement. From the point of view of governmental operations, these are "nondeci-
sions," because they are not raised to the level of public concern. The pluralistic
view is favored by a methodology which singles out decisions which actually
reach the point of consideration by various public committees and thereby
become the focus of struggle among legitimate competing groups and individuals.
The power-elite view is favored by a methodology which looks at "settled"
decisions, structural aspects of the economy, and other long-range aspects of
community organization. Thus, the pluralist rejects the significance of "non-
decisions," while the power-structure theorist assume them away as another set
of decisions made by the power elite.

To focus only on decisions that reach the public arena is to ignore two
significant contributing factors in public decision-making: (1) decisions made in
the private sector which have a public impact (i.e., private land-use decisions,
investment decisions, and so forth); and (2) decisions made within the structure
of government (often by staff personnel) which narrow the range of alternatives
(set the "agenda") in terms of the issues which emerge in the public arena.
Both of these categories of "non-decisions" provide important constraints to
the public decision-making process.

This leads to two other closely related areas of "agreement." Both
approaches have focused on *individual power* − on the question of whether
economic or public leaders are more important in making current public
decisions. Advocates of power-structure theory have fragmented the economic
structure and its effects by choosing to look at individuals holding high positions
in the economic and social system. The pluralists have also focused on individuals,
their influence, the use of their resources, and so forth. By choosing to focus
on individuals, both approaches have overlooked certain factors crucial to public
decision-making. Power elitists, concerned with the economic base of the
community with general patterns of distribution of values, tend to overlook
important political mechanisms which intervene between property and wealth
in a democratic society to constrain the upper classes. They fail to deal adequately
with the situational factors of political decisions which may alter considerably
the outcome of particular struggles over the allocation of resources. They are
concerned with structure and outcomes, not with situations. Pluralists, on the
other hand, take structure and culture for granted, as part of the consensus
at any given time. Structure and culture, being constant, do not enter into their
model of the decision-making situation or the contingencies of that situation.
Pluralists deal only with situational factors and outcomes of particular events
and controversies as variables.

The second related point arises from the fact that neither approach
establishes the possibility of serious debate over policy alternatives anywhere
in the political system. This is to be expected in the power-structure approach,
since consensus of an elite precludes debate over alternatives. But the question

must be raised in connection with the pluralistic approach as to whether "pluralism" exists if everyone agrees on major policies. Failure to include the possibility of debate over alternatives must again be attributed, in part, to the focus on issues in the public arena.

Although those of the pluralistic school would undoubtedly vigorously deny the fact, it may be suggested that both approaches admit the possibility of a monolithic power structure. As has been noted, the power-structure theory is built on this assumption. Dahl, on the other hand, speaks of Mayor Lee of New Haven as having "pyramided his resources" to achieve passage of his programs. It would seem, then, that elected officials, in the accumulation of such resources, could conceivably constitute a "monolithic" power structure. Frank Munger, in describing decision-making in Syracuse, implies that they do. In discussing the role of Mayor Rolland Marvin, Munger notes that there was a "high concentration of community authority in the hands of a single man, simultaneously a political leader and public official."[39] Thus he suggests that Mayor Marvin wielded an unprecedented influence over public decisions. Marvin's achievements, however, were not unlike those of Lee after he had "pyramided his resources." Dahl denies, however, that Mayor Lee's "executive-centered order" was a monolith: "The preference of any group that could swing its weight at election time — teachers, citizens of the Hill, Negroes on Dixwell Avenue, or Notables — would weigh heavily in the calculations of the mayor, for the executive-centered coalition was not the *only* important pattern of influence in New Haven."[40] The point, however, is that Lee successfully used his resources (recognizing the potential influences that could be exerted by other groups or coalitions) to circumvent opposition to his programs and thus continue in power.

Finally, as has been implied previously, both approaches bias their findings through the selection of issues on which to focus their investigation. The policy issues treated by Hunter were either trivial or of predominant interest to businessmen. Further, they were issues in which "top leaders" could function successfully: getting an international trade association to locate in Atlanta, attracting new industry, and so forth. On other issues of wider concern, the elite was either split or relatively ineffective: (1) the plan of development for the city; (2) the sales tax; (3) traffic control; and (4) race relations. Dahl's issues, on the other hand, were not typical; they did not divide the "few" from the "many," and therefore the exercise of influence remained diffuse.

Summary of Contributions

In summary, it may be suggested that while both approaches offer important insights into community decision-making, neither pursues the subject in sufficient depth to provide a complete picture of the public decision-making process. The ideological disputes over method and terminology are, in large measure, due to a failure of both sides to recognize that: (1) the power-structure theorists are not really testing the present role of community economic dominants but are concerned with the long-range impact of economic and political structure and culture; and (2) the "pluralists" are not really testing the impact of deeply embedded institutions but are concerned with the situational impact of many different factors impinging upon present decisions. What would seem to be the next logical step is to build on the positive contributions of both approaches, while at the same time attempting to alleviate some of the problems inherent in each. In particular, an effort should be made in building a model of public decision-making to facilitate further investigation of the question of the different kinds and levels of decisions and the relative influence exercised by various participants in these decisions.

Decision Analysis

In the light of the foregoing considerations, it would seem appropriate to formulate a model of public decision-making which would permit a fuller exploration of those areas in which the public administrator and planner might appropriately exercise their influence and technical expertise. At the same time, such a model should be tested against the present practices of public management that have achieved various levels of success in influencing public decisions.

Four Basic Characteristics of Public Decisions

As a point of departure in the development of such a model, it is important to return to the question of authority and responsibility for public decisions. As has been noted, the arbitrary classifications of "policy decisions" offer little assistance in resolving this question. There are, however, four basic characteristics which, in large measure, determine the nature of any public decision. Each of these characteristics should be examined in the early stages of decision analysis to ascertain the most appropriate level at which the actual decision can and should be made.

The first important characteristic deals with the *degree of futurity* of a given decision situation. For how long into the future does the actual decision commit the agency or government? How quickly can the decision be reversed should this become necessary? Many difficult and important decisions may involve a complex analysis of many factors and substantial commitments of public funds. However, if such decisions are almost immediately reversible, they should always be made at the lowest level of management at which the relevant facts are most readily available.

A second criterion relates to the *impact* of a decision on other functions, on other areas, or on government as a whole. If the decision affects only one function, it is of the lowest order. Otherwise, it will have to be made on a higher level, where the impact of all affected functions can be considered. To use more technical systems language: "optimization" of process and performance of one function or area must not be made at the expense of other functions or areas; decisions must not lead to "suboptimization" for the agency or government as a whole.

A third factor in identifying the character of a decision situation is determined by the *number of qualitative aspects* that enter into the actual decision: basic principles of conduct, ethical values, social and political beliefs, and so forth. As Simon has pointed out, the moment value considerations must be taken into account, the decision becomes one of a higher order and requires either determination or review at a higher level of authority. Frequently, the most important, as well as the most common, of qualitative factors are human beings and their expectations in decision situations.

Finally, decisions can be classified according to whether they are *recurrent* or *rare*. Both types must be made on the level in the organization that corresponds to the futurity, impact, and qualitative characteristics of the decision situation. Recurrent decisions require the establishment of general rules so that appropriate response mechanisms can be "programmed" into the decision system to deal with such situations when they reoccur. The formulation of such rules may require a decision at a relatively high level. The application of the rule to a specific case, while also a decision, then becomes a routine matter and can be placed at a much lower level. The rare or unique decision situation, however, must be treated as a distinct event. Whenever it occurs, it must be thought through from beginning to end. Unfortunately, all too often recurrent decision situations — those which could be dealt with through the application of decision rules — are treated as distinct, unique events.

Decision-Making and the Formal Structure of Authority

A decision should always be made at the lowest possible level within the organization and as close to the scene of action as possible. Moreover, a decision should be made at a level which ensures that all activities and objectives affected are considered fully. The first rule indicates how far down the hierarchy of an organization a decision *should* be made; the second rule, how far down it *can* be made. Together, these heuristic rules indicate which members in the organization must share in the decision and which must be informed of it. Analyzing foreseeable decisions, therefore, provides important insights as to both the required structure of management within an organization and the different levels of authority and responsibility called for within that structure.

These heuristic guidelines, however, leave unanswered important questions concerning authority relations and the role of communications in the decision-making process. Many writers have suggested that as an organization becomes more complex,[m] decision-making becomes decentralized, filtering down through the organization. As a consequence, those in the organization who have authority for decisions, that is, authority which comes from the hierarchical structure, become more dependent on those in the organization with technical competence to advise them on the alternatives from which choice can and should be made. At the same time, efficient and effective channels of communication within the organization and between the organization and other units in its decision environment become a critical factor in the decision-making process.

The primary purpose of the next two chapters, therefore, will be to examine further the concepts of authority and organizational communications as they relate to processes of public management. An attempt will be made in these discussions to formulate some general propositions concerning the role of these factors in public decision-making.

---

[m]Increased organizational complexity may arise from increased size and/or from increases in the responsibilities of the organization. In many public organizations, the latter phenomenon has occurred without a parallel increase in size, thereby increasing the problem of effective decision-making.

4 Authority Relations in the Decision-Making Process

Authority relations are an integral part of organizational behavior, and therefore clarification of the concept of authority is essential to the development of a systematic theory of public decision-making. In a sense, the study of public organizations involves a search for conceptual tools to assist in an understanding of the complexities of organizational behavior with its many functional and structural variations. An understanding of the concept of authority seems particularly important in this regard, since it provides useful insights into how public organizations formulate objectives and develop processes to achieve these ends. In order to gain their objectives, public organizations must utilize certain instruments of motivation and constraint, and the exercise of authority — both internal and external — is a crucial element in this equation.

It would seem evident, therefore, that if public management is to achieve the objective of greater rationality in decisions which affect the public sector, it will be necessary for members of the profession to develop a fuller understanding of the complex relationships which exist in modern organizations, public and private.

Three Models of Authority

Students of formal organizations — concerned as they are with structure, authority, leadership, and responsibility — generally advocate one of several theoretical models of authority relations in decision situations. These models, for the most part, are derived from the processes by which decisions are made by officials with hierarchical authority.

One model is based on the assumption that a decision is the result of some procedure, built into the organizational hierarchy, which sifts, winnows, and digests information concerning the decision situation. Through this process, attention of the decision-maker is focused on acceptable alternatives which fall within some prescribed area of discretion. This model maintains that decision-making is a cumulative process, requiring planning and coordination at all levels of an organization. A second model would seem to imply that while decision-making is a process which has its roots deep in organizational experience, it is not so much a planned activity as an indigenous and sometimes momentary expression of response to particular demand situations. A third model combines elements of the other two. This model focuses primarily on the influence exercised in decision situations by persons possessing technical expertise. As Pfiffner and Presthus have observed:

In government and large-scale enterprise generally, decision-making always involves technical and political considerations which necessitate consultation with experts in each area. As a result, the high official, in whom ultimate authority formally resides, often appears to have been manipulated in one direction, then another, by a variety of individuals who possess special knowledge.[1]

The Weberian Model of Authority

A thorough search for various conceptual models of authority in the literature of organization theory inevitably leads one to conclude that there is but one "true" model, the Weberian model, the rest being either interpretations of or reactions to it. The theories of Max Weber have survived the test of time and explication. In many basic areas, these theories are still valid in spite of (or perhaps because of) the many innovations and complexities that have evolved in modern organizations since they were first published over fifty years ago in *Wirtschaft and Gesellschaft*.

Weber was a prophet as well as a perceptive observer of the evolution in public administration in Germany during the second half of the nineteenth century. While the French were torn between indignation and amusement over *bureaucratie*, the Germans during this period made the term *bureaucracy* synonymous with a system of superior efficiency and accomplishment. Further, as Marshall and Gladys Dimock have observed: "Max Weber's world is the universe of the efficiency engineer, the systems planner, the specialist in operations research, the specialist in automation and computer technology . . . . American society in midcentury has become largely the environment Weber envisaged."[2]

Weber analyzed formal organizations as part of his theory of authority, or systems of legitimate social control. He pictured an evolution of organizational forms in terms of the kinds of authority relations to be found within them and in terms of the sources of legitimacy for this authority. Weber defined authority as ". . . the probability that certain specific commands (or all commands) from a given source will be obeyed by a given group of persons."[3] The group obeys willingly, because its members consider it legitimate for this source of authority to control their actions.

Charismatic, Traditional, and Legal Authority

At one extreme, Weber postulates a relatively simple, nonspecialized form of organization in which followers give almost unqualified obedience to a leader who is endowed with "charisma." Since charismatic authority depends on the qualities of an individual, it is relatively unstable and, as a rule, cannot be transmitted to a successor. Therefore, authority legitimized by the *sanctity of tradition* evolves as a means of routinizing the selection of a successor and securing prerogatives of authority for those closest to the leader. In traditional authority, the existing social order is viewed as sacred, eternal, and inviolable. The subjects are bound to their ruler by traditional feelings of personal loyalty and other cultural beliefs about the social order that reinforce his position.

The final stage in this evolution is approached when it becomes necessary to further extend the prerogatives of authority to a group of officials in order to carry out certain administrative functions necessary to the traditional system. This transitory phase, which Weber terms "status patrimonialism," frequently evolves into what he calls *legal authority* (and which others have labeled *rational-legal* or *bureaucratic* authority). For Weber, both the authority of the patrimonial prince and the trained administrator are forms of legal authority. The first he labels "substantive rationalization," while the second he calls "formal rationalization." It also should be noted that Weber does not suggest that bureaucratic authority is the only form of legal authority, merely the purest.

Legal authority is legitimized by a belief in the supremacy of the law. It assumes the existence of a formally established body of social norms designed to organize conduct for the rational pursuit of specific goals. In such a system, obedience is owed not to a person — a traditional or charismatic leader — but to a set of impersonal principles. These principles include the obligation to follow directives from an office superior to one's own, regardless of who occupies the higher office. Although superior officials command the obedience of their subordinates, they in turn are subject to the authority of the same body of impersonal regulations, and their authority is limited accordingly.

Weber's Model of Bureaucracy

Weber's model of bureaucracy can be characterized by: (1) impersonal social relations; (2) appointment and promotion on the basis of merit; (3) authority and obligations which are specified a priori and adhere to the job rather than to the individual; (4) authority organized on a hierarchical basis, focusing on impersonal discipline and rational expertise; (5) control through directives originating at the apex of the authority pyramid and transmitted through channels down to its base; (6) a formally established system of rules and regulations governing official decisions and actions; (7) separation of policy and administrative positions, with the membership of the bureaucracy being concerned primarily with administrative decisions; and (8) specialization and division of labor. The directives controlling a subordinate include the various administrative regulations of the bureaucracy, the professional and technical principles guiding his activities, and, particularly, the orders received from his superiors.

Weber further asserts that many of the characteristics attributed to bureaucracies are interrelated in particular ways. For example, specialization is said to promote expertise; the authority structure and the existence of formal rules are assumed to make vital contributions to the coordination of activities; and detachment is held to increase rationality. In general, Weber's treatment, like that of classic administrative theorists such as Gulick and Urwick, [4] emphasized the formal, rational, impersonal, "control from the top" aspects of authority.

Interpretations of the Weberian Model

There have been many interpretations and explications of what Weber really meant *or should have meant* in his discussions of bureaucratic authority. For Weber, authority is given consent because it is legitimate, rather than being legitimate because it evokes consent. Therefore, for Weber, consent is always a given to be taken for granted, rather than a problem whose sources must be traced. As a consequence, Weber never systematically analyzed the actual social processes which either generate or thwart the emergence of consent.

While Weber did not subject the dysfunctional aspects of bureaucracy to the same kind of systematic analysis he undertook in connection with the more positive aspects of his conceptual scheme, critics of Weber often tend to lose sight of the real value of formulating an "ideal type." As Weber envisioned this construct, it was to serve as a measuring rod with which to compare optimal aspirations against actual achievements. It is not intended as a descriptive model of how the bureaucratic authority system operates. While such descriptive analyses are vital to the development of a more systematic theory of organizations, Weber's failure to include this aspect in his theoretical analysis should not be viewed as a weakness in the conceptual framework.

Attempts to expand upon Weber's basic formulations also reflect a concern for his preoccupation with the formal aspects of bureaucracies and the lack of consideration given to the informal relations and unofficial patterns which develop in complex organizations. This concern, in turn, has led to an extensive body of theory dealing with the "informal" aspect of organizations, i.e., the areas in which reality departs from the ideal-typical characteristics of the Weberian model.

Presthus, in developing his interpretation of authority in complex organizations, attributes to Weber the statement that authority is validated by a legitimizing process analogous to socialization, i.e., learning and accepting the norms of the group or social system.[5] Presthus postulates a "transactional concept" of authority which rests on two propositions: (1) that the authority process is reciprocal, i.e., "the anticipated reactions of all actors become a datum in the behavior of each"; and (2) that authority is mediated by four types of legitimizing — technical expertise, formal role, rapport, and a general deference to authority.

Peabody extends this line of analysis by suggesting a distinction between formal authority and functional authority, the bases of the first being legitimacy, position, and sanctions inherent in office, while the second is based on professional competence, experience, and human relation skills.[6] Thus Peabody asserts that Presthus' categories of "generalized deference toward authority" and "legitimation by formal role or position" would fall under the heading of formal authority, while legitimation by "technical expertise" and "rapport" are forms of functional authority.

Other writers have attempted to reconcile the implicit contradictions in Weber's conception of bureaucratic authority. These writers have suggested that by emphasizing as the basis for bureaucratic authority both expert judgment — resting on technical knowledge — and disciplined compliance with directives of superiors, Weber implies that there is no conflict between the two principles. However, the conflict between disciplined compliance with administrative procedures and adherence to professional standards in the performance of duties is one of the central issues of contemporary organizations.[7] Thus, the search continues for a theoretical framework which can take account of these issues, while at the same time maintain the conceptual integrity of the Weberian model.

Two Fundamental Forms of Authority

The foregoing discussion of the Weberian model of authority and subsequent interpretations of the model lead to the suggestion that there are two fundamental forms of authority in complex organizations: (1) *structure-based authority* and (2) *function-based authority*. It may be further posited that: (a) the concept of formal authority based on position, legitimacy, and sanctions inherent in office may be subsumed under structure-based authority; and (b) the concept of authority stemming from technical competence (expertise authority) or from human relation skills (personal authority) can be subsumed under function-based authority.

Later in this discussion, an attempt will be made to show that increases in the level of applied technology available to an organization lead to a gradual shift in emphasis and orientation from long-range goals (ends) to intermediate objectives (means). This shift in emphasis, in turn, leads to a shift from structure-based authority to function-based authority. As a consequence, relative increases in potential authority accrue to functional positions most closely associated with intermediate objectives.

Whether authority is derived from the organizational hierarchy (structure-based authority) or results from technical competence or personal skills (function-based authority), in large measure its legitimacy depends on acceptance by individuals in authority relationships. This concept of acceptance will be explored further in the next section.

The Barnard "Bottom-Up" Model of Authority

While a number of theorists have attempted to build on the Weberian model of authority relations, a second group has raised fundamental questions as to whether authority flows from the top, as Weber suggests, or rises from within the organization as "consent of the governed." Perhaps the foremost challenge to the concept of top-down authority came in a series of lectures at Harvard University in the mid-thirites by Chester I. Barnard.[8] Barnard's interpretation of authority, like an earlier discussion of the "illusion of final authority" by Follett, comes close to turning the hierarchy of authority upside down.[a]

Processes of Compliance

While Weber focused on the structure of authority, Barnard was concerned primarily with the processes of compliance. For Barnard, authority is "legitimated" by the acceptance of those exposed to it.

The essence of the Barnard thesis is that people differ in the degree of effort they are willing to expend to achieve the objectives of an organization. At any given time, production will reflect the varying amounts of effort put forth by individual members. Hence, the organization must in some way secure a willingness to cooperate from the members of the organization. Contrary to most classical theories, the most important way to secure this cooperation, according to Barnard, is not through the use of financial incentives; rather, it must be brought about by executive leadership.

The degree of effective authority possessed by a leader in the organization is measured by the willingness of subordinates to accept such authority. Thus, Barnard's conception of authority refers to the social definition of others' expectations regarding compliance.

Organizational Consensus: Acceptance of Authority

Barnard introduces the concept of the "zone of indifference" to account for the seemingly unquestioning acceptance of orders by subordinates. He

---

[a]In developing his views of authority relations, Barnard built on the philosophy of Mary Parker Follett (*Creative Experience*, published in 1924), the then-current findings of social psychologists presented in the previous chapter, and his own perceptions of organizational behavior, based on his experience as president of the New Jersey Bell Telephone Company.

suggests that if all orders in a superordinate-subordinate relationship were to be arranged in the order of their acceptability to the persons affected, some would be clearly unacceptable and therefore not be obeyed, another group would be somewhat neutral, and a third group would unquestionably be acceptable. It is this last group in which the person affected will readily accept orders and will be relatively indifferent as to what the orders are so far as the question of authority is concerned.

Jackson, in interpreting this concept, asserts that this zone of indifference is the region in which a person with a given status expects, and is expected to accept, orders.[9] Jackson has termed this region "the range of tolerable behavior," thereby placing a greater emphasis on organizational consensus as to what is acceptable behavior given a specific authoritative command.

Herbert Simon presents a concept similar to that of Barnard's zone of indifference, the "zone of acceptance."[10] Simon wavers, however, between fully adopting the implications of Barnard's model of authority and supporting the more formal views of Weber and Urwick. On the one hand, he suggests that ". . . a subordinate is said to accept authority whenever he permits his behavior to be guided by the decision of a superior, without independently examining the merits of that decision."[11] Simon's definition of authority, however, as ". . . the power to make decisions which guide the actions of others," is more closely aligned with the formulations of Weber.

In applying his zone-of-acceptance concept, Simon asserts that when exercising authority, the superior does not seek to convince the subordinate but only to obtain his acquiescence. However, he also states that the magnitude of the zone of acceptance will depend on the sanctions which the person in authority has available to enforce his commands.

Among Simon's major contributions to the understanding of authority has been his development of four motivational bases conditioning the acceptance of authority: (1) confidence (technical skills); (2) social approval (identification, or what Presthus has called "rapport"); (3) sanctions and rewards; and (4) legitimization.[12] Simon's interpretation of authority has been widely disseminated and adopted. Thus, as with the Weberian model, advocates of the Barnard model of authority have sought to make a number of basic refinements in the original formulations.

While the debate over whether authority goes upward or downward has led to a number of empirical studies in organizational authority relations, it has generated more heat than light. It is apparent that the upward-downward dichotomy is an oversimplification of the complex dynamics by which authority is generated and applied in modern organizations. These relationships cannot be identified clearly in structural terms alone, but must also be studied in connection with the organizational processes in which authority relations are most relevant, i.e., in decision-making situations.

The Decision-Making Model of Authority

Simon, building on the formulations of Barnard, points to decision-making as the key to gaining insights into the structure and functions of complex organizations. It is clear from his writings, however, and in particular his classic *Administrative Behavior*, that while he views rational decision-making processes as the ideal, Simon feels that in the organizational context decisions are predominantly nonrational.

Who Has the Authority to Make Decisions?

Snyder, Bruck, and Sapin offer an interesting definition of decision-making which reflects many of the problems confronting proponents of the decision-making model.

Decision-making is a process which results in the selection, from a socially defined, limited number of problematical, alternative projects (objectives), of one project intended to bring about the particular future state of affairs envisaged by the decision-makers.[13]

In a slightly different context, Rossi has defined a decision as ". . . a choice among several modes of action which is made by an authoritative person or group . . ."[14] Thus Rossi suggests that a choice among alternatives can be considered a decision in organizational terms only if it is made by a person or group of persons with authority, i.e., the legitimate and recognized right to make the decision in question.

Lasswell and Kaplan define "power" as participation in the decision-making process, that is, the right to participate in the selection of an alternative.[15] This formulation suggests recognition of the fact that many persons may participate in decision-making situations and that organizational decisions are, as Simon points out, responsive to a complex structure of influence. Thus the problem becomes one of determining who exercises influence in decision-making situations and to what degree.

In Simon's view: "The function of the organization is to limit the scope of the decisions that each member must make; only in this way can rationality be approached."[16] Organizations limit decisions by defining the responsibilities of each official, thus supplying him with goals to guide his decisions; and setting up the mechanisms, such as formal rules, information channels, and training programs that help to narrow the range of alternatives the official must consider before making his decision. Vertical specialization, the division of labor based on authority (power) rather than work, provides the basis for establishing decision mechanisms. Decisions are made at several levels within an organization. General policy-making is concentrated at the top, policy specification is carried out by the middle ranks, and the actual work is performed by the lower ranks. Therefore, the higher the rank of an individual in the organizational hierarchy, the more his job consists of decision-making and the fewer the actual tasks he will be called upon to carry out.

Building on these observations, Simon asserts that once the overall objectives are established, the hierarchical structure of the organization serves as a framework for means-ends chains, specifying for each official the goals and objectives of his tasks; his duties may be confined to the selection of the best means for achieving these objectives. Procedural regulations, in turn, further limit the area of search for a "best solution." The combination of these two limits, according to Simon, permits rational decision-making in organizations.[b]

While this formulation is somewhat less rigid than more traditional views, it does not stand in conflict with the notion that authority for decisions is allocated on a hierarchical basis. Thus, as Thompson asserts in his comments on the theories of means-ends in decision-making: "Although many spontaneous, nonhierarchical, informal group decisions constantly take place in organizations, the decision which commit the organization, the official decisions, take place in hierarchically structured groups."[17]

William Dill has attempted to specify conditions under which decision-making responsibilities can be effectively allocated on a hierarchical basis.[18] He notes the essential argument of classical theory: as decisions become more complicated, more comprehensive in scope, and more significant to the organization, responsibility for decision-making must be shifted upward to higher-level personnel. A secondary argument is that disagreements between men or groups on one level in the organization should be resolved (decisions made) by a common superior at the next higher level.

Dill concludes that the assignment of decision-making responsibility on a hierarchical basis presumes several conditions not easily met in real organizations: (1) that roles in decision-making activities are assigned to individuals and groups in some uniform manner and are not simply assumed as opportunities present themselves; (2) that there are effective organizational means for recognizing the complexity and significance of decision problems and for routing them to the appropriate level within the organization; (3) that men in top-level positions are superior to men at lower levels in access to information, in analytical skills for diagnosing problems, and in their competence in rendering decisions and seeing that they are carried out; and (4) that the men at the top of the pyramid are assumed to have the time to deal with the problems that are shifted up to them.

---

[b]While these devices "permit" rational decision-making, they do not guarantee rationality. Success in their application depends wholly on the rationality of the initial objectives established within the organizational context and the manner in which procedural regulations are formulated and enforced.

Thus, while hierarchical status suggests official legitimacy, i.e., the right to make decisions, it does not necessarily mean that individual occupants of such status positions possess the capacity to see that their will dominates. Nor does the concept of the formal authority pyramid really reveal anything about the systems of influence, communication, and information exchange that prevail in decision-making situations.

Other Determinants of Authority Relations in Decision-Making Situations

Many studies of decision-making have emphasized the importance of technical competence as a major factor in determining the structure and processes of authority relations. There are other important determinants, however, which have been given only superficial treatment in these analyses. By implication, at least, it is generally assumed that individuals in decision-making situations must communicate with one another and with others outside the immediate situation. Thus, coterminous with any decision-making system is a communication system which also must be analyzed as a structural feature of the organization. The communication system consists of channels, links between points in the system, the sum total of these communication channels constituting the communication network.

Several rather basic functions are served by the communication network. It provides a means of support and confirmation of the structure of authority. It makes possible the circulation of orders and directives and the flow of data and information within the organization. It serves to initiate particular patterns of activity before and during decision-making situations. And, finally, the communication network makes possible more uniform definitions of the problems and issues requiring decisions.

Taking cognizance of the importance of the communication system in decision-making leads to several other important aspects which must be considered in authority relations. The first of these is the notion of access to the communication network. Any network will have several different points of access through which information enters or leaves the system. Some of these points of access are formal or structure-based, that is, prescribed by the hierarchical structure of the organization. Many others are function-based, stemming from more personal contacts and knowledge. In either case, acts of communication may be face-to-face, indirect (various forms of more formal written communication), or mediated through a third party. The manner in which access is gained to the communication system will have an important bearing on authority relations between individuals and groups. The greater the range of access points available to an individual (both in number and variety), the greater his potential influence in decision-making situations.

In addition to technical competence to analyze data and information which flows through the communication system, the informational resources of the organization will have an important bearing on decision-making processes. There are two kinds of information which are of particular concern in this regard. The first is information about the setting of the organization, i.e., its relationship to the broader environment. The second is concerned with the consequences of past decisions. Together, these may be viewed as providing feedback for the decisional system.[c]

Information is circulated through the communication network on the basis of a filtering process (classification, coding, and routing). The distribution of this information, therefore, may have a significant bearing on authority relations in any given situation. The participation (and relative influence) of an individual is conditioned, in part, by how much he knows. As a consequence, the withholding of information and the jealous guarding of informational resources are strategies frequently employed to gain greater influence in decision-making situations.

This suggests another important determinant of authority relations — the various expectations of participants, particularly those who must carry out decisions once they are made. Some individuals or groups are automatically included in a decision-making situation because of their position in the organizational hierarchy. Such individuals or groups can claim participation as a matter of right, whether this is given explicit expression or exists as a matter of general consensus. Their participation is based upon certain *inherent prerogatives*.

Other individuals or groups are included in decision-making situations because of their technical competence. Such individuals are brought into the system because of the need for special skills and information. Initially, at least, such participation is merely in an advisory capacity and involves neither claims nor actual authority or responsibility for the decisions made. As various writers have pointed out, however, much more is implied here than mere expertise, since the recommendations of experts may play an important role in establishing the basis of a decision. Thus, the line between advisory and prerogative-based participation often becomes blurred and, over time, advisory participants often become "prerogative" participants. Further, they come

---

[c]It is also useful to distinguish among three types of messages in the communication system: primary, secondary, and tertiary. A primary message is one that merely contains raw data; its contents need not be analyzed or interpreted. A secondary message involves the selection and analysis of certain items of raw data relevant to some objective. Some writers have suggested that a distinction be made between "data" and "information," the latter being analogous with secondary messages. A tertiary message occurs when either secondary or primary messages are classified or coded as part of the filtering process within the communication system, as, for example, when a report is stamped "urgent," "file," "circulate," "confidential," or when some other symbol is attached. Classification, or coding, results in the selection and rejection of information, and therefore, plays an important role in determining the routing of data and information through the communication network.

to expect this relationship to exist in any decision-making situation in which their technical expertise may be required. This situation seems particularly evident among those who will be called upon to translate decisions into action programs.

From these formulations, it may be concluded that the question of who participates in a decision-making situation depends on more than the traditionally defined dimensions of importance, comprehensiveness, and complexity of the required decision. Also included in this determination are such organizational aspects as: (1) the information from which the problems are formulated and the routes by which this information enters and is circulated through the organization;[d] (2) the specialized training and experience of individuals and groups and the distribution of these resources within the organization; (3) the amount of discretion and initiative granted to subordinate groups; and (4) the orientations of the people who will be called on to carry out the decisions once they are made and their expectations regarding participation in the decision-making process.

Relatively little study has been made of this last aspect of decision situations. It may be suggested with regard to "expectations" that a distinction be made between the "technocrat" and the "bureaucrat." The technocrat is a member of an agency staff with extensive contacts in professional organizations outside the structure of government. These contacts, in turn, provide him with certain codes of conduct as well as sources of information regarding innovative problem-solving. In consequence, the technocrat's expectations are conditioned, in part, by role definitions in the broader profession. The bureaucrat, on the other hand, is the career employee, oriented primarily to the hierarchical structure of the organization. Reissman, in a more elaborate discussion of this subject, has suggested four bureaucratic types: (1) the functionalist, oriented to an outside professional group; (2) the specialist, oriented both to a professional group and advancement within the hierarchy; (3) the service bureaucrat, who is oriented to the hierarchical structure but also follows a competing norm of service to a clientele group; and (4) the job bureaucrat, who defines his role largely in terms of self-interest and career advancement.[19]

---

[d]In public bureaucracies, the main sources of new programs and policies are the members of the several professions working at the technical levels within the organizational structure of government.

In sum, by generating policy alternatives and setting standards, professions may have an immense impact on an agency's ability to maintain and raise its aspirations; therefore on its budget; therefore on public policies realized through the budget . . . And if professions . . . play as large a role as I think they do in developing innovations in public policy and putting them into effect, then problem-evoking and problem solving in the professions are central to the policy making process.

(Rufus P. Browning, "Innovative and Non-Innovative Decision Processes in Government Budgeting," Annual Meeting of the American Political Science Association, New York, September 4–7, 1963, p. 18.)

Professionalism and the Bureaucrat

The conflict between professionalism and the role expectations of the bureaucrat constitutes a major issue in the field of public management.[e] In the context of modern public service, the professional in government is often faced with the problem of making a distinction between his role in establishing goal directives and his role in assisting decision-makers through the rational application of techniques of his profession. As the previously reported survey by Rabinovitz and Pottinger found, over 71 percent of the respondents stated that they purposely integrated policy advice and value judgments with their technical recommendations. Such an overwhelming response is in keeping with the education and training that most professionals receive in preparing for public service. The neophyte professional, while in the university, is led to respect the traditional independent goals and respected images of professional life — the ideal of independent public service ruled only by the practitioner's ethics or inner authority.

After he is employed, however, the budding professional soon discovers that goals, practices, and everyday demands are frequently established by "nonprofessionals" within an institutional and political framework. As Gamberg has observed: "The conflict of independent decision and dependent position, of power of knowledge and the authority of those without knowledge, of the ideal of self-sufficiency and the actuality of interdependence is a major source of tension in modern professional life."[20]

Government in middle-sized cities (50,000 to 250,000 population) offers the professional a particularly ambiguous base of operations. In some cases, one finds genuine antagonism to and mistrust of outside experts and "intellects" and a faith limited to home-grown officials without "fancy" educations or ideas. Paradoxically, because of frequent citizen apathy to public issues, the middle-sized city also can be quite amenable to the innovations of those professionals who define their roles politically and who possess the patience and perserverance necessary to prepare a conservative system for change.

However, as Gamberg has suggested, the professional who is content to do relatively little behind the smokescreen of expertise can usually have an easy tenure in the middle-sized city. The conflict in professional ideology between bureaucratic security and political involvement can be easily resolved in favor of

---

[e]A parallel issue centers on the countervailing forces which emerge with the rise of professionalism in government. As many current writings in the fields of public administration and political sociology suggest, citizen participation and interest in governmental affairs often decline as governments become more bureaucratic and professional. The implications of these countervailing forces have an important bearing on the success of governmental programs that rely on public support and participation. An interesting discussion of this problem is provided by Morris Janowitz, *et al.* in *Public Administration and the Public Perspectives Toward Government in a Metropolitan Community* (Ann Arbor, 1958).

the former. In the absence of vigorous community and political leadership, the professional can become an entrenched bureaucrat who does not even have to take orders.

Many professionals in public service are notoriously mobile. Advancement usually means a change in location. Under such conditions, it is often difficult for the professional to establish the necessary rapport with other government officials, civil or elected, and with the general public, to bring about necessary changes. Many professionals appear to be a band of "educated gypsies," frequently using their record of accomplishment in smaller communities to secure more lucrative positions in larger municipalities.[21]

Decentralized Decision-Making and Polycentralized Authority

Considerable emphasis has been placed in the field of operations research on the technique of factoring as a problem-solving mechanism. Factoring involves the breaking down of a general problem into more simple and more specific sets of activities until actual program solutions can be reached. While many organizations go about this factoring process in less than ideal fashion, there is considerable evidence to suggest that most problems which confront an organization are handled in this way. In some cases, programmed responses are called forth as a solution; that is, a decision is made on the basis of a successful response utilized in the past. Other problems, however, require totally new response mechanisms.

For the most part, the way in which a problem is factored will depend on the technologies required to achieve the goal of the organization, and the location of those technical resources in the communication network. To the extent that rational decisions are required to complete this factoring process, they will be, for the most part, the decisions of a group of technical specialists. This is because most of the questions involved are technical in nature. Kenneth Benne has suggested: "To the extent that we depend upon others with claims to expertness in specialized processes integral to our way of living, whether information, advice, or skill with respect to the conduct of those processes, to that extent we are subjects of the authority of experts."[22]

In bureaucratic organizations, in which the formal structure of authority is hierarchical, some mechanism must be found to legitimate the decisions made at the technical level in the process of factoring. Therefore, associated with factoring is the *delegation of jurisdiction*, that is to say, the creation of non-hierarchical or function-based authority relationships.

As Thompson and others have observed, the increased complexity of problems confronting modern organizations also led to an increased inter-dependence among specialists. The demand for adequate communication of information among these specialists tends to overload the more formal communication channels of the hierarchy and results in the creation of specialist communication channels and the development of specialized languages (jargon) and shorthand categories for the classification of large amounts of information.

Most problem-solving communication, consequently, takes place through specialist communication channels . . . . these communication channels are generally not officially recognized and legitimized by organizational hierarchies. As a result, most problem-solving communication is "illegal" and surreptitious, and protected from official notice by means of myths and fictions.[23]

In complex problem-solving situations, there must be a high degree of role specialization and task fragmentation in order to achieve a workable solution. Many writers have suggested that this, in turn, will result in a reduction of central coordination and a proliferation of specialists, undermining hierarchical authority and leading to a breakdown in centralization of decision-making.

It may be suggested that these writers are looking at the "end products" of a complex process of organizational adjustment to specialization. There is some evidence to support the notion that, while increased specialization forces organizations to decentralize decision-making authority, many of these decisions are strictly of a procedural nature. Major policy decisions, at least in the initial stages, are retained as a centralized function. In many organizations, as a countervailing force to the decentralization of decision-making authority, there is a parallel increase in formal procedures (in the form of operational rules and quality controls). These procedures are designed to limit the area of discretion within which decentralized authority can be exercised. Several examples come to mind to illustrate this, perhaps the most evident being in the military, where "the book" of rules and procedures grows to many volumes.

Increased application of such rules and controls often results in the multinucleation of the organization under function-based authority. The final step in the process is adjustments in the organizational structure to give recognition to these nodes of function-based authority which, in turn, produces a polycentralized structure of authority.[f]

Thus, one means of internal control of organizations is to "legitimate" the

---

[f]The concept of polycentralized authority was suggested by Charles Perrow's formulation of task structures in various organizations based on their technology. ("A Framework for the Comparative Analysis of Organization," *American Sociological Review*, Vol. 32 pp. 43ff.) Perrow suggests that organizations with high interdependence among technical and supervisory groups will have a high level of discretion among groups and that the power of both the technical and supervisory groups will be high, and not at the expense of each other. Coordination under these conditions will be through feedback. The suggestion here is that when these conditions prevail in an organization, adjustments will be made in the structure of authority to produce polycentralization.

processes of initiation and problem-solving through the allocation of these functions to specified positions within the hierarchical structure. Through this approach, the formal communication system is adjusted so that communication channels more nearly conform to the formal authority structure.

As Thompson has suggested, a number of developments are challenging the legitimacy of hierarchical authority in bureaucratic organizations. Particularly crucial is the gap which advancing specialization and technical complexity are creating between the right to take specific action and the knowledge needed to do so. Those who are traditionally empowered to make all decisions can no longer have the necessary range of knowledge. This gap, in turn, brings about a good deal of pretense in organizational activities.

Related problems created by this situation arise from the conflict of specialization and responsibility. Both within organizations and during their formal schooling, technical specialists are frequently indoctrinated with the notion that responsibility is a hierarchical or "administrative" function. The role or responsibility of the specialist is to point out the technical implications of proposals. However, since it must be concluded from the foregoing discussion that the hierarchical view of authority and responsibility does not and could not correspond to a one-to-one basis with practice in modern organizations, a fundamental conflict arises between the expectations of the specialist and the demands of reality. This conflict frequently results in an unwillingness of the specialist to make even procedural decisions and a "passing on" of this responsibility to those in the hierarchy who possess the authority for decisions. Those in a superior relationship to specialists frequently encourage this response, since to make a choice from among several alternatives increases the superior's influence in the decision-making process. This reluctance on the part of specialists to take responsibility for decisions further complicates the processes of decision-making.

Dyadic Formulations of Authority Relationships

While there is growing recognition of the inadequacy of the hierarchical theory of decision-making, relatively few attempts have been made to develop a more thorough basis for analysis. One exception is an interesting think piece written over fifteen years ago by Robert Dahl.[24] He suggests four broad classes of decision-making processes:

1.   The hierarchical process — where leaders are heavily influenced by the structure of the hierarchy itself
2.   The democratic process — where leaders are heavily influenced by nonleaders through such devices as nomination and election (Dahl framed his classes in a political context; however, in an organizational context, this process

might be related to the advisory role of nonauthoritative positions in
the system)
3. The bargaining process — where leaders, to some degree interdependent
    with each other, exercise reciprocal controls over each other through group
    decision-making
4. The pricing system — this process is qualitatively different from the first
    three and has only limited application in an organizational context.

Dahl's central proposition is that "leadership is somewhat specialized and
not monolithic, it is bargaining not hierarchical." Clearly, it is a necessary
consequence of the "process" approach to the analysis of decision-making that
decisions are not presumed to be made by one man after receiving all the facts
and alternative courses of action from a staff, but by a series of persons — many
of whom do not occupy formal hierarchical positions.

Two-Person Paradigm

In an effort to take account of these deviations from the traditional
hierarchical concept of authority in decision-making situations, a number of
authors have formulated models of authority in terms of the influence or power
that one individual can exercise over another in a decision-making situation.
In general, these formulations have been in terms of two-person paradigm. Dahl,
for example, defines power in terms of the probability of one person influencing
another's behavior.

One measure of A's influence might be the magnitude of the change in probabilities that B will perform an act within the scope, contingent on some action by
A. Individuals who have greater than average influence over a given scope are
"leaders."[25]

Caplow, adhering in part to the notion of hierarchical relationships, suggests
that the status of an organizational position is its place in the prescribed rank
order of influence in the organization: "By *status* we mean the quantitative
difference — however measured — between A's ability to modify B's behavior
and B's ability to modify A's behavior, when A and B interact."[26] Cartwright
presents a similar paradigm, defining influence as the maximum force that A
can bring to bear on B, less the maximum resistance that B can exert.[27]
This definition closely parallels Weber's conception of power (*Macht*) as the
probability that one actor within a social relationship will be in a position
to carry out his own will despite resistance.[28]
    These and similar conceptions try carefully in theoretical language to
specify definitions of power and influence, the amount available to participants,

and the scope through which it can be exercised. The difficulty is, of course, that power is so ubiquitous and complex that social scientists have differed, not only as to its definition, but with respect to the techniques appropriate for determining (let alone measuring the extent) whether in a given relationship A has power or influence over B.

Expansion of Dyadic Formulations

Jackson has suggested that dyadic formulations of power and influence relationships have little to offer organization theory unless it can be demonstrated conceptually and operationally how the two-person paradigm can be expanded to encompass a multiplicity of interacting individuals in a social system.[29] One such attempt has been made by French and Raven.[30] Building on Cartwright's definition of power, they have postulated a number of different types of power in terms of their source or base in an organization. These basic types — "expert," "referent," "reward," "coercive," and "legitimate" — appear to be a mixture of personal attributes and organization-derived qualities. Whether a person's expertise or popularity (referent power) entitles him to exercise authority may depend on a number of other factors, including the normative structure of the organization. It would appear that only legitimate power clearly refers to position in a group or organization. As these writers frame their definitions, reward power and coercive power seem to depend on legitimate power. French and Raven appear to assume that legitimacy can be conferred on a position only from above. Thus, they indicate that legitimate power is approximately the same as many concepts of authority.

In terms of the French-Raven analysis, role in the hierarchy still provides the most important power attributes: ". . . legitimate power in a formal organization is largely a relationship between offices rather than between persons. And the acceptance of an office as right is a basis for legitimate power — a judge has a right to levy fines, a foreman should assign work. . . ."

Robert Dubin has suggested a second form of power — functional power — which is allocated by the organization through specialization and division of labor. Specialization, according to Dubin, ". . . creates automatic dependence. A specialized job operating in isolation produces nothing useful." Power, therefore, becomes ". . . the effect that the kind of performance, or failure to perform, has on the rest of the organization."[31]

The model of power suggested by Raven and French closely parallels the concept of function-based authority; the fundamental element is the work performed rather than the status position occupied by an individual. As a consequence, this focus on functions suggests a model of power quite different from that represented by the formal organization chart. In the first place, it is assumed that everyone in the organization possesses some power (as opposed to the hierarchical model, which conceives of power as absolute at the top and nonexistent at the bottom). This being the case, there must be restraints on the exercise of power throughout the organization. Thus, Dubin suggests that the system of specialization minimizes the possibility of absolute powers being assumed by a single individual or small group.

Although every type of work possesses some power, the exact amount will vary from function to function. Some work is more important than other tasks in maintaining the system and enabling the organization to perform as currently desired. Therefore, function-based power does not follow hierarchical channels. Rather, such power increases as the importance of the particular functional activity to the maintenance of the total system increases.[g]

Dubin also suggests an important concept relating to the number of persons participating in a particular decision situation. He advances this hypothesis: "For any given level of functional importance in a system, the power residing in a functional agent (functionary) is inversely proportional to the number of other system functional agents capable of performing the function."[32] In short, if there are many agents participating in a decision situation, individual power will be less than if the function-based power were concentrated in one or relatively few persons. This sort of relationships is readily recognized with regard to high-ranking officials; presidents of corporations are powerful because they alone are responsible for the exercise of certain functional responsibilities. It is also applicable, however, to lesser positions in the organizational structure if these positions enjoy a monopoly in certain functional areas. The specialist, therefore, enjoys certain functional power as a result of his expertise.

This analysis has important implications for the structure of an organization and individual behavior within that structure. If different activities are assumed to possess differing amounts of potential influence, then it follows that the assignment of these functions within the organization will have a significant impact on the structure and exercise of power and authority.[h]

This discussion suggests a further proposition concerning the type of authority frequently assumed to be derived from technical competence. Authority of expertise or technical competence does not stem from the

---

[g]These concepts recall the previous discussion of regulation within an open system and the so-called Law of Requisite Variety.

[h]Pfiffner and Sherwood have suggested a second important implication stemming from this concept of functional monopoly (*Administrative Organization*, p. 338). The fear that power may accrue to certain individuals within the system can be circumvented by simply assigning the function to several people. The separation-of-powers doctrine and the proliferation of boards and commissions in state and local government and of committees in business are illustrative applications of this fundamental precept. While such multimember bodies are frequently criticized as cumbersome in decision-making, the avoidance or elimination of functional exclusiveness may be more important to the organization than certain other costs, in which case a structure with many multimember units may be more desirable than the usual tight organizational pyramid.

possession of knowledge and skills per se. Rather, it is accrued from the functional position occupied in the system which permits the use of this knowedge to influence the decision-making process.

While the decision-making model and its many variations have added a number of dimensions to an understanding of authority relations in complex organizations, these formulations have also clouded the issue somewhat by the looseness of the terminology used. As Robert Dahl has noted:

There is a long and honorable history attached to such words as power, influence, control, and authority. For a great many purposes, it is highly important that a distinction should be made among them; thus to Max Weber, *"Herrschaft ist . . . ein Sonderfall von Macht,"* Authority is a special case of the first and Legitimate Authority a subtype of cardinal significance.[33]

Summary and Conclusions

The question of whether authority is derived from the hierarchical structure of the organization (the Weberian model) or evolves from the consent of the governed (the Barnard model) has generated much debate. A basic conclusion to be drawn, however, is that this debate has resulted in a composite concept of authority somewhat analogous to models of the universe prior to the theories of Copernicus. That is to say, various theorists have built elaborate conceptual formulations on a set of basic assumptions without fully exploring or questioning those assumptions. Efforts to distinguish between formal and informal authority relations have added further confusion rather than clarity to our understanding of authority in complex organizations. The decision-model, while partially circumventing the question of authority sources by examining authority relations in process terms, also has suffered from the lack of clear conceptual definitions.

In the present work, it has been suggested that the question of who participates (has influence or authority) in decision-making situations depends on such organizational aspects as: (1) the information from which problems are identified and solutions formulated; (2) the routes by which this information enters and is circulated through the organization (the communication network); (3) the distribution of resources of problem-solving within an organization (specialized training and experience of individuals and groups); (4) the amount of discretion and initative granted to subordinate groups (functional independence); and (5) the expectations of participants in the decision process (including those who may be called on to carry out decisions). From these concepts, a dichotomy of structure-based and function-based authority has been formulated as a basic frame of reference.

Whether authority is derived from the organizational hierarchy (structure-based) or results from technical competence or personal skills in a particular situation (function-based), legitimation depends on acceptance by individuals in authority relationships. Without willing consent, the exercise of authority becomes either force, manipulation, or persuasion.

The discussion of function-based authority underlines the importance of the communication system within an organization. It has been said that an organization can be considered an elaborate system for gathering, evaluating, recombining, and disseminating information. It must be concluded, therefore, that communication is more than a secondary or derived aspect of organization. Communication is a basic process out of which many other functions derive. Therefore, the channels and apparatus for the transmission of information become a vital part of organizational structure.

5

Decision-Making and the Communication Process

In the previous chapter, the decision system was presented largely in structural and functional terms. The primary concern was with the way the system is organized — the arrangement of its component elements — and the functional performance of these elements. That which binds the decision system together and provides the means to move the system from one state to another was discussed only by implication.[a]

The emphasis in the foregoing discussion would suggest that, in seeking relatively stable processes of interaction in organizations, studies of decision-making might profitably focus on the networks of communication. Decision-making involves a complicated process of combining communication from various sources and results in the transmission of further communication. In this context, power may be thought of as the extent to which a given communication influences the generation and flow of later decision-oriented communication. Points in the flow of communication where this influence is exerted may be considered positions of authority.

The Communication of Information as an Operator

It should be clear, but it bears repeating, that a problem is no more or less than the words in which it is described. The solution of any problem depends on how clearly it can be given form by naming and describing it. Thus, as Hodnett has stated:

To diagnose a problem, you have first to put it into words or other symbols that define that problem exactly. Sometimes you will arrive at this statement quickly and easily. Sometimes you will find the hardest part of the problem is stating

---

[a]In systems theory, a dynamic system is often expressed schematically by means of a series of "boxes" linked by "arrows." The boxes represent the *operands* (the state of the system before change) and *transforms* (the state of the system after change), while the arrows represent the *operators* (those things which bring about change). In many applications of systems theory, knowledge about the operator often is not essential, since the analysis is concerned primarily with *what* happens and not *why* it happens. In the case of decision-making, however, it is important to identify and understand the actions of the operator, since it is a process variable which can be manipulated to increase the efficiency and rationality of the decision system.

91

it. Then you know that you have not yet identified it. . . . Your effort to identify a problem, therefore, is accompanied by a simultaneous effort to find an adequate statement of it. . . .

Unless you put a problem into words, you do not give it form. If it is formless, it does not exist in a manner that permits solution.[1]

Decision-makers seldom deal with the problem situation itself or with any aspect of the problem. They deal almost exclusively with *information* about the problem. In turn, they must make decisions which best satisfy not actual conditions, but information about those conditions. Ruesch and Kees have pointed out some inherent dangers in this aspect of decision-making:

. . . most of these men have rather limited contact with many of the processes they symbolically deal with or control. The danger of this remoteness from reality lies in the tendency to regard abstract principles as concrete entities, attributing body and substance to numbers and letters and confusing verbal symbols with actual events.[2]

Thus it may be suggested that *effective communication of information is the warp and woof of the decision-making process.*

Communication in an Organization Context

Decision-making depends on communication for its success and often for its very existence.[3] The importance of communication to the overall operations of an organization and, in particular, to the decision-making process, has been discussed in some detail by Herbert Simon.[4] As Bavelas the Barrett have observed: "The goals an organization selects, the methods it applies, the effectiveness with which it improves its own procedures — all of these hinge upon the quality and availability of the information in the system."[5]

Structures within an organization are differentiated and then redifferentiated again and again. As the organization is divided into specialized subunits, these units must use communications to coordinate their output. An organization can be conceptualized as a configuration of communication patterns which connect individuals and collectivities of varying sizes, shapes, and degrees of stability and cohesiveness and thereby establishes patterns of contact among individuals and groups.

Basic Functions of the Communcation System

As was pointed out in the previous chapter, several basic organizational functions are served by the communication system. Organizational communications: (1) provide support and confirmation for the formal structure of authority; (2) make possible the circulation of orders and directives and the flow of data and information within the organization; (3) serve to initiate particular patterns of activity before and during decision-making situations; and (4) serve as the vehicle for the exercise of influence in the decision-making process — both informal influence (as in persuasion) and more formal influence (as in authority). In addition to serving as the matrix which links organizational members in these various ways, the communication system serves as the instrument by which an organization is embedded in its broader environment. Finally, the communication system makes possible more uniform definitions of problems and issues requiring decisions. As Barnard put it: "In an exhaustive theory of organization, communication would occupy a central place, because the structure's extensiveness, and scope of the organization are almost entirely determined by communication techniques."[6]

Information Theory and Communication Flow

In recent years, important advances have been made in understanding the mechanics of communication flow. This work — pioneered by Dr. Claude E. Shannon of Bell Laboratories [7] and Professor Norbert Wiener, [8] the father of modern cybernetic theory — has evolved into a formal theory of information. In outline form, the elements of this theory are as follows:

1. Communication is treated as a problem in statistics
2. The primary focus is on the large-scale or gross aspects of communication
3. Units of measurement are provided for the amount of information required in broad classes of messages
4. It shows how to compute the maximum rate of transmission of error-free information over any system

The system considered by information theory is diagrammed in Figure 5-1.

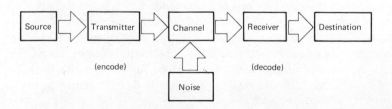

Figure 5-1. Information Theory. (Adapted from: David Slepian, in J. F. McClosky and F. N. Trifethen (eds.), *Operations Research for Management*, Vol. I (Baltimore, 1954), pp. 149-167).

The components of the system can exist in any communication situation, from one which involves the use of electronic equipment to a simple family discussion.

The inner core or "channel" consists of the actual mechanisms involved in the communication system, whether interaction is through direct word of mouth, by telephone or other electronic device, or via hand- or machine-written messages. The capacity of a channel is measured strictly by the maximum amount of information that can be transmitted through it in a unit of time — there is always such a maximum. The technology used in transmission has implications for organizational behavior involved in communication processes.[b]

Noise, Redundance and Content of Information

"Noise" is any form of interference which reduces the effectiveness of transmission by introducing errors into the flow of information. Noise may change a message to obvious nonsense. Often worse, however, is when noise converts a message into another meaningful but entirely misleading message. Communication channels are never without some noise. In addition to interference which may arise from outside the information flow (static in electronic channels, typing errors in written messages, and so forth), there are two other important sources of noise in any communication system: (1) semantic noise, which occurs between the information source and the encoding of messages at the transmitter; and (2) semantic reception noise, which occurs between the engineering receiver and the actual destination of the message.[9] These noise sources are related to the human factor in information distortion and misinterpretation.

The only effective weapon against noise is some form of redundance, which involves the tailoring of a message with respect to the capacity of a communication channel so that the channel will be exploited effectively without overcrowding. While redundance always lowers the amount of information that can be conveyed, this inconvenience is often tolerated in order to circumvent the masking effects of noise.

The particular characteristic of a message which distinguishes it from nonsense and from other messages is termed "content of information." One practical problem in all communication is the preservation of the same content of information from source to destination. The application of information theory to servo-mechanisms aids in the design of the circuits to take a given pattern of information at the source and reproduce it almost instantly at the receiver with a minimum loss due to noise.

---

[b]Perhaps the most basic influence of such technology is exhibited in the concept of a channel's signal-to-noise ratio. Certain types of channels are more susceptible to "noise" than others.

Application of Information Theory in an
Organizational Context

There are certain significant differences when attempts are made to apply information theory outside electronic circuitry, however. Information flow in human-channel communication systems is a much more complex and difficult activity. One major difficulty is that, typically, there are many more channels than in electronic circuitry. Even when a single channel is selected for use, there is a tendency for information to move "outside of channels." To use a computer effectively, it must be programmed; the problem must be clearly understood and coded into the equipment. There are many situations in organizations where the problems are not clearly understood or, if they are understood, the links with the system's "memory" are often incomplete. In the context of information theory, then, the need is one of problem clarification. Unless the problem is known and defined in detail, it is impossible to establish information needs to serve as guidelines in the identification of the parameters of the problem and the combination of information inputs and data from memory to arrive at a solution.

Types of Communication Networks[c]

While the discussion has centered on the notion of communication channels structurally organized in a communication network, it should be evident that the "network" involved in organizational communications is not a unidimensional structure. As Cherry has pointed out, organizational communications consist of "a number of networks superimposed."[10] Often the various networks can be separated for empirical analysis, even though they are superimposed. At other times, one set of channels carries messages that have multiple levels of meaning. In such instances, communication networks may be little more than analytic constructs. The sorting of messages into different networks often lacks refinement because of the tendency for individuals to use rewarding channels again and again, even though such use goes beyond the original intent for which the channel was established. It may be useful, however, to describe some of the different types of communication networks to be found in an organization, especially since the characteristics of each network may lead to different decision-making consequences.

---

[c]The author would like to acknowledge a debt to the excellent summary of theory and empirical analyses of this subject provided by Harold Guetzkow in his landmark article, "Communications in Organizations" (*Handbook of Organizations*, edited by James G. March (Chicago: Rand McNally & Company, 1965), Chapter 12).

The Authority Network

Traditionally, primary attention has been given to organizational communications involved in the exercise of authority relations. Channels in this
network are defined in terms of the legitimacy that one individual or group has
vis-à-vis others in the organization with respect to the issuance of directives,
commands, and decisions. A prevailing feature of such networks is their
directionality; orders usually flow vertically within the organization, from a
relatively few individuals at the top to the many in the lower regions of
the authority structure.

Barnard emphasized the primacy of the "system of communication" in
stressing its role as the repository for the "lines of authority." For Barnard,
authority "flowed" through the communication system of the organization.
Barnard abstracted from the total phenomena a network of superior-subordinate
role relations and conceived of an organization as the collective communication
structure associated with these relationships. He regarded authority as an
attribute of communication by virtue of which such authority is accepted by
members of the group as binding on their actions.

Information-Exchange Network

The information-exchange network of communication is sometimes
thought of as an inversion of the authority communication flow. Its messages
are usually concerned with knowledge about the state of affairs with respect
to the internal operations of the organization and the broader external environment. While its directionality is often assumed to be the opposite of that
involved in authority communication, this network is also often used by those
above to supply information for decisions to lower echelons in the organization.

In his empirical studies of British industries, Burns concluded that "The
'vertical' system [of communication] would be virtually unworkable without the
considerable flow of information laterally."[11] Burns also found that
communication circuits were maintained ". . . among groups of equivalent
status which crossed departmental boundaries; communication 'leaked' from
level to level through contact individuals (not necessarily in the direct executive
line concerned) and the ground at a lower level was prepared for likely
action."

Thus, when regularized channels fail to function adequately, new, highly
specialized channels sometimes develop. There is contradictory evidence,
however, as to the importance of the informal channels of communication (the
grapevine). Davis, in his study of the "Jason Company," concluded: "Formal
and informal communication systems tend to be jointly active, or jointly
inactive. Where formal communication was inactive . . ., the grapevine did not

rush in to fill the void . . .; instead, there simply was lack of communication."[12] These findings are contrary to the assertions of other writers that the grapevine ". . . thrives when other channels of information are closed."[13]

Task-Expertise Communication Networks

As Thompson has commented, as the technical base for organizational activities becomes increasingly salient, problem-solving communication seems to develop its own channels. The task-expertise network provides a vehicle whereby technical know-how can be brought to bear on the performance of organizational activities. An important feature of this network is its fragmentation; relatively unrelated islands of expertise are created throughout the organization. The evidence presented by Dalton in his study of lower-level management and union officials indicates that experts often avoid established authoritative channels in order to bring their knowledge about particular situations to bear on their specialized tasks.[14]

Trades and professions, existing in the larger society, provide an important basis for the development of task-expertise communication networks. Occupational groups socialize their members with the use of specialized jargons in handling the tools and techniques of their trades. Such groups also provide norms concerning work standards and levels of performance.

There is undoubtedly considerable overlap in communication structures involved in the transmission of messages concerned with authority, information, and expertise. All three networks tend to be involved in task specialization; however, quite different characteristics may be associated with each. For example, in the task-expertise network, the flow of messages would seem to be two-way and predominately lateral, whereas the direction of flow in the authority and information-exchange networks would seem to be more one-way and vertical.

Other Basic Communication Networks

Perhaps the most segmented of all the communication networks is that which exists as localized linkages among friends within the organization. These networks are generally smaller in scope than those occasioned by occupational groupings, although they are often congruent with such groupings, if not as extensive. Very often, messages devoted to communications involving authority, information, and expertise also carry implications of friendship relations. Such double usage of other networks illustrates the ease with which networks devoted to different kinds of messages may share the same communication channels.

Networks carrying messages about status may be even less well defined. Such networks are used by all members of an organization in their relations with one another. Rather than having directionality, status networks have many connections that are occasional and fleeting and cut across almost all other networks. Not only is information about status carried over networks; status is often attached to the network itself and to nodes within the network. Jackson's study of relations among professionals in a public welfare agency led him to conclude that the feedback mechanisms of communication served ". . . to provide individual members with social reality concerning others' expectations and evaluations, reinforcing approved behavior and extinguishing disapproved, and attracting or repelling them from membership."[15]

Perception of one's position within the status system also influences the extent to which one utilizes communication channels. Thus, Barnlund and Harland, summarizing their experimental work in small-group communication, suggest that ". . . the larger the status differential, the more restricted the channels of communication, the greater the tendency for information to flow from low to high status persons, and the more distorted the content of the messages."[16]

Implications for Decision-Making

The differentiation and overlapping of communication networks involved in the flow of authority, information, expertise, friendship, and status yield important consequences for decision-making. When networks are highly differentiated, isolation may be very costly, both in the demanding maintenance of duplicate channels for certain communication functions and in the loss of message content due to the high friction of transmission between channels. Such conditions frequently occur in public decision situations that require inputs from both the structure of government and the broader public. Interest groups may develop their own communication networks and gain entrance to the parallel networks of government at a variety of access points. Informal points of contact may supersede formal channels, as when an interest-group leader petitions an elected official for some decision at the "club," with the result that the more normative patterns of decision-making are circumvented or blurred. A parallel problem is that the demands of the members of various interest groups, which run the danger of becoming distorted in transmittal through the groups' communication channels, may be further distorted when transmitted from one system to another.

When communication networks are undifferentiated and overlap extensively, one set of messages may be submerged by another. Perhaps the most evident situation arises from an overlap of the networks of authority and friendship. Orders and commands, in such cases, may not carry sufficient force to be implemented effectively. By the same token, an undue overlap between the status and information-exchange networks may result in an information input receiving greater weight than it merits in a decision, simply because of the status enjoyed by the source.

Experimental Studies in Communication Networks

There is a substantial body of evidence to suggest that the location of an individual in a communication structure significantly affects his relative degree of influence and authority. Many laboratory experiments have been conducted with different communication networks, stemming largely from the original work of Bavelas the Leavitt.[17] While the results of these studies have not been totally conclusive, it can be said that, in small group situations, a communication network resembling a wheel, with the key individual at the "hub" and others forming the "spokes," seems to facilitate decision-making. These studies also suggest that a "two-level decision hierarchy" in which a certain amount of selective filtering of information takes place increases the effectiveness of decision-making in small groups.

From these experimental studies and from actual organizational situations, it is fairly clear that persons in central communication positions initiate a higher proportion of authoritative and influential communication than they receive from others. The orders, instructions, requests, and suggestions they make often result in the issuance of further authoritative communication by other persons. Left unanswered by these studies, however, is the question of how an individual achieves a central position in the communication process.

Basic Types of Communication Flows

From the foregoing discussion, it may be suggested that five basic types of communication flows are involved in the decision-making process.[d]

---

[d]For the purposes of this discussion, a segment of the total social communication within an organization has been singled out for further analysis. This segment differs somewhat from what Redfield and others have defined as administrative communication: "those segments of social communication within a formal organization that are institutionally determined by the organization" (Charles E. Redfield, *Communication in Management* (Chicago, 1953), p. 6). Lee O. Thayer suggests a four-way division of administrative communication as follows: (1) evaluative communication; (2) instructive communication; (3) persuasive communication; and (4) informative communication (*Administrative Communication* (Homewood, Ill., 1961), Chapters 9, 10, 11, and 12). Communication affecting the decision-making process includes administrative communication, as defined by Redfield, but also includes other forms of communication which may modify the information in the channels established and maintained by the formal organization or affect the capacity of those channels to handle information. In particular, the process of selective filtering, insofar as it is not "built into" the formal, institutionalized communication network, would fall in this latter category.

1. Expressive communication — largely directed to an external audience and
    consisting of annual reports, press releases, progress reports, and other
    materials designed to "educate and inform" persons outside the organization
2. Eductive communication — messages designed to draw forth or elicit
    information, generally transmitted in the form of questions directed at
    specific individuals within the organization
3. Informative communication — restricted, for the most part, to the trans-
    mission of data and information at various levels of interpretation and
    analysis, short of specific proposals or recommendations
4. Influential communication — advice, suggestions, recommendations,
    proposals, responses to eductive messages, and so forth; often supported by
    informative communication
5. Authoritative communication — orders, commands, directives; in general,
    communication designed to initiate action on the part of others

Expressive communication plays a role in the decision-making process in
that it may contain statements of policy, records of performance, or other
statements which, in turn, may elicit demand inputs from outside the system.
Expressive communication also includes certain internal documents designed to
bring about a greater awareness of and adherence to organizational goals and
objectives among members.

Eductive communication is very often the stimulus which sets the decision-
making process in motion. As Adrian McDonough has noted, the processing
of information in response to an open question accounts for the bulk of white-
collar manhours in any organization. Therefore, informative communication
is the principal means by which the decision-making process is moved from
stage to stage. Communication is informative *only* if it is acceptable as information to the receiver — if it provides him with something that he did not know
and was aware of a need to know. An operational definition of informative
communication might be: "Signals convey information only when they consist
of a sequence of symbols or values that changes in a way not predicted by
the receiver."[18] This definition implies more than mere receptivity on the
part of the receiver of the communication.

Whenever an individual communicates to evaluate, to instruct, to advise, to
persuade, or for any other purpose, his communication has the *potential of
being influential*. It is useful, however, to distinguish between two types of
influence, depending on the presence or absence of *intention* on the part of the
person who exercises the influence.[e]

---

[e]In decision-making situations, the information supplied by actor A may influence the
decision of actor B, even though the intention to do so was not present in the actions of A.
Such influence might be classed as *induced influence*. The case in which A does intend to
influence B's decision through his communication can be viewed as an attempt at *direct influence*.

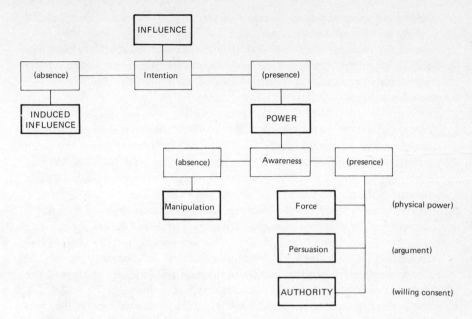

Figure 5-2. Relationships Among Various Forms of Direct and Indirect Influence.

It is possible to identify two basic types of direct influence, based on the awareness of actor B of the intentions of actor A. *Manipulation* occurs when B is unaware of A's intention to influence his decision, but A's communication, in fact, does manage to get B to pursue a certain course of action. If, on the other hand, A seeks to influence B's decision by presenting arguments intended to show why a recommended course of action is desirable, it may be said that A is using *persuasion*. B reviews these communications, evaluates them in the light of his own notions of what he considers best under the circumstances, and then accepts (or rejects) the recommendations as the basis of his actions.[f]

Authoritative communication, of course, embodies the official pronouncements of a decision made by those in a position to bring about desired courses of action. Actor A sends a message to Actor B, and B adopts this message as the basis of his own behavior without evaluating it in terms of his own standards of what is desirable under the circumstances.

The distinctions among these concepts can be summarized by the diagram presented in Figure 5-2.

---

[f]Two other forms of direct influence — force and authority — fall under the broader category of *power*. In the exercise of force, A influences the actions of B and, in a sense, B has made a decision: to act in a certain way rather than submit to punishment at the hands of A. Influence through the exercise of authority is covered under authoritative communication as it applies to decision-making.

Informative and Influential Communication

Of the five basic types of communication flows, the two which are most pertinent to the present discussion are informative communication and influential communication. There are four conditions which must be met to make a communication, or any portion of it, informative:

1. *The "information" being transmitted must have been previously unknown to the receiver.* A communication is informative to the extent that the receiver learns something from it — an idea, a concept, a point of view, or a relationship among these. The term "unknown" refers to the idea content of the message and not to the words or their usage
2. *The information offered must be acceptable to the receiver as information according to his own ideas, beliefs, needs, and attitudes.*[g] People are most likely to accept information which: (a) they are looking for; (b) they can use in some way (including psychologically) at once; (c) they can see some possible use for in the immediate future; (d) they fancy because of the physical or contextual conditions under which it occurs
3. *The content of the communication must be clear to the receiver.* If the message, or any portion of it, seems ambiguous to the receiver, to that extent it will be either noninformative or misinformative to him
4. *The message must be meaningful and useful to the receiver.* To be meaningful, the message content must be such that it can be readily assigned to any appropriate place in the receiver's knowledge of the subject and the relationship between ideas as the receiver sees them

With the possible exception of the first, these conditions also apply to influential communication. Recommendations or proposals can influence the decisions of others only if they are meaningful and useful, unambiguous, and acceptable to the receiver's system of values and attitudes.

Sources of Information: External and Internal

An individual's decision is influenced by the communication of information which he receives from two sources: those stimuli external to his organism and

---

[g]If the receiver perceives that his beliefs are likely to be challenged or their foundations questioned, he will probably ignore or at least misunderstand the content or intent of the communication. In a study by Cooper and Jahoda ("The Evasion of Propaganda: How Prejudiced People Respond to Anti-Prejudice Propaganda," *Journal of Psychology*, Vol. 23 (1947), pp. 15-25, the results suggested that people who come in contact with communication which does not fit their own beliefs will psychologically evade the issue by unconsciously misunderstanding the message.

those internal to it.[h] The second category includes memory, conditioned responses, physical and emotional states, a value system, and so forth. A decision is triggered by the receipt of information about some external situation, or by an information stimulus from within the individual. Frequently, these two decision-provoking events occur together, so that information from an external source is taken in combination with an individual's goals, plans, attitudes, drives, and so on to yield a decision. Karl Deutsch has described this relationship as follows:

The simplest way in which a decision system can be pictured from a communications viewpoint is to assume a message-receiving function as part of a system which has stored memories somewhere internal to it. Instead of having the stimulus-response act of the experimental psychologist who is watching the twitching of the frog's legs, we are dealing with human beings who have vast and deep memories and who will therefore respond to most of the information intake primarily in terms of what is recalled from memory. A *decision area* may be pictured as one where incoming messages are combined with recalled memories for determining the output of the system.[19]

What has be posited about the role of memory in the decision process of an individual can also be applied to organizational decision-making. Pieces of information may be stored in the minds of different group members as well as in material records. Items of information from all of these sources may be selectively recalled, combined with new incoming information, and communicated during the deliberation and decision process of the group. In this sense, groups act like individuals; however, in the process of drawing upon a range of memories, decisions are produced which differ from those of any one of the individual members.

Characteristics of Organizational
Communication Flows

Communication in organizations differs from ordinary social communication in a number of ways. Much social communication takes place between two individuals, a single source and a single destination. Even in the communication turmoil of the cocktail party, where messages appear to be buzzing about

---

[h]All stimuli are cybernetic agents, i.e., agents of control or communication. Stimuli include signals, signs, and symbols. Any stimulus is a signal; a sign is a symbol, the response to which has been modified by learning; a symbol is a sign produced by its interpreter and substitutable for a synonymous sign. Symbols include signs, and signs include symbols. (For a fuller discussion of these distinctions, see: John R. Kirk, "Communication Theory and Methods of Fixing Belief," *ETC: A Reveiw of General Semantics*, Vol. 10 (Summer, 1953), pp. 298–305.)

everywhere, there are usually identifiable clusters of two or three persons, each engaged in communication exchange (albeit transitory). In organizations, on the other hand, the destination of communication often consists of more than one person, as in the staff meeting, the briefing session, the memorandum issued simultaneously to all members of the organization, and so forth. By the same token, the initiators of communication may be more than one person, as when the findings of group problem-solving activities are passed up the decision hierarchy. When multiple initiations and multiple receptions are combined, one has the phenomenon of the conference. Thus, organizational communication may be characterized as "one-to-many," "many-to-one," or "many-to-many."

This variable characteristic of organizational communication has an important bearing on the effectiveness of transmission. As Ruesch and Bateson have noted:

Typically, in larger organized groups only the source or only the destination of many messages is distinct and known to the participants; the unknown part is related to the fact that individuals may either act as source and destination, or as channels which merely relay the message to the other individuals. The correctness of messages is therefore delayed and frequently is possible only by short-cutting the traditionally established pathways.[20]

The Importance of Timing in Communications

Another factor of the variable character of organizational communication is the timing with which messages are distributed through the system. Messages may be distributed either simultaneously or serially. When individuals communicate serially, messages spread irregularly throughout the organization and arrive at different locations at different times. This time differential may have important implications for the functioning of individuals in their relation to each other. For example, problems in coordination of action to carry out decisions often arise because time lags exist within the communication flow. Very often the undivided attention of the receiver is essential to a clear understanding of the information directed to him; so the allocation of his time and attention presents a constant potential barrier to effective communication.

When the communication is simultaneous (usually in the form of "one-to-many"), time differences in the arrival of the message are eliminated, or at least minimized. The time barrier in terms of attention paid the message is still present, however. Furthermore, because the "many" in the context of the one-to-many communication situation varies in composition — depending on the distribution of persons to whom the message may be relevant — the problem of determining the appropriate destinations of the message (who should be included in the "many") becomes critical. Errors of omission may constitute as serious a problem as errors of inclusion in producing a communication "over-load" in the system.

There is an important corollary to the problem of timing of communication as it relates to decision-making. A decision-maker may get all of the information he needs, or he may transmit all of the information in an acceptable manner, but it may be too late, or too soon. The timeliness of information is essential to its usefulness.

The technology involved in the transmission of messages (the channels utilized) also may influence their impact in the decision-making process. Certain kinds of information are best communicated in person, others by memoranda, still others by reports, and so on. Some types of information are communicated most successfully by utilizing formal channels, other kinds, using informal channels, and others by using the organization's "grapevine." For example, the use of the grapevine among executives, says Barnard, promotes the communica-tion of ". . . intangible facts, opinions, suggestions, suspicions, that cannot pass through formal channels without raising issues calling for decisions, without dissipating dignity and objective authority. . . ."[21]

The form of communication may also determine the extent to which messages are retained by the system. Messages may be relatively transitory, as in the case of telephone calls, or they may be more permanent, making it possible for them to be studied and digested over time. The transitory message, although it provides no permanent record (except for possible fragmentary notes taken down in haste), has the advantage of holding the complete momen-tary attention of the receiver. The more permanent record provided by written messages may produce a more sustained influence on the decision-making process, since they may be referred to again and again. However, such messages must compete not only with the demanding oral forms of communication, but also with other written messages. If circulation of written memos is not severely restricted, irrelevant memos may prevent the reading of relevant ones.

Thus, the characteristics of communication flows within organizations — the multiplicity of possible message sources and destinations, the possibility of serial or simultaneous message transfers, and the transitory or permanent nature of the messages received — interact in important ways with such qualities of the organization as its size, its differentiated structure, and its ability to handle decisions in a coordinated manner.

Organizational Barriers to Effective Communication Flows

The preceding discussion identified several barriers to effective communica-tion stemming from the nature and character of the messages themselves. There are, however, other barriers which arise from the nature, dynamics, and

functions of the organization itself. Physical distance between members of
an organization, both in terms of activity locus and organizational structure,
presents a very obvious barrier to communication. When persons requiring
a high degree of communication exchange are not in proximity to one another,
they must rely on indirect and alternative means of coordinating their activities.
Very often, devices and methods of indirect communication result in incomplete
or distorted transmission of information and fail to convey the true intent of
the sender.

Job specialization can complicate the exchange of information within an
organization. With job specialization comes a greater reliance on intentional
communication transmitted through established channels. However, as
Thompson has observed, the demand for adequate communication of information among specialists often overloads the more formal communication
channels of the hierarchy. This overload results in the creation of specialist
communication channels and the development of specialized languages and
useful shorthand categories for classifying large amounts of information.

Power and status relationships may also serve to impede the free flow of
information within an organization. Numerous studies have shown that the
subordinate tends to filter out of his communication with his superiors
all information which would make the boss look bad. The subordinate is even
eager to distort neutral information if it will be good news to the boss. Since
messages are processed and reprocessed at each node in the communication
system, there is ample opportunity to transform the meaning of messages as they
are transmitted within an organization. Executives are also responsible for
some information filtering, both wittingly and unwittingly. An executive
is frequently reluctant to communicate to his subordinates information that
would make him appear unimportant or incompetent.

A final organizational barrier to communication is that of information
ownership. The operation of this barrier depends on the intensity of the
aspirations of the persons involved and on their modes of achievement. As long
as more value is placed on achievement by position than achievement by
cooperation, there will appear to the competitors to be organization sanctions
of the power that accrues to the "owner" of vital information.

Selective Filtering — Omissions and Distortions

In organizations with sharply defined hierarchies it is easy to understand
why the recipients at the upper levels are unable to respond in one-to-one
fashion to the flood of messages from numerous lower levels. To date, however,
relatively little study has been made of the overall effects of this funneling of
information on the communication process. Shelly and Gilchrist, in small-group
experimental studies, speculate that:

Under pressure of greater amounts of required communication to be handled at once, the individuals in the group probably neglect to forward some problem relevant information and/or duplicate previously forwarded information; this in turn gives rise to information seeking questions. These questions, because answers are required, further increase the communication load (a) leading to greater probability of neglecting to forward information and/or (b) forgetting to whom certain items have been previously sent, etc.[22]

Thus, a central problem in communication systems centers on the determination of the fullness of meaning to be carried without overloading the system. This problem is particularly evident in decision-making situations, since the timeliness of decisions is often crucial, and delays are often encountered because of communication bottlenecks. As Cartwright has pointed out:

Units which correspond to articulation points of a communication network are likely to carry a heavy load of communication, because certain pairs of units of the organization cannot communicate to each (other) except through this unit. If such a unit becomes a "bottleneck" or if it systematically screens out certain types of information, parts of the organization will become poorly informed about matters that may be of importance to the organization as a whole."[23]

As messages are transmitted within an organization, the omission of detail may provide one means of reducing communication overload. When such omissions are systematic with respect to certain categories of information, the process may be labeled "selective filtering." Such selective filtering is often crucial to effective communication in complex decision situations.

Technical Jargon: A Basic Filtering Mechanism

Communication systems become more effective when languages are employed which carry larger amounts of meaning with relatively fewer symbols. Organizations find such communication devices as charts, diagrams, blueprints and other "graphics," coding and classification systems, occupational jargons, and so forth helpful in increasing the efficiency of communication. The degree to which knowledge relevant to a given decision alternative may be transmitted within an organization depends on the extent to which details may be summarized and condensed in an efficient shared language. Very often, however, technical jargon loses its "meaning" as it is transmitted upward in the decision-making process.

The omission of detail may take place at any point in the communication system. With more complicated data and information, however, a series of summarizations may occur, beginning early in the communication process. As March and Simon have suggested: "The more complex the data that are perceived, and the less adequate the organization's language, the closer to the source of information will the uncertainty absorption take place, and the greater will be the amount of summarization at each step of transmission."[24]

Other Mechanisms of Adjustment

Under conditions of input overload, increases in outputs are correspondingly demanded. In such situations, a number of other mechanisms of adjustment are often employed. Miller postulates that the proliferation of more channels of input or output (or both) is a typical way for organizations to respond to overloads in the communication system — as "by putting more people on the job."[25] Another response to overload is to reduce the intake, either by occasionally avoiding the processing of demands for communication or by ignoring them completely. Moderate overloads may also be obviated by queuing, which involves delaying responses during peak load periods and then attempting to catch up during lulls. Units may also adjust by making an approximation to the more precise or accurate response output. Sometimes the press of crisis situations induces bypassing, so that the usual linkages in the communication network are short-circuited in the transmission of messages within the organization.

Problems Arising from Selective Filtering

Selective filtering and the other mechanisms of adjustment, however, create the danger of either deleting important aspects of communication or introducing message distortions. Since it is extremely difficult to communicate about intangible and nonstandardized objects, message distortion is a common phenomenon of organizational communication. In decision situations, therefore, organizations frequently must make conscious efforts to develop means by which less objective communication contents can be handled. As Cyert and March observe:

Any decision-making system develops codes for communication about the environment. Such a code partitions all possible states of the world into a relatively small number of classes of states. . . . Thus, if a decision rule is designed to choose between two alternatives, the information code will tend to reduce all possible states of the world to two classes.[26]

Such rules for the codification of inputs, however, frequently introduce additional distortions.[27]

Taking a broader perspective, such systematic biasing of message content may not always be dysfunctional. Allport and Postman found, in experimental situations, that transmitted messages ". . . tended to grow shorter, more concise, and more easily grasped and told," and that there was ". . . selective perception, retention, and reporting of a limited number of details from a larger context."[28] In other words, the messages were often sharpened.

Omissions and inaccuracies may increase the ambiguity of messages; however, since ambiguous messages are open to multiple interpretations, more agreeable meanings may be attached to them by the receiver. Thus, while ambiguity may result in slippage between sender and receiver, such slippage may also promote consensus and agreement.

Storage of Communication — The Function of the Memory Bank

In discussing the characteristics of communication flows, it was noted that the more permanent record provided by a written message may produce a more sustained influence on the decision-making process, since it can be stored and recalled. What is stored, for the most part, is information. Information, however, is not subject to the laws of conservation of matter and energy. Information can be both created and wiped out — although it cannot be created from nothing or destroyed completely.

Since information has physical reality, its storage — memory — is a physical process which can be represented in seven distinct stages:[29]

1. Abstraction or coding of incoming information into appropriate symbols
2. Storage of these symbols by means of some appropriate recording device, such as patterns of electric charges in certain electronic devices, the activity patterns of cells in nervous tissues, or the distribution of written symbols on paper
3. Dissociation of some of this information from the rest
4. Recall of some of the dissociated items, as well as the combination of items into larger assemblies
5. Recombinations of some of the recalled items into new patterns that were not among the inputs into the system
6. New abstraction from the recombined items preserving their new pattern, but obliterating its combinatorial origin
7. Transmission of the new items to storage or to applications to action

A similar multistage sequence is involved in the matching of incoming patterns of information against stored patterns recalled from memory. Thus, the "memory bank" of the decision system is a repository for programmed decisions, for information concerning past experiences, for information by which "right" decisions are tested for their acceptability, and so forth.

Memory: A Selective, Dissociative, and
Combinatorial Process

Only part of past experience is selected for storage. In human memory, a selection of what we would like to remember is combined with a selection of what our subconscious mind chooses to emphasize.[30] In addition to being selective, memory is dissociative and combinatorial. Information and experience can be broken down into their component parts for storage, and then reassembled into new patterns quite different from the intake from the outside world.[i] Putting information together and estimating that a particular combination is worth pursuing is one of the fundamental activities of decision-making. It results in outputs which meet the needs of the situation better than before.

Functions of Memory in the Decision-Making
Process

Memory serves a number of important functions in the decision-making process. It is a major component in the screening and selection process by which demand inputs are sorted out and converted into *intakes*; selected information concerning a given intake is transmitted to memory and stored for possible recall at later stages in the decision process. In the process of defining the problem, selective recall serves to classify the general nature of the problem and identify the constraints and boundary conditions. This involves the recall of combined information from the system's memory bank during which further input is generated and stored for future recall. Deutsch has suggested that the area of dissociative and combinatorial memory is an implicit area of decision, since the forming of certain combinations and the omissions of others operates indirectly as a series of partial decisions.[31]

Once a preliminary decision is reached, selective recall of various information combinations is applied to modify the decision in the light of what are judged acceptable and feasible policies. In this process, the normative decision (what ought to be done) is measured against past experiences (drawn from memory) as to what might be the limits of action. This process of combining selected data and memories with the "right" decision to achieve an acceptable decision might be thought of as a second screening process, the screen being continuously modified by the system's output, i.e., the results of the final decisions which are translated into action.

---

[i]It seems reasonable to assume that the human memory is capable of making associations of relatively low probability as well as those of very high probability. If such improbable combinations and associations turn out to be highly relevant to a particular situation and lead to significant actions, they may be called strokes of genius, flashes of insight, or innovations.

With this conceptual development, it is possible to suggest a preliminary model which illustrates the relationships between memory and various stages in the decision-making process (Figure 5-3).

Expectations and Communication

Expectations play important roles in organizational communication. When messages are systematically sent and received, patterns of interaction develop among the communication nodes. Habitual usage of particular channels of the communication network, over time, generates expectations which have the force of custom. Messages are often carefully worded according to a certain set of expectations shared by the receivers. As Jackson has postulated, shared expectations within an organization become sanctions which normatively regulate behavior. Any message which does not conform to such shared expectations is likely to be ignored or produce negative responses on the part of the receivers.

By the same token, communications directed toward human beings are accompanied by the implicit expectation that, if the meaning is apprehended (and within the set of expectations of the receivers), responses within a given range of possibilities will be forthcoming.[j] If an appropriate response is not produced, the communicator has three possible courses of action.

1. He can ignore (or fail to notice) the discrepancy between expectations and responses and proceed as if there were no discrepancy
2. He can take note of the discrepancy and try again, perhaps by modifying the mode or content of his communication
3. He can take note of the discrepancy and revise his expectations to conform to the responses which he has observed

As a rule, either (2) or (3), or a combination of them, is the usual outcome of such situation; and these operations, in which the communicator modifies his behavior (either "internally" or "externally") on the basis of his observations, are examples of *feedback* in human action.

Expectations and the systems which they constitute are built up, reinforced, or modified by the operation of feedback as a person experiences his environment, both internal and external. It is the interaction of expectations and the resulting feedback which make communication possible. Expectations act as standards by which each participant can gauge the extent to which he under-

---

[j]Dorsey (*op. cit.*, p. 313) has suggested that when we are receiving or about to receive a communication, we often have more or less definite expectations as to the probable form or mode or tenor, if not the content, of such communications.

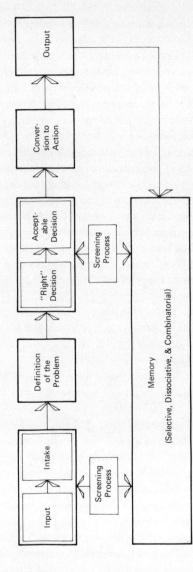

Figure 5-3. Preliminary Model of Decision-Making, Showing Relationship of Memory to Various States in the Process.

stands the other and is in turn understood. Feedback permits self-correction or adjustment in behavior in the light of comparisons between responses and expectations.

Applying these formulations to decision-making situations, it may be assumed that the initiator of a decision will have a set of expectations as to the receptiveness of the system when the decision is communicated to others. If the responses are not in accord with these expectations, the discrepancy can be ignored (usually with dire consequences), the decision can be modified and resubmitted, or the decision can be disregarded in view of the negative responses to it. This is the operation that takes place as decision alternatives are refined in the search for a "best" solution and an acceptable decision. In both instances, the process is one of communication.

In most decision-making situations, however, expectations are more complex than the expectations of each person concerning the other's probable overt behavior in response to communication. As has been noted, there exists a set of expectations in the system against which decisions must be tested. In other words, the initiator of a decision also has expectations about what he thinks are the expectations of the system, and his expectations about the expectations of the system will influence his behavior in presenting a decision. By the same token, those in the system to whom the decision is presented will try to interpret the initiator's expectations, which in turn will influence their behavior. Thus the relationship between the expectations of both the initiator and the respondents in an ongoing decision-making system are reciprocal, or complementary. Interaction takes place within the framework of these complementary expectations and both influences and is influenced by them.[32]

The Role of the Communication Intermediary

As several studies have suggested, when one of the regularized networks of communication is not employed or does not function effectively, communication may take place within the organization through ad hoc linkages, crosscutting regularized channels. These ad hoc linkages, in turn, may give rise to special roles for those who transcend the boundaries of prescribed communication networks. To date, however, the evidence concerning the role of the "intermediary" or "go-between" in the communication process is fragmentary and inconclusive.

Dalton, in a study of union and management relations, suggested that the role of the intermediary or go-between is to ". . . communicate things that no one wants to assume responsibility for knowing, doing, or being associated with."[33] According to Dalton, persons are selected for this role because of their reputation for "talking out of turn" and for carrying "secrets" to the right people, which assures almost predictable communication. Thus the informal communication network is utilized to achieve the ends of the formal system through the spreading of well-placed "rumors."

Caplow's study of communication of rumors in the military illustrates that the go-between or intermediary frequently serves this function.[34] However, as Norton Long has observed in his thesis on the community as an ecology of games, there is a more fundamental and positive role for such persons to play in linking the total system through their bridging communication.[35]

The relatively limited empirical evidence available indicates that those who serve most effectively as "intermediaries" are not marginal to two (or more) communication networks which they bridge, but instead are well linked into multiple networks.[36] Jacobson and Seashore, for example, give particular emphasis to the importance of liaison roles in their empirical analysis of interunit communications within the federal government.

. . . some individuals appear to function as "liaison" persons between groups, and characteristically have many, frequent, reciprocated, and important contacts which cut across the contact group structure.

This last class of persons . . . participate widely in the communication system but are not identifiable in any simple way with a single sub-group . . . . They are found at all status levels in the structure.

These liaison persons appear to be of critical importance to the conceptualization of organization in communication terms as they are in a position to influence significantly or to control the communications to and from certain groups.[37]

Catanese and Steiss, in their empirical study of decision-making in middle-sized cities, [38] found that influence in public decision situations is seldom evenly distributed through the system. Rather, it tends to occur in "clusters" — groups of persons or representatives of institutions capable of influencing the course of public decisions. These "decision clusters" are linked by a network of communication maintained by intermediaries who have membership in or access to more than one cluster.

These empirical studies would seem to be in accord with the position taken by Long in his studies of community decision-making.

The staff man in the civic field is the typical protagonist of things in general — a kind of entrepreneur of ideas. . . . Lacking both status and a confining organizational basis, he has a socially valuable mobility between the specialized games and hierarchies in the territorial system.[39]

From this somewhat fragmented evidence it may be postulated that the more effective public management personnel are in serving in an intermediary role, the greater their likelihood of success.

Implications for Public Management

As Thompson, Hage, and others have observed, the increased complexity of the problems confronting modern organizations — and public agencies in urban government — has resulted in a high degree of role specialization and task fragmentation in order to achieve more workable solutions.[40] In the public sector, the information required for any particular decision is dispersed among numerous individuals and groups in diverse positions. Generally, no one person has sufficient information to make a decision by himself without first engaging in an extensive communication process. The necessary information is generated at many different points within government, with much of the information relevant to a decision originating at operating levels. Information from outside government must enter the communication system via various "sensory mechanisms." While these mechanisms may take the form of routinized reporting devices, these "sensors" are frequently individuals who maintain formal and informal contacts with the broader decision environment. In this connection, the public manager's role as a sensory mechanism often stems from his contacts outside the community structure — in professional societies and associations, through such information sources as professional journals, conferences, and so forth. A new program or a solution to an existing problem may be evoked by the experience of other members of the profession in other organizations.

As McDonough has observed, management personnel stay clean because the material they handle is information. They acquire, use, retain, and transmit information through a complex communication network.

Messages, conferences, bull sessions, grumbles, notes, memoranda, phone calls — these are flowing and bumping around in any organization continuously and in all directions — up, down, and sideways. They get people irritated or satisfied, they confuse or clarify, they lead or they mislead. To make these myriad communications each contribute some constructive effect to the objective of the organization is the job of management.[41]

Management personnel either produce the raw material for decision (information) or the actual decisions. The existence of management depends on the open question which someone in the organization has asked. To provide answers to such questions, certain information must either exist or be "produced" and then must be communicated to the appropriate decision point in the system. Thus, much of public administration is concerned with getting and transmitting information. The degree of influence exercised by public management in the decision process often depends on technical competence to supply information.

When one unit holds an acknowledged monopoly over incoming messages, its communication to other parts of the decision system tends to be uniform, thereby reducing contradictions within the organization. By the same token, it may be assumed that when multiple end-points or sensor are provided for the reception of communication, the variation in interpretation of a given message is greater. Therefore, uniformity in reception would seem to be a desirable objective in public management; such uniformity, in turn, would seem to depend on the extent to which a common frame of reference exists within a public agency and government as a whole.[k]

Various Forms of Communication: A Summary

In addition to information, various amounts of influential communication of various degrees of importance flow in all directions through public organizations. This influential communication has an important bearing on the public decision-making process and must be distinguished from strictly informative and expressive communication. Informative communication, for the most part, is restricted to the transmission of raw data (primary messages), although it may include messages containing various amounts of interpretation and analysis, short of specific proposals or recommendations. If such communications are used in decision-making situations, their influence must be considered under the category of *induced influence*, i.e., where exercise of influence is unintentional. Expressive communication is generally directed to an external audience and consists of annual reports, progress reports, and other materials designed to "educate and inform" the general public. Also included in this category are certain internal documents designed to bring about a greater awareness of objectives among members of the organization.

A focus on the patterning of communication relationships cuts across the so-called formal and informal aspects of organizational activities. With each decision, or category of decisions, different patterns of communication will be evident. It may be suggested, then, that a continuum or scale of communication could be constructed in any organization, at one end of which would be "authoritative" communication and at the other the various forms of "expressive" communication evident in any organization. Between these two extremes would be found the varying degrees of "influential" communication.

Programmed and Nonprogrammed Communication

In part, communication channels are deliberately and consciously planned in the programming of public organizations. In part, however, these channels

---

[k]This common frame of reference may take many years to develop and may require the application of training programs and a gamut of other devices used to ensure conformity to organizational norms.

develop through usage. Simon and March advance two propositions concerning
the development of the communication network.[42] First they suggest
that the greater the communication efficiency of a given channel, the greater the
use of that channel. Channel efficiency is facilitated by a common understanding
of the problems and a shared "language" for dealing with these problems.
Links between members of a common profession — such as public management
— tend to be used in the communication system.

Second, channel use tends to be self-reinforcing. When a channel is used
frequently for one purpose, its use for other, unrelated, purposes will be
encouraged. In particular, informal or special-purpose channels tend to become
general-purpose channels whenever a hierarchical or formal channel does not
exist or access to such channels is denied the communicator. The self-reinforcing
character of channel use is particularly strong if it brings individuals into
face-to-face contact. In this case, informal communication, much of it social
in character, develops side by side with task-oriented communication. The use of
the channel for either kind of communication tends to reinforce its use for
the other.

As a corollary to these two propositions, it may be suggested that the more
often a particular communication channel is used, the more central becomes
its position in the communication network. This corollary would seem to hold
whether or not the hierarchical structure considers the channel a central one. As
a result, persons linked by the communication channel have a relatively high
potential source of influence in decision situations.

A second factor which relates to the achievement of a central position in the
communication network evolves from the functional differences among
communication channels. Individual decision centers and channels are often
specialized as to the kinds of information they handle and the ways in which
they handle it.[1]

Since communication is such a dominant factor in the processes of
decision-making, a major objective of public managers should be to remain at
the center of a system of "signals" that run through the organizational structure.
Such a system is the vital link between the executive and the various jurisdictions
of delegated authority in the middle range of the organization, where most
managerial duties are centered. In seeking such a position in the communication

---

[1]In large organizations, specialized communication functions are reflected in the
division of work. Among some of the specialized communication units typically found are:
(1) units specializing in the physical transmission of communications; (2) units specializing
in recording and report preparation (bookkeeping and other record maintenance functions);
(3) units specializing in the acquisition of raw information (often referred to as research or
intelligence units); (4) units specializing in the retention of information (files, archive units,
etc.); (5) units specializing in the interpretation of policy and organizational goals; and (6)
units specializing in the provision of technical premises for decisions (various technical
specialty groups).

structure, the basic propositions offered by Simon and March and their corollaries should be borne in mind.

Problem-Solving and Innovative Communication

It must be concluded from the foregoing discussion that the success of problem-solving efforts in organizations depends on the adequacy of communications as well as on skills and knowledge. Much of the previous work in organization theory has focused on decision-making which involves a selection from among fairly well-defined alternatives. The more complex and abstruse activities involved in the initiation of tasks or in creative problem-solving, where alternative solutions are not immediately available, have seldom been studied and are little understood.

As noted in the previous chapter, Simon and March have distinguished between "programmed" and "nonprogrammed" decision-making; the latter includes the discovery, elaboration, and institution of new organizational activities. One of their conclusions is that both the rate and type of innovations depend on the location of individuals in the communication structure. The man who recognizes a problem or the need for an innovation and introduces the subject into the communication system of an organization exercises important influence in the decision-making process.[43] The person who is in a position to perform a "broker function," i.e., to filter and select from the flow of innovative communication, shares substantially in this influence.

These conclusions support the notion that each position in the communication network provides its incumbent with certain types and amounts of potential influence and authority. In the next chapter, in which a model of public decision-making is presented, particular attention will be given to the avenues open to public management personnel in securing these favored positions in the communication system.

6 Decision-Making as a Multistate Process

A fundamental problem associated with most case studies of public decision-making is that they provide relatively little insight into decision-making *as a process*. For the most part, these studies have concentrated on an examination of patterns of influence at a given point in time. A "static" picture is thus presented, although the dynamic characteristics of the decision process are often acknowledged. While pluralists discuss shifts in influence, historically and in terms of various public issues, they pay minimal attention to changes over time in the patterns of influence associated with a particular decision. By focusing only on issues in the public arena, the pluralists' model ignores the screening activities of the private sector and the decisions made within the structure of government — activities which tend to narrow the range of alternatives (set the public agenda) in terms of the issues which emerge in the public arena.

Martin, Munger, *et al.* conclude from their studies of public decision-making that decisions do not arise from individual choices but from a flow of choices; a decision to take a particular action involves a series of acts.[1] This view of decision-making has received considerable support from writers in the field of management. As Robert Tannenbaum has noted:

In making a decision, an individual must become aware of relevant behavior alternatives, define them, and finally evaluate them as a basis for choice. To understand what is involved in the making of a decision, it will be helpful carefully to examine each of these steps in the decision-making process.[2]

It may be suggested, therefore, that patterns of decision-making can be best viewed in terms of a *multistage process*. Simon and March suggest a three-stage process, beginning with a disaggregation of the problem to permit a solution of the parts; a search stage, which may be physical, perceptual, or cognitive; and a screening stage, in which the items identified in the search stage are examined to see if they qualify as possible solutions (or possible components of solutions) to the problem at hand.[3] They acknowledge, however, that the elementary components of the decision-making process are characterized by a good deal of randomness; that is, except in strictly economic situations, decision-making operates in a stochastic fashion, like a Markovian machine. There is considerable arbitrariness in the sequence in which these steps are taken. There are, however two elements in the decision-making process that give it structure and permit it to yield a relatively well-organized product. They are: (1) the broad procedural programs recognizable in most problem-solving situations;[a] and (2) the substantive programs, i.e., the structuring of the decision-making process that comes about as a reflection of the structure of the problem.

The Classic Equilibrium Model of Decision-Making

Some writers have questioned the concept of an orderly multistage decision-making process. They suggest that such procedures are merely the means used to formalize and proclaim decisions, not to cast them. William Gore has stated this position in this way:

Classical theory sets decision-making off as a sequence of independent choices made by executives with formally delegated powers. Acting in the name of the organization with the assistance of top staff and through consultation with their subordinates, these men were said to carry out decision-making functions. They do this through the rational process of defining a problem, identifying the alternatives, selecting the most appropriate and acceptable alternative, translating it into a course of action, and initiating the implementing activities.

Though instances where this pattern occurred were observed, they were exceptions. We do not have one case history that shows the executive *making* the decision through a formal mechanism.[4]

Gore thus concludes that since decision-making as a mode of organization behavior is "so completely integrated with the rest of collective activity," the "classical model" of a rational decision-making process must be rejected.

The Issue of "Formal Mechanisms"

There is little in the writings of modern interpreters of so-called classical decision theory to suggest that decision-making is considered a separate, specialized function, somehow existing apart from the broader organizational context. Rather, inherent in these efforts to identify and analyze the multistage process by which decisions are formulated is the recognition that decision-making is an integral part of all phases of organizational activity. Decision-making is not a "distinct and independent" function of a select few. It is a major leap in logic to suggest that efforts to identify the stages of decision-making are akin to the development of "formal mechanisms." While these efforts, in large part,

---

[a]Simon and March observe that most of our descriptions of temporal patterns in problem-solving go back to John Dewey's analysis of the problem-solving process and to Gestalt theorizing about productive thinking.

are motivated by a desire to improve the process of decision-making, only the purist would maintain that decision-making could be reduced (or elevated) to a "science," governed by strict rules and "formal mechanisms."

Most advocates of the so-called "classical model" are in accord with Gore when he observes:

The roots of the decision-making process are deep in the subsoil of an organization. Hidden from common sense observation, they lie far below the forms and rituals of formal organization and the crust of rationality. Therefore the full character of decision-making is not easily perceived.[5]

Contradiction of the Classic Model

An effective decision-making system does not merely seek equilibrium in the sense of the classic model. The classic equilibrium model of decision-making assumes that, in the face of change, a decision system is compelled by some overriding force to reestablish some preexisting state of equilibrium. This concept of equilibrium, however, is incapable of describing an important range of dynamic phenomena. On the basis of empirical observation, it must be concluded that a decision system does not merely have static continuity at some fixed level of equilibrium.[6] Rather, in responding to forces of change, a decision system frequently strives to create conditions that, under favorable circumstances, permit it to achieve some new level of stability. At times, positive action may be taken to destroy a previous equilibrium or even to achieve some new point of continuing disequilibrium.

A Dynamic, Open, Goal-Directed System

Adaptation to change is more than simple adjustments to events which impose themselves on the structure of a decision system. A primary characteristic of all open systems is that they are able to manifest a wide range of actions of a positive, constructive, and innovative sort for warding off or absorbing forces of displacement.[b] In short, open systems need not simply react to change by oscillating in the neighborhood of some point of equilibrium or by shifting to a new one.

A growing awareness of these "dynamic" qualities of open systems must lead to a concern for a more thorough examination of the temporal sequences in which the structural configuration of a system shapes its functions; and,

---

[b]As defined in Chapter 1, an open system is one that interacts continually with its broader environment and possesses the quality of equifinality. Throughout this presentation, the public decision-making processes will be considered an open system.

conversely, the processes by which the structure is in turn altered by functional change. At the same time, recognition must be given to the fact that an open system interacts continually with its broader environment.

Viewed in systems terms, public decision-making can be considered as an open system which acts through a stochastic search process in seeking relative stability. Even though the decision-making system appears to act through trial and error, its behavior is teleological, or goal-directed. In the search process, the system may pass through a number of critical stages, until it eventually settles down in a "field," or region where conflicts with its broader environment are minimized. Expressed and unexpressed demands, emanating from the broader environment and from within the decision system, continue to act as disturbances to the stability of the system, however. These disturbances force the system to develop and employ regulatory devices to counter these "dysfunctional" aspects.

The Character of Regulation in Decision-Making

Regulation in decision-making situations can take one of three basic forms: (1) it can rely on programmed decisions by adopting an approach which has proved successful in other decision-demanding situations; (2) it may lead to adaptive decisions which may not get at the root causes underlying the demand but may "satisfice;" or (3) it may seek a more innovative response to decision demands. Programmed and adaptive decisions return the system to the same relative set of states in which it existed prior to the disturbance (i.e., before the demand for a decision). Innovative decisions, on the other hand, result in an alteration of the structural configuration of the system or produce new states, that is, introduce new courses of action not evident prior to the disturbance. Adaptive decisions *may* yield revisions of expectations among the participants in the decision system. Innovative decisions, on the other hand, produce new expectations both within the system and in the broader decision environment.

Demands as the Inputs of a Decision System

As a rule, decision-making becomes a more orderly and identifiable process when it reaches the stage in which alternative solutions are formulated and considered. The earlier stages, in which demands for decisions are identified and categorized and the problem is first defined, require an equally systematic approach. As Northrup so aptly pointed out: "One may have the most rigorous of methods during the later stages of investigations but if a false or superficial beginning has been made, rigor later on will never retrieve the situation."[7]

Therefore, in considering decision-making as a multistage process, it is necessary to begin at a point in advance of the stage where general recognition of a decision-demanding situation exists.

While a particular system under study often is set apart from its broader environment, it must be recognized that many aspects of this environment have an important impact on the system. These enter the system in the form of *inputs*. In the case of a decision system, these inputs take the form of *decision demands*. Since the concept of demands is central to the model of public decision-making being developed here, it is important at the outset to clarify this term.

A demand has been defined by Easton as ". . . an expressed opinion that an authoritative allocation with regard to a particular subject matter should or should not be made by those responsible for doing so."[8] In this definition, demand takes on a neutral connotation,[c] in that it is not necessarily associated with some set of value preferences on the part of the demand-maker. In fact, demands may be used to conceal true preferences, as when alternative programs are promoted for the purpose of generating support for some other, unexpressed, course of action.

In the context of the present discussion, however, such *expressed demands* represent only part of the overall demand inputs of the decision-making process. There are also those demands which arise from dysfunctional conditions of a given situation, but which may not take the form of an "expressed opinion." Such conditions may be interpreted from within the system as constituting demand inputs, even though they have not been identified or verbalized as such "outside" the system. This broader definition of demands is analogous to the systems concept of disturbances in that it includes anything "out there" that is interpreted as potentially dysfunctional to the system.

A demand may be quite narrow, specific, and relatively simple and direct in nature, or it may be highly general, vague, and complex. Expressed demands may take the form of specific grievances and discontents, relevant to a given experience or situation. At the other end of a continuum of expressed demands are such highly generalized demands as broad pleas for better government, more vigorous fiscal policies, victory in war, the alleviation of poverty, and so forth. Such generalized demands seldom include any specific courses of action. "Causes," stemming from various ideologies, are frequently among the principal sources of such demands, although they embody ill-defined, all-encompassing, programs of action.

---

[c]Easton makes a distinction between authoritative outputs and associated outputs. The former includes "binding decisions, laws, decrees, regulations, orders, and judicial decisions," while the latter covers "policies, rationales, and commitments" (Easton, *op. cit.*, p. 353). In the present discussion, all outputs of the system are dependent on a decision (including the "decision" not to decide). Therefore, the term "decision" can be substituted in this definition for "authoritative allocation."

Expressed demands may be directed to some specific individual or group in the decision-making system, or they may be ubiquitous in their orientation. In either case, associated with every expressed demand is some set of expectations concerning the responses that should come from the system. Unexpressed demands also arise from a variety of sources and assume multifacet characteristics. They are like expressed demands in that someone within the system must recognize the conditions giving rise to such demands as being "out of phase" with some set of acceptable conditions. In other words, before demands can gain entry to the decision system, they must be "sensed" as demands.

The Stage of Uncertainty and Doubt

It is this perception or "sensing" of a demand as being "out of phase" with some set of acceptable conditions which sets the decision-making process in motion. Very often, this perception is merely a sense of uncertainty or doubt which exists because the constituent elements in some segment of the broader environment are unsettled or not unified. As John Dewey has observed ". . . it is the very nature of the indeterminate situation which evokes inquiry to be questionable . . . to be uncertain, unsettled, disturbed."[9]

This concept of uncertainty is a positive one. It does not mean a mere lack, absence, or deprivation in a purely negative sense, such as would exist if the doubts were simply subjective states. Uncertainty stems from a particular, uncertain, objective situation.[10] The objective observations of the situation do not coincide with the definition of what *should be*. The latter may itself be either subjectively or objectively defined.

Examining this "stage of uncertainty" in terms of an individual's response to an indeterminate situation, Blanshard has suggested that the immediate stimulus to reflection or thought is the appearance of an "island" which declines to be incorporated into an individual's "mainland of thought". The problem is always one of integration; how to bring these "islands" into an intelligible whole.

The movement of reflection starts when we are presented with something . . . which we need for any reason to fit into the system we carry about in our minds, and which yet resists inclusion. An island appears demanding union with the mainland; we must bridge the gap, but are at a loss how to do it; tension arises, and from that tension, reflection.[11]

Here again, the concept of "tension" is suggested as a motivating force in decision-making, provoking action to return the system to a steady state (a state where tensions have been resolved, at least temporarily).

In psychological terms, the gap between the "mainland of thought" and the "island" is a gap in the conceptual structure of an individual (or a collection of individuals), which is brought about by an awareness of an uncertain situation. The gap is alien to the present conceptual framework. Therefore, the decision-making process is initiated to seek some resolution of these conditions.

Every sane mind approaches any situation with a conceptual structure or frame of reference into which he attempts to fit his objective observations. This conceptual framework is a dynamic thing, continuously built upon through education and experience. A certain background and training may provide an individual with a well-constructed system of ideas which makes him more sensitive to problems that others might not notice. That is to say, an individual's conceptual frame of reference governs, in large measure, the way in which he will approach an uncertain situation. Further, this frame of reference will contribute to the identification of a situation as "out of phase" with the currently acceptable system.

Thus the role of the trained professional, as an "initiator" in the decision-making process, may be identified more clearly. He must continually appraise various aspects of the accepted system and identify any element in the broader environment that may seem to be a potential disturbance to this system. This role might be likened to that of a regulator which acts as a warning device against conditions that threaten to drive the system out of some desirable set of states i.e., a stable region.

Beyond this initial stage, the role of the professional may vary considerably depending on the trajectory that the decision system assumes. For this reason, this stage of the decision-making process is frequently overlooked or deemed to be outside of the actual process. Such a view, however, fractionalizes the decision process unduly, producing somewhat distorted conclusions as to the nature of the final decision. A clerk who recognizes some discrepancy in sale procedures which has resulted in reduced profits (an unexpressed demand) and brings it to the attention of his superior, may not be in on the final decision to make major modifications in sales operations. Nevertheless, the decision came about through his initiative.

It should be noted that the "demands" for decisions may arise from within the system itself as well as from sources external to the system.[d] It may be suggested, however, that these internal and external inputs or demands are handled within the system in much the same way.

Screening Demands to Determine Intakes

This development permits a further elaboration of the distinctions between programmed decisions and adaptive and innovative decisions. Once a situation has been identified as uncertain (or potentially uncertain), there are four possible

---

[d]Easton makes the distinction between "inputs" and "withinputs;" the second means demands which are generated from within the system (Easton, *op. cit.*, pp. 21 ff).

responses. Each response involves a further degree of commitment to the decision-making process.

The first possible response is to disregard the uncertain situation; to decide to do nothing about it. Such a response is likely when the demand (input) is below some threshold of tolerance. If, for any number of reasons (such as time, cost, or effort) this response is invoked, then the process is cut short and abandoned. In this analysis, there is no discussion of such negative behavior except to observe that it is a possible response.

The second response is to identify the uncertain situation as one which can be handled through programmed decision mechanisms. This would suggest that the system contains a "memory bank" in which these programmed decision mechanisms are "stored" and against which uncertain situations are tested to determine if an appropriate programmed decision is available. Here again, the process is cut short by the application of a programmed response.

If either of the two remaining possible responses is invoked, the decision-making process moves to the next stage — classification and definition. It may be suggested, therefore, that inputs are "screened" to determine the actual *intakes* into the system. This screening process filters out those demands on which no further action is to be taken at present and those which can be handled through programmed decision mechanisms.

The Stage of Classification and Definition

"Uncertain situations," as discussed in the preceding section, are not the same as "problematic situations." Although uncertainty is essential to the initiation of the decision-making process, more is required before a problematic situation arises. As Dewey has stated, the uncertain situation ". . . becomes problematic in the very process of being subjected to inquiry."[12] Analysis does not begin with the uncertain or unsettled situation — this is anticipatory to analysis — rather, it is initiated with the identification of the problematic situation in which the problem implied in the uncertain situation is made explicit.

Northrup, like Dewey, emphasizes the importance of the problematic situation by asserting that decision-making must begin with an analysis of the situation which generates the problem. Northrup presents his own formulation of the decision-making process as follows:

In the handling of any specific problem certain stages are to be noted . . . (1) the analysis of the problem which initiates inquiry, (2) the Baconian inductive observation of the relevant facts to which the analysis of the problem leads one, and (3) the designation of relevant hypotheses suggested by the relevant facts.[13]

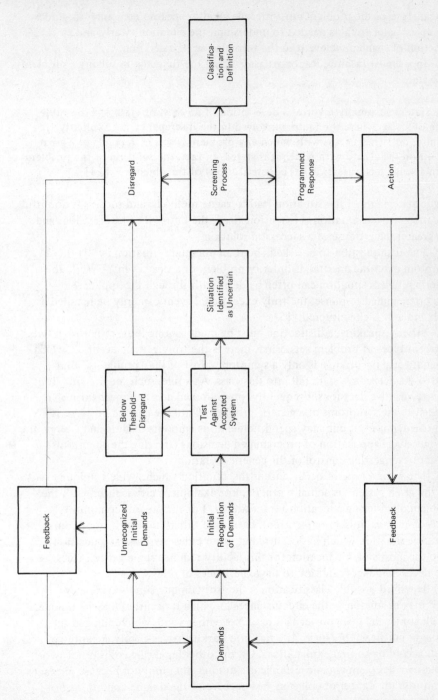

Figure 6–1. The Stage of Uncertainty and Doubt and the Screening Process.

The analysis of the problem must precede all else, because such analysis guides the investigator to facts needed to understand the situation clearly and to selection of elements relevant to the formulation of a decision.

In a similar fashion, Rapoport asserts that the first step in solving a problem is to state it.

The statement usually involves a description of an existing state and desirable state of affairs where the factors involved in the discrepancy are explicitly pointed out. The success with which any problem is solved depends to a great extent on the clarity with which it is stated. In fact, the solution of the problem is, in a sense, a clarification (or concretization) of the objectives.[14]

Vague statements of the situation lead to vague methods, and success is doubtful. The more a given situation is extensionalized, the better the classification, and the greater the promise of a successful solution.

The first question to be asked about an uncertain situation is: "Is this a symptom of a fundamental disorder or problem or a stray event?" While the generic problem situation can often be dealt with through the application of a programmed response, the truly exceptional event can only be handled as such and as it is encountered.[15]

Strictly speaking, a distinction must be made among four, rather than two, different types of problem sets. First, there is the truly generic event, of which the individual occurrence is only a symptom. Most of the "problems" that confront a decision system fall into this class. As a rule, such generic situations require adaptive decisions. Frequently, programmed decision mechanisms are applied to the symptoms of a generic problem. Until the generic problem is identified, however, one may spend tremendous amounts of time and energy in the piecemeal application of programmed decisions (treating the symptoms) without ever getting control of the generic situation.

The second type of occurrence is the situation which, while a unique event for the given system, is actually generic. For example, a city is faced with the problem of choosing a location for its airport. For the present community decision-makers, it is a nonrecurrent, or unique, situation. But it is, of course, a generic situation which has occurred in other cities. Arriving at a decision as to the most suitable location for this facility requires some general rules. The decision-makers can look to the experiences of others.

The third possible classification is the truly unique situation. The event itself may be unique or the circumstances in which it occurred may be unique. To illustrate: the huge power failure of November 1965, which plunged the whole of northeastern North America into darkness, was a truly exceptional event according to first explanations. On the other hand, the collision of two airplanes miles from any air terminal is a unique situation, not because airplanes do not run the danger of collision, but because of the unique conditions or circumstances under which the event occurred.

Truly unique events are rare. When one appears, however, the question must be asked: "Is this a true exception or only the first manifestation of a new generic problem?" This, then, is the fourth and last category of events with which the decision process must deal — the early manifestation of a new genus. For example, both the power failure and the isolated collision of two aircraft were only the first occurrences of what, under conditions of modern technology, are likely to become fairly frequent occurrences unless generic solutions are found.

General rules, policies, or principles can usually be developed or adopted to deal with generic situations. Once the right policy has been found, all manifestations of the same generic situation can be handled fairly pragmatically through the adaptation of the rule or principle to the concrete circumstances of the situation, that is, through adaptive decision-making. The unique problem and the first manifestation of a generic problem frequently require greater innovation to arrive at a successful solution. Figure 6-2 illustrates the relations between these four categories and the two fundamental dimensions of *availability of rules and principles* for dealing with such problem situations and the *frequency of encounter* of these situations.

By far the most common mistake in decision-making situations is to treat a generic problem as if it were a series of unique events. The other extreme, treating every problem incrementally through the application of programmed decision mechanisms (treating a unique event as if it were just another example of the old problem to which the old rule should be applied) can have equally negative results.

The role of the experienced professional at this stage of the decision-making process should be evident. To avoid incomplete solutions to only partially understood problems, the technical expertise of those closest to the situation

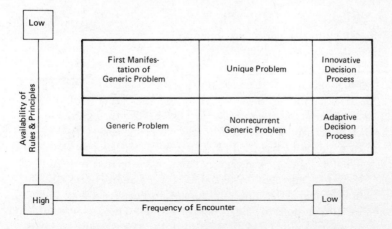

Figure 6-2. Basic Categories of Problems Demanding Decisions.

should be utilized to classify the problem. Once a problem has been classified, it is usually fairly easy to define. A further danger in this step, however, is not the wrong definition, but a plausible but incomplete one. Here again the technical expertise of the professional is required to safeguard against an incomplete definition by checking it against all the observable facts and discarding any definition the moment it fails to encompass any of them.

This approach, in essence, is what is included in Northrup's second stage — Baconian inductive observation of relevant facts to which the analysis of the problem leads one. As Northrup states the approach: "The second stage of inquiry comes to an end when the facts designated by the analysis of the problem in the first stage are immediately apprehended by observation, expressed in terms of concepts with carefully controlled denotative meanings by description, and systematized by classification."[16] These are the rules laid down by Hippocrates for medical diagnosis over 2,000 years ago. They are the rules for scientific observation first formulated by Aristotle and reaffirmed by Galileo over 300 years ago.

The outcome of the analysis of a problematic situation should be a clear definition of the problem. If the problem cannot be stated specifically, preferably in one interrogative sentence which includes one or more goals, then the analysis of the problematic situation has not been adequate or of sufficient depth. Emotional bias, habitual or traditional behavior, or the common tendency of human beings to seek the path of least resistance may result in a superficial analysis, followed by a statement of the apparent problem instead of the real problem. An excellent solution to an apparent problem, of course, will not work in practice because it is the solution to a problem that does not exist. Consequently, short-circuiting this stage of analysis may result in more time being spent later to get at the real problem when it becomes painfully evident that further analysis is required.

Identification of Constraints and Boundary Conditions

The next major step in the decision-making process involves the establishment of clear specifications as to what the decision must accomplish. In so doing, six basic questions must be answered: (1) What are the existing or potential constraints to an effective solution to the problem set? (2) What objectives must the decision meet? (3) What are the minimum goals to be attained? (4) What measure(s) of efficiency can be used relative to each of the objectives? (5) What standard(s) can be applied for evaluation of possible courses of action? (6) What definition of "most effective" is to be applied in judging the possible solutions to any given problem set? These questions aid in the establishment of "boundary conditions." To be effective, a decision must satisfy a clearly identified set of boundary conditions. In the field of quantitative decision-making, where techniques of operations research (such as linear and dynamic programming) can often be applied, boundary conditions can be identified clearly and given numerical values. In most decision-making situations, however, the identification of boundary conditions may be a most difficult undertaking.

Nevertheless, this stage is crucial in decision-making, for a decision that does not meet the boundary conditions is worse than one which wrongly defines the problem. It is all but impossible to salvage the decision that starts with the right premises but stops short of the right conclusions. Furthermore, clear thinking about the boundary conditions is needed to recognize when a course of action brought about by a given decision must be abandoned. A common cause of failure in a decision lies in the inability to recognize a subsequent shift in goals — in the specifications — which makes the previously "right" decision suddenly inappropriate. In the words of Drucker: ". . . unless the decision maker has kept the boundary conditions clear, so as to make possible the immediate replacement of the outflanked decision with a new and appropriate policy, he may not even notice that things have changed."[17]

Often decisions are made in which the specifications to be satisfied are essentially incompatible. In other words, to achieve Goal A through the course of action prescribed by the decision precludes the achievement of Goal B, or at best makes it highly unlikely. This represents a classic case in which boundary conditions were not fully and clearly identified. By the same token, a decision is often made which involves a "gamble" or "calculated risk." This is the type of decision that might work if nothing at all goes wrong. Such decisions often arise from something much less rational than a gamble — namely, a hope against hope that two or more clearly incompatible specifications can be fulfilled simultaneously.

The establishment of the boundary conditions of a decision clearly *is not* something that can or should be undertaken by the professional alone. His role should be to articulate sentiments and identifiable "felt needs" and to translate these into terms which will make possible a comparison among an array of goals and objectives. The choice of goals must rest with those authorized to act on behalf of the community, i.e., the public decision-makers.

As a rule, however, the articulation of community goals and objectives is seldom sufficiently specific to be of real value in establishing boundary conditions for any particular decision. Therefore, decisions are made with the vague hope that they will implement the overall goals and objectives of the community. What is required is some mechanism whereby these overall goals can be translated into more specific program goals and through which identifiable boundary conditions can be tested against the more general (and remote) goals and objectives. In deterministic decision situations, such mechanisms are generally available; in stochastic situations (which constitute the majority of public

decision situations), it is unlikely that such mechanisms can be readily developed.
The best device continues to be experience, coupled with a careful delineation
of the problem and the objectives associated with the required decision.

Formulation of Alternatives

Once the problem and the boundary conditions have been specified, with
what is believed to be a sufficiency of the relevant facts, it is possible to pass
on to the next stage of the decision-making process — the formulation of
alternatives.[e] It should be an invariable rule to develop several alternatives for
every situation. Otherwise there is the danger of failling into the trap of a false
"either-or" proposition. There is a common confusion in human thinking
between a true contradiction which embraces all possibilities, and a contrast
which lists only two out of a number of possibilities. This danger is further
heightened by a tendency to focus on the extremes.

Alternative solutions are the only means of bringing the basic assumptions
concerning a given situation up to the conscious level, thereby forcing examination and testing of their validity. Alternative solutions are no guarantee of
wisdom or of the right decision. But at least they prevent making what would
have been known to be the wrong decision had the problem been thought
through.

To Dewey, searching for and considering alternatives is a "progressive"
matter.

A possible relevant solution is . . . suggested by the determination of factual
conditions which are secured by observation. The possible solution presents
itself, therefore, as an *idea*, just as the terms of the problems (which are facts)
are instituted by observation. Ideas are anticipated consequences (forecasts)
of what will happen when certain operations are executed under and with
respect to observed conditions. Observation of facts and suggested meanings or
ideas arise and develop in correspondence with each other. The more facts of
the case come to light in consequence of being subjected to observation,
the clearer and more pertinent become the conceptions of the way the problem
constituted by these facts is dealt with. On the other side, the clearer the idea,
the more definite . . . become the operations of observation and of execution
that must be performed in order to resolve the situation.[18]

Alternative approaches relevant to the possible solution of a problem differ
in grade according to the level of reflection reached. At first, they are relatively

---

[e]In discussions of this phase of decision-making, the terms "alternative," "hypothesis,"
"suggested solution," "tentative solution," "concept," and "idea" are frequently used interchangeably.

vague; but as the alternatives operate to direct further observation, they become more suitable in their capacity to resolve the problem. As alternatives become more appropriate, observations likewise become more acute. Perception and conception continue to work together until the former locates and describes the problem, while the latter represents a possible method of solution.[19]

This description differs somewhat from the more typical alternative formulation phase in the public planning process. One gets the impression that alternatives presented in a comprehensive planning program are often taken as "givens" to be shaped to the particular needs of any community. While this is an oversimplification, there is an inherent danger in the selection for analysis of a "standard" set of alternative "models" in that this procedure tends to limit the evolutionary nature of alternative formulation.

The next step in this stage is to develop an understanding of the possible consequences, byproducts, and side effects associated with each of the suggested alternatives. As Dewey puts it:

. . . developing the meaning contents of ideas in their relation to one another . . . is reasoning. When a suggested meaning (idea) is immediately accepted, inquiry is cut short. Hence the conclusion reached is not grounded even if it happens to be correct. The check upon immediate acceptance is the examination of the meaning as a meaning.[20]

This examination consists of an identification of the implications of particular courses of action in relation to other alternatives in the system. The relationship so formulated constitutes a proposition. If such and such a relation is accepted, then we are committed to such and such other courses of action because of their membership in the same system. Through a series of such intermediate examinations, an understanding of the problem is finally reached which is clearly more relevant to the situation at hand than the original conception. It indicates operations which can be performed to test its applicability, whereas the original conception is usually too vague to determine crucial operations.

Thus, the examination of suggested alternatives with reference to their operational fitness involves an investigation to determine their capacity to direct further observation to secure additional factual material. This examination may result in the rejection, acceptance, or modification of ideas in an attempt to arrive at more relevant alternatives. The possible range of alternatives will vary with the problem. It must be recognized, however, that alternatives are a function, in part at least, of the data and concepts of one's disposal. When these are sufficient, fruitful alternatives are likely to emerge.

One possible alternative should always be considered: to take no action at all. This alternative is seldom recognized as a "decision," although it is as much a commitment as taking some specific positive action. An unpleasant or difficult

decision cannot be avoided merely by doing nothing. The consequences of
a decision against any action must be clearly spelled out. By carefully considering the alternative of doing nothing, the traditional ways of doing things —
which reflect past needs rather than present — can be more fully examined.

Frequently, in the search for alternatives an impasse will be reached. In such
cases, the restructuring of the problem may provide new or additional insights
into the possible alternative solutions. Problem restructuring means the manipulation of elements of the problem; it may involve a change of viewpoint, or a
permissible modification of objectives, or a rearrangement of the other elements
of the problem as it is stated.

Framing and analyzing alternatives and their consequences in view of the
problem and the relevant facts is a major part of all rational decision-making.
In spite of its prime importance to the decision-making process, there are no
simple hard and fast rules for finding the right set of alternatives.

The Search for a "Best" Solution

Only after a number of alternatives have been formulated is it possible to
determine the "best" solution. If an adequate job has been done to this point, it
will be found that either there are several alternatives to choose from, each
of which would solve the problem, or there are half a dozen or so which fall
short of perfection, in different ways. Rarely is there one and only one solution.
Such a solution may be nothing more than a plausible argument for a precon-
ceived idea.

There are two basic modes of operation for finding the "best" solution
from among several alternatives, depending on the general class of decision
sought — adaptive or innovative. Since adaptive decisions merely require that the
alternative meet the minimal expectations sanctioned by the system, and do
not require the substitution of new expectations, the "best" alternative can be
selected on the basis of relatively simple criteria. The selected alternative should
be one that provides "satisfactory" solutions to the problem (thereby alleviating
pressures created by the demand), while creating a minimum disturbance of
established expectations. No single alternative may satisfy these conditions;
it may be necessary, therefore, to combine elements from several alternatives to
achieve these objectives. The innovative decision requires a more rigorous
analysis and testing, since it will result ultimately in modification of expectations.
In seeking the "best" solution to a situation requiring innovation, there are five
criteria which may provide helpful guidelines. They are techniques for: dealing
with uncertainty, examining risks and gains, identifying economy of effort,
specifying the timing of alternatives, and establishing the limitations of resources.

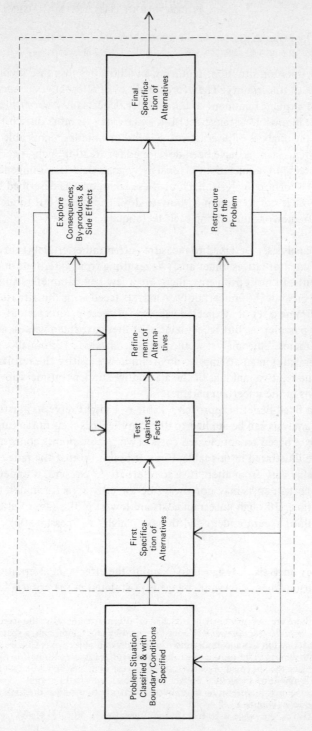

Figure 6–3. The Formulation of Alternatives.

Treatment of Uncertainty

Most of the decision situations requiring an innovative response involve
major conditions of uncertainty. Therefore, analyses of alternatives in such cases
must provide for explicit treatment of uncertainty. Uncertainty about the future —
typically present in most long-range decision situations — is most difficult to take
into account in the analysis of alternatives. Several techniques, applicable
under varying circumstances, have been developed for treating such uncertainty,
however. These techniques include: (1) sensitivity analysis; (2) contingency
analysis; and (3) a fortiori analysis. Each of these techniques is described briefly
below; the purpose is not to present a "how-to-do-it" approach but to identify
the conceptual framework underlying each technique.

Sensitivity analysis. Designed to measure (often rather crudely) the
possible effects on alternatives under analysis resulting from variations in
uncertain elements. In most problems, there are a few key parameters about
which there is a great deal of uncertainty. Analysts faced with this situation first
attempt to determine a set of "expected values" for these parameters, as
well as all other parameters. But recognizing that these expected values, at best,
may be "guesstimates," the analyst would use several values (optimistic, most
likely, and pessimistic) in an attempt to ascertain how sensitive the results
might be (i.e., the relative rankings of the alternatives under consideration) in
light of variations in the uncertain parameters.

Assuming a fixed-benefits approach,[f] Table 6-1 might serve to illustrate
how sensitivity analysis can be applied to disclose the variations in rankings
among alternatives based on anticipated costs. Two related points concerning
uncertainties are illustrated in this table. First, it points up that the range
of uncertainty may vary from alternative to alternative.[g] Second, it underlines
the fact that uncertain costs may not always be the critical factor in determining
the "best" solution; although uncertain costs are lowest in the case of alternative
C, it still ranks third except under conditions of "high" or "pessimistic"
uncertain costs.

Contingency analysis. Designed to examine the effects on alternatives
under consideration when a relevant change is postulated in the criteria for

---

[f]In general, there are two principal approaches to alternative analysis: the *fixed-benefits
approach* and the *fixed-budget approach*. Under the fixed-benefits approach, a specific level
of benefits to be attained in the accomplishment of some given objective is first established.
The analysis then attempts to determine that alternative (or feasible combination of alternatives) likely to achieve the specified objectives at the lowest cost. The fixed budget approach
involves the establishment of a specified budget level to be used to attain some given objective. The analysis attempts to determine that alternative likely to produce the highest level
of benefits for the given budget level.
[g]For alternative A, the range is 10 to 110; for alternative B, 30 to 115, and for alternative C, 5 to 90.

Table 6–1
Illustration of Sensitivity Analysis under Various Uncertain Cost Levels

	Alternatives		
Cost Levels	A	B	C
"Expected Value" of "Certain" Costs	90	80	100
"Expected Value" of Uncertain Costs (medium)	60	40	70
"Expected Value" of All Costs	150	120	170
Ranking of Alternatives	2	1	3
"High" value of Uncertain Costs	110	115	90
"Expected Value" of All Costs	200	195	190
Ranking of Alternatives	3	2	1
"Low" value of Uncertain Costs	10	30	5
"Expected Value" of All Costs	100	110	115
Ranking of Alternatives	1	2	3

[a]Adopted from: Catanese and Steiss, *Systemic Planning: Theory and Application* (Lexington, Mass., 1970), p. 92.

evaluating the alternatives. This approach can also be used to ascertain the effects of a major change in the general environment of the problem situation. In short, it is a form of "with and without" analysis. In the field of public health, for example, various alternative approaches to a state agency's responsibility for environmental health programs might be evaluated with and without a major new program of health-code enforcement. In a local context, various possible park sites may be evaluated under conditions of existing population distribution and the configuration of access routes. Additional evaluations then might be made, assuming different population distributions and under various route configurations.

A fortiori analysis. A method of deliberately "stacking the deck" in favor of one alternative to determine how it might stand up in comparison to other alternatives. (The Latin term means "with stronger reason.") Suppose that in a particular decision situation the generally accepted judgment before analysis strongly favors alternative C. In performing the analysis of C in comparison to other feasible alternatives, the analyst may choose deliberately to resolve the major uncertainties in favor of C and then determine how each of the other alternatives compares under these adverse conditions. If some alternative other than C looks good, the analyst may have a very strong case for dismissing the initial

intuitive judgment concerning alternative C. Such analysis might be carried out
in a series of trials, with each alternative, in turn, favored in terms of the
major uncertainties.

While these three techniques for dealing with uncertainty may be useful in a
direct analytical sense, they may also contribute indirectly to the resolution of
problem situations. Through sensitivity and contingency analysis, for example, it
may be possible to gain a better understanding of the really critical uncertainties
of a given problem area. With this knowledge, a newly designed alternative
might be formulated that would provide a reasonably good hedge against a range
of the more significant uncertainties. While this is often difficult, when it can
be accomplished it may offer one of the best ways to offset the uncertainties of
a problem situation.

Risks and Expected Gains

The second of the five available criteria has to do with the *risk* involved in a
series of alternatives. The risk of each proposed course of action must be
weighed against the *expected gains*. The terms "risk" and "gains" are used here
instead than the more conventional concepts of costs and benefits for several
reasons. While any public decision represents a choice of one alternative over
another and therefore involves quantitative analysis (cost-benefit analysis), efforts
to convert the positive and negative aspects of any alternative into dollars-and-
cents terms frequently results in too narrow a frame of reference. In this case,
costs means something more than that which shows up in a profit-loss statement.
Often, however, in developing a cost-benefit matrix items are omitted because
they are "intangibles." But many of these "intangibles" are important "risks"
which may seriously affect the ultimate outcome of the decision. Risks and gains
must be weighed only after they have been completely listed. Assessment of
benefits, on the other hand, frequently involves double accounting. Direct
benefits, for which dollar figures can be derived, are often counted again in
terms of the more indirect benefits. Thus, in arriving at a "net gains" figure,
such indirect benefits must be "discounted" in order to avoid an unrealistic
assessment.

There is no riskless action nor even riskless nonaction. But what matters is
neither the expected gain nor the anticipated risk, but the ratio between them.
Every alternative should therefore contain an appraisal of the "odds" it carries.
The value of such an analysis lies not in the end results but in the process which
must be carried out in arriving at these end results. If no alternative is found
suitable in terms of risks and gains, then it is necessary to return to the previous
stage in an effort to formulate more suitable alternatives. This process may
have to be repeated many times before it is possible to pass on to the next phase.

Economy of Effort

The third criterion involes an assessment of the *economy of effort*. Which of the possible courses of action will give the greatest results with the least effort, will obtain the needed change with the least necessary disturbance of the total system? As Peter Drucker has observed, too often decision-makers pick an elephant gun to chase sparrows; too many others use slingshots against forty-ton tanks.[21] It must be recognized that grandiose schemes have many hidden risks which, if carefully considered, would reduce the economy of effort. By the same token, solutions which fall short of producing optimal results may result in a series of incremental decisions, which in the long run will involve a much higher expenditure of effort.

Timing of Alternatives

The fourth criterion is concerned with the *timing* of the possible alternatives. If the situation is urgent, the preferable course of action may be one that dramatizes the decision and serves notice that something important is happening. If, on the other hand, long, consistent effort is needed, a slow start that gathers momentum may be preferable. In some situations the solution must be final and must immediately lift the vision of those involved to a new goal. In others, what matters most is to get the first step taken. The final goal may be shrouded in obscurity for the time being.

Decisions concerning timing are often extremely difficult to systematize. They elude analysis and depend on perception. But there is one guide. Whenever a public decision requires a change in vision to accomplish something new, it is best to be ambitious, to present the complete program, the ultimate aim. Whenever the decision necessitates a change in people's habits, it may be best to take one step at a time, to start slowly and modestly, to do no more at first than is absolutely necessary.

Limitations of Resources

The final criterion deals with the *limitations of resources*. This evaluative guideline is closely related to the concept of *systems readiness*. A basic problem of decision-making, whether in the public or private sectors, is the achievement of a balance in the programs and allocation of resources so as to ensure a systems readiness in the short-, medium-, and long-range futures. Achieving this objective requires a posture of sufficient flexibility to meet a wide range of possible competitive actions.

Perhaps the most important resource to be considered is the personnel
that will be required to carry out the decision. No decision can be better than
those individuals or agencies responsible for carrying it out. A course of action
may well require more competence, skill, and understanding than those affected
possess. Efforts must be made — and provided for in the decision — to raise
the ability and standards of the people who must carry out the programs associated with the decision. Decisions are often made, procedures developed, and
policies enacted without first asking the questions: (1) Are the means available
for carrying these things out? and (2) Are the people available? A less-than-
optimal decision must never be adopted simply because the competence to do
what is right is lacking at the moment. The "best" decision should always lie
between genuine alternatives, that is, between courses of action which will
adequately solve the problem.

Modification to Gain Acceptable Decision

The effective decision-maker must start out with what is "right" or "best"
rather than what is acceptable or possible, precisely because he will always
have to make compromises in the end. This observation relates back to the
specification of boundary conditions, for if it is not clearly known what will
satisfy the boundary conditions, the decision-maker will be unable to distinguish
between the right and the wrong compromise — and may end by making the
wrong choice.

In framing innovative decisions, it is a waste of time to begin by worrying
about what will be acceptable and what should or should not be done so as
not to evoke resistance. Things one worries about seldom happen, while
objections and difficulties no one thought about may suddenly turn out to be
almost insurmountable obstacles. In other words, the decision-maker gains
little if the innovative decision-making process starts out with the question:
"What is acceptable"? For in the process of answering this question, the
important aspects are usually overlooked and any chance of coming up with an
effective solution — let alone the right answer — may be lost.

After the "best" solution has been identified, the first step in seeking an
acceptable decision is to make a reconnaissance of the expectations of the
system. Unlike adaptive decisions, innovative decisions nearly always require
that expectations be altered and modified. Therefore, a careful appraisal
must be made of the expectations (both internal and external to the decision
system) that must be accommodated by the decision. This is the painful
process of self-examination, which, as Gore has suggested, often produces
internal stress and tensions (internal demands).

It may be anticipated that, upon matching the proposed solution against the system's expectations, one of three conditions will be found: (1) the expectations are in accord with the proposed solution, in which case an acceptable decision has been found; (2) the expectations are ambivalent to the proposed solution; or (3) the expectations are hostile to the proposed solution. In the last two cases, some means must be devised to create support for the proposal. If no acceptable means are found, internal demands will be heightened, and a further reconnaissance of the system's expectations will be required.

This process of modification and compromise is somewhat akin to what other decision-making models have identified as "accommodating the power structure."[22] The somewhat more neutral notion of *system expectations* has been used here to give recognition to the role of the internal structure of the decision-making process, as well as to provide a model which is adaptable to both the "power structure" and "pluralistic" approaches to community decision-making. Thus the term "expectations" can include all of these factors internal and external to the decision system.

Converting Decisions into Actions

While thinking through the boundary conditions is perhaps the most difficult step in the decision-making process, converting the decision into effective action is usually the most time-consuming one. Yet a decision will not become effective unless the action commitments have been built into it from the start. In fact, no decision has been made unless carrying it out in specific steps has become someone's work assignment and responsibility. Until this is accomplished, the decision is only a good intention.

The flaw in so many policy statements is that they contain no action commitments — they fail to designate specific areas of responsibility for their effective implementation. Converting a decision into action requires that several distinct questions be answered: (1) Who has to know of the decision? (2) What action has to be taken? (3) Who is to take it? and (4) What does the action have to be so that the people who have to do it can do it? The first and the last of these questions are too often overlooked — with dire consequences.

As has been noted, the action must be appropriate to the capacities of the people who have to carry it out. The action commitment becomes doubly important when people have to change their behavior, habits, or attitudes to make a decision effective. Care must be taken not only to see that the responsibility for the action is clearly assigned, but also that the people assigned are capable of carrying it out. The measurements, the standards of accomplishment, and the incentives associated with the proposed action must be changed simultaneously with the introduction of the decision.

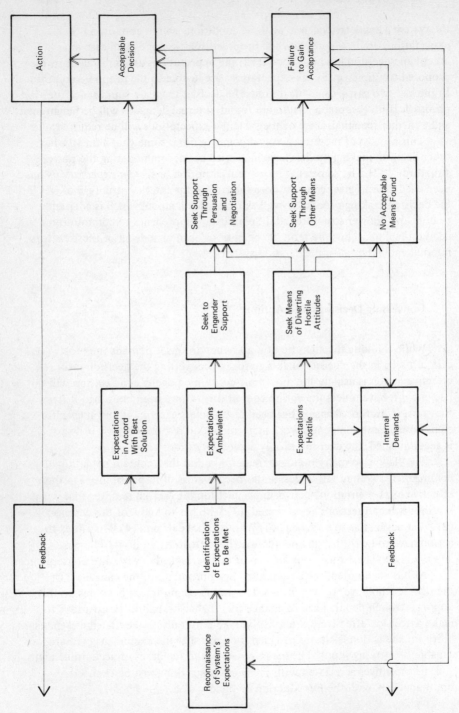

Figure 6-4. Achievement of an Acceptable Decision Through Modification and Compromise.

142

The Feedback Stage

To complete the model of the decision-making system, provision must be made throughout the process for "feedback." Feedback occurs, intentionally or unintentionally, at many stages in the decision-making process. Much of this feedback is internal to the process, resulting in a recycling of a particular phase in order to achieve further refinements and modifications. The feedback which has an impact on the entire system generally occurs at two points: (1) after the decision has been made and action programs have been initiated; and (2) whenever internal demands are created within the system. In both cases, new demands (inputs) may be generated, causing the total system to recycle.

Information monitoring and reporting are particularly important after a decision has been reached in order to provide continuous testing of expectations against actual events. Even the best decision has a high probability of being wrong; even the most effective one eventually becomes obsolete. Failure to provide for adequate feedback is one of the primary reasons for persisting in a course of action long after it has ceased to be appropriate or rational. While the advent of the computer has made it possible to compile and analyze great quantities of feedback data in a relatively short time, it must be recognized that computers can handle only abstractions. Abstractions can be relied on only if they are constantly checked against concrete results. As Drucker has observed, unless decision-makers build their feedback around direct exposure to reality, their decisions may result in sterile dogmatism.[23]

A basic aspect of the decision-making process is the development of a predictive capacity within the system to identify changing conditions which might necessitate modifications in the selected courses of action. Controls should be developed for a given solution by: (1) defining what constitutes a significant change for each variable and relationship which appears as a component in the decision; (2) establishing procedures for detecting the occurrence of such significant changes (providing modifications in the screening devices); and (3) specifying the tolerable range within which the solution can be modified if such changes occur and beyond which new solutions must be sought. In applying these controls, the information gained through "feedback" serves as a central component.

Summary

In the preceding analysis, it has been suggested that the patterns of decision-making include the following eight stages:

1. The Stage of Uncertainty and Doubt and the Screening Process
2. The Stage of Classification and Definition

3.   The Identification of Constraints and Boundary Conditions
4.   The Formulation of Alternatives
5.   The Search for a "Best" Solution
6.   The Modification of the "Best" Solution to an Acceptable Decision
7.   The Conversion of the Decision into Action
8.   The Feedback Stage

Figure 6–5 illustrates the relationships among these eight stages in terms of a general systems model.

The Stage of Uncertainty and Doubt is dependent on the overall structural configuration of the decision-making system. A well-developed structure – one in which there are extensive couplings among critical components – will be highly sensitive to doubtful and uncertain situations. On the other hand, a less well constructed system may fail to provide the necessary awareness of an unsettled situation and, subsequently, its accompanying problems. Thus, this stage of the decision-making process can be likened to the early warning devices in servo-mechanisms. The system is alerted to the possible impingement of some demand situation requiring a decision – the effectiveness of the regulatory device being governed by the Law of Requisite Variety.

In Stages Two and Three, an attempt is made to discover the relevant facts of the problematic situation and to define and delimit the problem. These stages of the decision-making process taken together parallel the construction of a regulator, i.e., the forming of the mechanism R so that when R and T (the environment of the system) are coupled, they will act to keep the overall system within some set of desirable states – to maintain stability – in the face of the impinging demand.

The statement of the problem and the identification of the conditions which the solution must meet, plus a sufficiency of relevant facts, may then be used to suggest relevant alternatives – Stage Four. Most public decisions involve stochastic situations. Therefore, activity in this stage resembles the seek-and-find or trial-and-error behavior characteristic of a Markovian regulator. A Markovian regulator, named for the mathematician who first made an extensive study of its properties, seeks to direct a system to a stable region by "vetoing" states which are not in the stable field for the system. Thus a system guided by a Markovian regulator appears to "wander" about a set of stable states, trying one combination after another.

In Stage Five, a testing of the possible alternatives is made in an effort to arrive at the "best," or maximal, solution. This solution is then modified in Stage Six to take into account the adjustments and compromises necessary to establish the chosen course of action in view of the expectations of the system. Out of this stage of the process emerges an optimal solution, given the political realities of the situation.

In Stage Seven, the decision is converted into action by making specific

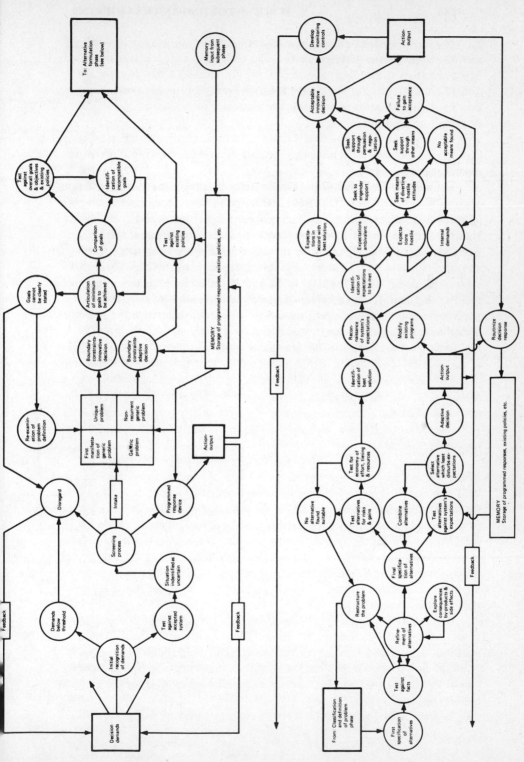

Figure 6–5. A General Cybernetics Model of the Decision-Making Process.

assignments of responsibilities. These assignments, in turn, may require adjustments in the structural configuration of the system, so that in effect the next demand acts on a "new" system. In fact, the structural configuration of the system may be altered at any time during the course of the decision-making process — this alteration may be necessary in order to achieve an acceptable decision.

Although the preceding model of decision-making is presented in eight distinct stages, it would be misleading to assume that in real life problems are so obliging as to permit an easy, logical sequence of attention. Alternatives are not usually created by moving in an orderly sequence from the first to last stage. It is not uncommon for a new alternative to occur from time to time while data about the problem are still being collected. Moreover, in a complex situation, different phases of the process may develop at different rates. For example, the stage of alternatives may be reached for one aspect or subsidiary problem of a more complex problem situation, while other parts of the same problem are still in the stage of definition and analysis. Thus in a complex, difficult problem, various stages may appear in different aspects of the same problem simultaneously. Nevertheless, it is necessary to approach the patterns of decision-making, stage by stage, in order to adequately analyze the process and to uncover some meaningful and useful insights.

7 The Evolution of Modern Public Budgeting

Scarcity of financial resources is a principal constraint in the public sector. Regardless of its fiscal position, no government can avoid the need for compromise among objectives — both for the present and the future. Governmental policies can be determined most effectively, however, if rational choices are made among alternative courses of action with full knowledge of the implications of each alternative. To achieve such knowledge, quantitative and qualitative management information must be collected, organized, and analyzed in some systematic manner in order to cast light on the consequences of spending limited public resources in various directions. As Cotton and Hatry have noted:

The widening of the scope and the increased complexity of the public services offered by the several areas of government have been matched by the difficulties of guiding and coordinating functions of government. Because the context in which a government — whether it be federal, state, or local — seeks to provide services for its citizens is one of scarcity of public resources in relation to over-all demands and objectives, the decision-makers in government are forced to choose among many competing programs. A rationally discriminating decision as to how best to serve the public interest can only be reached through the use of improved tools of public decision making.[1]

It must be recognized that budget analysis, budget-making, and financial planning and management involve areas of administration which require significant long-term professional training, particularly in connection with fiscal programs in larger political jurisdictions. It is most important, however, that all public management personnel gain a fuller appreciation and understanding of the budgetary process in government. It is the purpose of the next several chapters to provide such an understanding.

The Objectives of Public Budgeting

Public budgeting provides an effective means of organizing management information to make correct decisions concerning the allocation of limited fiscal resources. A budget may be defined as: "A comprehensive plan, expressed in financial terms, by which an operating program is effective for a given period of time. It includes estimates of: (a) the services, activities, and projects comprising

147

the program; (b) the resultant expenditure requirements; and (c) the resources usable for their support."[2]

Budgeting provides a system of communication that is regularized and cyclical. The purposes of the public budget are both *policy* and *administration*.[3] The budget is much more than a financial document; it represents a process by which: (1) public policy is made; (2) public action programs are put into effect; and (3) both legislative and administrative controls are established. A budget must be interwoven with and be a product of the entire public management process. It is influenced by the same social, economic, and political processes that affect the conduct of all public affairs.

A budget document provides a common terminology for describing the plans and programs covering diverse public operations. It can offer an effective vehicle for the periodic reevaluation of governmental purposes and objectives and can facilitate comparisons of public programs and their costs in the light of these objectives. The budget serves as the legal basis for public spending and fiscal accountability. Through the budget process, financial authority and responsibility can be delegated while appropriate central control over these matters is retained.

Public Planning and Budgeting

At the heart of modern budgeting lies the need for public planning. Reflecting on the functional objectives of budgeting outlined above in this context, it may be concluded that three basic forms of public planning are required: (1) strategic planning; (2) management (tactical) planning; and (3) operations planning and control.

Strategic planning is the process of identifying public goals and objectives, determining needed changes in those objectives, and deciding on the resources to be used to attain them. It entails the evaluation of alternative courses of action and the formulation of policies that govern the acquisition, use, and disposition of public resources.

Management or tactical planning is the process by which steps are taken to assure that resources are obtained and used effectively and efficiently in the accomplishment of public objectives. It involves: (1) the programming of approved goals into specific projects, programs, and activities; (2) the design of organizational units to carry out approved programs; and (3) the staffing of those units and the procurement of necessary resources. Management planning encompasses program analysis, capital improvements programming, administrative control, and so forth. The process of management planning is spread over the entire budget cycle. Ideally, it forms the link between goals and objectives and the actual performance of public activities.

Operations planning or (scheduling) and control is the process of assuring that specific tasks are carried out effectively and efficiently. It refers to the measures taken to accomplish the policies, plans, and programs established elsewhere in the budget cycle. Operations planning and control is predominant during the execution and audit stages of budgeting, although the form of budget estimates and appropriations is often determined by control procedures. In its more advanced form, operations planning involves the application of such management tools as PERT and CPM. Operations control, on the other hand, involves such control and reporting procedures as position controls, restrictions on transfers, requisition procedures, and travel regulations, to mention the more common devices. These control mechanisms have the purpose of securing compliance with policies made by central authorities.

The "Mix" of Planning Processes

Every budget system — even the most rudimentary — incorporates these basic planning processes. Operationally, they are often indivisible. The "mix" and relative emphasis among these processes, however, varies considerably. As a practical matter, strategic planning, management planning, and operations planning have tended to be viewed as competing processes in budgeting with no neat division of functions among the various participants.[a] Moreover, these planning processes often require quite different skills and result in different ways of handling the budget mission. As a consequence, one type of outlook frequently dominates.

Most important, perhaps, are the differential information requirements of each of these basic modes of planning. Information needs differ in terms of time spans, levels of aggregation, linkages with organization and operating units, and the input-output foci. The apparent solution is to design a management information system that can serve the multiple needs of planning and budgeting. Historically, however, there has been a strong tendency to homogenize information structures and to attempt to rely on a single classification system to serve all budgetary purposes. For the most part, the informational system has been structured to meet the purposes of control. As a result, the type of multipurpose budget system envisioned by contemporary advocates of budget reform has been almost impossible to achieve.

----

[a]Since time is one of the scarce resources in budgeting, central authorities must be selective in the things they do and the elements they emphasize. This scarcity would suggest that the control responsibilities should be decentralized to operating levels, while strategic and tactical planning is retained in a more central position. However, the lack of reliable and relied-on internal control systems has forced central authorities to assume many of the control functions, often at the expense of strategic planning.

Changing Attitudes Toward Public Budgeting

Contemporary attitudes differ considerably from those of the past on the question of what constitutes prudent public policy in fiscal affairs. The proper role of government in providing public facilities and services has also come in for considerable reevaluation and redefinition, as has the question of what government can or should do to foster sound economic growth and development. These shifts in attitude concerning fiscal policy have caused and been the cause of changing attitudes toward public budgeting. As Charles Beard once observed: "Budget reform bears the imprint of the age in which it originated."

It is possible to identify three successive stages of budget reform. The emphasis in each stage has a close parallel with one of the three basic modes of planning outlined above. In the first stage, dating roughly from 1920 to 1935, the dominant emphasis was on developing adequate mechanisms for the control of expenditures. The second stage, which began with the New Deal of the Roosevelt administration and reached its peak in the early fifties with the introduction of performance budgeting, provided a focus on management considerations. The third stage can be traced to the current efforts to link strategic planning and budgeting in a multipurpose budget system.

The Era of Fiscal Controls

Historically, the fiscal aspects of budgeting have received the greatest emphasis. In most governments, the budget has been primarily considered a financial and accounting device, in which expenditure estimates for various departments and agencies are submitted and reviewed in monetary terms. Under this approach, requests are supported by detailing *objects of expenditures* — tabulations of the myriad items required to operate an administrative unit, such as salaries and wages for personnel, rent, office supplies, equipment, and other inputs. Technical routines for the compilation and review of estimates and the disbursement of funds are built on these "line itemizations." The validity of requests is judged primarily on the basis of comparisons with previous levels of expenditures. During the era of fiscal controls, annual balancing of the budget was regarded as a fundamental principle of sound fiscal policy. This policy, however, frequently resulted in serious constraints on economic growth and development.

Leaders in the movement for executive budgeting during the early part of this century envisioned a system of functional classifications that would focus on the work to be accomplished. They regarded objects of expenditure as subsidiary data, to be included for informational purposes only. This preference for functional accounts reflected those underlying concepts discussed previously, in connection with the dichotomy between politics and administration.[4] The Taft Commission, in its landmark report on the need for a national budget in 1912, vigorously opposed object-of-expenditure appropriations and recommended that expenditures be classified by class of work, organizational unit, character of expense, and method of financing.[5]

Early efforts to develop functional accounts, however, were relatively unsuccessful. Such accounts were designed primarily to facilitate rational program decisions; they did not provide adequate protection against administrative improprieties. Therefore, after some experimentation with functional accounts, most early budget agencies settled on detailed itemization of objects, which was believed desirable not only ". . . because it provides for the utilization of all the machinery of control which has been provided, but it also admits to a much higher degree of perfection than it has at present attained."[6]

One of the fundamental problems that continues to plague the typical line-item budget is the large number of items of appropriation. In an effort to mitigate the adverse effects of multiple classifications, the Bureau of Municipal Research, in establishing the basis for budgeting in New York City in 1917, proposed a fundamental distinction between the purposes of budgets and appropriations, and between the types of classifications suitable for each. Appropriations were to be used as statutory controls on spending, whereas budgets were considered instruments of planning and publicity. Budgets were to include all of the details underlying plans of work and the specifications of costs to accomplish that work. Total costs were to be classified by functions in an effort to determine questions of policy having to do with the services rendered and to establish a foundation for appraising results. Thus, the Bureau recommended the establishment of *work programs* which were to provide a detailed schedule or analysis of each function, activity, or process within each governmental agency.

This was a far-sighted conception of budgeting, one that embodied many aspects of a multipurpose budget system of the type found in Planning-Programming-Budgeting-Scheduling systems today. However, the approach failed to gain acceptance, and the Bureau was left with object accounts oriented to a control function. The distinction between budgets and appropriations was not well understood, and the work program idea was rejected on the ground that it lacked adequate accounting backup.[7]

By the early twenties, the object-of-expenditure approach to budgeting was widespread. The founding generation of budget personnel concentrated on perfecting this approach with its control orientation, and thus the era was marked by a preoccupation with forms and factual descriptions of actual and recommended procedures.

The Management Orientation

As many of the administrative abuses that had given rise to object controls were regulated by statute, and as more reliable systems of accounting were installed, the budget was gradually freed from its unidimensional role of fiscal watchdog. The rapid growth of government activities and expenditures made it exceedingly difficult and costly for central budget officials to keep track of the many objects in the budget. Activities began to be aggregated, and increased attention was given to the formulation of management devices for controlling the continued proliferation of administrative and operating agencies.

At the same time, with the advent of Keynesian concepts in economics, it became evident that governmental spending could serve as a means to increase wealth, as well as to redistribute it, without displacing private investment. As long as government involvement in economic affairs was considered a "necessary evil," and as long as there was little recognition of the social value of public expenditures, the main function of budgeting was to keep public spending in check. Outputs were seen in terms of limited and fixed values, and therefore the budget was used as a central control mechanism to govern inputs. However, as the work and accomplishments of public agencies came to be regarded as "benefits," the task of budgeting was redefined to include the effective marshalling of fiscal and organizational resources for the attainment of those benefits.

All of these factors converged in the New Deal years of the thirties. In 1939, the Bureau of the Budget was transferred from the Department of the Treasury to the newly created Executive Office of the President, marking a major shift in the federal approach to budgeting, away from the control orientation toward a management orientation. The staff of the Bureau was increased tenfold, with significant additions from the ranks of public administration. Added to the Bureau's budgeting activities were functions in administrative management, statistical coordination, and apportionment procedures for budget execution.

The scientific management movement, with its historical ties to public administration, also hastened the adoption of budget processes for appraisal and improvement of administrative performance. But far more relevant applications of managerial cost-accounting were developed during this period in connection with government operations: government agencies sought to devise performance standards, and rudimentary techniques of work measurement were introduced in several federal agencies.

By the end of the Second World War, the management orientation was firmly established in all but one aspect of federal budgeting — the classification of expenditures. In 1949, the Hoover Commission called for modifications in budget classifications so as to be in accord with the management orientation. The term *performance budgeting* was first used by the Commission in recommending the adoption of improved budgetary techniques by the federal government. The Commission report stated:

We recommend that the whole budgetary concept of the federal government should be refashioned by the adoption of a budget based upon functions, activities, and projects; this we designate a performance budget. Such an approach would focus attention upon the general character and relative importance of the work to be done, or upon the service to be rendered, rather than upon the things to be acquired, such as personal services, supplies, equipment, and so on. These latter objects are, after all, only the means to an end. The all important thing in budgeting is the work or the service to be accomplished, and what that work or service will cost.[8]

Performance budgeting has a strong management orientation; its principal objective is to assist administrators in their assessment of the work-efficiency of operating units. It seeks this objective by: (1) casting budget categories in functional terms, and (2) providing work-cost measurements to facilitate the more efficient performance of prescribed activities. Generally, its methods are particularistic, with the reduction of work-cost data into discreet, measurable units. Performance budgeting derives much of its conceptual and technical basis from cost accounting and scientific management. Budgeting is a tool of management and the budget is envisioned as a work program. Mosher has stated that ". . . the central idea of the performance budget . . . is that the budget process be focused upon programs and functions — that is, accomplishments to be achieved, work to be done."[9]

Performance budgeting led to the introduction of activity classifications. Activities are related to the functions and work responsibilities of distinct operating units; hence their classification ordinarily conforms to organizational lines. This type of classification is most useful for an administrator who has to schedule the procurement and utilization of resources for the production of goods and services. Activity classifications gather under a single rubric all the expenditure data needed by an administrator to manage his unit. The evaluation of programs, however, requires an end-product classification oriented more directly to the mission and purpose of government. This latter type of classification may not be very useful to the administrator, but it is of great value to the budget-maker who must decide how to allocate scarce funds among competing claims.

Narrative descriptions of programs and performance were also added to the budget document. These statements give a general picture of the work that will be done by the organizational unit requesting funds. The narratives have a descriptive and justificatory function; they do not provide an objective basis for evaluating the cost-utility of an expenditure, however. There is little evidence that such narratives have been used for decision-making. Rather, they seem best suited for giving the uninformed outsider (legislators and the public) some glimpses of what is going on inside an agency.

Performance budgeting resulted in a multitude of work-cost measurements. The most widely applied of these techniques were detailed workload statistics assembled by administrators to justify their requests for additional funds. Attempts also were made to apply the techniques of scientific management and cost accounting to the development of work and productivity standards.

The Next Major Innovation – Program Budgeting

The weighing and evaluation of alternative programs are important factors in modern budgeting policy. The same dollar spent on different programs may yield greatly varied results, both in economic and social achievement. Wise budget policy generally seeks to spend public resources where they can produce the greatest net benefits. As Page has observed: "A budget should be a financial expression of a program plan. Setting goals, defining objectives, and developing planned programs for achieving those objectives are important, integral parts of preparing and justifying a budget submission."[10] Thus, the decisive problem confronting all levels of government, as well as agencies within government, involves the allocation of limited public resources – in an optimum fashion – to meet selected physical, economic, social, and cultural needs and demands.

Perhaps the innovation in the budget process that has received the greatest attention in recent years is the Planning-Programming-Budgeting-Scheduling system (P.P.B.S.). Heralded as an innovation in comprehensive budgeting procedures, P.P.B.S. was first brought to public attention in August 1965, when President Johnson proclaimed that by fiscal year 1968, all federal departments would adopt the budgeting procedures that had been followed successfully for some years in the Department of Defense.

In spite of the attention that P.P.B.S. systems have received, the fundamental concepts are not radically different from earlier program evaluation methods. As David Novick, who often is credited with formulating the P.P.B.S. approach, has observed, the concepts of program budgeting "have rather ancient and hoary origins."[11] These concepts did not start in the Department of Defense or The Rånd Corporation, as many have suggested. Rather, there are two basic roots, one in the federal government, where program budgeting concepts were introduced as part of the wartime controls systems by the War Production Board in 1942. The other root – an even longer and older one – is in private industry. There is evidence to suggest that large corporations such as DuPont and General Motors were applying program budget techniques in the early twenties.

The basic concept underlying program budgeting – presenting budgetary requests in terms of program "packages" rather than in the usual line-item format – has been adopted as a central focus of the P.P.B.S. system. However, this concept has been broadened to encompass a structuring of programs according to objectives regardless of agency responsibility. Further, under the P.P.B.S. approach, a conscious effort is made: (1) to state end objectives; (2) to seek a wider range of alternatives; and (3) to link program and financial plans.[12] In short, P.P.B.S. systems recognize that planning and budgeting are complementary operations. The need for planning, programming, budgeting, and scheduling arises from the indissoluble connection between the allocation of resources and the formulation and conduct of government policy. When undertaken in the proper "mix," these processes constitute the means by which objectives and resources — and the interrelations among them — are taken into account to achieve a more coherent and comprehensive program of action for government as a whole.

Program budgeting and P.P.B.S. are oriented to a strengthening of the role of strategic planning in the budget process. The primary goal of program budgeting is to secure a more rational basis for decision-making by providing: (1) data on the costs and benefits of alternative approaches to the attainment of proposed public objectives; and (2) measurements of output (effectiveness or performance) to facilitate a continual view of programs designed to attain chosen objectives. As a policy device, program budgeting departs from more basic models of efficiency in which the objective is fixed and quantities of inputs and outputs are adjusted to secure an optimal relationship.[13] In program budgeting, policy and program objectives may be considered variables — analysis may lead to new statements of objectives.

Program budgeting focuses on aggregates of expenditures (broad program classifications which may cut across agency lines of responsibility). Such a focus facilitates the evaluation of alternative courses of action in terms of costs and benefits (or effectiveness). Detailed itemizations of expenditure categories are brought into play only as they may contribute to the analysis of the total system or in terms of their potential impact on marginal tradeoffs among competing proposals. In program budgeting, the emphasis is on comprehensiveness and on the grouping of data into categories that facilitate comparisons among alternative mixes of public expenditures. The program budget is viewed as a statement of public policy.

Major Components of Program Budgeting

While the concept of PPBS burst on the public budget scene in the sixties amid general enthusiasm, heralded as the Holy Grail of over a half century of budget reform crusades, its future in the seventies remains in doubt. As with many innovations introduced by dictum, inadequate groundwork was laid for the introduction of PPBS into the federal budget process. What proved to be highly successful in the evaluation of weaponry systems in the Department of Defense had only limited application to other public agencies. Very quickly, proponents of PPBS were faced with strong arguments concerning its "failures" even in the Defense Department. Much heat but little light arose in the ensuing discussions of PPBS that look place in legislative chambers, agency conference rooms, and the classroom.

It is of no particular concern to this author whether the term PPBS survives these continuing debates. What is important, however, is that the underlying framework — a more systemic and comprehensive approach to budget-making — be further refined and perfected as an important mechanism of public management. It is with these objectives in mind that this and subsequent discussions will attempt to circumvent the PPBS controversy by returning to the more basic concepts of program budgeting.

There are five major components to a program budget. The first involves an identification of major public goals and objectives in program terms. This component, of course, is the essence of strategic planning and, as was said in Chapter 1, strategic planning can mean the difference between success and failure in the delivery of vital public services. Unfortunately, the concepts of strategic planning are the least developed of the three basic modes of public planning.

A second major component of program budgeting involves the structuring and analysis of public programs "across the board," i.e., without concern, initially, for the variety of agencies that might be involved in the processes implementation. The across the board structuring of governmental programs is an ideal to strive toward — in reality, such a goal should be considered a long-range rather than an immediate objective. Such a structure would focus the process of goal identification in terms of the total activities of government, regardless of where these activities may be carried out within the organizational structure. Some agencies simply cannot make the shift to such a program structure in a short time. In other cases, a significant effort must first be launched in the development of a management information and program evaluation system (MIPES) before the interdependencies of various agencies can be examined and the goals of government can be programmed in a more comprehensive manner.

The third component of program budgeting involves an extended time horizon and multi-year program and financial plans. The extended time horizon is necessary to establish a long-range process which can circumvent the "crisis programming" characteristic of many public activities. This longer time horizon serves to guide the total activities of government in a more coherent and comprehensive fashion. The multi-year program plan is needed to indicate the proposed outputs of public facilities and services according to the objectives outlined in the strategic planning stage. The magnitude of each program is determined through this phase of the budgetary process. The multi-year financial plan serves to project costs for each program as outlined by the decisions that are made. Cost estimates, outlined in varying levels of detail according to the time span covered, must be matched with estimates of revenue sources required to support the proposed programs. Only through such an examination is it possible to determine the adequacy of current sources of revenue in the light of future demands.

Program analysis — the fourth component — is the cornerstone of program budgeting. Through this systematic analysis of alternatives, programs are selected for multi-year plans. While program analysis may take several forms, in essence it involves the reduction of complex problems into their component parts or segments so that each can be studied in greater detail, followed by a synthesis of these parts back to the whole. Program analysis recognizes the basic problem types involved in the allocation of limited resources: (1) the problem of maximizing benefits given the costs involved; (2) the problem of minimizing costs to achieve a certain given level of benefits; or (3) the combination of the above two problem types in which both costs and benefits vary. The analytical task in program analysis involves the use of existing resources or the generation of additional resources to create new means-ends patterns to resolve conflict over problems of choice. In general, this task involves: (1) identification of questions relevant to the inquiry; (2) operationalization of vaguely stated objectives; (3) elimination of imprecise factors; (4) ascertainment of quantifiable variables; (5) specification of assumptions; (6) selection of models and other tools of analysis; (7) specification of alternatives; and (8) selection of the "best" or "optimal" course of action or program. These steps will receive further discussion.

The final component in program budgeting involves program updating procedures. Through such procedures, the program analysis techniques are applied to determine needed program modifications and improvements once programs are implemented.

What Is a Program?

While the concept of program budgeting has been described above in general terms, one of the most critical aspects of this budgetary technique has been left undefined — namely, what is a program? In governmental budgeting parlance, the terms *operation, activity, function,* and *performance* have often been used in place of the word *program.* To achieve some specificity of meaning and fuller understanding of the basis for program budgeting, it is necessary to regard a *program* as a *group of interdependent, closely related services or activities which possess or contribute to a common objective or set of allied objectives.* Designation of an activity or operation as a program must take into account the following aspects:

1. A program should permit the comparison of alternative methods of pursuing an imperfectly determined policy objective
2. Even if the objectives are clearly defined, a program should seek alternative means of achieving these objectives
3. Programs may consist of a number of complementary components, some of which may be effective without others and some of which are highly interdependent on the whole

4.   A program defines an element within a larger process and is usually tied or linked to other program elements
5.   Programs may have overlapping structures, where these overlaps are used as means to meet certain objectives
6.   A program is concerned with the time-span of expenditures

Program Preparation

Programming and budgeting are different but complementary cyclical processes and should be consistent with one another. In his analysis of these functions, Mosher points out: "Budgeting is tied in with programming in a number of ways, but the processes are fundamentally distinct; the organization and individuals concerned differ in part; and the procedures, the timing, the philosophy, and the classifications differ."[14] Good program preparation depends on the programming and budgeting systems used. In some cases, there is little difference between the two systems; in other instances, however, a radical difference does exist. When the latter situation occurs (as it often does when the techniques of budgeting and programming develop at different rates and achieve different levels of sophistication), particular care must be exercised to ensure consistency in the total effort.

An Iterative Process

Organization of the decision-making process and its relation to the general framework of government plays an important role in program preparation. Basic considerations in this connection include: (1) the organizational position of decision-initiating agencies (either centralized or decentralized); and (2) the time span required to complete the decision process. The development of the program preparation phase must not be conducted within a closed-system context. Cognizance must be taken of the feedback mechanisms and subsequent revisions and reevaluations of the program definitions as part of an *iterative process* which seeks precision in the input phase of the system. The probability of change in programs increases as the time-span of decisions increases. In short-term or tactical planning, the probability of revision and reevaluation is less than in the longer-term strategic planning. One particular approach to strategic planning that recognizes the possibility of changing goals and objectives within an open system is the concept of systemic planning, which seeks other than optimal alternatives to very long-range planning problems.[15] In practice, however, the usual range of time for public programs is between five and ten years.

Who Is Responsible for Program Preparation?

Assignment of responsibility for the preparation of public programs involves consideration of the organization of the initiating body and its policy development processes. Questions of organization involve consideration of structure-based and function-based authority relations within the initiating unit and the communication positions of personnel with planning and budgeting responsibilities. The policy development process may be predetermined either by accepted agency policy or by the organization of authority within the agency. Often the policy development process is conservative in nature, since it involves decisions as to what superiors within the agency will accept and approve. Responsibility becomes more centralized when policy development depends on a clear perception of policy preferences in the executive branch as reflected in past decisions, or when it depends on legislative policy as reflected in laws and legislative reports.

The allocation of responsibility for program preparation plays an important part in determining the overall effectiveness of program budgeting. As noted previously, there are three major planning activities involved in program budgeting: (1) strategic planning; (2) tactical planning; and (3) operations planning. Each agency or department must develop a coordinating function in an attempt to synthesize these three planning processes. This coordinating function should interface with both larger and smaller decision-making units within the political system in a hierarchical manner. At the federal level, such a structure is suggested by the development of the Office of Executive Management, which ". . . was created in order to integrate separate agencies. OEM was formed to analyze governmental structure, provide assistance to agencies in developing information systems, coordinate operations with state and local programs, and to assist in fiscal affairs related to PPBS."[16]

Program Structure

A program structure is developed as a format for the presentation of budget information. As such, it provides a framework within which resource allocations are made. In the development of program structures, agencies must determine appropriate output-oriented (performance-oriented) categories which cover the work of the agency. To do this, the program structure often must be broken down into program categories, program subcategories, and program elements. This hierarchy can be illustrated by the "program tree" or "decision tree" shown in Figure 7–1. The development of such program trees owes much to the work done in military planning and programming. Hartley in his article on the applications of PPBS as a systems concept has provided

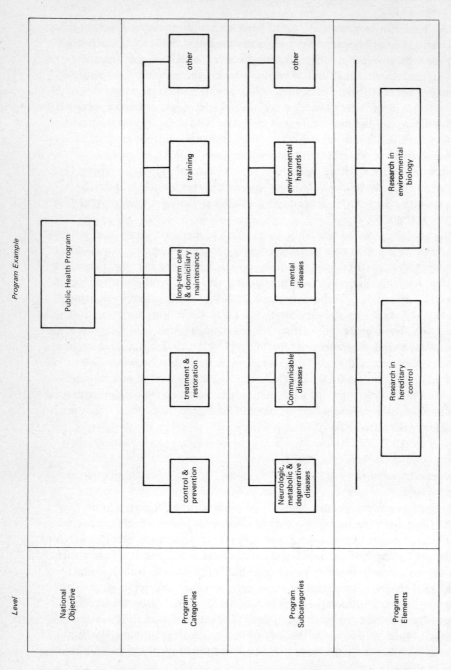

Figure 7-1. An Example of a Program Tree as Applied to the Field of Public Heath. Adapted from: Robert U. Ayres, *Technological Forecasting and Long-Range Planning* (New York: McGraw-Hill Book Company, 1969), p. 180.

a number of significant illustrations of actual program structures with civilian applications.[17]

An apparent paradox exists in the program budget concept. Much of the literature on the subject carries an implicit assumption that basic classifications of an agency's program are, or should be, identical with its organizational structure. It follows, then, that if the structure of the agency is not in accord with the "logical" program structure, the agency should be reorganized. However, the directives of the Bureau of the Budget on program structuring have indicated that the program structure *may or may not reflect* the organization framework of the agency. This paradox would seem to indicate that, through program directives, a relatively slow reorganization of existing agencies, in accord with functional requirements of program budgeting, is more appropriate and more realistic than a direct frontal attack. This suggested methodology for reorganization recognizes the basic conservative nature of government agencies and their unwillingness to undertake radical changes in operations.

As indicated earlier, the design of a program structure can be viewed as a *hierarchical ordering problem*. Such designs require the determination of the number of levels of organization within a particular agency. Once the levels have been chosen, program analysts may begin to state objectives, select program categories, and prepare descriptive statements for each component of the structure. The statement of objectives and the selection of categories must take into account the iterative process involved in the systematic development of the program structure. As broad descriptive statements are developed, they must be translated into clear program objectives that are analytically based and operationally useful. The analysts' view of the developing structure must involve the objectives of the structure (the top-down model) and the activities or functions which take place (the bottom-up model).

There are two general types of factors which influence the design of a program structure: (1) factors concerning the overall approach (structured, unstructured, or ex cathedra); and (2) factors influencing the response of individual agencies. The first category of factors includes: (1) the size of the organizational structure, the number of agencies or commissions reporting to the chief executive, and the degree of autonomy prevailing within the organization; (b) the constitutional or statutory powers of the chief executive with respect to the budget-making function; (c) the personality and management philosophy of the chief executive and the acceptance of these factors within the organization; (d) the understanding of and sympathy for the operational philosophy of program budgeting on the part of responsible agency heads; and (e) the ability, size, prestige, and organizational location of the central staff agency responsible for program budgeting. The factors influencing the response of the individual agency are more diverse. They include: (a) the understanding of and sympathy for the program budget approach and an explicit understanding of the guidelines involved in program structuring; (b) the perception of the

agency head as to the support of program budgeting principles by the chief
executive; (c) the structure and complexity of the agency and its allocation of
responsibility; (d) the nature of the agency mission or missions and the range
of activities to be carried out; (e) the types of programs towards which the agency
is directed and the diversity of these problems; (f) inertia and tradition within
the agency; (g) the political popularity of agency programs and the agency's
relationship with key legislators; (h) the relations between the bureaus or
divisions within the agency (and the possibility of competition); (i) statutory
obligations of the agency and the nature of its clientele groups; and (j) the
characteristics of the agency's existing management information system and the
competence of its program budgeting staff.

Program Analysis

The first basic element in program analysis is the definition of a public
problem. This definition may be concerned with the establishment of goals and
objectives or may involve the establishment of criteria and quantitative measures
to improve the effectiveness of an existing program or activity. As the definition
of the problem proceeds, a projection of the determinants must be made in
terms of future social and economic factors which may influence or have an
effect on the problem. In systems terminology, this step involves the delineation
of system boundaries and the determination of exogenous and endogenous
variables. Once the system has been defined in a tentative fashion, the analysis
must shift to the generation of alternative approaches which might be applied in
attacking the problem. Evaluation of the effectiveness of alternatives may be
carried out through the use of cost-benefit or cost-effectiveness analysis. These
forms of analysis require the generation and application of quantitative measures
of performance or effectiveness in terms of stated objectives. Reliance on
quantitative data requires that the analyst be aware of the limitations of these
techniques and his understanding of the uncertainties involved.

Establishment of objectives at the outset of the analysis provides the basis
for determining which programs and activities are related. Reduction of agency
activities through the use of program trees requires that these objectives be
stated clearly, since they are the necessary information inputs involved in the
development of a program structure. Achievement expectations are determined
on the basis of the stated objectives, and objectives provide a basis for developing
criteria of performance that permit accomplishments to be quantified.

The establishment of criteria involved in the establishment of objectives
may be viewed as analogous to the behavior patterns established in game theory.
In this case, two basic criteria are involved: (1) the *maximin criterion*, by which
the minimum possible gain is maximized regardless of the actions taken by
the agency or others in the decision system, and (2) the *minimax criterion*, by

which the maximum regret possible is minimized regardless of the possible actions taken by the participants. Although the above criteria have been developed from rather simplistic two-person games, more complex models may be developed which consider internal and external constraints limiting the achievement of objectives.

Analytic Approaches in Program Budgeting

The spectrum of methodology available to the analyst in program budgeting points up both the limitations and sophistication of this budgetary approach. Viewed within a continuum (Figure 7–2), the major thrust of cost-benefit or cost-utility analysis is towards suboptimization within a defined range of quantification. At present, much of the sophistication in analytical techniques is found at the far right hand side of the continuum, including the developments of the Critical Path Method, PERT, and the methodologies of operations research (basic tools in operations planning and control). Towards the left hand end of the continuum (the conceptual foundations for strategic planning), however, the use of qualitative information serves to limit our present capabilities of measurement.

For the most part, intuition, judgment, and experience play an important role in major allocation decisions. When models of the system under analysis are formulated, the analyst must be cognizant of the differences in modeling techniques. If the models are viewed in relation to real-world situations, a continuum based on abstraction can also be identified. As we move along this continuum from real-world situations, the first technique encountered is the use of an operational exercise as a model, next the use of gaming techniques, and then simulation models. At the far end of the continuum are the analytical models. Increasing the abstraction involved in modeling results in an increase in the speed of the analysis, while increasing the realism of the modeling increases the costs involved.

Cost-Utility Analysis

The techniques of cost-benefit, cost-effectiveness, and systems analysis differ slightly in application; however, for the purposes of this presentation and to avoid confusion in terminology, the term *cost-utility analysis* will be used in place of the above terms. Cost-utility analysis is essentially an analytic tool used to sharpen the decision process of intuition and judgment. It involves the following characteristics: [18]

1.   Systematic examination and comparison of alternative courses of action to

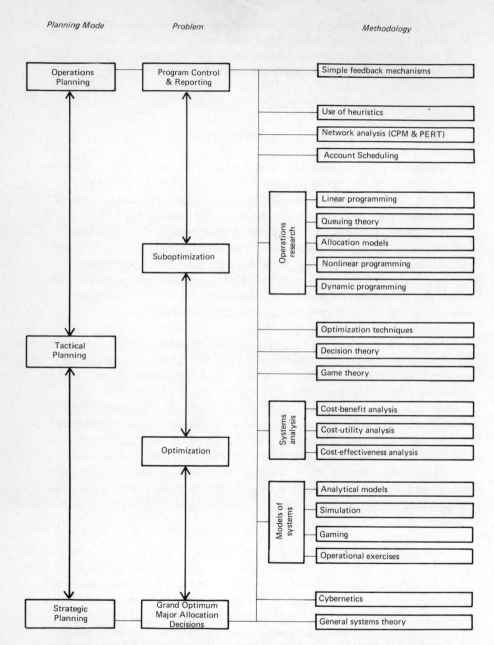

Figure 7-2. The Planning-Problem-Methodology Continuum. Adapted from: Roy F. Kenzie, "Program Planning and Program Analysis: The Essentials of Effective PPBS," unpublished manuscript, March, 1970.

achieve specified objectives — in this context, objectives may be altered
or new objectives created
2. Critical evaluation of alternatives in terms of cost (economic resources
required) and utility (the gains or benefits)
3. A future time context
4. Explicit treatment of uncertainty
5. Multi-variable problem environment
6. Use of both quantitative and qualitative information
7. An output which is geared to investment-type decision problems and/or
research and development activities

The output orientation of program budgeting is emphasized by the structuring of cost-utility models and their relation to the goal structure. The purpose
of cost-utility analysis is to identify the effect on output (performance or
effectiveness) of different levels of input (resources). In the private sector, this
analysis is carried out through the identification of production indifference
curves (transformation curves or isoquants) [19] and the Engel curve.[20] The
Engel curve is described by a series of points of tangency of successive production
indifference curves as resource inputs are increased (see Figure 7-3).
The difficulty of measuring costs and utility, especially in the public sector
and in nonprofit organizations, does not prevent analysis of resource allocation
within this framework. In fact, such analyses are made routinely through the
adoption of implicit assumptions concerning costs and utility functions and their
relationships. While it is difficult to identify precisely the output from public
activities such as hospitals, libraries, recreational facilities, and the like, such
output can often be approximated. In practice, such approximations are made
through crude *surrogates*. Further refinements can be made through the process
of program structuring, in which information is developed to ascertain how
participants view the mission of the program and the referents or "proximate
criteria" [21] (empirically measurable, it is hoped) that are used in identifying
the performance of the program. Using this information, it is possible to describe
different levels of output in terms of the expectations of participants in the
decision process.[b]
One of the major considerations in undertaking cost-utility analysis is the
proper structuring of the problem and the design of the analysis. Although
application of conceptual approaches such as *fixed utility* (or fixed benefits) and

---

[b]Paul Rigby, in an unpublished paper entitled "Identifying Effect of Potential Budgets
on Program Output", has constructed a methodology for determining "consumption indifference curves," curves which describe the decision-maker's preferences in buying inputs to
achieve goals. This approach is based on an interview technique in which empirical referents
of the respondents are recorded and analyzed to determine the input tradeoffs in terms of
various levels of output or performance.

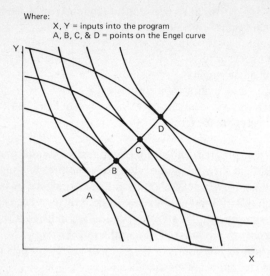

Figure 7–3A. Expressed Trade-Off Between Two Program Inputs Producing an Engel Curve.

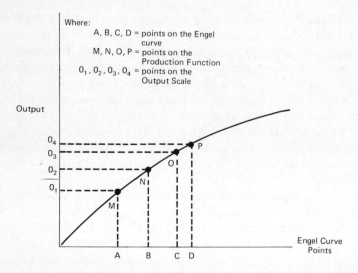

Figure 7–3B. Assumed Relationship Between Program Input and Output (Production Function).

fixed budget has met with some success in problem situations where such fixed levels can be established, there are no formal rules for this most critical phase of the analysis. Much of this analysis depends on the use of experience, skill, imagination, and intuition. Further, since the analysis involves a feedback mechanism, an iterative process permits the continuous redefinition of this formative stage.

The Problem Identification Stage: Model-Building, Uncertainty, and Timing

There are a number of major difficulties which may be encountered in the problem identification phase. Among these considerations are: (1) the level of the system or the level of the organization of the system elements; (2) the size of the problem in terms of the number of variables, externalities, and constraints; (3) the problem order or sequence of operations; (4) problem complexities and the structure of the decision trees involved; (5) the types of analytical techniques applied (some techniques require more explicit first-run inputs than others); (6) the number of systems and subsystems involved and the problem environment of these systems; (7) the information sources involved in terms of problem completion and prediction; and (8) the linkages and networks involved within and between the systems and subsystems.

Once the tentative problem identification phase has been completed, the next major consideration in program analysis is the building of a model of the system. Models are abstract representations of reality which help the analyst perceive significant relations in the real world, to manipulate those relationships, and so to predict other relations. There are essentially two types of models: (1) the formal mathematical model, and (2) the informal nonmathematical model. Model-building is an art and not a science and is the result of an experimental process. In the model, relevant variables are highlighted, and those variables not relevant to the problem are consciously suppressed. Sets of explicit assumptions are established within the model to develop a set of relationships among objectives, costs, and utility.

Treatment of uncertainty is another major consideration which must be taken into account in program analysis. There are two general types of uncertainty: (1) uncertainty as to the state of the world in the future, and (2) uncertainty arising from the use of statistical methods. Techniques for dealing with the first type of uncertainty were discussed in the previous chapter. A further examination of these techniques and approaches for dealing with the second type of uncertainty will be taken up in a later chapter.

Time also plays an important role in program analysis. Problems may be treated as either static or dynamic. If the model is dynamic, or operates through time, then the analysis will be more complicated due to the larger number of variables involved. Further, the selection of criteria for identifying alternative courses of action will be more complex.

Checking the Validity of the Model

As noted earlier, models are often constructed to test and predict various aspects of the generated alternatives. Major consideration must be given to checking the validity of the model. To do this, the following questions should be asked:

1. Can the model describe known facts and situations reasonably well?
2. When the principal parameters involved are varied, do the results remain the same (consistent and plausible)?
3. Can the model handle special cases where there is some concept of what the output should be?
4. Can it consign causes to known effects?

Qualitative supplementation is another major consideration in program analysis. In cost-utility analysis, such supplementation is an integral part of the analytic effort and is applied in the interpretation of quantitative work. When certain qualitative considerations cannot be used in the formal analysis, they should be discussed when alternatives are presented to the decision-makers.

Summary and Conclusions

During the past fifty years, there have been a number of significant shifts in emphasis in the processes of public budgeting. With each shift has come a change in the roles and responsibilities of participants in budget-making. Current efforts to develop and implement a more systematic technique to ensure sound policies and decisions in the allocation of public resources have produced the concept of program budgeting. Program budgeting holds the potential of providing a very useful interface between the activities of long-range planning and decision-making and the day-to-day operations of government. As such, it is essential that public management personnel be fully involved in the further development and sophistication of these concepts and techniques.

In general, there are three aspects of program budgeting that must be understood. The first involves the *structural* questions, including the setting of end objectives and the determination of the time horizon for the planning and budgeting period. Second, there are the *analytical* aspects, through which alternative courses of action are examined systematically in terms of costs and utility. This analysis clarifies the range of choices available and the implications of choice for the decision-maker. The third aspect of program budgeting relates to *data and information needs*. The structural and analytical aspects of program budgeting must be supported by a highly developed management information and program evaluation system (MIPES). Such a system must involve the participation and support of all involved agencies of government.

It must be recognized that the political process is one of adjustment and compromise. The allocation of fiscal resources can be further illuminated by the continuous assembling and analysis of data on the nature and capacity of the economy and the objectives and needs of government and its policy. There is, however, an inherent danger of becoming mesmerized by the techniques of a "systems" approach, It is better to have fiscal decisions that are *nearly right* than ones that are *perfectly wrong*. This is not to minimize the potential contributions that can be derived through a program budgeting approach. Rather, it is to suggest that program budgeting must be taken in proper perspective in relation to other components in the public decision-making process.

8 Effective Preparation of Public Budgets

The interactions of all elements, public and private, in a given jurisdiction are part of the governmental process that results in policy formulation. It is in this connection that budgeting takes its place among the principal mechanisms for the formulation of public policy. When seen in this manner, budgeting becomes a process that is continuous, dynamic, and extremely influential.

A complete budget — including an enumeration of all proposed programs, expenditures, and revenues — makes it possible for decision-makers to compare the relative needs for various public services and to weigh the desirability of proposed services against the tax burden required to finance public programs. The publicity of actions taken in reviewing the budget furnishes the public with important guidelines in judging the work of legislative and administrative officials. A well documented and thoroughly explained budget can inspire public confidence more effectively than any other action taken by a legislative body or chief executive.

In the presentation of the budget, administrators have an opportunity to explain management programs and policies. Attention can be focused on the many decisions required to determine appropriate standards of service. Management problems that require legislative action or backing for solution can be discussed. In the process of preparing the budget, the public manager has an excellent opportunity to appraise the competence of agency personnel, review the organizational structure and operating methods of public agencies, and formulate and initiate improvements. The execution of the budget provides one of the most important devices for directing and controlling activities for which public management personnel are responsible.

Program Budgeting in Local Government

To date, program budgeting has had relatively limited application outside the federal government, even though many of the concepts of program budgeting are particularly adaptable to the decision needs of local governments. The primary mission of local government is service, and therefore public activities at the local level can be readily identified and often can be measured in programmatic terms. Local resistance to the modifications necessary to initiate a program budget approach, however, can frequently be traced to the assumption that a high degree of technical expertise is required to undertake sound program analysis. This assumption is valid at the federal level, where the overlapping and complex program missions of a multitude of agencies make the task of program analysis extremely difficult. At the local level, however, the structuring and analysis of programs can be carried out with relative ease. Program budgeting does not involve any radical departures from previously accepted budget methods. Rather, it embodies a reemphasis of long-accepted principles of building a budget on the basis of sound appraisals of need. Program budgeting and traditional object budgeting can be quite compatible, with the two approaches complementing each other.

As a general rule, however, it is neither practical nor desirable to adopt all features of program budgeting overnight. Initially, emphasis should be placed on making necessary revisions in the budget document so that an explanation and justification of expenditures is presented in terms of public-service programs. Such a presentation, in the early stages of conversion, may be based on the more traditional object-of-expenditure approach; an aggregation of object-of-expenditure data in programmatic terms should provide the basis for the necessary reorientation to a program budget approach. Within the limitations of time and data available, attention should be focused during budget preparation and review on the development of factual data about the output or performance of public programs to support all fiscal requests. At the same time, a long-term effort should be initiated to improve work records and reports, accounting methods, program structuring (with the development of preliminary program trees), and other elements important to the management and budget process. All of these procedures must be analyzed and adjusted according to program dimensions appropriate to a given jurisdiction.

Limitations of the Budget Process

It should be understood, however, that the budget does not offer any automatic or magic solution to the complex problems and issues which surround the control and direction of public affairs. As Mosher has stated: "Budgeting, like other social processes, is a human undertaking, carried on by people who are subject to a wide variety of influences and motivations."[1] Public management personnel should be well aware of the limitations within which they must operate and the hazards which must be faced.

The first problem is one of definition. The term "budget" is commonly used to identify different aspects of financial planning. Sometimes it designates financial and operating programs recommended for consideration by local governing bodies; in other cases, the budget is the program approved by such bodies from which controlling appropriations are established. It is necessary, therefore, to distinguish between a proposed and an adopted budget. The definition problem also involves the time span covered by the budget document. The current budget generally covers operations for a fiscal year (or in some cases two) and is frequently called an *operating* budget. As such, it may be contrasted with the *capital budget*, which is concerned with the forecasting of capital improvement needs and long-term programs of operational services. Capital budgets generally cover a five-to-six-year period and are supported by capital improvements or capital investment programs.[2]

One of the most significant values of the annual budget is that the cycle is repeated every year, requiring regular reviews of activities and service policies. The danger inherent in cyclical budgeting, however, is that it can result in short-run thinking and a tendency to postpone necessary expenditure increases or revenue measures to some future budget period. Failure to look beyond the current budget can result in a significant multiplication of future problems.

Budgeting is essentially a planning process. However, no plan can anticipate unknown factors. The problem of an uncertain future must be countered by a comprehensive approach to strategic planning, by careful program analysis, and by continuous efforts to improve available projection techniques.

Governments do not operate in a vacuum. The budget process will always be affected by political, economic, and social forces originating outside government, in the broader decision environment. Whether the budget-makers like it or not, government must be responsive to many of these forces. At the same time, most local governments have existed for many years. Older, established organizations within governments build up systems of values, beliefs, and traditions that are slow to change. The budget for any current cycle will inevitably be significantly affected by past commitments, established standards of service, existing organizational structures, and current methods of operation. Any of these factors may not be entirely satisfactory from the standpoint of effective budget-making. Through budget analysis, the public manager may find many areas in need of improvement; however, it may not be possible to effect such improvements immediately. Budgeting should be a continuous process and it may be necessary to program reforms over a long period of time.

Public management personnel must give particular attention to personal relationships with members of the official family. Since justifiable expenditure requests often exceed available resources, some aspects of budgeting are competitive in nature. Conflict between persons concerned in the budget process can be damaging to future efficiency and morale. While there are no sure-fire methods for avoiding such conflicts, every effort should be made to keep participants fully informed as to the basis for allocation decisions and to avoid decisions which might be interpreted as arbitrary or capricious.

Factors Determining Public Expediture Requirements

Revenue analysis is a vital phase of budgeting. All too often, however, the budget process is unduly influenced by the constraints established by revenue analysis, and in consequence public programs become a reflection of the funds

available rather than of true community needs. It must be remembered that
in the long run revenue totals must reflect expenditure needs. Therefore, a
major effort in the budget process must be directed toward the estimating of
expenditure requirements, particularly those relating to definable public
programs.[3] The fundamental conditioning factors that influence program
costs may be classified as follows: (1) the scope and quality of services provided;
(2) the volume of activity required to render the services; (3) methods, facilities,
and organization for performing these activities; (4) qualities and types of
labor, materials, equipment, and other cost elements required by public programs;
and (5) price levels of the various cost elements.[4]

The budget process must be directed to the analysis and review of these
cost-conditioning factors as they relate to each program, function, activity, and
operation performed. While allocation decisions may be made on programmatic
information, budget requests must be supported by the more detailed cost
information outlined above. The analysis of cost must be a continuous process,
with each annual budget representing only a relatively short time cycle in the
long life span of the community and its public-service programs. An adequate
budget system must provide comprehensive and effective procedural devices
for controlling expenditures and thus establishing the price citizens must pay for
public services. Here again, however, there exists a potential conflict between
the "economic watchdog" attitude adopted by some budget officials and the
more progressive service orientation necessary to provide programs geared
to the needs of the community.

Foundations of Effective Budget Preparation

If a program budget is to provide orderly and regularly recurring means for
determining and revising public service policies and implementing administrative
controls, it must be established on a firm foundation. The success of program
budgeting is dependent on many ingredients; among these, seven are particularly
important.

Progressive Management Programs.   Local governments, to a large extent,
are production-oriented; therefore, basic techniques and activities of progressive
public management other than budgeting should be given adequate attention
and development.

Continuous and Comprehensive Operations Analysis.   Management research
is an essential tool for determining budget requirements. Such research involves
the compilation and analysis of facts concerning governmental operations
to be used as a basis for decisions and action programs. Budget-making must be
based on a constant scrutiny of services performed, operating methods, organiza-

tional structures, and the utilization of facilities. These research activities are an integral part of the operations planning and control process.

Legal Basis for Budgeting.   The budget is so important to the proper function of government that its place and continuity must be assured in organic law. Such legislation should indicate the date on which the fiscal year begins, date of budget transmittal, date of budget adoption, general scope of the budget, and responsibility and authority for budget preparation and execution. Details as to budget procedures and the content of the budget document, however, should be incorporated in ordinances and administrative rules and regulations that are subject to modification and improvement.

Adequate Accounting System.   The system of public accounts must be adequate not only for fiscal control but also for the provision of important budgetary information. First priority should be given to the establishment of revenue and activity account classifications tailored to local needs. "Model" classification systems should be considered only as guides and must be interpreted with regard to the needs of a particular community and its "inventory" of services and activities. An accounting system, as a minimum, should include: (1) comprehensive procedures for expense distribution; (2) unit cost accounting procedures; (3) general ledger accounts for work in progress; and (4) suspense accounts for distribution of such expenditures as compensation insurance, retirement contributions, etc.

Inventory of Public Service Activities. Such an inventory must be developed and maintained along with a system of records and reports to provide information on volume of activity and program output or performance. These records and reports provide data for the preparation of program justifications. While the need for such data is closely akin to the underlying concepts of performance budgeting, the types of measures applied differ considerably. Figure 8–1 provides a suggested approach to the establishment of a record and reporting system.

Long-term Service and Capital Improvements Program.   The annual budget is actually only a part of a long-term operating and capital program. Each annual budget provides an opportunity for fulfilling a portion of these long-term programs. The procedures for long-term financial planning, therefore, should relate carefully to current budgeting procedures.

Scheduling Procedures, Instructions, and Forms for Compilation, Review, and Presentation.   Viewed as a process, budgeting may be described as a formalized system of communication. The extent of formalization in the process will vary depending on the size of the organization, but the basic

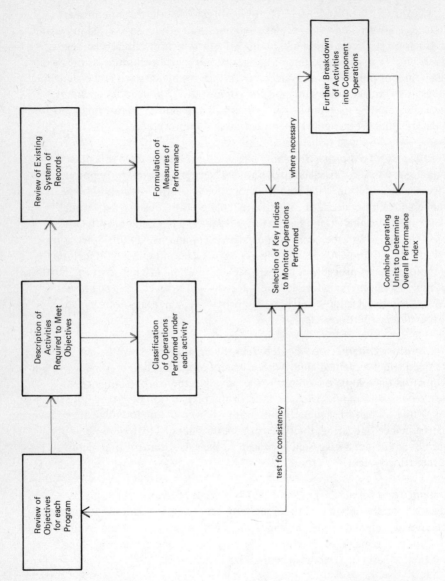

Figure 8-1. Procedures for Establishing Improved Record and Reporting System.

outlines of the program will be the same. Every device of communication —
formal and informal — comes into play, including written instructions, schedules,
forms, personal and group conferences, and so on.

The Budget Calendar and Operation Schedule

Budget-making requires careful scheduling if public officials are to be given
adequate time and complete information for sound decisions on budget policy.
If the mass of detail required is to be coordinated and deadlines are to be met, all
steps in the process must be taken in logical sequence. The responsibility for
performing each step must be clearly assigned. To ensure that requests are
submitted in a uniform and complete manner, it is essential that well-designed
forms be provided. It also is desirable that policies and special instructions
for the guidance of agency heads be set forth specifically in writing.

A budget calendar should be established in advance and should set forth,
in chronological order, the key dates and assignments of responsibilities. At
the local level, the controlling dates of the budget calendar are often set by
state law, city charter, or ordinance, and serve as deadlines for submission of the
budget to city council, for its adoption, and for setting the annual property
tax levy and rate.

The budget calendars suggested in Table 8-1 are based on a fiscal year
starting on January 1, with property taxes falling due on the same date. The
actual dates, of course, will have to be adjusted to the fiscal year of the
municipality. The total time for the annual budget preparation will vary from
four to six months in a large city to two to three months in a small city. The
time interval allowed for each step will vary somewhat in accordance with
the size of the municipality and established legal requirements.

Figure 8-2 illustrates the program budget cycle adopted in the sixties by
the State of New York.[5] There are seven basic steps in this cycle.

Preparatory Phase.   Preparation for long-range programming takes place
immediately following the submission of the executive budget to the legislature
in January. Revised central forecasts of population and economic trends are
prepared to guide agency planning and programming. Previous program projections are also reviewed.

Agency Long-Range Programming.   Before the beginning of the new fiscal
year, each agency begins the preparation or revision of its long-range program
projections. Departmental planning intentionally overlaps the start of the
new fiscal year to ensure that legislative alterations in the executive budget are
reflected in the new program projections.

Table 8–1
Suggested Budget Preparation Calendars for Large and Small Cities

Large City	Small City	Budget Requirement	Responsible Official
Time Period			
Feb. 1–July	June 15–Aug. 15	Preparation of long-term program of services and capital improvements	Chief administrator and dept. heads
Prior to July 15	Prior to Aug. 15	Preliminary work, including entering prior and current-year financial data on estimate forms and preliminary revenue estimates	Chief finance officer and budget officer
July 15	Aug. 15	Issue budget instructions and estimate forms	Chief administrator
July 15–Sept. 1	Aug. 15–Oct. 1	Prepare work program and budget estimates	Dept. heads
July 15–Sept. 1	Sept. 22–Oct. 1	Prepare revenue estimates	Chief finance officer and budget officer
Aug. 15–Sept. 7	Oct. 1–Oct. 15	Check mathematical accuracy of estimates, compile, and summarize	Chief finance officer
Sept 1–Oct. 15	Oct. 15–Nov. 15	Investigate and review requests; determine final recommendations	Budget officer and chief administrator
Oct. 15–Nov. 1	Nov. 5–Nov. 15	Prepare budget document	Chief administrator & budget officer, chief finance officer
Nov. 1	Nov. 15	Submit budget into city council	Chief administrator
Nov. 1–Nov. 22	Nov. 15–Dec. 1	Legislative consideration of budget	City council
Nov. 7–Nov. 15	Nov. 19–Nov. 23	Public budget hearings	City council
Nov. 22	Dec. 1	Budget adoption by enactment of appropriation and revenue ordinances	City council
Nov. 22–Jan. 1	Dec. 1–Jan. 1	Prepare and mail tax bills	Finance dept.
Dec. 15–Jan. 10	Dec. 15–Jan. 5	Prepare, review, and establish budget allotments	Dept. heads and budget officer
Continuous	Continuous	Budget administration and management research	All administrative & staff officials

June Conferences. Program projections are presented to the governor's staff agencies before June 1. Conferences are scheduled during June to discusss the major policy issues and administrative aspects of each program projection. A general analysis and evaluation of major trends in state programs are sent to the governor and his immediate advisors.

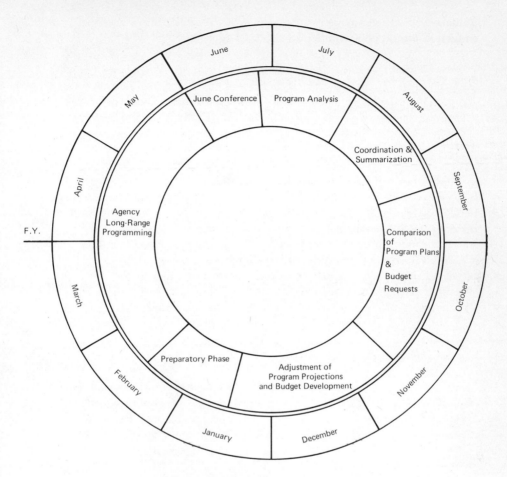

Figure 8–2. The Program Budget Cycle of the State of New York. Adapted from: *Guidelines for Integrated Planning Programming Budgeting* (Albany, New York, 1966), p. 4.

Program Analysis and Evaluation. Following the June conferences, the program plan projections are analyzed in depth. Followup work on existing or potential policy issues and administrative problems begins in accordance with priorities established during the June conferences.

Coordination and Summarization. Following analysis on a departmental basis, program plans are combined and analyzed on a coordinated basis by the central budget staff. Proposed programs are related to development trends in both the public and private sectors. Unadjusted summaries of personnel, capital, and fiscal requirements are prepared. Areas of existing or potential conflict and unnecessary overlap are reviewed carefully.

Comparison of Program Plans and Budget Requests. When budget requests are received from individual agencies in September, they should include a comparison of the budget request with the projected requirements of the first year of the long-range program projections. During formal budget hearings, departments present their budget requests in the context of the long-range goals of their programs.

Adjustment of Program Projections and Budget Development. Program projections of the various agencies are adjusted to reflect the changes, if any, in their budget requests. The proposed executive budget is then developed against the priorities and requirements of the long-range program projections.

With some modest modification in timing, these procedures could be applied at the local or county levels of government. Here again, the key to successful application of these procedures centers on stages two and four — the long-range programs developed by individual agencies and the program analysis and evaluation procedures carried out by the central budget staff.

Six Interacting Cycles in the Budget Process

Although emphasis was placed in the preceding discussion on the development of a budget cycle based on a calendar year, the process of program budgeting may be envisioned as six interacting cycles, or iterative activities (as shown in Figure 8–3), the time schedule for each of which varies considerably. The basic components of each of these cycles can be summarized as follows:

Strategic Planning
S1 Basic Research and Analysis
S2 Diagnosis of Trends and Needs
S3 Statement of Goals and Objectives
S4 Formulation and Analysis of Alternatives
S5 Policy Alternatives and Recommendations

Development Planning
D1 Projections and Forecasts
D2 Resource Plans (Natural, Economic, Human)
D3 Plans for Facilities and Services
D4 Land Use and Transportation Plans
D5 Comprehensive Development Plans

Financial Planning and Capital Improvements Programming
F1 Long-Range Financial Plans

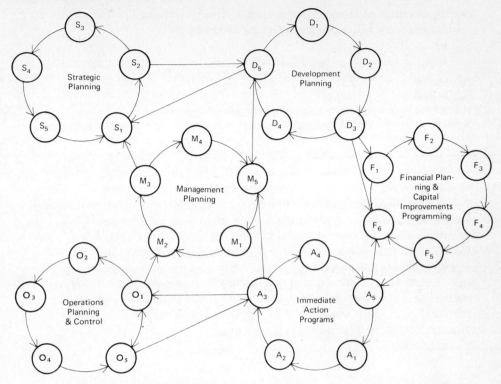

Figure 8–3. Schematic Representation of Interrelationships Among Major Elements in Program Budgeting.

F2 Financial Analysis
F3 Alternative Fiscal Policies
F4 Establishment of Resource Needs
F5 Assignment of Priorities
F6 Operating and Capital Budgets and Capital Improvements Program

Management Planning

M1 Detailed Studies of Program Needs and Program Structuring
M2 Program Analysis
M3 Analysis of Service Standards
M4 Estimates of Volume of Activities and Forecasts of Shifts in Rate or Flow of Activities
M5 Development of Operational Programs and Assignment of Program Responsibilities

Operations Planning and Control
O1 Definition of Alternative Means of Achieving Programs
O2 Network Analysis and Program Scheduling
O3 Quality Analysis and Control

O4 Coordination of Management Services
O5 Promotion of Efficiency and Economy of Operations

Immediate Action Programs

A1 Operational Needs Analysis
A2 Operational Policy Decisions
A3 Scheduling of Activities
A4 Administration of Day-to-Day Governmental Operations
A5 Administration of Operating Budget

The successful implementation of program budgeting, in large measure, depends
on the success with which each of these cycles is operated and coordinated.
Of particular importance is the interface among these six cycles, shown by the
connecting arrows in Figure 8–3. In the previous chapter, considerable attention
was given to procedures for program structuring and analysis (M1 and M2). In
subsequent chapters, the component processes of strategic planning, development
planning, and operations planning and control will be discussed in further detail.
The remainder of this chapter will focus primarily on considerations relating
to management planning and financial planning. Four aspects, in particular, are of
central concern to these iterative processes and to the overall development of a
program budget — the analysis of service standards (M3) estimates of volume
of activity (M4), establishment of resource needs (F4), and long-range financial
planning (F1).

Analysis of Service Standards (M3)

One of the most important factors in determining public expenditure
requirements is the range and quality of services to be provided. Closely related
to the standards of service are organization, facilities, and methods utilized
in their performance. A large part of the management planning process and the
closely related budget process must be devoted to an evaluation of service
standards and a search for better methods for accomplishing program objectives.
Total resources available for financing the budget are always limited. It is
inevitable, therefore, that judgments be made as to the comparative value of
various public services currently provided or proposed. Comparative judgments
as to priority are necessary when considering activities performed within a
single functional area. Priority judgments are also required between entirely
unrelated functions and services.

Decisions on standards of service and judgments concerning effectiveness of
performance must be made regardless of the budget philosophy adopted.
Where a strict "fiscal" approach is followed, budgets all too often are built
primarily on the basis of review and projection of past expenditure. Unfortunately, data on the flow of dollars in and out of the public coffer provide very
little objective information for making all-important service decisions fundamental to the budget. Where the philosophy of performance or program budgeting

prevails, emphasis is placed on analysis of the underlying factors, such as service standards, which will determine the flow of dollars. In planning a program to improve budgetary techniques, initial emphasis must be given to: (1) preparation of an inventory of activities or functions classified by programs, with identification of subactivities and operations; (2) analysis of each activity in terms of objectives, with description of facilities and methods used in its accomplishment; and (3) assembly of data which will be useful in evaluating each public service program.

Inventory of Activities

To be of maximum value, the activity inventory must be comprehensive. It should include systematic compilation of pertinent information relating to objectives, means, and methods of accomplishment for each public activity. The inventory process should also include a search for clues to the measurement of performance and volume of activities. Once the activity inventory has been completed, it can be kept up to date with relative ease as part of the annual budget process. The initial tasks of compiling the inventory can be accomplished most expeditiously if there is participation at all levels of the organization.

Evaluating Standards of Service

An inventory of public activities will provide a clear picture of present service standards and methods, but it provides no automatic formula for determining appropriate service standards for the future. Final decisions on such standards are properly the responsibility of elected officials. However, public management personnel must assume the responsibility of recommending changes in public programs when desirable. They also have a responsibility for furnishing full information concerning services currently performed, results achieved, probable results, and cost of additional services.

Comparisons of service levels with those of other localities and with "model" standards may be helpful. While such comparisons can never be taken as conclusive due to local variations, they frequently raise important questions and thereby bring to light instances where local service standards are either too high or too low. Although such standards are useful, they are more or less arbitrary goals designed to fit ideal situations.

Analysis of Methods of Operations

Information compiled in the preparation of the activity inventory provides a starting point for evaluating important factors which influence operating cost and program effectiveness. There are no simple answers to the problems of evaluation of methods of operation. All levels of management should give continuing attention to the improvement of work programs and work methods. The results, as a part of the budget process, can be a valuable means of focusing attention on the problem.

Activity Inventory in the Annual Budget Process

The inventory of activities and program analysis are basic to the development and presentation of a sound budget. When the initial survey has been completed, each distinct program should be identified and briefly defined in descriptive terms. A comprehensive code can then be prepared, classifying activities and programs by agencies and functions. In the case of major programs, it may be desirable to break down activities into subactivities or even functional operations. The code thus established will provide a basis for compilation of budget estimates with separate estimates prepared for each activity or subactivity, along with supporting data on program performance.

Refinements in estimating methods can only be accomplished over a longer period as progress is made in long-term research on methods of operation and as agency heads become skilled in such techniques of administrative analysis. Nonmeasurable activities will always remain. Work programs for nonmeasurable activities, therefore, must be developed and evaluated primarily through the descriptive type of analysis. Even for measurable activities, data on the volume of activity cannot be used as the only determining factor until sufficient research has been completed to validate the significance of the data and to establish standards for the cost estimates based on actual performance.

Estimates of Volume of Activities (M4)

One of the major factors determining cost is the volume of activity involved in providing a given public service at the standard of quality desired, using a particular organization and methods established for its performance. In program budgeting, therefore, a great deal of attention must be given to the development of record and reporting systems that will provide reliable data on the volume of activities.

A variety of methods has been developed for compiling such data and relating these measures to expenditure estimates. Each of these methods is equally valid, and each should be utilized where appropriate in order that the volume of activity can be analyzed properly. Further refinements are possible where cost-accounting installations have been made or where standards have been established through extensive research for converting volume standards to standard units of personnel and material. Some of the approaches currently utilized are described below.[6]

Cost-Accounting Basis

Where a system of cost accounting has been instituted, units of accomplishment, as well as unit costs, can be derived directly from the program records. Under such a system, therefore, the development of expenditure forecasts as a function of the volume of activity is quite easy. Such experience data provide a relatively sound foundation for projecting future costs for the direct cost portions of the cost-accounting distribution. Adjustments must be made for any change expected in prices of cost elements such as salaries and materials.

Man-Hour Basis

The man-hour approach to estimating requirements based on volume of activity differs from the cost-accounting approach only in that personnel requirements, not all cost factors, are computed. A major advantage of the man-hour approach is that an extensive accounting installation if not required; attention is focused only on the major cost element, which can be recorded much more cheaply than all cost elements.

The Ratio-of-Personnel Basis

Under this approach, the number of personnel required to perform a particular function is related to a definite organizational index. Most commonly, such ratios have been used to determine service and staff needs, e.g., one clerical support position for every x professional staff members. The same general principle may also be applied in certain line activities in governments that have well-established organizational configurations.

The ratio-of-personnel technique establishes a base of personnel needs as related to certain basic functions, e.g., number of men required to operate firefighting equipment in each fire company within the municipality. These figures are then modified to take account of extra personnel needs arising from vacations, sick leave, operational shifts, and so forth.

The Point-Grading System

In many situations, it may be necessary and desirable to proceed beyond the types of analysis described above. In the field of recreation, for example, standard units of operation may be more difficult to obtain than is the case with many other public services. In the case of recreation, there are at least four variables: size and number of facilities, population served, record of use, and hours open.[7] Consequently, a point-grading system, which is more complex than the ratio-personnel approach, is particularly useful where personnel needs must be related to more than one index or criterion.

The point-grading system requires a thorough operations analysis in order to establish the basis for personnel allocations. Essentially, the idea is to set up an ideal facility and determine its personnel requirements. Then each existing facility is "graded" in relation to this optimum. Personal allocations are then fixed for each facility according to its point score.

Estimating Expenditure Requirements by Fiscal Analysis (F2)

While emphasis in the budget process should be placed on evaluation of service standards, review of operational methods, and justifications of public programs, allocation decisions must ultimately be converted to monetary terms. For many programs — those unsuited to program analysis or those for which sufficient data are not yet compiled — fiscal analysis is a major budgetary device. This analysis includes the compilation of expenditure data for each activity, including at least one previous year, the current year, and estimates for the coming year broken down by object of expenditure.

Where a thorough accounting for costs is made in terms of activity along with careful review of program performance, most jurisdictions adopting such techniques have found that is is no longer necessary to break down expenditures by as many detailed object account codes as was common practice in the past. In some cases, it may be desirable to make detailed examination of actual expenditure documents, which will often produce budget information that cannot be obtained merely by reviewing books of account. Sometimes a study of expenditures on a "cross-section" basis (examining a particular object classification in all agencies, such as automobile maintenance, transportation allowance, printing, or office supplies) may reveal possibilities for savings.

Budget and Expenditure Estimate Forms

Standard forms, with explanatory instructions, should be provided for presentation of the financial estimates of each agency in an orderly fashion. The forms should be designed to supply necessary detail for analysis and review of the budget, for preparation of the final document, and for establishing budget control accounts after the budget is adopted.

The appropriate expenditure estimate forms and procedures for program budgeting will vary from jurisidction to jurisdiction. The following is a brief description of some of the more important expenditure estimate forms: [8]

Budget Summary: condenses all subsidiary budget requests into totals under appropriate program headings, with categorical breakdowns such as personal services, nonpersonal expenses, capital outlay, seasonal and regular employment, and so forth.

Agency Personnel Summary: summarizes personnel requests by both program and division, giving position titles, numbers of employees in each category, and funds requests.[a]

Object Account Summary: distributes program expenditures, budgetary appropriations, and requests into three broad classifications — personal services, nonpersonal expenses, and capital outlay.

Account Detail: substantiates in detail the nonpersonal expense and capital outlay requests summarized in the Object Account Summary.

Other budget forms: A capital outlay request may be required for items over a certain acquisition cost (usually $25 to $50), having a useful life of more than one year, and/or having a permanent character. A budget revenue estimate may be required of agencies collecting revenues.

Some of the forms listed above can be combined. Irrespective of the design and number of budget forms, they should cover revenue estimates, all personal service costs, expenditures for nonpersonal services, and capital outlays.

Long-Range Estimates of Expenditure Requirements (F4)

The preceding discussion of expenditure estimating procedures applies to all budgeting approaches, whether they are based on "line itemizations" or programmatic considerations. What sets program budgeting apart from more traditional approaches are the procedures which have been established for developing long-range estimates of expenditure requirements. These procedures are designed to provide a basis for: (1) the development and evaluation of program policy; (2) the establishment of specific program plans and targets to support recommended program policy; and (3) estimates of the manpower, facilities, and fiscal resources needed to carry out recommended program plans. The first of these objectives relates to the mission of strategic planning; the second focuses on the longer-range aspects of management planning (program structuring); and the third is concerned with the process of financial planning.

---

[a]As a subsidiary to the Agency Personnel Summary, it may be necessary to require a Personnel and Salary Detail Sheet. This form contains a listing of all monthly employees as shown on the master payroll and provides detailed information by quarters for full-time monthly employees and seasonal, monthly, hourly, and daily employees.

Figure 8-4 provides a summary of these component elements and their
relationships.

Basis for Program Policy

In the development and evaluation of program policy, four major elements
should be considered: external factors influencing public programs, total needs
and demands, relative roles of various development interests both public and
private, and interagency allocation of responsibilities. The information developed
in this long-range analysis provides the basis for preliminary statements of
overall program objectives.

The first element is designed to identify external forces that have a present
or potential impact on the direction, magnitude, scope and content, and success
of public programs, and to evaluate that impact. Such external forces should
include anticipated shifts and changes in the population, other significant
demographic characteristics, projected changes in economic activities, social
trends, scientific and technological changes, and other meaningful long-term
trends. Definition, projection, and evaluation of these trends will aid in the
identification of programs which should be changed or phased in or out. To the
extent possible, these projections should span a period of twenty to twenty-five
years.

A statement of total public needs and demands should be developed in
order to establish levels of program activity or services to be further structured
in the program planning phase. *Needs* are defined as quantifiable conditions
or problem areas which require action if the maximum welfare of the general
public is to be served. *Demands* are requests for action or services to meet needs,
articulated by organizations or individuals that reflect citizen wants.[b] All
public needs and demands should be considered, regardless of the responsibilities
of various levels of government or of private initiative required to meet the
needs. In developing such statements, the assumptions, standards, and criteria
used to quantify and project needs and demands should be described briefly.
As with the previous element, twenty- to twenty-five-year projections should be
made.

The third step focuses on an evaluation of the present and future roles of
various levels of government and private enterprise within designated functional
areas. The purpose is to encourage and strengthen intergovernmental relations,
identify existing and potential areas of complementary action, and evaluate

---

[b]The distinction between expressed and unexpressed demands made previously applies
here.

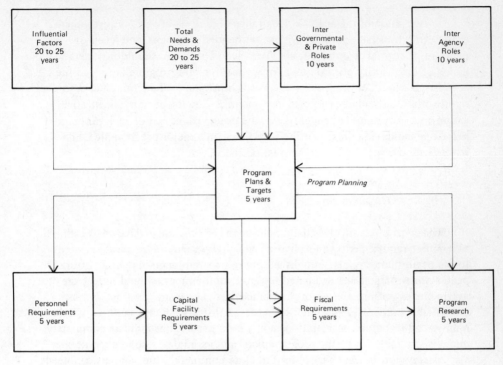

The Basis for Program Policy

Figure 8–4. Major Components in Long-Range Estimates of Expenditure Requirements.

areas of concern where additional emphasis should be expended by one or more levels of government. Projections should span a ten-year period.

The purpose of the final input to the evaluation of program policy is to identify agency activities in relation to one another and to those activities of other agencies with closely related areas of responsibility. Agency responsibilities should be delineated in terms of the total public needs and demands. Respective roles and the statutory or other coordinating mechanisms should be described where responsibilities are shared by two or more agencies. Areas of significant overlap that might be eliminated through formal coordination or realignment of responsibilities should be identified. Projections should span a period of ten years.

Establishment of Program Plans and Targets

In this phase of the analysis, long-range objectives of various governmental agencies are translated into specific recommended programs, and levels of program performance or output are identified. This phase should include a listing of the priority position of all programs in major program areas and the current, modified, or proposed status of each program. The requirements for new legislation should be outlined, and major policy issues or administrative problems, if any, should be identified. The potential impact of each program should be indicated in terms of the total needs in a major program area. Projections should span at least a five-year period.

Resource Requirements

The third phase involves the development of long-range (five-year) estimates of resource requirements. This phase of the analysis should be closely related to the performance targets established in the program planning phase. Both the program plan targets and estimated resource requirements should reflect the best judgments of optimum levels of program service, considering general limitations on available manpower and other resources. Arbitrary ceilings should not be imposed on resource considerations nor should projections indicate completely unrealistic targets. Thus, the program plans and estimated resource requirements *may or may not* indicate a capability to close completely the gap between needs and current levels of service. Where the identified gap between the capable level of service and a proven need should be closed at a faster rate but requires removal of limitations beyond an agency's control, projected target levels of performance should be qualified with statements to this effect.

Three of the four elements included in this phase — personnel requirements, capital facility requirements, and fiscal requirements — are quite similar to those estimates outlined previously in connection with annual expenditure requirements, the major difference being the time span of five years. The fourth element — program research — provides added information on agency activities designed to support program goals and program directions.

Special Accounts and Funds

The methods outlined to this point should be applied in some manner regardless of whether operations are financed from general funds or from special earmarked revenue sources. Two problems arise from the use of special revenue accounts: (1) there is a tendency to allow unnecessary expenditures to take place within special revenue funds; and (2) such funds are frequently exempted

from the regular budgetary process. Both of these problems should be avoided
if possible.

There should be only one general fund tax levy for all general operating
purposes. The idea behind special tax levies was that they would guarantee
a minimum level of support for a given activity and also provide a means of
controlling expenditures. But in practice such procedures have made it difficult
to make proper allocations of the monies at hand. In some years a special
tax levy may provide too much money and in others not enough. It has also
been found that expenditures can be controlled better through proper budgetary
measures than through separate levies.

The Long-Range Financial Plan (F1)

A long-range financial plan is a comprehensive program, covering a period of
perhaps twenty to twenty-five years. It comprises estimates of the jurisdiction's
expenditures for the operation and maintenance of public services and for
capital facilities, together with estimates of revenues from all forms of taxes,
borrowing, and other sources that will be needed to finance those expenditures.
Long-range financial planning must go hand in hand with the preparation of
a comprehensive plan. Only through consideration of the costs associated with
the execution of the comprehensive plan in relation to available resources
and to ordinary operating and maintenance costs of government can the plan
be properly "scaled." Without a financial plan, it is virtually impossible to
determine whether the comprehensive plan is too conservative — forgoing
desirable public improvements that well could be afforded —or too grandiose —
proposing improvements on a scale well beyond public resources.

Components of the Financial Plan

A truly comprehensive long-range financial plan must be based on the
following program components: (1) a program of operating and maintenance
expenditures for public services; (2) a capital improvements program based
on the comprehensive plan; and (3) a comprehensive revenue program. Once the
financial plan has been formulated, it is carried out with the aid of three other
administrative devices: (1) a priority list of proposed capital improvements;
(2) a capital budget; and (3) the annual operating budget.

In developing a financial plan, consideration must be given not only to
those activities and facilities that are controlled directly by local government,
but also those activities of all overlapping governmental jurisdictions or units
within the environs of the community. If the financial plan does not take
into account all of these activities, there is a very real danger that the sum total

of all programmed expenditures for the overlapping units will constitute an excessive drain on the financial resources of the area.

In practice, the formulation of a financial plan is carried out with consideration given to two separate categories of expenditure: (1) operating and maintenance expenditures; and (2) expenditures for capital improvements. In making this separation, however, care must be taken to ensure that appropriate attention is given to their interaction. Too often a major capital facility is planned and constructed without taking cognizance of the long-term commitments involved in the operation and maintenance of the facility.

The major physical facilities required for the rendering of public services comprise the capital plant of the jurisdiction. This may include streets, public parking facilities, parks, playgrounds, water, sewage and other utilities and distribution systems (delivery systems), street-lighting systems, public buildings — schools, libraries, police and fire stations — and the necessary major equipment for their operation. The initial construction or acquisition, together with improvements and additions to the facilities, is called "capital improvement." Funds expended for such facilities are usually referred to as "capital expenditures." Such facilities are properly designated as capital improvements regardless of the manner in which they are obtained or the methods used for their financing. For example, a park may be obtained by gift, purchase, or condemnation, and the development may be financed from current revenues, from the proceeds of bond issues, or by other methods.

The Capital Improvements Program (F6)

The capital improvements program (CIP) consists of a comprehensive list of capital improvements that are or will be needed by the jurisdiction within some specified time period, in order to carry on the program of public services that has been agreed upon. The CIP thus constitutes a bridge between the program of services, on the one hand, and the comprehensive plan, on the other. The usual practice is to derive the list of capital improvements from a preliminary comprehensive plan, to study this list in relation to the public services program and financial plan, and then to employ the revised list in modifying the comprehensive plan.

As a part of the capital improvements program, the projects to be undertaken are usually arranged in the order of proposed priority of execution, with estimates of the probable cost of each improvement, the method of financing, and other pertinent information. The development of a priority list of capital improvements can be one of the most critical and difficult phases of the CIP process, since various quantitative and qualitative considerations must be brought into play.

The Capital Budget

Programs that extend over a period of twenty years or more are obviously subject to many uncertainties. It is neither necessary nor possible to be as specific and exacting in programming over a long period as in determining programs for the more immediate future. The more immediate portions of the capital improvements program, therefore, are generally developed in greater detail than the entire program, and are then incorporated into a six-year *capital budget* that is extended annually by adding to it the program components for another year.[c] There is no magic in the number six, but communities have found that this provides a convenient period for the detailed programming of public improvements. In general, six years are required to develop a major facility from initial conception to actual construction. The authorization of capital improvements, as well as of operating and maintenance expenditures, is accomplished by adoption of an annual budget and the enactment of appropriation ordinances. The annual budget, therefore, is a one-year slice of the long-range program.

Estimating Budget Revenues

Revenue estimates should receive the same careful consideration as the expenditure and program performance side of the budget. Estimated receipts from present rates of taxes and miscellaneous charges must be calculated after a thorough analysis of collection trends and conditions affecting the yield from each source. The rates of all service charges must be compared with changes anticipated in the cost of rendering services, and consideration must be given to possible adjustments in rate schedules. If revenues will be inadequate to finance the expenditure program proposed, consideration must be given to: (1) further reductions in expenditures; (2) changes in existing rates of taxes and charges; and (3) adoption of new types of revenue sources.

Each source of revenue may require a different formula in order to forecast a reliable estimate to be included in the budget. Some revenues may produce practically the same amounts from year to year; other revenues fluctuate violently and cannot be relied on to yield the same levels from one year to another. However, for each revenue source, there will be a rate of charge and an item subject to levy of tax, license, or charge. The yield must be estimated by determining *how frequently the item subject to tax will occur.*

---

[c]In some quarters, the six-year document is called a capital improvement program, with the annual or biennial document referred to as the capital budget. Either convention implies the same basic principles.

summaries carefully, and through the use of charts and tables to explain
service programs. In many jurisdictions where the program budget has been
accepted by decision-makers and citizens, budget documents have been revised
completely to make them primarily explanations of service programs, with
detailed object-of-expenditure data largely eliminated or greatly simplified.

The Budget Document

The budget document is normally presented in at least two major parts. The
first part contains the budget message and summaries of revenue and expense
information on all funds which have a direct bearing on "cost." Part II, which
contains the detailed supporting data, may be divided into several sections. The
first section contains program objectives, volume-of-activity data, and expenditure requirements for each agency. The second section may contain details
on the long-term capital improvement program for the current budget period.
The third section may contain information concerning special funds not directly
involving "cost" to the taxpayer, such as trust funds and revolving funds.[e]
Some jurisdictions add a Part III which includes the drafts of ordinances to be
passed by the legislative body to adopt the budget program, such as the appropriation ordinance, tax levy ordinance, and the borrowing ordinance (if bond
issues are proposed).

The Budget Message

The chief executive's budget message is the primary vehicle for conveying
a clear understanding of the problems to be faced in implementing the budget
program. The message should outline the fiscal policy proposed and the basic
premises underlying the estimates. Note should be made of any major changes
recommended in public services; important changes in program objectives,
costs, revenues, and financial trends should be explained. To add emphasis, a few
carefully selected charts and graphs may be interspersed throughout the written
text. Brief comments may be made in the message concerning some important
items of increase or decrease in agency budgets. The budget message, however,
must be concise and maintain reader interest. The purely monetary side of
the financial plan should be set forth in summary tables which follow the
message.

---

[e]Revolving funds for internal service enterprises should be supported by work-program
data. The capital required for each revolving fund should be analyzed in the budget-making
process. Any additional capital required or excesses that can be returned should be reflected
in the operating budget. Full detail concerning each revolving fund operation should be incorporated in the budget document.

The purpose of the budget message is to give life and meaning to the budget figures and to highlight salient features. It should include a summary of financial operations during the past year and the current year to date, an analysis of the financial situation at the present time, a description of the proposed financial and activities program, and an explanation of the principal budget items.

The budget message should summarize the financial and operating programs embodied in the proposed budget, pointing out items in which the principal changes occur and factors which prompt the increased or decreased requests. Reference should be made to the relationship between capital outlay items in the proposed budget and the long-term capital improvements program. If there is no long-term capital improvements program, and it is the policy of the jurisdiction to authorize improvements chiefly on the basis of competing pressures from interest groups, the chief executive is remiss in his duty if he does not point out the difficulties arising from such a policy. Stress should be given to the advantages which could be derived from the systematic programming of public improvements and long-term financial planning.

Summary Statements and Detailed Budget Estimates

A series of summary statements of revenue and expenditures should follow the written budget message. The exact form of these statements will vary depending on the legal funding structure of the jurisdiction. Among the more commonly used summary statements are the following:

General Budget Summary: preferably a one-page statement indicating the balance between proposed expenditures and resources; this statement may be divided into several sections, one for each fund.

Summary of Expenditures: provides a summary breakdown of expenditures by program, function, agency, and fund.

Summary of Property Tax Revenues: shows a tabulation for several years of important data concerning property taxes, including assessed valuation by class of property, tax levy, tax collections, distribution of receipts by funds, and details of tax rate.[f]

Summary of Miscellaneous Revenues: shows tabulations for several years of revenues collected and analyzed by source and by fund.

Bonded Indebtedness Statement: shows data concerning amount of bonds

---

[f]This summary statement, of course, applies only to local jurisdictions which derive the majority of their revenue from property taxes. For state governments, a similar statement would be prepared for such major revenue sources as the state income tax or sales tax.

outstanding, bonds authorized and unissued, condition of sinking funds, and analysis of legal debt margin.

Part II of the budget document, which follows the section containing the budget message and summaries, gives a detailed analysis of each agency's programs and expenditure requests. The amount of detail and form of presentation vary a good deal depending on the desires of the budget-makers and, to some extent, on legal requirements.

Publicity on the Budget

The first publicity should be given the budget when it is submitted for legislative review. After it has been transmitted to the legislative body (city council, county commission, or state legislature), sufficient copies of the budget document should be distributed to newspapers, libraries, and civic organizations. A limited number of copies should be available for citizens who request them and extra copies should be on file for public inspection. The budget message and summary sections are often printed in adequate quantity for wide distribution. These sections of the budget can be passed out to persons present at public meetings on the budget.

Legislative Action on the Budget

The first step in the legislative review of the budget is for the legislative body to consult with the chief executive and his staff for detailed explanations of the proposed programs and means of financing them. It is neither necessary nor desirable, however, for the legislative body to concern itself with minor details of the work and finances contained in the proposed budget except as they relate to major policies and programs.

Next, public hearings are held so that citizens may express their sentiments. These hearings should be widely publicized so as to ensure all citizens an adequate opportunity to present their views. Public hearings on budgets have generally proven dismal failures, if their purpose is to ascertain the attitudes of lay citizens on the proposals of the budget. Relatively few citizens attend these hearings unless a group is irate over some aspect of the budget that it thinks is detrimental to its interests. Too often, the only nonofficials attending budget hearings are representatives of taxpayers' organizations, vested-interest groups pushing their pet projects, and others with time on their hands. Officials should be prepared for surprises, however. Citizens may decide to attend the hearing, and public officials must be ready and able to answer any questions. At the local level, a public hearing is generally required by the charter, and a summary of the tentative budget may be published, together with a notice of the time and place of the hearing. Even if it is not required by law, a brief budget summary should be published for wide distribution — wider than the complete document receives.

Following the public hearings, the budget should again be discussed in executive session. Agreement on an overall budget program should be reached in these sessions. Every effort should be made to provide the legislative body with a full understanding of the budget in terms of the public programs which it represents. Legislators should receive more than a thick book, with page after page of tables, providing little or no explanation of the services or the intent of the administration. Under such circumstances, members of the legislative body may feel obliged to check details of expenditures, such as the amount for pencils, cost of paper, and so forth. Such nit-picking over details arises from the absence of any broad explanation of the public programs to be undertaken. As a result, important policy decisions involved in setting the level of public services may never be faced directly.

Adoption of Appropriation Measures

In some jurisdictions, budget appropriation and other measures must be adopted by ordinance; in others, by resolution. Sometimes the law requires an extremely detailed and inflexible appropriation measure. When the ordinance or resolution is written around a detailed budget in such a way as to make the detailed statements of the budget document a part of the ordinance, each item then becomes a control item and is unchangeable except by legislative action. This is always unfortunate. Since the appropriation measure is the basis for conducting operations during the year, considerable flexibility is desirable in order that the chief administrator may be free to employ that combination of labor, equipment, supplies, and materials which appears most suitable and economical in any given situation which develops during the year.

Appropriations should be in lump-sum form to each agency for current expenditures and capital outlay. Further details, of course, will appear in the budget document to support and explain the items in the appropriation ordinance or resolution. These detailed items need not, and should not, be written into the appropriation measure. The legislative body should be empowered to reduce appropriations during the year or to transfer unencumbered balances from one appropriation to another. Except for expenditures from the emergency appropriation and large contracts requiring specific legislative approval, all appropriations should become available for expenditure at any time at the discretion of the chief administrator without further action by the legislative body.

Budget Administration and Expenditure Controls

When the legislative review is completed and the appropriation and tax levy measures for the next fiscal year have been adopted, the budget, in effect, is returned to the chief executive for execution, the second half of the budget cycle. All the steps of formulating and reviewing the budget are of relatively little importance if the financial plan is not administered properly.

To enforce a budget properly, an effective system of budgetary controls must be established. Such a system should be built around two essential elements: *fiscal control* and *management control*. Effective fiscal control involves: (1) an allotment system for all expenditures from appropriations; (2) adequate appropriation and expenditure accounting; and (3) frequent and regular financial reports on receipts and expenditures of each fund. Management control involves: (1) cost and performance control procedures;[g] (2) performance reporting and review; and (3) continuous operations analysis and management research dealing with work methods and organization.

Regardless of the special assignments of budget duties, the chief executive, in large measure, must rely on agency heads and their subordinates to achieve the necessary economies in day-to-day operations and to conform to the overall budget program. In the final analysis, costs must be controlled at the point of origin. The devices of budget administration, such as the allotment system, the budgetary accounting procedures, and the many management control procedures, will be of limited value without the full understanding and active cooperation of operating supervisors. Indeed, excellent cost control procedures improperly administered can quickly degenerate into burdensome red tape instead of expediting action and improving the quality of administrative decisions.

Budget administration can work successfully only when it is based on teamwork between staff aides and agency executives. The primary objective of all staff agencies should be to strengthen management on the operating levels through the provision of technical assistance in analyzing procedures, methods of operation, and special cost problems.

Concluding Remarks

In the preceding discussion, an attempt has been made to integrate the concepts of program budgeting and established procedures of more traditional forms of budget-making. As such, the procedures set forth are not dependent on a highly developed program-analysis approach based on techniques of cost-benefit or cost-effectiveness analysis. At the same time, however, these more sophisticated techniques can be applied within the framework outlined, thereby making possible an orderly transition from more traditional approaches to budgeting to the more comprehensive and systematic approach of program budgeting.

---

[g]In larger jurisdictions, these control procedures may include top-management approval before agencies are permitted to fill personnel vacancies, to initiate certain expenditures, or to proceed with some types of activities.

9 A Framework for Strategic Planning

Public officials at all levels of government are frequently criticized for shortsighted decisions. Elected officials may be accused of looking forward only as far as the next election and of placing narrow, parochial interests above the general welfare. To some extent, such criticism may be justified; however, even the political novice recognizes that his stay in office will be short if he does not take some positive action in the public interest.

Short-range decisions often have important long-range implications; if overlooked or ignored, these longer-range aspects may have serious repercussions. Decisions of expediency frequently become institutionalized; emergency tax measures have a way of becoming permanent. Traditions in government are easy to form and difficult to break.

The primary objective of strategic planning is to broaden the base upon which to make public decisions having long-range implications. Strategic planners must attempt to identify long-range needs stemming from growth and development (or the lack of growth), explore the ramifications and implications of public programs designed to meet those needs, and formulate development plans which permit a maximization of positive aspects of growth while minimizing the negative aspects.

The Traditional Approach to Public Planning

It is common practice in public planning to formulate a plan for some specific target date twenty-five to forty years in the future. Under this approach, population is projected and future growth is assigned to a defined period of time, suggesting that by 1985 or in the year 2000 the population of a particular jurisdiction will be of such a magnitude (usually expressed as a range). Based on these projections, it is then suggested that public services and facilities will have to be enlarged accordingly, land consumption by new development will be of a given magnitude, employment opportunities will have to be provided in a given quantity, and so forth. As a rule, in these plans considerable attention is also devoted to the identification of more immediate problems of growth (or lack of it) and suggested solutions to those problems.

201

A Cumulative Process

Under such an approach, planning frequently becomes a cumulative process; that is, all the component parts are added up to determine what the whole will look like. Problem-solving often takes precedence over the establishment of effective long-range goals and objectives to guide future development. Planning proposals are frequently based on "anticipated population and economic conditions."

Under such circumstances, where proposals are made to provide solutions to the more immediate problems of growth, a short-range situation is created. It may be suggested that this approach does not deal realistically with the long-range problems of growth and development or necessarily provide an adequate basis for long-range policy decisions. Granted, the actual period of time — twenty to forty years — is relatively long, but the concept of planning for the ultimate assurance of adequate resources, such as land, water, open space, and so forth, a vibrant economy, and a more harmonious social system requires a more farsighted approach than can be achieved by such a cumulative process. By definition, the cumulative process is short-range planning over a long period of time. The results, benefits, and profits to be gained from such plans will not be assured in the long run and, in fact, may be lost in the crises of problem-solving.

Perhaps this discussion may appear overly critical of short-range planning. This is not the case, however, for as pointed out in the previous chapter, short-range planning is an important ingredient in the policy planning process. The real criticism is against short-range planning which is not based on a long-range plan or a long-range set of goals and objectives.

A plan is of limited value if it does not look far enough into the future to permit change to be rationally and logically anticipated. A more dynamic method of strategic planning is required to achieve the objectives of effective and rational long-range decision-making. Such an approach should involve the *systematic combining and extending of facts and possibilities* to point out policy alternatives for long-range development. This evaluation should be undertaken in such a manner that deliberations may be subjected to *constant correction and refinement* in establishing a desirable range within which public choice can and should be made.

Greater Coordination Between Theoretical and Practical Planning

Two basic factors are reflected in the failure of public planning to satisfy growing demands for increased comprehensiveness: (1) deficiencies in methodology and in the formulation of viable work programs; and (2) fragmentation of research and an emphasis on applied studies oriented toward "practical" planning. As a result, many theoretical studies and analyses are performed without a clear program for application, while actual planning studies often place too much emphasis on pragmatic concerns. Thus, improved analytical methods adopted by the planning profession have not resulted in immediate improvements in the conceptual basis of the public planning process.

The planning method advocated in the present work seeks a greater coordination between the two processes of theoretical and practical planning and in particular the transformation of research findings into plan formulations. The need for this emphasis arises from the observation that too often existing conditions, rather than a well-conceived formulation of goals, are accepted as the basis for future planning. Consequently, strategic planners should seek to delimit an ideal picture of a future jurisdiction through the development of testable hypotheses. The formulation of long-term planning goals, therefore, serves as an integrative element in the development of the strategic plan. The theoretical basis for strategic planning represents a summary and coordination of the goals and trends by which a given jurisdiction or area should develop. It thus serves as the basis for the transformation of those trends and goals into more definitive development plans. Much of the appeal of this approach derives from the conscious inclusion of these elements as safeguards against the tendency to develop future plans as mere extensions of the present or as extrapolations of the past.

A Systemic Model for Strategic Planning

The approach outlined in this chapter focuses on a goal-oriented, systemic model for strategic planning as a conscious departure from the more conventional processes of public planning which are largely cumulative and linear in nature. It is a composite model, embodying the theoretical formulations of the Swedish planner, Ingrid Jussil, the Swedish economist, Folke Kristensson, and Professor Leo Jakobson of the University of Wisconsin, as well as the author's own work in horizon planning and systemic planning.[1]

The implementation of this model depends on the orderly development of five interacting component elements:

(S1) Basic Research and Analysis
    a. Basic data collection and inventories
    b. Studies of the factors determining a planning horizon
    c. Identification of the planning horizon and levels of population to be served by the plan
(S2) Diagnosis of Trends and Needs
    a. Technical and applied studies
    b. Macro-level trends and related considerations
    c. Formulation of effectiveness measures

(S3) Statement of Goals and Objectives
    a. Delineation of significant structural changes
    b. Formulation of hypotheses concerning conceptual aspects of the planning area
    c. Definition of the desired state of the system
(S4) Formulation and Analysis of Alternatives
    a. Development of a multi-dimensional goals matrix
    b. Redefinition of the desired state of the system
(S5) Policy Alternatives and Recommendations
    a. Translation of hypothetical goals into policies
    b. Formulation of zone-specific policy sets
    c. Identification of basic quadrants of policy action.

The conceptual bases for the systemic model are schematically expressed in Figure 9-1. Fundamental to the model is the concept that theoretical constructs — derived from a concentration of data concerning the jurisdiction under study and the formulation of preliminary goals and objectives concerning the desired state of the system — must be completed as a pivotal step in the strategic planning process. These theoretical constructs, in turn, serve as a basis for policies and decisions. The process of plan formulation, then, consists of a fusion of the ideal with practical information that evolves through various inventory studies and technical analyses.

    The goal formulation process serves as a vehicle for avoiding the basic tendency to posit future plans on existing conditions. Furthermore, theoretical goals can play a vital role in the day-to-day process of political decision-making and in successive refinements of the strategic plan by providing a more clearly articulated focus around which these activities can operate. Applying this approach, the danger of sacrificing the basic merits of a strategic plan to technical or political complications can in great measure be circumvented. Through a goal-oriented model, *policies* — factual premises representing what *can* be done — are tested against *goals* — value premises representing what *should* be done. The outcome of this interface should be an incorporation of ideal and practical elements in the public policy formulation process.

Departures from the Conventional Linear Approach

    In the systemic model, a three-pronged, simultaneous program with scheduled points of contact is substituted for the conventional linear progression of more traditional forms of public planning. Recognition is given in the model to value inputs in the formulation of hypothetical goal sets, as well as in the establishment of alternative policy sets. An attempt is made to minimize the negative impact of these inputs. The test of hypothetical goals provides informa-

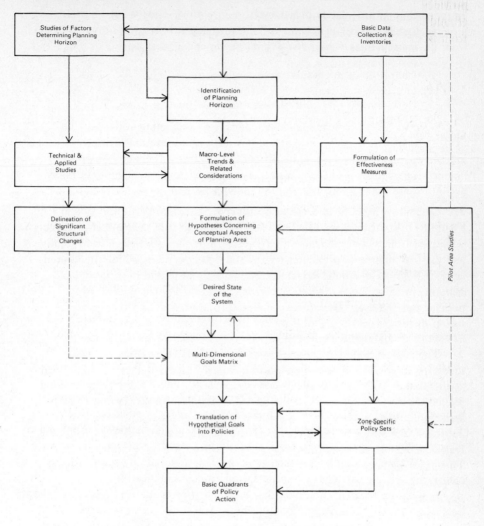

Figure 9-1. Schematic Diagram of the Strategic Planning Process.

tion necessary to reduce or diffuse errors in judgment and selectivity. Through
an a priori polarization of representative value positions, most viewpoints
can be accommodated in the proposed framework without impairing their
simplicity and degree of abstraction.

The systemic model provides a basis for testing hypothetical goals prior
to policy formulation. The model also incorporates recognition of nonscheduled
policy concerns arising in pilot studies — concerns which may not conform
to policies anticipated in the goal-formulation process. Thus, a structure is

provided that permits the development of policy sets formed against a background of goals, basic data inventories, and practical information drawn
from technical studies.

The Horizon Concept

Basic to the systemic model is the concept of a planning horizon — the
farthest point which can be anticipated based on interpretation of what is
presently known about development trends. Applying this concept, a series of
"plans" can be developed for a given level of population at some undetermined
point in time: the planning horizon. As time passes and the planning horizon
draws nearer, it becomes possible to see more and to anticipate a point farther in
the future. Just as with the natural horizon, as the specified level of population
is approached, the planning horizon continues to recede, making adjustments
in long-range goals and objectives both necessary and possible. Therefore,
the *horizon concept* provides a dynamic approach to strategic planning; the
horizon can be changed, revised, or dismissed as the body of knowledge on
which it is based is enlarged.

It is possible to establish both objective (measurable) and subjective
criteria for determining the planning horizon of any given area. For example,
Wesley Bellis has suggested that there is a measurable "tolerancy of congestion"
which can be expressed in terms of population densities.[2] When the population
of an urban area exceeds this density level, economic and social linkages tend
to break down because people and goods can no longer be moved efficiently.
According to Bellis, the tendency is for such areas to lose population through
out-migration until a more "tolerable density" once again is achieved. Applying
this criterion to a specific urban area, it would be possible to establish an upper
limit or "horizon" population which could be exceeded only by substantially
modifying existing patterns of transportation and communication.

It should be evident, however, that such specific criteria are products of the
level of technology at any given point in time. The "tolerancy of congestion"
in an area where the primary mode of transportation is by foot is quite different
from an area in which motorized vehicles provide the principal means of moving
people and goods. Thus, changes accrue gradually, so that there is no actual
"point of decision" at which living conditions, as we know them today, will have
to be abandoned in favor of some other form or pattern of human settlement.

As suggested, a planning horizon can also be established by more subjective
criteria (some of which can also be measured). For example, it may be deemed
desirable to provide a full range of recreational opportunities to the population of
a given area. Applying certain open-space standards (which are frequently
drawn on a subjective basis), it is possible to determine what portion of the total
land area of the jurisdiction would be required to accommodate the desirable
recreational activities of a given population. It would also be possible to determine, within the limits of the jurisdiction's total land area, the ultimate or

"horizon" population that could be accommodated under such recreational standards. Thus, if the population were permitted to exceed this level, adjustments in the overall recreational objectives of the jurisdiction would have to be made.

A plan formulated upon the horizon concept is not a master plan, comprehensive development plan, or general plan in the usual sense. Rather, it yields a series of policy statements to guide long-range future growth and development toward some desired state of the system. As such, strategic planning, based on the concept of a planning horizon, deviates from the traditional cumulative approach to the formulation of development plans. The horizon concept offers the basis for a *thesis* rather than a *synthesis*.

Levels of Population

One important deviation from the traditional cumulative approach to planning lies at the foundation of the horizon concept. As has been pointed out, master plans or comprehensive plans generally are tied to a "year-population" basis, i.e., populations are projected on the basis of current trends to some specific future point in time. The projected level of population is then translated into physical terms (housing requirements, employment opportunity needs, land use consumption, service and facility needs, etc.). Plans drawn on this basis are highly dependent on the accuracy and validity of their population projections. This, of course, is why it is common practice to provide a range of projected populations for the target year of the plan.

One of the most evident shortcomings of the earlier work in the field of public planning was that estimates of future populations were extremely conservative. As a result, the actual level of need exceeded the provisions of the "plan" well before the established target date.

The horizon concept avoids this problem and achieves flexibility by drawing up its proposals on the basis of assumed levels of population. While it is difficult to predict, with any degree of accuracy, the level of population that will be reached in certain prescribed time periods, it is reasonable to assume that the population will reach certain levels at *some* future point in time. In the traditional approach, a time period and target date are selected for planning purposes and the level of population serves as the variable. Under the horizon concept, the year in which some predetermined population is to be reached becomes the variable.

There are several distinct advantages to this approach. Most public facility and service needs are a function of numbers of people first, and of time second. In other words, a population of a given size and composition will require certain facilities and services, will consume a given land space for housing, and will require a given level of economic activity to provide an adequate supply of job opportunities, regardless of when in time this population level is reached. As the level of population is approached, the time dimension can continually

be refined without destroying the overall validity of the strategic plan. Interim
levels of population can also be established to provide incremental objectives
which, in turn, can be factored into the long-range plan as the time dimension is
refined. Since about six years of lead time are required to plan and construct
most capital facilities, it is necessary only to make more detailed projections of
population on a short-range basis rather than over a twenty-five-year period.
As these more refined and detailed projections are made, the planning and
construction of capital facilities can be accelerated or decelerated in the light of
current conditions and trends. It must be recognized, of course, that wide
fluctuations in the rate of construction of capital facilities is highly undesirable
from a capital improvements programming standpoint. Therefore, techniques
must be developed to ensure that the long-range projections of population
provide an adequate basis for these shorter-term projections.

Population Projection Techniques

The horizon concept permits the application of several population projection techniques which are not feasible under the more traditional cumulative
approach to development planning. The use of these techniques provides greater
detail as to the composition of future populations while at the same time
affording the flexibility generally sought in the cumulative approach through
the provision of a range of projections.

It is generally assumed (and so stated in making population projections on
a cumulative basis) that the direction and size of the net migration for a given
area in future decades will approximate the rate for some previous decade
or other period of time. Recent studies have shown, however, that this is at best
a tenuous assumption. For the most part, the direction and size of future net
migrations are a function of the level and vitality of economic activities and the
resultant rate of increase in employment opportunities, as well as the percentage
of unemployment in a given area, relative to rates and percentages in other
areas. Furthermore, assumptions of future net migration must be related
to detailed statistical analyses of impending changes in the age distribution of the
population, both of the United States and of the areas for which the assumptions are made.[a] The age distribution of the population, both in the areas which
the migrants leave and in those to which they move, is of considerable importance
not only in the projections of net migration, but also in projections of natural
increases.

In recent years, techniques have been developed to provide the necessary

---

[a]For example, the age distribution of migrants differs significantly from that of non-
movers. As would be expected, young men and women in the age groups twenty to twenty-
nine have relatively higher migration rates than any other age group. Since these age cohorts
span the early years of the family formation stage of the life cycle, it might be expected that
the movements of these age groups would have an important bearing on the rates of natural
increase in a given area.

inputs to produce more accurate assumptions as to net migration rates for
any given jurisdiction.[3] These refinements in the earlier methods of population
projections, however, add other variables which further complicate projections
made on the basis of a year-population target date, since it becomes necessary
to vary the range of projections on three dimensions (fertility rate, death rate,
and migration rate). Thus for any future point in time, the use of only a high and
low assumption for each dimension would produce eight possible projections;
using a three-level rate assumption, twenty-seven projections could be developed,
and so forth.

Since the horizon concept is not tied to a specific point in time, this
problem can be circumvented. Rather than generating a number of projections
for a specific target date, the application of these population projection techniques under the horizon concept produces estimates as to the point in time
when a specific level of population will be reached. Thus, based on the assumptions of a relatively high birth rate and a low death rate, coupled with a
vigorous economy which will attract a high level of in-migration, the "horizon"
population for a given area may be reached in 1990. On the other hand, a
relatively low birth rate and a high death rate plus a low rate of in-migration
(or possibly out-migration) might indicate that the same "horizon" population
would not be reached until the year 2025. Further, it is possible, through
the use of a relatively simple computer program, to factor in all of these various
possible assumptions and to produce time estimates for any given level of
population under any combination of circumstances.[b] The population distributions under these differing assumptions, of course, will show considerable
variation.

Thus the horizon concept and its corollary, levels of population, provide
important tools for the strategic planning process. Using these techniques,
some of the implications of initial policy objectives can be tested and necessary
modifications made.[c] Further, with improved data gathering and analysis,

---

[b]The author, in conjunction with Anton F. Gross and the staff of the Rutgers Center
for Data Processing, has participated in the development and testing of such a computer program. The program is designed to accept a wide variety of assumptions as to survival rates,
birth rates or fertility rates, migration rates, and so forth. These assumptions serve as input
"parameters" in the program. Data cards are then fed in, giving the current age-sex cohorts
of the population under study. The computer is instructed to act on these data according to
the parameters established by the rate assumptions and to continue to do so until a given
level of population is reached. The printout from the computer provides the age and sex
breakdowns of the population for five-year intervals plus the number of "loops" (years) required to reach this configuration and the total population. By varying the parameters, any
number of combinations of assumptions can be run through this program and analyzed.

[c]For example, a "desired" level of population may be established for a given jurisdiction. The approach outlined above could then be applied to test the feasibility of attaining
this "desired" level of population. Through such an analysis, it may be determined that the
vitality of the economy is insufficient to achieve the desired level in an appropriate time
period, with the result that many problems unanticipated at the outset would be a byproduct of this level of growth and the resulting configuration. The policy implications in
terms of capital facility needs and public service programs required could also be explored
through this approach.

it would be possible to assess not only long-range policy objectives and goals but the implications of short-range policy decisions as well.

The Factors Determining the Horizon

The planning horizon of any area (i.e., the farthest point in the future that can be perceived today) is determined by a number of factors relating to the long-range availability of basic resources vital to desirable living conditions. These major determining resources include: *land*, for urban uses, for recreation, for agriculture, etc.; *natural resources*, particularly water; *economic resources*, such as employment opportunities, productivity, markets, etc.; and *public facilities and services*.

The way in which land resources are employed is a critical factor in the future growth and development of any area. While the supply of land is fixed in its spatial dimensions, land productivity depends not only on its area, but also on the intelligence, skill, technology, and balance of uses which are applied to the fixed land space. The forces of change necessitate continuous adjustments in the manner in which our land resources are utilized.

While it must be acknowledged that the concept of an ideal "balance of uses," as it relates to land resources, must be flexible and continuously adjusted to meet changing conditions, certain basic statements can be made as to what constitutes a desirable distribution of available land resources. The amount of land to be reserved to meet foreseeable demands for residential, industrial, and commercial development, for leisure-time activities, to accommodate transportation and other public facilities needs, and so on, all serve as important inputs in the determination of the development "horizon" of any jurisdiction. Such assumptions may be related to the concept of overall "holding capacity." They must include much more than this, however, in that these assumptions as to future allocation and distribution of activities must take cognizance of the concept of a "desirable" balance. To determine what is "desirable" for a particular jurisdiction, it is necessary to formulate a series of meaningful goals and to test these goals in the context of a specific population. This is perhaps the most critical phase in the public planning process. Unfortunately, it also is the least sophisticated in its development and application. Too often, goals are a reflection of either limited aspirations or of a value system held by the goal-makers but not necessarily shared by the polity.

Procedures for the Development of Goal Sets

A survey of the planning literature demonstrates that the methodologies most often employed in the process of goal formulation build upon an *inductive approach*. These methods are usually based on a survey of public attitudes, opinions, and objectives. In application, these techniques seem to lead to such self-evident objectives as the desire for decent housing, beauty in the environment, the elimination of pollution, economic opportunities, and so forth.

In the systemic model for strategic planning, a *deductive approach* replaces more typical inductive techniques. Through the use of a deductive approach, the planner's task becomes one of forming tentative goal sets and effectiveness measures and testing them in the context of a specific population, thus allowing new factors to emerge. In this manner, the goal formulation process becomes an educational device as well as a political tool. It increases the awareness of the population with respect to the changes that may be taking place in society, but also allows the population to react to these changes in accordance with their own values, norms, and expectations. The set of goals which eventually emerges through this process of testing and feedback should be representative in general of the attitudes of the specific community and, in particular, of its level of tolerance with respect to change in values, norms, customs, and the modernization of institutions.

The process of goal formulation must be addressed to the changing patterns in society, rather than acting merely as an extension or reflection of past or present trends. The model for strategic planning proposed here requires the development of hypothetical goal sets based on trends in society at large. The formulations are followed by the application of tests to determine the acceptability or unacceptability of these goals by the specific population.

Explicit Statements of "Conflict Positions"

In this context, *goals* may be defined as *codifications of desirable patterns of performance*, as exhibited by individuals and/or institutions or by physical, social, economic, and cultural variables. This definition perceives goal sets as describing the *desired state of the system*; it implies that the planning and decision-making processes must be capable of *manipulating and controlling systems variables in order to achieve this desired state*. This definition also makes clear that goal sets are not mutually exclusive; a single set of variables may be common to a number of goals. This complicates the strategic planning and decision-making processes, since primary variables of a low-priority goal may be secondary variables of a high-priority goal. Under such circumstances, it might be rational to maximize the low-priority goal if shifts in the variables would advance the achievement of high-priority goals.

In the systemic model, explicit recognition is given to the fact that value inputs are likely to occur at critical points in the strategic planning process, namely, in connection with the formulation of goals. Specific safeguards are required to minimize the influence of personal biases (values) which may be projected into the initial goal statements. This tendency can never be completely eliminated. Therefore, public goals must be formulated within a concise conceptual framework, incorporating a set of clearly identified "conflict positions," statements of existing or potential areas of value conflict. If such a framework is adopted, the influence of personal viewpoints held by members of the goal formulation team can be held to a minimum. As a consequence, the overall model should provide a better approximation of reality.

The Use of Effectiveness Measures

In order to measure goal achievement, effectiveness measures must be formulated and applied. Effectiveness measures involve a scoring technique for determining *the state of a given system at a given point in time*. They are indicators which measure direct and indirect impacts of specific resources in the pursuit of certain goals.[d]

Under the "effectiveness" approach, goals are defined by: (1) establishing current levels and types of performance in discrete categories; (2) estimating the current impacts of resources upon this performance; and (3) then defining desired levels and types of performance (i.e., long-range goals). The development of positive statements of performance provides a base from which change may be defined and evaluated. Normative statements of performance — hypothetical goals — can then be defined as deviations or changes from the current state. This approach is based on the concept of marginal change from the current state of the system.

It is important to stress the fundamental assumptions which underlie this further modification to comprehensive planning:

1. Hypothetical goal sets can be viewed as normative statements of performance
2. Performance can be defined in output-oriented terminology based on a vocabulary of understandable program and policy variables
3. Policy and program variables identify administrative and legislative policy and those interests — individuals and groups within the study area — which make up the patterns of performance to be affected

Policy and program variables must describe the relationships between all components of the system as they represent the patterns of performance under study and as they are to be affected by the allocation of resources. Analysis

---

[d]Careful selection and use of effectiveness measures can go a long way in overcoming some of the difficulties and ambiguities of local decision-making. This does not imply that the more traditional concept of goals is to be discarded, but only that there are a number of advantages to analyzing the effects that resources have upon system variables before commitments are made to specific goals.

of the relationships between program and policy variables and the various categories of performance permits the statement of normative performance and the subsequent development of output-oriented programs.

An important assumption in the development of normative statements of performance is that they can be derived, or inferred from current conditions (but are not limited by those conditions). This means that current operations and their effects must be continuously under surveillance, i.e., the basic data-collection element of the systemic model cannot be a "one-shot" survey. This continuous evaluation is probably the most effective means available for initiating a goal-oriented planning and decision-making system in an existing organizational structure.

The Structure of the Planning Area

In the process of formulating hypothetical goals, the need for comprehensiveness becomes a matter of primary concern. This need emphasizes the importance of taking into account the possible goals held by all manner of groups and individuals and of dealing with all aspects of the planning area. A comprehensive overview of the planning area must include: (1) future possible structural changes; (2) the variety of needs and demands evident in the polity; and (3) the effects of demands for spatial areas of various sizes and densities from the point of view of people and establishments. A differentiation is made in the systemic model between the *goals of the people* — those concerning welfare — and the *goals of institutions and establishments* — those goals aimed at efficiency. Having made this distinction, the presumptions or conditions necessary for both elements to achieve their goals then must be described. In the complete model, both the demands affecting regional structure and the influence of structure on the demands are described.

The description of significant structural changes over time is both a prognosis and a historical evaluation. Changes seem to be initiated directly by the underlying forces of development and these changes, in turn, influence people's demands for changes in the regional structure.[e] To judge future development, a complete data and information set is not sufficient, since changes that may be expected are likely to be so revolutionary that information on past development trends will often be of limited value.

---

[e]For example, in the past, people sought locations on the basis of proximity to place of work. However, changes in regional structure related to transportation and communication conditions have affected people's demands to the extent that they now are (and will be) more interested in freedom of choice among various components (place of work, social environment, desired amenities, etc.) and would rather take advantage of a larger assortment of employment opportunities that a larger and more densely populated region presents than the possibilities for a reduced amount of travel.

The systemic model explicity recognizes the necessity of taking into account new factors emerging from changing patterns of society, so that future goals and demands are not interpreted as mere extensions of the present. The crucial task is to predict future desires and needs of people and establishments and the possibility of satisfying those desires within the limitations imposed by technical, economic, and social developments and public policies in general.

The systemic model also focuses on the delineation of certain neutral factors which may have an impact on the equilibrium of demands and structural changes.[f] These factors can exercise influence on the size and structure of a jurisdiction or region in addition to and parallel with influences produced by the demands of people and establishments. These "neutral factors" can be regarded as restrictions on or limitations to the manner in which the general demand-influence structure of a region is developed. Inclusion of these factors results in deviations in regional structure from that which would have evolved given the sole influence of demands.

A Conflict Model of Goal Sets

A particularly valuable aspect of this approach is the direct attention given to the interaction and potential conflicts among goals, as well as the effects that fulfillment of one goal has on the possibility of fulfilling others. In the systemic model, an attempt is made to direct attention to strong interdependent relationships. People, establishments, and governments, by their actions, affect each other's choices. From an overall point of view, it is important that these relationships are taken into consideration, especially in the case of decisions with long-range effects.

The most obvious source of conflict arises from the fact that basic needs of people and those of establishments and institutions are often in opposition. People are concerned primarily with *welfare*, while establishments and institutions focus on *efficiency*. In addition, people constitute a resource, demanding goods and services, while establishments produce goods and services but demand resources. Identification of conflict situations in posing goals has special merit in that it points up weak spots at the outset and, therefore, makes possible the development of more realistic public policies.

A Multidimensional Goals Matrix

The basis for the identification of conflict situations is a multidimensional goals matrix through which basic conflict areas are given more specific recogni-

---

[f]Examples of such neutral factors are symbols, such as "small-town atmosphere," or ethnic preferences that are held in such high value by certain minority groups that their lack cannot be compensated by a more generous share of other components.

tion. The previous discussion provides the basis for the initial conflict division, i.e., the separation of individual goals from those expressive of institutional and establishment interests, which require collective action for their implementation.

A second level of possible goal conflict arises from geographic considerations. It must be recognized that goals for any jurisdiction cannot be formulated in isolation, focusing on the particular limited issues of a geographically constricted area. Therefore, for any planning area, a multilevel geographic division is required. At the local level, attention must be given to regional and state goals and policies; at the regional level, state and subregional goals must be factored into the analysis. National goals, as well as regional and local goals, must be considered in the formulation of a strategic plan at the state level.

Geographic levels of interest also suggest that the goal-formulation process should take account of the *nature* of the goals to be formulated for each of these levels. At the state level, for example, goals are likely to be developed in terms of long-range implications and in the context of broad national-regional trends. Statewide goals, therefore, find expression in broad, general terms. Their purpose would be to provide a basic background and understanding of the issues involved. Although no single vehicle for implementation currently exists at the regional level, there are various politically sensitive governmental mechanisms capable of goal implementation. However, the multitude and scope of governmental concerns suggest that regional goals should be framed within the context of other governmental programs. Therefore, the nature of regional goals remains fairly general, although their time perspective may be restricted to levels that can be related to the political process. They should be expressed in terms that allow for more specific policy and program formulation, two major components of goal implementation at the regional level. Finally, at the subregional or local level, concerns may be more clearly focused. High priority should be given by public officials and private interests to clearly articulated concerns. The more tangible qualities at this level with regard to physical properties and to social, economic, and political issues require that goals be stated in specific terms. Such goals should also be of such a nature that they promise results within relatively short periods of time. In other words, goals must be expressed at this level in terms of more pragmatic concerns and must be oriented towards action programs and projects which will permit implementation within the more immediate future.

A third level of possible conflict emerges with regard to development issues and the various viewpoints that can be brought to bear on their resolution. Thus, a logical division of goals can be established to express social, environmental, economic, and political-administrative emphases. By their very nature, these emphases introduce various manifestations of both value conflict and congruence. Social and environmental goals generally seem in accord in their concern with quality, welfare, and "the good life." By contrast, the economic and political-administrative concerns gravitate toward the more pragmatic issues of efficiency, growth, and production cost and returns. Thus, in the goal matrix, a division line between social-environmental goals and political-economic goals provides a second major conflict threshold of the magnitude represented by the conflict between institutional and individual goals.

The Specificity of Goal Sets

The changing nature of goals at the various geographic levels introduces still another conflict dimension, resulting from the specificity levels of the various goal sets. It is reasonable to assume that goals expressed in broad, general terms are within easy reach of consensus. However, when goals are stated in much more precise and action-oriented terms, subsets of opposing interests are likely to emerge within the general framework of the goals matrix. On the side of individual goals, for example, a conflict may be apparent at the subregional level between individuals who own property and those who see property only through the eyes of the user.[g] On the institutional side, a similar polarization can be assumed to exist between economic-business interests on the one hand and political-governmental interests on the other. This conflict may not be limited to the subregional or local level, but may begin to surface in discussions of regional goals. At the state level, in part because of the more general nature of the expressed goals and in part because of the nature of the operational structure of state government, it may be assumed that the traditional dichotomy between business and government will be minimal. In many instances, particularly at the national level, new institutional coalitions have emerged or are in the process of formation.[h] At the local level, however, it must be assumed that the conflict situation still exists and that a harmonious partnership of business and government will not be established for some time.

The design of the goals matrix (Figure 9–2) represents a hypothetical situation. In reality, the suggested framework is not so clear cut, nor can

---

[g]A classic example of this type of conflict situation can be found in the use of recreational lands. Owners of shoreline property around a lake, for example, are often in conflict with individuals seeking access to the water-oriented recreational facilities. A similar situation arises in the conflict between landowners adjacent to public recreational facilities who may wish to develop commercial interests to take advantage of their location and conservationists who seek out-of-door experiences "unspoiled" by these commercial "intrusions."

[h]In a continuing study conducted on behalf of the General Electric Company concerning the social, political, and economic trends of the next decade [*Our Future Business Environment: Developing Trends and Changing Institutions* (April, 1968)], the growing interdependence of institutions is cited as one of the eight most significant trends determining social change in the United States over the next decade. The study forecasts ". . . a gradual blurring of the traditional division between public and private sectors . . . with government intervening in the private sector, but also with private business entering fields traditionally associated with governmental activity." The impact of this trend, however, is expected to be most forceful in terms of broad societal problems or in terms of problems which formerly were "local" but are assuming regional and national importance, such as pollution and urban renewal.

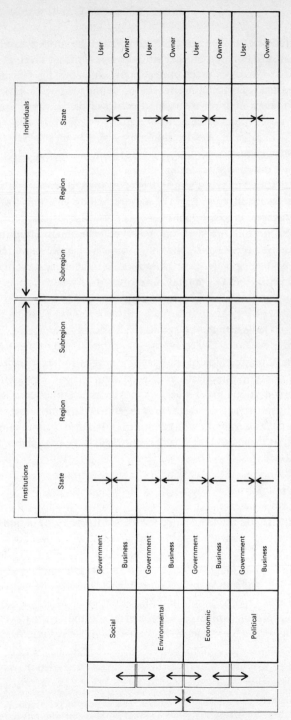

Figure 9-2. A Schematic Representation of the Multi-Dimensional Goals Matrix.

217

individual or aggregate goals be neatly compartmentalized into the cells of the matrix. The attempt to polarize conflict situations is simply a methodological device, designed to bring out a range of responses which can be ordered and positioned on continua. This concept provides a vehicle that will allow for systematic development of alternative goal sets, however. Such goal sets will not only describe areas of general agreement, but also areas of conflict and latent opposition. As a consequence, the decision-maker should be in a better position to make choices from among alternatives when the degrees of conflict and coalescence in each instance are more apparent.

Finally, the test of the hypothetical goals formulated within the framework of the matrix can reveal different levels of understanding in regard to the goals themselves, as well as to the goal formulation process. Internal respondent conflict, therefore, must be expected and analyzed. The general hypothesis underlying the goals matrix suggests that information regarding internal individual conflict among the respondents will be valuable in identifying levels of comprehension with respect to complex developmental issues.

Translation of Goals into Public Policies

To this point, the discussion of the systemic model for strategic planning has been focused primarily on questions of goal formulation. To be effective (to achieve implementation), goals must be translated into public policies. For purposes of this discussion, *policies* may be defined as *statements pronounced by authorities having the power of implementation*, i.e., the power to identify and commit means whereby agreed-upon goals can be achieved.

Five Categories of Policy

Policy statements are intended to cover the entire range of actions required from the actual establishment of a goal to the point at which the goal is attained. The formulation of policy can be considered to embrace various points on a *continuum of means*, ranging from long-range, general, and educational objectives to more immediate, specific, and action-oriented programs. The number of policy steps along this continuum, of course, will vary from task to task. In his analysis of policy planning, Beal suggests three distinct categories of policy, focusing on the basic questions of *what is to be accomplished* (objectives), *where is it to be accomplished* (locus), and *how is it to be accomplished* (means).[4] In addition to these three categories, it also may be suggested that policy must address questions of *priority* and *standards of accomplishment, evaluation and control*.

These five categories of policy span a range of statements, from norms and

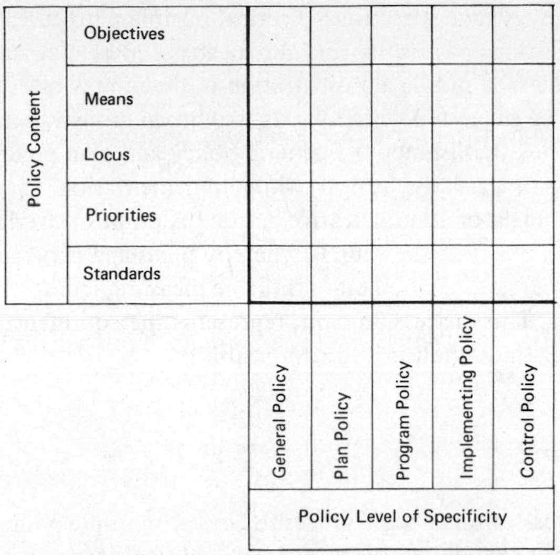

Policy Content		General Policy	Plan Policy	Program Policy	Implementing Policy	Control Policy
	Objectives					
	Means					
	Locus					
	Priorities					
	Standards					

Policy Level of Specificity

Figure 9–3. X & Y Coordinates of a Multiple Policy Matrix.

values on the one hand to guidelines on the other. Taken as a set, however, they do not provide a complete categorization of policy concerns. An important element not included is the degree of generality or specificity of action required to implement each policy. An analysis of various kinds of public policy statements would suggest that this latter consideration can best be described in terms of the types of action involved in policy implementation. Such action may fall within the realm of general policies at one end of the spectrum and control policies at the other. Between these extremes might be arrayed plan policies, program policies, and implementation policies. Taken together, the five categories of policy and the five divisions on the generality-specificity continuum provide the X and Y coordinates on a multiple policy matrix, as shown in Figure 9–3.

Modes of Planning and Levels of Policy Action

If the analysis is pursued further with respect to the issues to which various policy sets are addressed and the modes of planning under which the various levels of action are developed, three broad groupings emerge. Policy content may be seen to involve strategic, tactical, or operation planning inputs. Objectives and priorities generally require strategic planning, while means and standards express the inputs of operations planning. Locus – the place where implementation is accomplished, be it a physical locale or an administrative unit – provides a tactical bridge between strategy and operations. Tactical planning, however, also requires attention to questions of priority and the means of implementation.

Drawing on the basic tenets of public administration outlined previously, yet another continuum may be suggested which yields two broad groupings in the levels of policy action. The establishment of general policy and plan policy are primarily the prerogatives of legislative action, while implementation and control fall within the domain of administrative action.[i] A point of overlap occurs at the level of program policy — the vehicle whereby plans and programs are translated into action. Program policy emerges, in large measure, from the process of budget-making. This process, in turn, represents the confluence of both administrative and legislative action and responsibility.

The Multiple Policy Matrix

Bringing all of the various continua together results in the multiple policy matrix shown in Figure 9-4. In examining this matrix, several significant observations may be made. First, legislative policy is primarily strategic; thus, the upper left quadrant is termed Basic Policy. Second, legislative action is required to establish operational means and standards within the framework of general and planning policy; policy statements in the lower left quadrant therefore deal with Legislative Policy. Third, the objectives and priorities of implementation and control are part of the strategy of administrative action; thus, the upper right quadrant represents statements falling within the realm of Administrative Policy. Finally, the lower right quadrant deals with administrative and tactical concerns — the means and standards of implementation and control. Since these concerns, in most instances, are technical in nature, the label Technical Policy seems appropriate to policy statements within this quadrant.

The four quadrants are demarcated by the cross-shaped area formed by legislative and administrative trade-offs in the vertical plane and by the horizontal plane, which denotes the overlap between strategical, tactical, and operational considerations. This area corresponds to what Beal calls "the intermediate level of policy planning."[5] This level, in Beal's view, is the most critical area of policy formulation because ". . . at the middle levels conflict between policies is, practically speaking, inevitable."

Within the conceptual framework for strategic planning outlined in this presentation, specific provisions can be made for these potential policy conflicts.

---

[i]Used in this context, the term "legislative" is not meant to be limited to actions of the legislative branch of government, but embraces legislative and executive action which is broadly identified with *policy-making* in the dichotomy of public administration theory. Since policy is formulated at several levels in the conceptual framework outlined above, the result is a continuum rather than a dichotomy.

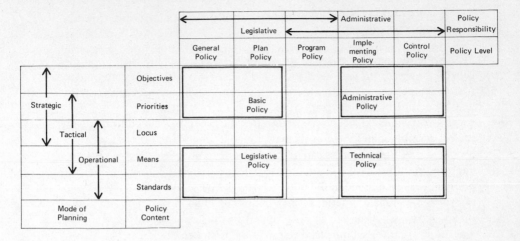

Figure 9-4. Multiple Policy Matrix.

The methods of analysis embodied in the goal matrix and the processes of systematization contained in the policy matrix should permit the formulation of internally consistent intermediate-level policy sets. Each policy set should represent an alternative course of action. In this approach, the conflicts can become the determining measures for the alternatives, allowing for the emergence of true alternative plans, rather than mere variations on the same basic theme.

The Political Value Input

The process of selecting among alternative plans provides a third type of value input of a political nature in addition to the two other types previously identified: (1) the values of the planner, which enter into the processes of formulating hypothetical goals and alternative policy sets; and (2) the values of the public, which emerge during the process of testing the preliminary goals. The political value input reflects the standards and objectives inherent in the legislative and administrative structure responsible for policy implementation. In combination with the impact of the values of the plan-makers and the public, this third type of value input becomes a structural link in the total planning process. The recognition of these three basic types of value input and their inclusion in the systemic model serve as a means of balancing the inevitable impact of values in the planning process and mitigating their effects, so that the values of no one individual or group will receive undue emphasis.

Reentering the Critical Dimensions of Comprehensiveness

While the matrices outlined above provide a basis for the translation of general policies from goal statements, two critical dimensions of comprehensiveness have not been recognized explicitly: (1) geographic comprehensiveness; and (2) comprehensive coverage of societal concerns. Regarding the latter — social, environmental, economic, and political concerns — the multiple policy matrix accommodates these concerns through a series of iterations. Each goal in any of the categories can be translated into policy through a separate application of the matrix. Thus, each social, environmental, economic, and political goal established in the initial matrix is "passed through" the second matrix and evaluated in terms of the various continua in the translation into policy and action. Conflicts in the goal matrix thus establish different policy sets and the alternatives should stand out with a fair degree of clarity.

Geographic Comprehensiveness

Geographic comprehensiveness, however, offers a different problem. When applied to a specific jurisdictional level, the cells in the multiple policy matrix for other than the unit of government under study become unidimensional. As an example, take the situation where the systemic model is applied at the local level. It should be obvious that only general policy, stating broad objectives, is feasible at the state level, since such policy might be applied to any specific locality within the state. At the regional level, because of the lack of legislative or administrative mechanisms for policy implementation, regional policy would have to be promulgated at the subregional level by appropriate units of government. Such policy would become an expression of extraterritorial concerns, void of standard means of implementation, but useful for its educational impact or even possibly attainable through cooperative action among concerned units of government. In contrast, legislative as well as administrative machinery exists for policy implementation at the local level. A full range of policies, therefore, is possible. If the focus of policy formulation is shifted to the state level, mechanisms exist for the implementation of state policy having uniform application; in this case, however, the regional and local applications of the matrix become unidimensional.

Zone-Specific Policy Sets

Any state or region can be divided into a number of environmental and developmental zones. These zones, in turn, may fall under a multiplicity of governmental jurisdictions. A uniform policy set, applicable to all areas or zones, is highly unlikely to be very meaningful. In addition, such policy would be very difficult (if not impractical) to formulate.[j] Therefore, a concept may be suggested which provides for the division of the state or region into "policy zones" based on local jurisdictions. Such an approach would permit the development of zone-specific policy sets.

The rationale of this approach is to eliminate, insofar as possible, multi-jurisdictional zones at a geographic level where a high degree of specificity would otherwise be required. The policy concerns or contents could then be set forth in the form of a single set of technical, administrative, and legislative policy statements which, in turn, could be applied selectively to each policy zone. Assume that a region can be divided into $Z1$ through Zn policy zones. Thus, if the policy content sets were to include administrative policies $A1$ through An, legislative policies $L1$ through Ln, and technical policies $T1$ through Tn (the assumption, stated previously, is that basic policies would have uniform application), the applicable policy set for any particular zone (say $Z3$) might include $A1, A3, A5, L2, L4, T1, T5, T7, Tn$, and so forth. Another zone ($Z5$) might have certain administrative and legislative policies in common with $Z3$, say $A3, A5$, and $L4$, while requiring other policies for its particular problems. The delineation of unique problem sets results from *pilot area studies*, stemming from the basic data collection and inventory phase of the strategic planning process, as shown previously in Figure 9-1.

It may be suggested that the proposed framework for policy formulation could provide the degree of uniformity necessary for dealing with each problem requiring policy on a state or regional basis, while at the same time allowing for flexibility in the application of policy at the local micro-level. For example, it might be assumed that for any region or state there would be a general policy regarding the conservation of critical environmental resources. Within the terms of this general policy, a number of technical policies could be framed to deal with the conservancy of particular resources, development of conservation areas, extraction of minerals or other economic uses of resources, and so forth. These technical policies would not necessarily apply to all of the areas within the region or state. On the contrary, as a matter of administrative

---

[j]Although the establishment of uniform policy is a most difficult undertaking, it is common practice in most contemporary governmental programs to strive for this objective. Thus, federal and state guidelines outlining the "policies" surrounding a particular public program are often couched in very general terms, permitting considerable administrative latitude in their application. Unfortunately, many administrators choose to "go by the book" (even though the "book" may be purposely general and vague), often with disastrous consequences. For example, many programs aimed at the mitigation of poverty require the establishment of minority group participation in the decision process. Many bureaucrats interpret "minority group" as Blacks. Where the Black population does not represent the disadvantaged minority, as is the case in many parts of Appalachia, communities may be held up for long periods in the application phase or may be unduly restricted in the administration of these programs.

policy, it may be desirable not to include a particular technical policy in a local situation where the policy in question has no current applicability. The zonal policy approach would allow for a discriminatory choice from among the many technical, legislative, and administrative policy sets, focusing on those schemes which have more immediate, practical application in a given zone.

It should be pointed out that the need may arise for certain functional policies which do not conform to the systemic model as outlined above. For example, the model suggests that policy inputs from the pilot studies may take place. If such policy issues, in fact, should emerge, however, the model does not preclude their incorporation into the various policy sets to be formulated. On the contrary, the proposed framework would facilitate their integration with other policies in the policy formulation process. The method of systematization provided by the model for strategic planning should aid in the integration of such exogenous needs into an overall framework as well as in the translation of those needs into meaningful policy.

Summary and Conclusions

The approach to strategic planning presented in this discussion represents a composite of several basic models which focus on the critical processes of goal formulation and policy determination. This systemic approach offers many important features often lacking in the more traditional linear process of planning. It involves a conscious effort to achieve greater coordination between theoretical and practical planning and, in particular, the process by which research findings are transformed into plan formulations. This is achieved through the formulation of hypotheses concerning the theoretical aspects of the plan, which, in turn, establish a framework for the delineation of long-range goals. In developing these long-range goal sets and alternative policy sets, specific provision is made to minimize the influence of value biases.

The identification of a *planning horizon* is a first important step in the application of the systemic model. Both objective (measurable) and subjective criteria should be established for the determination of a planning horizon for any given area. The horizon concept and its corollary, levels of population, provide important tools for the strategic planning process. Using these techniques, implications of initial policy objectives can be tested and necessary modifications made. The horizon concept offers the basis for a goal-oriented *thesis* as to future development rather than a *synthesis* of past development trends.

Central to the conceptual basis of the systemic model is the attention given in the goal formulation process to the changing patterns in society and the identification of desired patterns of behavior or performance. Application of effectiveness measures as a "scoring technique" provides the basis for deter-

mining the state of a given system at a given point in time. A deductive approach
(in contrast to the inductive methods used in many planning models) is used
in the formulation of tentative goal sets and in testing these goals in the context
of specific population.

Another major component of the systemic model for strategic planning
is the differentiation between goals of the people and goals of establishments.
Certain neutral factors which may influence the equilibrium of demands and
structural changes are also delineated. These component processes lead to
the formulation of a multidimensional goal matrix which incorporates basic
conflict areas influencing the development of a particular jurisdiction.

In the conversion of broad goals into more specific policies, a categorization
of policy content is made in terms of objectives, priorities, locus, means, and
standards. Through this process, four basic quadrants of policy action can
be identified and critical areas of overlap and conflict can be highlighted in the
policy formulation process.

The model also gives recognition to the different nature of goals formulated
at various geographic levels, i.e., state, regional, subregional, and local. A
conceptual approach for the identification of zone-specific policy sets serves
as an integrative element in the model. The background for establishing the
parameters of zone-specific policy sets comes about through a series of pilot area
studies.

To date, the systemic model for strategic planning set forth in this discussion has not been completely tested in actual application. Component inputs
to the model, however, have been applied by Jussil and Kristensson in Sweden
and adaptations have been used in conjunction with planning studies in
Wisconsin, New Jersey, Maryland, and Hawaii. While it yet remains to fully
verify the composite approach, the systemic model holds the promise of an
important breakthrough in the development of a more effective basis for long-
range public decisions. Further, the internal consistency of the systemic model
is such that various component parts, such as the horizon concept, the multi-
dimensional goal matrix, the multiple policy matrix, and the zone-specific
policy sets, can be applied separately in existing strategic planning processes.

10 The Use of Effectiveness Measures in Public Decision-Making

While concepts of goal-oriented decision-making can be described in some detail, relatively few attempts have been made to realistically apply program budgeting and techniques of systems analysis to decision-making in local government. Attempts to translate current decisions and programs into systems-like frameworks, however, continue to be made. These "systems" approaches then frequently are used to "prove" that the old decision-making techniques (and decision-makers) are just as good as any new techniques.

Proposed changes in governmental processes of decision-making and resource-allocation must be evaluated in view of the ambiguities and conflicts which, in a very real sense, represent the nature of contemporary local government.[1] Attempts to bring greater rationality to decision-making in local government — through the application of program budgeting, systems theory and analysis, operations research, and so forth — must be based on the assumptions, concepts, and criteria which represent the current state of local government.

New Techniques for Optimizing Public Resource Allocations: A Critical Need

The most significant decision problem confronting local government involves the allocation of resources, in an optimal fashion, to meet physical, economic, social, and political needs and demands. To date, the professional in government has had relatively little involvement in the resolution of this problem. The complexity of the resource allocation problem is well illustrated by underlining some of the critical factors necessary to resolve this problem: (1) unambiguous, quantitative indicators of physical, social, economic, and political needs and demands; (2) a social, democratic mechanism for identifying constituency preferences in a jurisdiction; (3) unlimited public fiscal resources; and (4) reliable information on the performance capabilities of available alternatives to meet specified needs and demands.

Resources are allocated in government through the budget process, which basically involves an adversary-type relationship among agencies. Significant criteria and controls employed are usually of a financial nature, focusing on the expenditure of money. Under such conditions, public decision-making is *input-oriented*. The analysis of objectives and alternative methods of achieving

227

these objectives is based on money-related rather than policy issues. If there
are sufficient funds to pay for the "inputs" — the resources requested by the
various agencies — there is no major budget problem in government. Seldom, if
ever, are projections or estimates made of the effects these inputs will have in
meeting the public needs and demands of the jurisdiction. There is no guarantee
that the public decision process is coherently responsive to comprehensive
objectives. At the same time, there is a clear lack of explicit mechanisms to
assure responsiveness to comprehensive objectives at the interagency level.

These indictments of current practice point up the critical need for new
techniques for optimizing the allocation of public resources. One such technique
that holds considerable promise is cost-effectiveness analysis.

The Role of Cost-Effectiveness Analysis

Cost-effectiveness is an analytical device employed in the process of
program budgeting. In this context, it must be distinguished from the structural
aspects and information system considerations of program budgeting. The
structural aspects of program budgeting are concerned primarily with the
establishment of program categories oriented toward the end-product activities
that are meaningful from a long-range, strategic planning point of view. Information system considerations, on the other hand, deal with (1) providing data
and information to serve as a basis for the analytical process, and (2) progress
reporting and control.

Analytical process considerations pertain to various study activities
conducted as an integral part of the program budgeting system. The analytical
process in program budgeting covers the entire spectrum from long-range
planning, through programming, to budgeting. Various analytical techniques
must be employed at each stage in this process.

Cost-effectiveness analysis, although not restricted in application to long-
range planning problems, is a most useful tool for such planning, particularly
when a wise range of alternative future courses of action needs to be examined in
a broad context. Prest and Turvey define cost-effectiveness analysis as ". . . a
practical way of assessing the desirability of projects, where it is important to
take a long view (in the sense of looking at repercussions in the further, as well as
the nearer, future) and a wide view (in the sense of allowing for side-effects of
many kinds of many persons, industries, regions, etc.). i.e., it implies the
enumeration and evaluation of all the relevant costs and benefits."[2]

Attributes of Cost-Effectiveness Analysis

Cost-effectiveness analysis provides the basis for the development of a
decision-making process which is output-oriented and which considers the impacts

of resources rather than resources themselves. Under this approach, a distinction is made between *efficiency* and *effectiveness* in an attempt to discard financial-type controls in favor of unambiguous and nonpecuniary accounting techniques to measure the output of public programs. This output orientation of cost-effectiveness is its most notable attribute; however, a number of other character-istics set this approach apart from other types of budget analysis techniques. While any list of these features is somewhat arbitrary, the more important of these attributes include the following: (1) end-product orientation; (2) extended time horizon; (3) life-cycle costs; (4) examination of total systems costs; (5) measurement of goal achievement; (6) development of management information system; and (7) analytical approach and techniques. Attributes 5, 6, and 7 will form the primary basis for the presentation which follows. First, however, it may be useful to review briefly the first four attributes, which are characteris-tic of all forms of cost-utility analysis.

End-Product Orientation

A basic modus operandi of cost-effectiveness analysis involves the identifi-cation and analysis of alternative "systems" to achieve some agreed-upon objective or set of objectives.[3] In program budgeting, the selected system becomes a *program element* — an integrated activity which combines personnel, other services, equipment, and facilities.[4] The end-product orientation of cost-effectiveness analysis is thus reflected in this systems approach. It is a basic principle that requirements for diverse resources be identified and associated with end products. The immediate problem is to identify all costs associated with the achievement of a particular level of performance that defines the desired state of the system at some future point in time. The cost of a system should reflect the total resource impact of the decision relating to that system, identifying and indicating the magnitude of all relevant costs of a particular alternative course of action (or system).

Extended Time Horizon

As stated previously, cost-effectiveness analysis is a tool for long-range strategic planning — for taking a long view and a wide view. In particular, development decisions are often required five to ten years or more before a system can be brought into being. The span of time covered in cost-effectiveness analysis must be sufficiently long to take cognizance of such lead times. Further-more, the time horizon must cover the full period of a system's operation and the period of its benefits. The horizon concept, therefore, becomes an integral part of cost-effectiveness analysis.

The extended time horizon has important implications for the development of cost estimates and estimates of program performance in terms of accrued benefits. A great deal of uncertainty surrounds such long-range analysis, and the farther out in time the analysis is addressed, the greater the uncertainty. Such analyses of systems often involve new materials and equipment never before produced, operations never before attempted, new processes, and new training concepts — all of which make their costing difficult and the estimates of benefits uncertain. Thus, emphasis must be placed on the comparability of estimates rather than on their absolute values.

Life-Cycle Costs

Another of the distinctive features of cost-effectiveness analysis (and the other basic forms of cost-utility analysis) is the use of cost categories. Systems costs are identified and grouped as follows: (1) research and development — costs associated primarily with the development of a new system or capability to the point where it is ready for operational use; (2) investment — costs beyond the development phase to introduce new systems or a new capability into use; and (3) operations — recurring costs of operating, supporting, and maintaining the system or capability. These cost categories reflect the life cycle of the system under study. Life-cycle costing results from the concept that the funds necessary to initially undertake a program are not the primary consideration, nor are the funds required in any particular time period. A decision to undertake a particular course of action should take into account the total cost impact over time.

A system's research and development costs are one-time costs and, in effect, a function of the nature of the system. Research and development costs are essentially insensitive to the number of units of the system that will be made operational or the length of time that the system will be in use. Investment costs, on the other hand, are a function of the number of units planned for in the system. The greater the number of units introduced into the program, the higher the investment cost. Such costs are generally one-time costs per unit. Operating costs depend on both the number of units in the program and the length of time that such units are operated, supported, and maintained. R & D costs are concerned with development decisions and the choice among feasible alternatives. Investment costs concern the extensiveness of the system's employment or the relative importance that the system will occupy in a larger program. The operating costs concern the manner and length of time that the system should be operated (this may be a function of effectiveness and thus in some systems is a variable cost). Figure 10-1 depicts cost categories over the life cycle of a system.

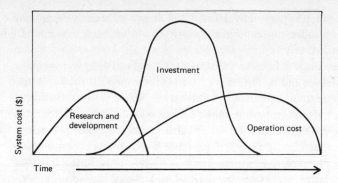

Figure 10-1. Life Cycle Costs Plotted Against Time.

Examination of Total Systems Costs

A central purpose of cost-effectiveness analysis is to develop estimates of future resource requirements for systems. Resource requirements are stated in terms of equipment, personnel, real facilities, supplies, and so forth. A total system cost, however, cannot be developed by summing over such heterogeneity of resource needs. Nor is it possible to make understandable comparisons between systems if their costs are expressed solely in terms of varieties of real resources. Dollar cost of such resources can serve the purpose and, therefore, must serve as the measure for cost estimations. In estimating the cost of a system, it is important to spell out the quantities of important resources. Critical resources, the supplies of which are quite limited (e.g., technical personnel), must be given separate attention in the analysis. It also is important to note that constant dollars are nearly always used in cost estimating.[6] Rarely is an attempt made to predict future price-level changes in comparing or evaluating alternatives in cost-effectiveness studies. Such predictions are extremely difficult to make and many problems remain to be solved.

Effectiveness Versus Efficiency:
Their Relations to Goals

Decision-making and analytical mechanisms of government are designed to pursue efficiency at the expense of effectiveness. This characteristic of public decision-making can be observed in continual efforts to achieve economies without decreasing service. The focus is on the elimination of waste: with fixed resources, to produce more of A without decreasing the production of B.

Questions of efficiency are generally defined and answered strictly in economic terms. Minimum consideration is given to priorities and/or relative worth of the programs pursued.

It must be recognized, however, that many (if not most) governmental activities must produce and be responsive to noneconomic returns. The effects of analyses which consider economic variables while ignoring noneconomic variables are seen today in irrelevant public school systems, destructive highway and freeway systems, and irrational public health and correctional programs. Further effects are seen in the analytical pretense which treats governmental programs as mutually exclusive entities. There is no purely technical basis for deciding the relative importance or merit of an Upward Bound program versus an on-the-job training program for adults. By pretending that technical analyses — analyses which focus on efficiency — are sufficient for political decisions, decision-makers lose the very information necessary to determine effectiveness. It is possible to have an efficiency transportation link which, for example, moves traffic from Point A to Point B with little or no waste. Such a link, however, is irrelevant if the need is to go to Point C. Effectiveness considers the relevant worth of Point B versus Point C with reference to specific values and variables. Consideration of this relative worth — the actual effect of resources — represents effectiveness.

Measuring Goal Achievement

In this context, *goals* may be defined as *codifications of desirable patterns of performance*, as exhibited by individuals and institutions, or by physical, social, economic, and political variables. Goals describe the desired state of any system. The public planning and decision-making processes must be capable of manipulating and controlling system variables in order to achieve this desired state. The decision-making process is complicated by the fact that goals are not mutually exclusive. A single set of variables may be common to a number of goals; the primary variables of a low-priority goal may be secondary variables of a high-priority goal.

Effectiveness measures must be developed and applied to determine the level of goal achievement. *Effectiveness measures* are defined as *indicators which measure the direct and indirect impacts of resource allocations*. They involve a basic scoring technique for determining the state of a given system. Careful selection and application of effectiveness measures can go a long way in overcoming some of the difficulties and ambiguities of public decision-making. This does not imply in any way that the concept of a goal is to be discarded, but only that there are a number of advantages to analyzing the effects resources have upon system variables before commitments to goals are made.

A Systemic Decision-Making Model:
The Use of Effectiveness Measures

The first step in the application of effectiveness measures to problems of public decision-making and resource allocation is the development of a management information and program evaluation system (MIPES). The emphasis of such an information system is on the identification, definition, isolation, and manipulation of specific variables as they relate to public goals. These variables can be used as effectiveness measures if consideration is given to the effects that resource allocations have upon them.

A management information and program evaluation system must be based on an examination of structural and operational characteristics of the agency or agencies in question. For purposes of analysis, a series of discrete program categories must be defined in terms of agency goals and objectives. For example, a law enforcement agency, broadly speaking, is organized to achieve two general goals: (1) the control of criminal behavior; and (2) the control of non-criminal behavior. A health agency may be seen as having two broad goals: (1) a remedial health mission; and (2) a preventive health mission. These broad categories of activity, of course, must eventually be further subdivided. Initially, however, it may be feasible to establish only rather broad program categories.

Goals are defined by: (1) establishing *current levels* and types of performance in each discrete program category; (2) estimating the *current impacts* of agency resources on that performance; and (3) defining *desired levels* and types of performance. The development of positive statements of performance provides a base from which to define and evaluate change. An approach based on the concept of marginal change from the current state [7] yields normative statements of performance — goals — which can be defined as deviations from the current level of operation. A fundamental assumption of this approach is that performance may be defined in oriented terminology based on program and policy variables.

It is assumed that normative statements of performance can be derived, or inferred, from current conditions. Current operations and their effects must be under continuous surveillance. Continuous program evaluation is the most effective means available for initiating a goal-oriented decision-making system in an existing governmental structure.

Isolation of Broad Alternatives for Control

Policy and program variables which define performance represent what is wanted, i.e., they are directly related to needs and demands. Analysis of the relationships between these variables and categories of performance permits the formulation of statements of normative performance. These statements, in turn, lead to the subsequent development of output-oriented programs. The next important step, therefore, in the development of MIPES is to list all possible categories and subcategories of performance under study. This preliminary identification begins to isolate broad alternatives for control. Each category and subcategory should be defined carefully so as to minimize overlapping characteristics and to identify gaps in the program descriptions.

A thorough analysis of the nature and extent of program output (performance) must be undertaken so that practical effectiveness measures and organizational and operational criteria can be defined. These measures and criteria have three basic functions: (1) the identification of desired ends, i.e., desired levels and patterns of performance; (2) the establishment of a structure which facilitates the evaluation of alternative methods of resource allocation; and (3) the creation of a planning and management framework which permits reevaluation and modification of criteria and measures as well as program structure. These criteria, or measures of effectiveness, can be defined as policy and program variables. Such variables (1) identify administrative policy and policy alternatives, and (2) are representative of those interests — individuals and groups within the jurisdiction — which comprise the patterns of performance and/or are to be affected by these patterns. This set of policy and program variables must describe the relationship between all of the critical components in the system, as they represent the patterns of performance under study and as they are to be affected by the allocation of public resources.

Defining Positive-Normative Performance:
an Analytical Framework

With the specific classification of policy and program variables, an analytical framework for goal definition and analysis can be structured. The use of policy and program variables to describe performance is required if an output-oriented decision process is desired. These variables do not directly consider agency activities or inputs; rather, the focus is on the effects of those agency activities (outputs) in the achievement of established goals.

Program performance can be classified by a number of factors. Agency programs involve identifiable persons (clientele) and/or events, and while programs are often considered continuous, certain milestones, or occurrences, can be identified. Therefore, the broad categories of information required to define patterns of performance might include the following items of data: (1) number and frequency of occurrences — the number of reported and estimates of the number of unreported occurrences in a given time period for a particular event toward which a given program is directed; (2) characteristics of persons or events involved in each occurrence; (3) relationships among persons or events involved; and (4) circumstances surround the occurrence of events.

One useful approach to the analysis of these characteristics is through the development of a matrix for each major subcategory of performance in which all of the pertinent variables are listed. Such a matrix is presented in Figure 10-2. This matrix represents a hypothetical description of one category or subcategory of performance. It would be necessary to perform similar analyses for each category or subcategory.

If the program under analysis deals with water pollution, for example, "characteristics" might refer to the types and sources of pollution, "relationships" might encompass the geographic location of the pollution sources or outflows, levels and types of pollutants, current levels of treatment given to the effluent, and so forth, while "circumstances" might pertain to weather conditions, stream flow, calendar period of pollution, and so on. The more extensive the listing of these factors, the more complete the analysis possible.

To illustrate how this approach might be applied analytically, several quick observations can be made from the hypothetical matrix. First, the dominant pattern is exhibited by events occurring with characteristic C1, relationship R1, and under circumstances A1. This combination accounts for fifty occurrences, followed by the combination of C2, R2, A1, which accounts for twenty occurrences. Over half of the occurrences (130) exhibit characteristic C1 or C2, and nearly half (120) share characteristic C1. Similarly, over half of all occurrences (150) exhibit relationships R1 and R2. Of the forty occurrences exhibiting characteristic C4, only thirty exhibit a second characteristic. None of the occurrences with C2 exhibit C4 or C5. Similarly, R2 is mutually exclusive with R3 and R4, and R4 is mutually exclusive with R2, R3, and R5. Finally, it may be observed that A5 and A6 occur simultaneously. These are but a few of the numerous observations that can be derived from this hypothetical matrix.

Positive statements of performance define the current state of the system; goals or normative statements of performance can be defined by specifying deviations from the current state. Program and policy variables similar to, if not identical with, those used to define the *current* nature and level of performance also can be used to define the *desired* state of the system. Performance can be defined in normative terms by stating the total number of characteristics of the events involved, and by expressing the desired circumstances of performance.

The next step in establishing the basis for analysis is to divide each cell of the matrix into four sectors, as shown in Figure 10-3. One sector of each cell is devoted to a record of the *reported* associations between the two variables which form the coordinates of that cell. A second sector is used to identify the *estimated* (reported plus unreported) associations among variables. The third sector is used to identify the desired or acceptable levels of association. The fourth sector can be applied to record the *actual* association between two variables after a period of time has elapsed. This last sector is for purposes of evaluation of program performance, once a new program is initiated.

Normative definitions mean, simply, that choices are to be made in concert with desired, or perhaps acceptable, levels of performance. It should be clear

	Number of Occurrences	Characteristics					Relationships					Circumstances					
		C_1	C_2	C_3	C_4	C_5	R_1	R_2	R_3	R_4	R_5	A_1	A_2	A_3	A_4	A_5	A_6
Number of Occurrences	250	70	60	50	40	30	90	60	40	20	40	80	60	40	50	10	10
C_1	70	X	60	50	10	10	60	10	0	0	0	50	20	0	0	0	0
C_2	60	50	X	10	0	10	10	20	15	15	0	20	10	10	10	10	0
C_3	50	10	10	X	20	10	10	20	10	0	10	10	10	10	20	0	0
C_4	40	0	0	20	X	10	5	5	10	5	15	0	10	10	20	0	0
C_5	30	10	0	10	10	X	5	5	5	0	15	0	10	10	0	0	10
R_1	90	60	10	20	5	5	X	30	20	20	10	60	0	0	10	10	10
R_2	60	10	20	20	5	5	30	X	0	0	10	20	40	0	0	0	0
R_3	40	0	15	0	10	5	20	0	X	0	0	0	20	0	0	0	0
R_4	20	0	15	0	5	0	20	0	0	X	0	0	0	0	20	0	0
R_5	40	0	0	10	15	15	10	10	0	0	X	0	0	40	0	0	0
A_1	80	50	20	10	0	0	60	20	0	0	0	X	40	10	30	0	0
A_2	60	20	10	10	10	10	0	40	20	0	0	40	X	20	0	0	0
A_3	40	0	10	10	10	10	0	0	0	0	40	10	20	X	10	0	0
A_4	50	0	10	20	20	0	10	0	0	20	0	30	0	10	X	0	0
A_5	10	0	10	0	0	0	10	0	0	0	0	0	0	0	0	X	10
A_6	10	0	0	0	0	10	10	0	0	0	0	0	0	0	0	10	X

Figure 10-2. Analytical Matrix Showing Pertinent Variables for a Major Subcategory of Performance.

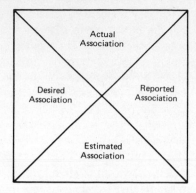

Figure 10-3. Sector Division of Each Cell in the Analytical Matrix.

that some forms of dysfunctional performance cannot be eliminated totally through the actions of governmental agencies. Therefore, in such cases, agencies must recognize the limits of their resources and responsibilities and be prepared to accept levels of performance that may not be totally functional in all circumstances.

Policy-Level Responsibilities of Agencies

This method of defining goals provides a means for distinguishing many of the subtleties present in the complex roles of government in contemporary society. Taken together, the completion of analyses for each category and subcategory of performance defines the goals of the jurisdiction. The values used to define these goals must be determined by a policy-oriented decision process. The definition of goals is a process of iteration and must be related to the likely costs to be incurred in achieving desired or acceptable levels of performance.

A continuing analysis and reevaluation of patterns and levels of performance and the policy and program variables used to define this performance must take place through formal, administrative-level mechanisms. The establishment of priorities should reflect the conception that governmental departments are administrative agencies with important policy-making responsibilities. It is naive to define a governmental agency as merely an administrative unit which reflects codified laws and rigidly pursues goals defined by other sectors or agencies of the community. Nor can a governmental agency be held to a system or procedure of decision-making which involves no risk-taking. The policy-level responsibilities of any governmental agency must represent several distinct dimensions: (1) they must assure that the agency reflects both administrative priorities in government and the needs and demands of the constituency;

(2) they must assure that the agency is aware of social and economic trends; and (3) they must assure that the expertise and knowledge of the agency become a part of the policy-making efforts. It is the policy formulation process which defines categories of performance, determines how these performance patterns are to be measured, establishes priorities on the various levels for each category, and assigns measures of effectiveness to each catetory.

The Nature of Program Analysis

Program analysis is concerned with the determination of programs and program levels which are most effective in achieving specific goals. It involves an evaluation of total program costs and anticipated program effects. Both costs and effectiveness are measured and analyzed in quantitative terms. While costs are usually expressed in dollar terms, the unit of measurement for effectiveness is that of the goal; it may or may not be pecuniary. Policy and program variables represent the nonmonetary units of measure. The use of these variables should not be confused with the more typical forms of cost-benefit analysis — methods for determining whether a program is *economically* worthwhile by comparing costs and benefits, both of which are measured and analyzed in monetary terms. The development of many public programs, clearly, must be based on more than monetary terms.

The Problem of Feasibility

Programs are time-phased plans for allocating resources. They involve the combination of manpower, equipment, and procedures available to affect and manipulate policy and program variables. Programs must be postulated and evaluated with reference to unambiguous statements of desired levels and types of performance. Initial statements of goals are not fixed or static. Goals must be continually evaluated and revised according to the outcomes available through various allocations of resources. At this stage, problems of feasibility are confronted. It may be necessary to make rather drastic modifications of the initial goal statements after the potential of available resources is thoroughly understood.

The question of feasibility must consider directly the costs of analyzing and measuring policy and program variables. For example, it is meaningless to consider programs affecting certain clientele groups if no efforts are made to collect and analyze the data which describe these particular clients. Program analysis, therefore, requires not only consideration of the direct costs of affecting performance, but also the cost of measuring any shifts in this performance. The information collected by other agencies, both public and private, must

be considered. In a budgeting sense, the cost incurred by other agencies in
collecting and analyzing data which describes various types of performance of
interest to the agency must be recognized. Attempts to develop high levels
of complementarity in data collection and analysis with other agencies also serves
to identify information voids. This approach also aids in the identification of
substitutes for certain program and policy variables, which have costs of
collection and analysis that are not justified.

Types of Program Analysis

Program development requires three types of decisions and supporting
analyses: (1) cost-goal analysis is concerned with the identification of feasible
goals; (2) cost-effectiveness analysis serves to assist in the identification of the
most effective program alternative; (3) cost-constraint analysis determines the
cost of employing less-than-optimal programs. Ideally, program analysis should
be an iterative process. In the early development of a goal-oriented budget
structure, however, it probably will be desirable (and necessary) to make these
analyses more or less independently. With additional sophistication in data
and techniques, iterative refinements can be made in the analysis.

Cost-Goal Analysis

Cost-goal analysis assists in establishing program goals and program levels
by determining the shape of program cost curves through the specification
of input-output relationships. This analysis indicates the likely changes in
program costs as program goals are changed. This technique has immediate use,
since it usually requires an analysis and assessment of existing programs. Once
the program cost curve is determined for each existing program, alternative
programs can be considered and their impacts assessed. Figure 10-4 presents this
type of analysis graphically. O1, O2, and O3 represent goals (outputs) and
C1, C2, and C3 represent program costs.

The program cost curve represents the sensitivity of cost (input) to
changes in the program's desired level of effectiveness (output). Unless program
cost relationships are understood, it is not possible to know what will happen
as the desired level of effectiveness — the goal — is raised or lowered. Costs
may change more or less proportionately. However, if costs do not increase as
rapidly as effectiveness, then the program is operating at a level of increasing
returns (represented by a positively sloped curve accelerating at an accelerating
rate). If costs increase more rapidly then effectiveness, the program is operating
in an area of diminishing returns.

Increasing returns do not mean that a program should be expanded or,

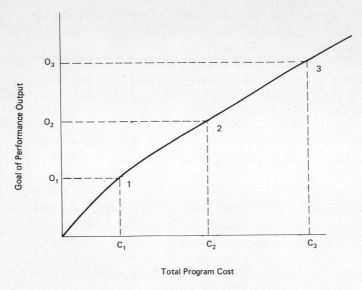

Figure 10-4. Cost-Goal Analysis in Graphic Form.

conversely, that it should be contracted if it is operating in an area of diminishing returns. A public program can be of such importance that it should be expanded even though it is operating with diminishing returns. However, it is useful to know that an additional commitment of $200,000 to one program will carry it twenty percent toward its goal, while the same resources added to another program would carry it only five percent closer to its goals.

Determining what might happen to program costs if the characteristics of the goal are changed is not an easy task. Frequently, only one point is known, that which relates the current cost to the current level of effectiveness. Cost-goal analysis requires the construction of a model which can relate incremental costs to increments in effectiveness.[a] Construction of program cost curves should become increasingly more sophisticated as these relationships are better understood. For some types of program, it is probable that practical models can now be developed. For others, program cost curves can be approximated from historical data.

A very crude first approximation can be obtained by plotting program costs against achieved levels of effectiveness for the recent past. A curve can then be drawn through these points. The construction of a historical curve in this manner represents a simple correlation analysis of independent and dependent variables. While it is very crude, it may be sufficiently accurate to judge whether the program under analysis appears to be operating in an area of increasing

---

[a]The problems of incremental costing will be discussed further in a later section.

or decreasing returns. In the future, it undoubtedly will be necessary (and possible) to resort to multiple correlation analysis in order to fully substantiate the shape of program cost curves.

Cost-Effectiveness Analysis[b]

There is usually more than one way to achieve a goal or set of goals. The objective of cost-effectiveness analysis, therefore, is to determine the most effective program for achieving each identified goal or goal set. An analysis of alternative program curves, representing either single programs or sets of programs, can reveal the preferred program for a given goal or set of goals.

This type of analysis is illustrated graphically in Figure 10–5. PA and PB

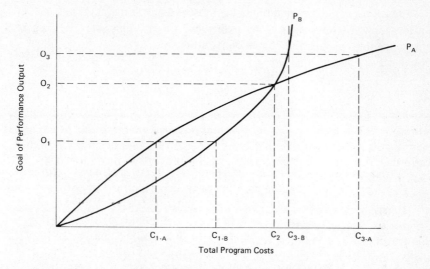

Figure 10–5. Cost-Effectiveness Analysis in Graphic Form.

represent alternative programs; O1, O2, and O3 are three different goals; C1-B and C1-A are program costs associated with goal O1; C2 is the program cost associated with goal O2; and C3-A and C3-B are program costs associated with goal O3. For goal O1, PA represents the most efficient and effective program

---

[b]Although it may create some confusion, both the entire process described here and this particular phase of the analysis have been labelled cost-effectiveness. Cost-effectiveness analysis, in the more narrow sense, begins with identified goals or normative statements of performance. The broader definition encompasses the recommended techniques for developing these statements. Other techniques, however, can be applied as a precedent to cost-effectiveness analysis in the more restricted sense.

since C1-A is the least cost. On the other hand, if the "higher" goal O3 is desired, PB is the most effective program at cost C3-B. If goal O2 were selected, the analyst would be indifferent between the two programs, since both have the same cost, C2.

Normally, comparison of alternative programs is made between an existing program and a proposed alternative. Since it is difficult enough to construct the cost curve for the existing program, it is frequently impossible to develop detailed cost curves for largely theoretical alternatives. Initially, therefore, it may be useful to undertake only a partial comparison. Based on an established goal, it is necessary to know only which program would achieve that goal most effectively; it is not necessary to know the actual shape of the alternative program curve but rather, only the *tendency* of the curve. Consider, for example, that in Figure 10–5, PA represents an existing program and PB an alternative. If O1 is the current goal and O3 is selected as the new goal, then C3-B and C3-A must be compared to determine the most effective program. That O3 can be achieved with fewer resources under the new program illustrates the dangers of assuming that one program, based on its superiority at one point, is the most effective program at all levels.

Cost-Constraint Analysis

In pratice, governmental programs may be adopted which do not represent the most effective programs technically available. Legislative constraints, intergovernmental relations, union rules, employer rights, community attitudes, and so forth are among the more obvious reasons. The purpose of cost-constraint analysis is to illustrate the cost of these constraints. This is accomplished by comparing the cost of the program that could be adopted if no constraints were present with the cost of the optimum program that can be employed given existing constraints. The analysis, shown graphically in Figure 10–6, starts with the expressed goal O1 and two programs (P constrained and P not-constrained). P not-constrained represents the most effective program as determined by cost-effectiveness analysis. The other program may be constrained by some legal, political, economic, or social factor. The constrained program may be the only program available. The cost of the constraints to the agency is the difference between the program cost of P not-constrained and P constrained. Once this cost is identified, decisions as to the importance of attempting to remove the constraints can be made. On the basis of this analysis, public managers can confront policy-makers with the facts on how much the relaxation of a given constraint would save the program. The cost of the constraint is also indicative of the amount of effort that might be made to overcome a constraint, if such effort were acceptable. In some cases, supporting a constraint would be more valuable for social or political reasons than a more effective program.

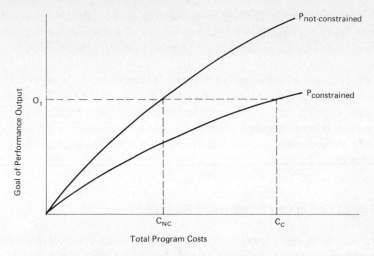

Figure 10–6. Cost-Constraint Analysis in Graphic Form.

Total Program Costs and Benefits

Program analysis must consider total costs and benefits. A *cost* is any resource input into a program; a *benefit* is any desirable impact arising from the operation of a program. Cost-benefit analyses are difficult because of the problems of separating and measuring direct, indirect, and induced benefits and costs. Direct costs are defined as those resource inputs made by the agency in question; indirect and induced costs are those incurred by other agencies, programs, or individuals, based on the goals in question. Desirable program effects accruing directly to the groups toward which a program is aimed are direct program benefits, while all other desirable effects of the program are indirect and induced benefits. Measuring indirect costs and benefits is a most complex and difficult undertaking. However, categorizing programs according to performance characteristics makes it possible to avoid some of the inherent conceptual problems of cost-benefit analysis.

Since most public programs affect the total community, it is probable that total benefits can be only roughly estimated. Total benefits must be calculated according to those areas of performance for which the agency has been given responsibility. The agency is accountable for the control or development of specific categories and subcategories of program performance, although it is understood that other agencies and groups may be concerned with influencing this performance. Analysis of the benefits of these categories will hold the task to manageable proportions.

It is necessary, however, to have some understanding of the contributions that other agencies and programs may make. These benefits accrue through the action of others and should be held separate from the benefits arising directly from the programs of the agency.[c] It also is necessary to distinguish among the benefits provided by the agency as they accrue to various other interests and groups.

A similar rationale must be applied to costs. Management, by being officially responsible for contributing to the influence of program performance, should logically account for any program costs induced in those areas. Thus, accountable costs should constitute the current operational definition of total costs. For any particular analysis, the benefit and cost tables should include the same categories.

The Role of Cost in Cost-Effectiveness Analysis

Cost-effectiveness analysis assists in identifying the most desirable approach among alternative means to some specified end. To make a meaningful choice, however, criteria, or tests of preferredness, must be formulated. Generally, the most suitable criterion is the maximization of the present value of all benefits to be derived less that of all costs, assuming both can be expressed in the same unit.[d] If costs and benefits cannot be so expressed, then the suitable forms are maximization of gain for a specified cost or the minimization of cost for achieving a specified gain.[8]

A Hypothetical Case Study

These criteria can be illustrated by a hypothetical case study. Assume that in Appalachia some 3,000 workers become unemployed each year due to technical obsolescence, that is, the job for which they are trained and skilled is eliminated through mechanization of industrial processes. The federal government has established an objective to retrain some or all of these workers to new skills by means of a one-year intensive training course. Through this program, it is anticipated that the workers will be employable at a certain skill level ten years sooner than if they had to attain the skills on their own. Therefore, the benefits

---

[c]An exception to this general rule may arise in cases where the objective of the agency's program is to induce action on the part of others. In this case, a part of the accrued benefits arising from the action of others may be appropriately considered in the agency's calculations.

[d]Money invested at some rate of interest will increase in value over time. For example, $100 invested today at six percent will amount to $106 one year from now. Looking at it in another way, $106 one year in the future is worth only $100 at present, if money is worth (can be invested at) six percent. The sum $100 is called the *present value* of $106 one year in the future if money is worth six percent. The $106 is *discounted* at six percent to determine the present value.

of this program will run for ten years. To provide this training, it is necessary to develop regional training centers. build new facilities or significantly upgrade existing facilities, hire new instructional personnel, and so forth. It is anticipated that the program will continue to operate over a ten-year period.

Developing Cost-Goal Curves

After considerable study, it is determined that there are two alternative means to achieve the program objectives. Each of these alternatives can be considered a system. In this context, a system can be viewed as any combination of resources brought together to achieve a specific objective. System A is an equipment-oriented approach, involving extensive use of programmed learning techniques, tape libraries to upgrade basic skills in reading, use of computers, and so forth. It has only five instructors per training center and a trainee-instructor ratio of sixty to one. System B is a teacher-oriented approach, involving team-teaching techniques. It requires twenty instructors per training center and has a ten-to-one trainee-instructor ratio. The trainee capacity at training centers for System A is 300 and for System B, 200. Assume further that the costs for each system can be summarized as in Table 10-1.

It is now possible to examine how costs and benefits (program effectiveness) are related in the tests for preferredness. First, assume that the benefits and costs cannot be measured in the same units, that is, they are incommensurable. In the case at hand, gains are measured in terms of the number of workers retrained, and costs are measured in dollars. Since decision-makers do not know the level of training they wish to support (or can afford to support given limited resources), it is necessary to develop a schedule of costs and benefits over the full range of workers to be trained (i.e., 0 to 3,000). For convenience, it may be assumed that the costs are of a continuous nature, that is, training centers can be constructed and operated at various sizes.

The trainee load capability is charted on the top part of Figure 10-7. System A would require ten training centers for 3,000 trainees and System B requires fifteen. The systems costs (development, investment, and ten years of operating

Table 10-1
Alternative Program Costs (in thousands)

Item of Cost	System A	System B
Development Costs	$15,000	$1,000
Investment per Training Center	500	400
Operational Costs per Year per Training Center	1,500	3,000

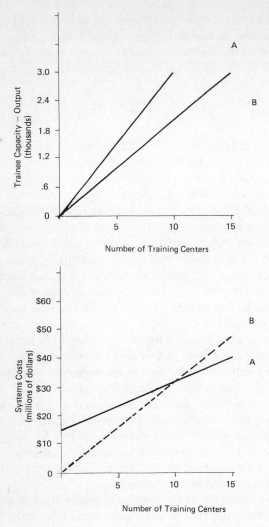

Figure 10-7. Trainee Capacity and Systems Costs Versus Number of Training Centers for Alternative Systems A and B.

costs) are charted on the bottom part of Figure 10-7, and are summarized in Table 10-2. It is now possible to combine benefits (trainee capacity — assumed to be equal to workers trained) and costs into one chart (Figure 10-8) by eliminating the common denominator, number of training centers.

Recognizing that nonquantifiable factors may enter into the final decision — the discussion of which will be omitted here for simplicity — it is possible to choose the best system, given either a fixed budget or a specified level of benefits. The envelope of optimum costs to benefits is indicated on Figure

Table 10–2
Total Costs over Ten Years (in thousands)

Centers	System A			System B		
	0	10	15	0	10	15
R & D	$15,000	$15,000	$15,000	$1,000	$ 1,000	$ 1,000
Investment	–	5,000	7,500	–	4,000	6,000
Operation	–	15,000	22,500	–	30,000	45,000
Total	$15,000	$35,000	$45,000	$1,000	$35,000	$52,000

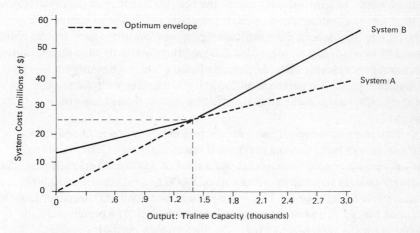

Figure 10–8. Trainee Capacity Versus System Costs for Alternative Systems A and B.

10–8: for all budgets under $24.2 million, System B is preferred because it will have a greater trainee capacity; conversely, for all trainee loads less than 1,360, System B is preferred because it will cost less than System A. For budgets above $24.2 million or for trainee loads above 1,360, System A is preferred. For example, at a $20-million budget, System B has a capacity of about 1,100 trainees, while A has about 800 trainees. At a trainee load of 2,400, however, System A will cost $31 million, whereas System B will cost $41.8 million. Although these illustrations have been extremely simplified, they show how cost and benefits interact when they are incommensurable.

Calculating Program Benefits

Using the same hypothetical case study in connection with program costs, assume that each worker trained will increase his earnings such that, for the ten-year period, taxes paid to the government will be increased by $250 each year and unemployment benefits of $250 per year will not have to be paid. The government, therefore, has the opportunity to use this $250 in some other way. The net gain to government, therefore, is $500 per trainee per year, or $5000 for the 10-year period.[e]

Discounting Costs and Benefits

The criterion for choice, for a given investment, is the maximization of present worth, i.e., the present value of the benefits less that of the costs. It now is necessary to compute the time-phased benefits and, using an appropriate interest rate, to discount the benefits to a present value.[9] Again, system costs would be developed as before, but in this case they would be time-phased and discounted to a present value. Such time-phased costs and benefits for one level of trainee capacity are portrayed in Table 10-3, together with the present value of each, based on the arbitrary assumption that money is worth six percent.[f]

Two years have been allowed for the period of development and testing and one year to build training centers and install equipment. The training centers operate for ten years, graduating a total of 3,000 workers each year. The graduate trainees build up in increments of 3,000 to a maximum of 30,000 graduates receiving benefits. This group phases down by 3,000 decrements as the assumed benefit period of ten years ends for each class. The present value of the costs for the total program (over the thirteen-year period) would be $27.25 million, while the present value of the benefits (assuming only the direct benefits outlined previously) would be $68.24 million, resulting in a present worth of approximately $41 million.

Developing Cost-Effectiveness Curves

Similar calculations for other levels of trainee capacity can be made, resulting in the chart of outputs (benefits) and costs shown in the top of Figure 10-9. These data, in turn, are presented in present worth terms in the bottom part of Figure 10-9. By comparing these diagrams with Figure 10-8, it will be noted that there is a shift in the crossover point for preferring System A to System B from the undiscounted case. This shift occurs because of the shape of the time streams of costs and benefits and the discount rate selected. The

---

[e]Clearly other benefits can be derived from this program. However, these two benefits are the ones most directly associated with the program objectives.

[f]The discount rate selected above is meant to reflect only the time preference for money and not the risk associated with the project.

Table 10-3
Present Worth Calculations – Six Percent Discount Rate Alternative System A – 3,000 Trainee Capacity (in millions of dollars)

Year	Centers in Operation	Costs Dev.	Invest.	Op.	Total	Present Value	Benefits Total	Present Value	Present Worth
1	–	7.5	–	–	7.5	7.08	–	–	–
2	–	7.5	–	–	7.5	6.68	–	–	–
3	–	–	5.0	–	5.0	4.20	–	–	–
4	10			1.5	1.5	1.19	–	–	
5	10			1.5	1.5	1.12	1.5	1.12	
6	10			1.5	1.5	1.06	3.0	2.11	
7	10			1.5	1.5	1.00	4.5	2.99	
8	10			1.5	1.5	.94	6.0	3.76	
9	10			1.5	1.5	.89	7.5	4.44	
10	10			1.5	1.5	.84	9.0	5.02	
11	10			1.5	1.5	.70	10.5	5.53	
12	10			1.5	1.5	.75	12.0	5.96	
13	10			1.5	1.5	.71	13.5	6.36	
14	–						15.0	6.66	
15							13.5	5.63	
16							12.0	4.72	
17							10.5	3.90	
18							9.0	3.15	
19							7.5	2.48	
20							6.0	1.87	
21							4.5	1.32	
22							3.0	.83	
23							1.5	.39	
Total		15.0	5.0	15.0	35.0	27.25	150.0	68.24	40.99

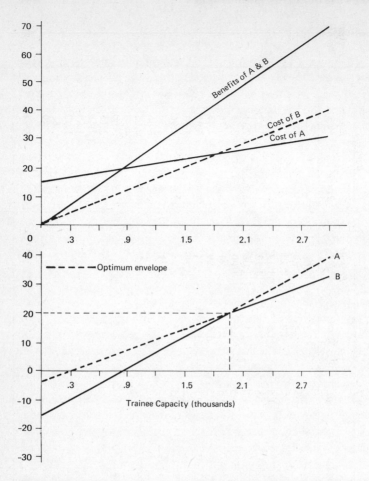

Figure 10-9. Present Worth of Alternative Systems A and B (at Six Percent Discount Rate).

crossover in the discounted data occurs at about 2,000 trainees, rather than 1,360. Both systems have a negative net worth (negative effectiveness) under 80 trainees, and System A continues to have a negative net worth up to about 750 trainees. All others things being equal, it is again possible to draw an envelope showing the best course of action. If money is worth six percent, it would not pay to invest in the program for less than eighty trainees per year. System B would maximize the returns for trainee capacity up to 2,000 and System A would maximize returns thereafter. Conversely, funds of about $22.5 million or more should be invested in System A, and funds of less than this level in System B.

Incremental Costing

In cost-effectiveness analysis, the cost analysis phase can be viewed as an application of the economic concept of marginal analysis. The analysis always must move from some base that represents the existing capability (the present state of the system) and the existing resource base. The problem is to determine how much in additional resources will be required to achieve some specified additional performance capability (the desired state of the system), or, conversely, how much additional performance capability would result from some additional expenditure. Therefore, incremental costs are the most relevant factors in cost analysis. The economic concept of marginal analysis must be distinguished from the accounting concept of associating total costs, including an allocated share of indirect expense, to an end item. Ideally, the incremental cost of a system is the difference between two total programs, one with the improved system and one without it.

Exclusion of "Sunk" Costs

In measuring incremental costs, care must be taken to exclude "sunk" costs.[g] Sunk costs, or costs which have been expended in the past, are not relevant to the question: "What will it cost in the future to acquire a future performance capability?" No matter how unfair it may seem, past costs, say for older systems, should not be included in the analysis, regardless of how much money may be involved. This is not to say that the resources acquired by past expenditures should be excluded from the analysis, however. Should sunk costs result in inheritable assets (i.e., resources which will become available only to the system under analysis), the sunk costs of those assets should be excluded. Inheritable assets can result from sunk costs on many systems, not just the ones under obvious consideration. It is for this reason that explicitly costing a total program is best because all systems can be examined and a better picture of resources available for other systems can be revealed. Conversely, all the systems competing for these assets are revealed and thus a more accurate picture of net asset requirements can be shown.

These points can be illustrated by reference to the previous hypothetical case study. It may be recalled that System A had an estimated development cost of $15 million for some complicated program learning equipment. If the study of this problem was delayed by two years, and in that period, $3 million per year

---

[g]While sunk costs should be excluded from the cost analysis, they should form a part of the total program analysis in program budgeting, i.e., in examining the program structure of an agency, past costs levels should be evaluated in terms of effectiveness, as well as the "new" costs to be incurred in seeking a more desirable level of performance.

was invested in the program to further develop this capability, then, at the time of decision, the relevant costs would be $9 million ($15 million less $6 million) assuming no change in the total program estimates. The $6 million would be a "sunk" cost and irrelevant. Looking at this question from a more realistic viewpoint, it is possible that several millions of dollars have already been spent on the development of the program learning approach. If it is assumed that these expenditures amount to $20 million, then the $15 million represents "future costs" of a development program whose total cost will be $35 million. However, only the $15 million to achieve the new capability is relevant to the cost analysis; the previously expended $20 million is not.

Dealing with Inheritable Assets

Regarding the question of inheritable assets, assume that a System C now exists and has a capability of training 1,000 displaced workers, although it is not judged to be worth further expansion. This system has five teachers per training facility and a twenty-to-one trainee-instructor ratio. While the buildings and equipment of System C could be used by System B, the capacity of System C is only 100 students per facility. System A cannot use System C facilities because new facilities are needed for the advanced equipment of System A. If it is assumed that $.3 million can be saved per training center if System B utilizes the facilities of System C, the systems costs shown in Table 10-1 can be converted to the information shown in Table 10-4.

The data on System C could be added to the diagrams in Figure 10-7, resulting in the diagram shown in Figure 10-10. Unfortunately, the investment savings for System B are not very significant, so that the break in the system costs after the tenth training center is put into operation is not sharp. It should be noted that the cost curve for System C stops at 10 because it is not planned to expand the system. The cost curve for System A is unchanged from the previous situation because it cannot inherit any resources, and the cost curve of System B breaks after unit 10 when facilities can no longer be inherited. To complete the analysis, the envelope of optimum cost to benefit for the three

Table 10-4
Alternative Program Costs (in thousands)

| Item of Cost | System A | System B | | System C |
		1st 10	Addition	(10 Centers)
Development	$15,000	$1,000		—
Investment/Center	500	100	400	—
Operations/year/Center	1,500	3,000	3,000	1,000

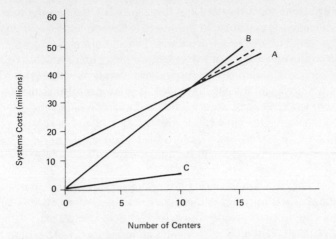

Figure 10-10. Systems Costs Versus Number of Centers for Alternative Systems A, B, and C.

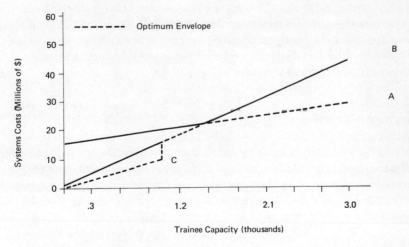

Figure 10-11. Trainee Capacity Versus System Costs for Alternative Systems A, B, and C.

systems is shown in Figure 10-11. System C is preferred for all trainee loads up to 1,000, System B from 1,000 to 1,580, and System A from 1,580 to 3,000. Conversely, for budget levels of about $16.5 million or less, System C is preferred (even though only $10 million can be spent on C); System B is preferred from $16.5 million to about $25.5 million; and System A thereafter.

Output-Oriented Resource Allocation:
A Summary

The elements of program analysis must be treated as interdependent processes. The definition of output-oriented categories of performance, specification as to levels of performance, and the development of programs to achieve these levels of performance, all build on one another. Decisions cannot be made as to the levels and types of performance unless the costs of the resources which are required for such performance are known. The methodology of program analysis requires that resources, or inputs, be explicitly related to goals, or output.

In each of these analyses, outputs — the nonpecuniary quantification of goals — can be defined as sets of policy and program variables. Alternative sets of variables, each representing a subcategory of performance, can be placed according to their relative position on the ordinate, as in Figures 10–4, –5, and –6. In some cases, finding the relative position will require trial-and-error efforts. But since prescribed levels — types and combinations of variables — represent outputs, attempts must be made to order these sets. Simple values representing the analytical matrices which describe each subcategory of performance can be placed on the ordinate and the resources which can achieve this performance capability can be identified. Through this process of trial and error and permutations, programs can be analyzed as they produce goals, i.e., input-output relationships will be understood along with the cost-level required to achieve various levels and types of performance.

Program Structure

Programs — time-phased plans for allocating resources — are exemplary and can be modified or revised according to their contribution towards the achievement of agency goals. Such programs represent the resources which are required for: (1) the determination of those levels and types of performance deemed desirable; (2) the collection of information describing program and policy variables; (3) the influence of those variables; and (4) the monitoring of those variables.

A major problem in program selection will be gaining an understanding of the interrelationships among all of the categories and subcategories of performance. Current efforts of the agency must be related to the basic programs postulated. Administrative decisions must be made which translate current operations into a general program format.

Criteria for Program Selection

In a very practical sense, it may be impossible to evaluate simultaneously a large number of alternative programs as they might affect all categories of performance. It is practical, however, to evaluate the effect of a program by defining that program with the capabilities represented in a specific proposal. Ideally, actions which achieve some goals while detracting from none are preferred. An approximation of this theoretical alternative is the conditions of Pareto optimality, i.e., conditions that exist when an action leaves some "one" better off and no "one" worse off. This criterion, however, is politically unfeasible.

Another criterion would approve decisions if the total gain is such that the "winners" could compensate the "losers." This is basically the political mechanism of "log-rolling." Here, pursuit of one goal would be made at the expense of another if it were believed that the benefits of the former more than compensated for the losses of the latter. This criterion — the Kaldor principle — has the "winners" compensating the "losers" when actions do not automatically leave some better off while leaving none worse off.

These criteria offer some rough guidelines for program selection. By estimating the shifts of the policy and program variables which result from any proposed allocation of resource, different programs or projects can be evaluated. If a new project provides the desired influence of a number of high-priority performance capabilities without changing others, a decision for selection would have a fairly high degree of rationality compared to a decision which requires a major allocation of resources with little or no perceptible effect on the performance capabilities of the agency.

Program selection also may often require changes in policy and program variables. It may be shown that the desired levels of control or influence cannot be achieved through the available alternatives of resource allocations. In such cases, either adjustments in goals are required, more resources must be obtained, or new methods for allocating current resources must be postulated.

As with the other techniques of program budgeting outlined previously, the cost-effectiveness model need not be adopted whole cloth. A number of subroutines in this model may be introduced initially into ongoing procedures of analysis. Of particular importance would be considerations developed through the more narrowly defined technique of cost-effectiveness curve analysis. As the complexity of the resource allocation problem becomes more evident, other techniques may then be adopted, depending on the availability of data and the needs and capabilities of analysis.

11

Operations Planning and Control

A high degree of inefficient organization continues to plague the programming of governmental operations. This continued inefficiency is somewhat ironic in light of general administrative objectives of economy and efficiency which have been a watchword in government since the early thirties. Readily available evidence of the above indictment, however, can be found in: (1) the number of project deadlines that are missed, often because they are unrealistic in view of the scope of work, (2) public programs which require substantial extensions to accomplish their objectives or which are dropped because they have not shown results in the anticipated time period (again the problem may be an unrealistic time schedule for accomplishment), and (3) the familiar practice of omitting work items from a project schedule in order to meet overall work deadlines.

New management techniques must be employed if public agencies are to achieve the objectives of greater effectiveness and efficiency in carrying out their ever-increasing responsibilities. The final mode of planning — operations planning and control — is most pertinent in this connection.

Application of Management Science Techniques

Management, both in the private and public sectors, is turning increasingly to newer "scientific" methods of problem-solving. Scientific methods are rarely the result of chance. They are the product of a systems approach to the definition of a problem and the development of a solution. In general terms, this method of analysis and solution can be described as follows:

Definition and clarification of current and future problems and their interrelationships, including an identification and analysis of the fundamental component elements of the problems or problem sets.

Determination of the rules governing the interrelationship and interdependencies of these elements.

Identification of parameters, boundary conditions, or constraints which determine the range of possible solutions to the totality of problems.

Determination of goals and objectives at varying levels of achievement.

Restructuring the elements of the problem into a new system through the formulation and evaluation of alternatives.

Determination of the implementation sequence for each feasible alternative.

Selection and implementation of the best alternative and the development of a predictive capacity (through the monitoring of performance feedback) to identify changing conditions that might necessitate modification in the selected course of action.

Contrary to prevalent myths about inventors and their inventions, solutions to complex problems are not merely "discovered;" they are worked out in a painstakingly systematic fashion. Management science involves the same kind of systematic approach in seeking solutions to complex administrative problems.

Two basic tools of management science are mathematics and the computer. While mathematics and computer technology can be esoteric pursuits, in management science nontechnical personnel must be able to understand and use both. A mathematically ordered system is desirable, but management must be able to use such a system without need of any special skills beyond basic arithmetic. In other words, mathematics should be limited to testing and justifying the method that is developed; implementation should required no special knowledge of mathematics. The same is true with regards to the computer. Managers should not be concerned with the details of programming and other technical aspects of electronic data-processing. Yet they must have some knowledge of the capabilities and limitations of data-processing equipment; and, whenever possible, they should take advantage of the speed and savings realized through the use of the computer.

What Is Operations Planning and Control?

Operations are the activities or jobs which must be performed to meet the objectives of a public program. Of vital importance is the sequence or order in which these activities are performed. In any program, certain activities can or must be done before others, while some activities can be carried out concurrently with others. In addition to determining the sequence of activities, project managers must establish the method, time, and cost of performing each activity. These factors constitute the basic resource requirements for carrying out public programs. Once a program or project is initiated, management of the activities involves adherence to some performance schedule. Operations planning is the determination of requirements for program resources and their necessary order of commitment in the various activities that must be performed to achieve program objectives. Operations control involves the monitoring of these activities to ensure that they adhere to a performance schedule. An important difference between operations planning and control and other methods of program management is that planning and scheduling are treated as separate but interdependent functions.

PERT/CPM: The Basis for Effective Operations Planning

Complex management demands are present whether the program involves the supervision of a research project, construction of a single home, management of a business, direction of a voyage into space, or development and maintenance of a public service program. Such techniques as PERT (Program Evaluation and Review Technique) and CPM (Critical Path Method) were developed in industry and the military in recognition of the need for better program management — for better operations planning and control. These techniques are equally applicable to the planning, monitoring, and control of any type of public program provided the following concepts are continually kept in mind: (1) planning must be geared to the operations to be performed; that is, the plan must be activity oriented; and (2) reporting can be geared to the completion (whole or part) of activities, or it can be geared to the arrival at a *milestone* in the program; however, if an event orientation is selected, then such a system can be properly established only from an activity-oriented plan.

These two points must be underlined at the outset, since the failure in application of these techniques to government programs so often arises from a failure on the part of program analysts and managers to recognize the need to express their programs in activity terms.[a]

Since PERT and CPM first appeared in the late fifties, their apparent differences have all but disappeared. In fact, features of each have been incorporated into the other. The arrow diagram, or network, is common to both methods. Differences may appear in the calculations made and in the emphasis placed on various aspects of the network. But again, the variations between the way two users employ either PERT or CPM may be greater than the actual differences between the techniques themselves. The important point is that a working model of a program is developed by creating an operations plan from which a realistic time schedule can be prepared. This is true no matter which method is used; the application of the basic approach is more important than the specific rules by which either technique is applied.

---

[a]This failure, in turn, may be traced to the inability or reluctance of public management to think in terms of strict time constraints. Although time is frequently overlooked as a public program resource, it may prove to be the most valuable of all resources and the one to be spent most wisely. Business management has long recognized that getting something done requires a concomitant specification of a time period for accomplishment if the objectives are to be met effectively. Governments have been slow to adopt this parallel requirement for public programs.

Evolution of the Network Analysis Concept

Reduced to their fundamental components, CPM and PERT are essentially more advanced forms of network analysis. The application of network theory to problems of operations planning and control is not new. Scientists and engineers have been visualizing networks and using network concepts since the earliest days of the Industrial Revolution. The present applications of network theory are modern manifestations of an evolutionary process begun many years ago.

Managers of industrial processes have used many of the terms and concepts of network analysis in their production planning work. Prior to World War II, industrial engineers developed process flowcharts and such industrial programming techniques as line-of-balance charts. These techniques are quite similar in concept to the network theory underlying PERT. Similarly, mathematicians have for years utilized a topological approach in industrial programming which parallels the network algorithm in both CPM and PERT.

Contemporary applications of networks as tools of planning and control are actually an offshoot of production scheduling sheets and control charts. These production control and planning tools — essentially bar charts — are the basis for many of the management information and control systems, such as milestone charts, that preceded the network-based system. Thus, the evolution of the network-based system can be traced back to the work of pioneers in the field of scientific management, such as Frederick Taylor and Henry Laurence Gantt. Taylor's time and motion studies are familiar to every student of industrial engineering and administration. Gantt charts (bar charts) form the basis for many modern production scheduling systems.

Origins of the Technique – Gantt Charts

Gantt charts have been widely used in industry since Henry Gantt first formulated the technique around 1900. The Gantt chart is premised on the notion that management is concerned almost entirely with the future. The task of management is to decide on policies and to take action in accordance with those policies so as to bring about a desired condition or set of conditions, i.e., to achieve certain goals and objectives. Decisions which affect the future, Gantt reasoned, must be based on a knowledge of what has happened in the past. While a record that certain events have taken place or a certain amount of work has been done is of value in making such decisions, it does not give the manager sufficient insight into the future. Gantt concluded that the manager must also know *when* those events took place or the *rate* at which work was done. In other words, his initial contribution was the recognition that the *relation of facts to time* must be made clear.

If management is to satisfactorily direct the operations under its supervision in the face of ever-increasing complexities, its decisions and its action must be based not only on carefully proved facts but also on a full appreciation of the importance of the momentum of those facts. The Gantt chart, because of its presentation of facts in their relation to time, was one of the most notable contributions to the art of management made in the first several decades of this century.

Advantages of the Gantt Chart

The use of a Gantt chart makes it necessary to have a plan of action. Recording the plan on a chart where it can be seen by others has a tendency to make it more definite and accurate. It also facilitates the assignment of clear-cut tasks to individuals. The objectives are presented clearly on the charts so that they can be understood in some detail and as a whole, not only by the executive who formulated the plan or program, but also by his subordinates.

The Gantt chart compares *what is done* with *what was done* — it keeps management advised as to the progress made in the execution of organizational plans, and if the progress is not satisfactory, it begins to uncover the reasons why. Thus, the manager's time can be used more efficiently, because each time a figure is received, he does not need to compare it with past records and decide whether it is good or bad. He has determined what figures (as to output or progress) will be satisfactory and has recorded them on the Gantt chart. The comparison of the accomplishment with the plan then becomes largely a clerical task, and the manager is left free to study the tendencies and to take action indicated by the chart. Thus, the Gantt chart was the first tool of management which permitted the application of the principle of management by exception: to focus attention of management on the deviations from the plan and to take the necessary action to bring operations back in line with the projected program, rather than to monitor each and every activity or step in the process.

The Gantt chart emphasizes reasons why performance falls short of the plan and thus attempts to fix responsibility for success or failure. Cause-and-effect relationships and their time dimensions are brought out more clearly than in previously applied techniques, thereby making it possible for the manager to foresee future happenings with a great deal more accuracy. The relative simplicity of the Gantt charting techniques — anyone with average intelligence can be trained to make these charts — is one reason why this technique continues to receive widespread application in contemporary program management.[b]

---

[b]Another important feature of the Gantt chart is its compactness. It has been estimated that the information concentrated on a single sheet or single Gantt chart would require as many as thirty-seven different charts if shown on the more traditional curve charts. There also is an element of continuity in the Gantt chart which emphasizes any break in records or any lack of knowledge as to what has taken place. Gantt charts are easy to read; records move with time across the sheet from left to right and no lines cross.

The Principle of the Gantt Chart

In the Gantt chart, a division of space represents both an amount of time and an amount of work to be done in that time. Lines drawn horizontally through that space show the relation of the amount of work actually done in that time to the amount scheduled. This feature distinguishes the Gantt chart from all other charts. Equal divisions of space on a single horizontal line represent at the same time: (1) equal time divisions; (2) varying amounts of work scheduled; and (3) varying amounts of work accomplished. Thus, the chart shows the relation of time spent to work accomplished. Furthermore, since knowledge of what has happened and when it happens results in action, the past is projected into the future. Records charted in this manner become more dynamic.

A single example may make the method clear. Assume that a work schedule for a given week is adopted as shown in Table 11-1. The variation in numbers may be the result of differences in daily work staff available for the project, travel time (if the project involves field staff), availability of equipment or supplies, or any of a number of reasons.

A sheet is ruled with equal spaces representing the days of the week, and the amount of work planned is shown on the left side of the day's space (see Figure 11-1). The numbers at the top of the chart represent: (1) daily production on the left, and (2) total production scheduled to date on the right. To record the work accomplished, a second line is drawn through the daily spaces to show a comparison between the schedule and actual accomplishment (second line in Figure 11-1). On Monday, the space represents 100 work units; only 75 were done, so a light line is drawn through 75 percent of the space. On Tuesday, 125 units were planned; 100 were completed, so a line is drawn through 80 percent of the space. On Wednesday, the 150 units scheduled were completed and therefore a line is drawn through the entire space. On Thursday, 150 units of work were scheduled and 180 were done, i.e., 120 percent of the schedule; a line is drawn therefore all the way across the space as a representation of the 100 percent and an additional line is shown through 20 percent of the space. On Friday, 150 work units were planned, but only 75 completed; a line is accordingly drawn through 50 percent of the space. The chart now gives a day-by-day comparison of the amount of work done and the amount scheduled and the relation of both schedule and accomplishment to time.

It is desirable, however, to know how the whole week's work compares with the schedule, and so the figures representing the cumulative schedule are entered to the right of the daily space. At the end of the day on Friday, for instance, the total amount of work to be accomplished up to that time was 675 units. A heavy line, therefore, is added to the chart to show a comparison between the *cumulative work done* and the *cumulative schedule* (bottom line in

Table 11–1
Weekly Work Unit Schedule

Days of Week	Work Units
Monday	100
Tuesday	125
Wednesday	150
Thursday	150
Friday	150

Figure 11–1). On Monday, the heavy line is the same length as the light line. Of the 100 work units completed on Tuesday, 25 must go to make up the shortage for Monday. The remaining are applied to Tuesday's schedule and the heavy line is drawn through 60 percent of the Tuesday space. Of the 150 work units completed on Wednesday, 50 are required to meet the schedule to Tuesday night and the remaining 100 are applied to Wednesday's schedule of 150, the line being drawn through 67 percent of the space. Of the 180 units completed on Thursday, 50 are used to meet the schedule to Wednesday night and the line representing the remaining 130 is drawn through 87.5 percent of the day's space. Of the 75 completed Friday, 20 go to meet Thursday's schedule, leaving 55 to be applied to Friday. The cumulative line, therefore, shows that by Friday night the work is two-thirds of a day behind the schedule.

The completed chart shows the relation of the schedule to time, the work completed each day in relation to both time and the schedule, and, finally, the cumulative work done and its relation to time and the schedule.

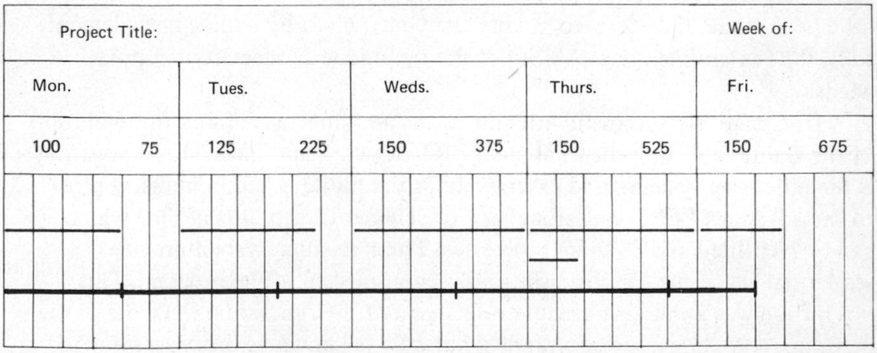

Project Title:				Week of:
Mon.	Tues.	Weds.	Thurs.	Fri.
100 75	125 225	150 375	150 525	150 675

Figure 11–1. Gantt Chart Showing Work Schedule and its Relation to Time and Accomplishment.

Shortcomings of the Original Charting Techniques

The advent of "concurrency," i.e., overlapping or interrelated activities and large-scale systems engineering projects soon revealed some fundamental weaknesses in the original Gantt bar chart as a management tool in an increasingly dynamic and changing management environment. These weaknesses include:

The inability of the chart to show interdependencies which exist between the efforts represented by the bars. This is a serious deficiency when planning a program in which various tasks are scheduled with a large degree of concurrency. Often, using only a bar chart as reference, a manager will overlook critical interdependencies between two or more tasks because conventional Gantt charts cannot display such relationships.

The inflexibility of a bar chart plotted against a calender scale, which prevents it from easily reflecting slippage or changes in plans.

The inability to reflect uncertainty or tolerances in the duration times estimated for the various activities. In contemporary management, this deficiency can be critical. Developments in technology have created projects of unprecedented size and complexity, in which primary time and costs are uncertain. This is illustrated most dramatically, of course, by modern space systems programs, which are characterized by extensive research, development, and engineering efforts, and by relatively insignificant production time in the traditional sense.

Milestone Charts: An Important Step Forward

The complex environment of modern management has tended to seriously impair the effectiveness of the Gantt chart as a management tool. Attempts have been made, therefore, to modify the Gantt chart by adding new elements to it, thus extending the capability of the technique to meet contemporary needs.

One relatively successful attempt forms an important link in the evolution of the Gantt chart into the CPM and PERT network approach: this innovation is the milestone system, used extensively in the military and in industry prior to the advent of PERT. Milestones are key elements or points in time which can be identified as a program progresses. The milestone system provides a sequential list of the various tasks to be accomplished in the program. This innovation was important because it recognized the functional elements of the program, reflecting more accurately what now is known as the *program work breakdown* or the *product indenture structure*.

The milestone system approach also increased *awareness* (if not effective display) of the interdependencies between tasks. The list of tasks and milestones are displayed on charts adjacent to a time scale. Symbols on the time scale identify the dates (or times) that each milestone is scheduled, when it is completed, if it has slipped, and so forth. The milestone system also makes it possible to accumulate this information in machine-readable form, and to code the data for various "sorts" or arrangements. Thus, data can be presented to management in various ways: by organization, by project and subproject, by performance status, and so forth.

An Example of the Milestone System

To see how the milestone approach provides a bridge between Gantt charting and CPM/PERT, assume for the sake of simplicity that there are three activities, A, B, C, which must be carried out in sequence in order to achieve some objective. The duration times (length of time to be spent on each activity) are as follows: activity A, four weeks, activity B, six weeks, and activity C, five weeks. Figure 11–2 is a milestone chart showing these three activities. This chart clearly shows how work should progress on these activities in sequence. Thus, by the end of week 8, the whole of activity A and two-thirds of activity B should be completed.

To show how work is actually progressing, a bar or line can be drawn within the uprights of the activity symbol, the length of the bar representing the amount of work completed. This gives a very simple and striking representation of work done, particularly if a number of activities are represented on the same chart.

Figure 11–3 illustrates such a chart for a project involving seven related activities. Activities A, B, and C are the same as illustrated in the previous example. The initiation of activity C, however, depends on the completion of activity D, which has a duration of eight weeks. In addition, activities F and G

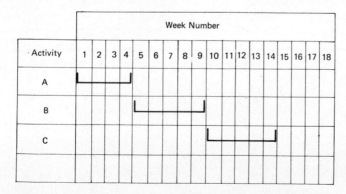

Figure 11–2. A Milestone Chart for Three Activities.

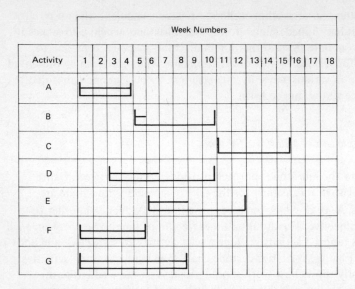

Figure 11–3. Milestone Chart Illustrating Seven Related Activities to be Undertaken over a Fifteen-Week Period.

must be undertaken and can be initiated at the outset of the project, while activity E is dependent upon the completion of activity F.

If the chart has been filled in correctly and is examined at the end of the seventh week (denoted by the two small arrows at the top and the bottom of the chart), then the following information should be readily apparent:

Activity A should be completed and in fact is
Activity B should be fifty percent completed, but in fact is only seventeen percent finished
Activity C should not be started, and, in fact, has not been
Activity D should be sixty-two percent complete, but is only fifty percent finished
Activity E should be thirty percent complete but in fact is approximately forty-three percent complete
Activity F should be and is completed
Activity G should be eighty-seven percent complete and in fact is totally completed

In short, bars to the left of the observation line represent underfulfillment, while those to the right represent overfulfillment. By the use of codes and/or symbols, the reasons for any delays can be displayed, and the whole chart can be very succinctly informative, combining both the planning and recording of progress functions. For many tasks, the modified Gantt milestone chart is unsurpassed, and its use has been very highly developed.

Difficulties with Milestone Charts

The Gantt milestone system is not without limitations; these include:

The relationships among milestones are still not clearly established. Milestones are merely listed in chronological sequence, not related in a logical sequence. Hence, all important interrelationships are still not displayed.

Full use of the computer is not achieved, although the use of data-processing equipment provides a greatly enhanced sorting and listing capability. The system does not allow for measuring the *effect* of changes and slippages, but merely improves the reporting of them.

As an example of these limitations, consider a project which is complete only when three activities, G, H, and I, are complete. Activity H cannot start until activity D is complete, and I cannot start until activities E, F, and G are complete. Activity G cannot start until D is complete, which in turn cannot start until activity B is complete. Activity E must follow activity B and activity F must follow yet another activity, A. The whole project is initiated with activities A, B, and C being started. The duration times of the various activities are shown in Table 11-2. With some effort, this project can be represented on a Gantt/Milestone chart (Figure 11-4). Such a chart, however, would not indicate that activity I necessarily depends on activities E, F, and G, or that the whole project must wait on the completion of activity G. In Figure 11-5, the same information is displayed through the use of a simple arrow

Table 11-2
Duration Times for Nine Activities

Activity	Duration (weeks)
A	16
B	20
C	30
D	15
E	10
F	15
G	3
H	16
I	12

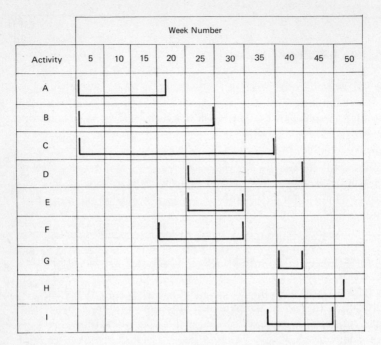

Figure 11–4. Milestone Chart for Nine Activities.

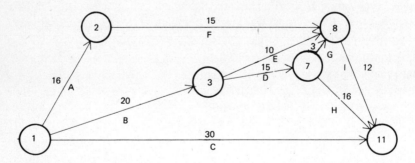

Figure 11–5. Arrow Network for Activities Shown in Milestone Chart.

network. A comparison of these two figures should illustrate the relative strengths of the arrow network in showing dependency and sequential relationships among activities.

The Line of Balance Technique

While efforts were being made in various fields to build upon the Gantt milestone system, industrial engineers began to perfect the so-called line of balance (or LOB) approach. Line of balance is a system for planning and controlling production that concentrates on the time aspects of key events required for completion of the entire project. As with other techniques, graphic displays are used to monitor the progress of the program and to illustrate where some objective or objectives are not being realized. In this manner, the graphic display allows a certain amount of management by exception and thus is quite useful.

The line of balance chart consists of three parts, generally recorded on a single display sheet. The main part of the sheet consists of a simplified network illustrating the more pertinent linkages among key elements and drawn on a time scale which reflects the overall project duration. This network represents something of a compromise between the milestone approach and the more detailed arrow network which underlies CPM and PERT.

The second part of the diagram is an overall schedule of starts and completions, generally represented by a bar graph similar to that used in early Gantt charts. The third portion of the chart shows the line of balance, which is represented by a vertical bar chart, divided into each of the component parts or activities of production. A stairstep line on this chart represents the actual line of balance. The reported completions are plotted vertically against the cumulative scale and are graphically compared with the required number of completions for each activity, shown by the line of balance. When the reported actual completions fall below the line of balance for a given activity, that activity is behind schedule, and when the actual completions go above the line of balance, the activity is ahead of schedule.

The LOB chart is a useful tool for a project manager who is not in daily contact with the project. Line of balance techniques also may be used in connection with PERT or CPM. Frequently, these latter techniques are used to plan and control a project up to the point where the first article or unit is completed (through the R & D and prototype stages). It is at this point that the uncertainty concerning time values has been minimized and project control can be shifted to the line of balance approach.

Line of balance may represent a more appropriate alternative at this point for several reasons. It can generate historical information faster, which in turn can be used in further reduction of project lead time. In general, LOB is not so involved or as detailed as PERT: it does not require the use of a computer and thus may be considerably less expensive.

From Gantt Charts to Networks

As the milestone approach was being perfected and widely applied, the network-based management system was emerging. In 1956, E. I. DuPont de Nemours undertook a thorough investigation of the extent to which a computer might be used to improve the planning, scheduling, rescheduling, and progress reporting of the company's engineering programs. A DuPont engineer, Morgan R. Walker, and a Remington-Rand computer expert, James E. Kelley, Jr., worked on the problem. Late in 1957, they ran a pilot test of a system using a unique arrow-diagram or network method. This network approach came to be known as the Critical Path Method.

In 1957, the U. S. Navy Special Projects Office (SPO), Bureau of Ordinance, established a research team composed of the members of SPO and the management consulting firm of Booz, Allen and Hamilton. The assignment of the research team was project PERT (Program Evaluation Research Task), aimed at finding a solution to what was at that time a common problem. The Special Projects Office was faced with the task of developing a program on Polaris. The Polaris project was a typical product of the times: a huge, complicated, weapon system development program, being conducted at or beyond the state of the art in many areas, with activities proceeding concurrently in hundreds of industrial and scientific organizations in different areas. What emerged was an approach to the solution of some of the fast-multiplying problems of large-scale systems projects in which technical innovation, complex logistics, and concurrent activity must be integrated: PERT (Program Evaluation and Review Technique).

PERT was employed on the Polaris program and is credited (along with a dedicated, project-oriented, management) with making it possible for the Navy to produce an operational ballistic missile-firing nuclear submarine years ahead of schedule. The actual benefits of PERT in Polaris are subject to question; a great deal of press agentry surround the PERT effort at that time. Subsequently, however, the original network concept has been adapted and extended to hundreds of management situations, where it has set a pattern for management information and control systems of the future.

By early 1961, literally hundreds of articles, reports, and papers had been published on PERT and PERT-like systems, making it perhaps the most widely publicized, highly praised, sharply criticized, and widely discussed management system ever invented. Enthusiastic proponents of the technique, eager to identify with progress, spawned a multitude of acronyms in addition to PERT. Appendix 11-A is a brief list of these techniques.

As these acronyms multiplied, responsible industrial and military leaders became increasingly concerned about standardization. Although many of these systems had minor differences, they were all network based. Various high-level efforts were mounted to minimize the differences and to develop a more or less standard system and nomenclature. This has now largely been accomplished, with PERT and CPM emerging as the standard.

Differences Between PERT and CPM

The CPM arrow-diagram network was developed from more detailed bar charts which were *job-* or *activity*-oriented. Linking jobs or activities together in a sequence of dependence, often without special identification of the connecting points, produced the arrow diagram. The environmental factors which had an important role in determining the elements of the CPM technique were: (1) well-defined projects; (2) one dominant organization; (3) relatively low levels of uncertainty; and (4) one geographical location for a project. The CPM activity-type network has been used widely in the process industries, in construction, and in single-project industrial activities.

PERT is an *event*-oriented network. It evolved from a combination of bar charts and milestone charts, on which milestones were identified as special events or particular points in time, which were of interest to management. Milestones are useful for progress evaluation; with them, it is possible to determine if a job is ahead, behind, or on schedule while it is in progress. Some of the environmental factors which affected the development of the PERT techniques were: (1) massive programs with hard-to-define objectives; (2) multiple and overlapping responsibilities divided among several organizations; (3) a high degree of time and cost uncertainty; and (4) wide geographic dispersal and complex logistics.

As both these methods were revised for improvement, the attractive features of one were soon incorporated into the other. Thus, while many of the techniques and concepts associated with CPM have been incorporated into PERT (e.g., it is possible to identify a "critical path" in the development of a PERT network), the Critical Path Method is able to stand on its own merits as a work-programming device. PERT techniques require substantially more sophistication in computer hardware and software, as well as more extensive computer programming experience. For the purposes of operations planning and control in government, therefore, CPM would seem to offer greater promise, especially in those cases where no previous programming experience is evident.[c]

---

[c]No attempt will be made in this discussion to provide a step-by-step outline of the technical procedures of the Critical Path Method. Such an outline is provided, however, in Catanese and Steiss, *Systemic Planning: Theory and Application* (Lexington, Mass.: D. C. Heath and Company, 1970), Chapter 7. Readers wishing to pursue this technique of network analysis in more detail may find a useful starting point with this description.

Network Analysis in the Public Sector

Network analysis was developed as a computer-oriented project planning, scheduling, and control technique through the use of higher mathematics. For this reason, many public officials and technicians have resisted the application of network analysis to the planning and scheduling of public programs. They insist that there are too many subjective variables and too much uncertainty in such undertakings to permit an effective application of these techniques. More time and money would be spent in their application, the critics assert, than could be justified by the improved efficiency in performance.

These arguments are fallacious by their very nature. The terms "mathematics" and "computer" do not restrict, in any way, the application of CPM and PERT to public programs. The computer is a tool; while CPM and PERT calculations are often produced by the computer, they can be figured just as well by hand. The only time a computer should be used is when speed is required for a large mass of calculations or when it is cheaper.

Mathematics of the order required to devise these techniques is not used in the application of CPM and PERT, nor is any sophisticated knowledge of mathematics required to apply these tools. Mathematics was used to develop, justify, and prove the rules associated with these techniques; these rules, in turn, require only simple arithmetic to apply. In summary, mathematics justifies the rules, and computers can speed the results. Neither is imperative, however, to the application of these operations planning and scheduling techniques in the public sector.

The frequently heard argument that techniques developed for private enterprise are not applicable directly to public activities — particularly non-product-oriented functions — also is fallacious. While it may be valid to say that many activities of government are process-oriented and therefore do not result in an end product as such, it must be recognized that these processes have (or should have) some objectives which can be analogous to a project completion. Further, a range of cost and time constraints can be associated with most governmental activities. Through effective programming, these activities, in turn, can be organized in an optimal manner so as to minimize activity cost and to utilize the constraints of time more effectively. Assuming that such a program is followed, it will also mean that the time saved through the elimination of inefficiencies will enable the staff to undertake new and varied activities without an increase in size.

The justification for the application of operations planning and programming techniques should be obvious to any progressive public manager. Decisions often commit government to major outlays of limited resources. The programs such decisions set in motion lead to a need to coordinate the myriad interrelated functions that must be considered to produce a plan and schedule. Even more important is the need to be able to incorporate changes as they occur and to know immediately the effect of change. What is required, therefore, is a dynamic planning and scheduling system which will not only produce the best possible initial plan and schedule but will be sufficiently dynamic to react to changing conditions and still maintain the best plan and schedule.

Uncertainty: The Problem of Stochastic Time Durations

The problem of uncertainty, frequently cited as a justification for not applying network analysis techniques in the public sector, is a very real problem; but it is a problem that has been faced and dealt with in the private sector with a fair degree of success. In applying network analysis, seldom will a program manager or analyst be able to predict the exact time duration of any given activity. The time estimate chosen will reflect the most likely duration, which is the most probable value (m) of an unknown distribution function (see Figure 11-6). If the variance of this distribution is small, the duration may be considered to be approximately deterministic.[d] If the variance is large, however, the duration is said to be on the verge of being stochastic (nondeterministic).[e]

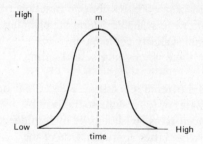

Figure 11-6. Most Probable Value (m).

The "Divide and Conquer" Technique

Detailed analysis can indicate ways to relax a stochastic case in order to provide greater validity in time estimates. For example, suppose an analyst estimates that a program or project will take one year to complete. If the probability distribution for this time estimate is assumed to have a standard

[d]A decision problem in which the choice of a set of variables can be assumed to lead invariably to a specific value of the function is called *deterministic*.
[e]A decision in a *nondeterministic* problem leads to a set of possible outcomes under conditions of uncertainty.

deviation of one month, the time estimate may be off by thirty days either way. Suppose, on the other hand, that the analyst can break the program or project into a series of twelve related tasks, each having a one-month duration with a standard deviation of two and a half days for each task duration (the total deviation remains the same — thirty days). Under these conditions, the standard deviation for the whole project can be computed by the following formula:

$$\sqrt{\sum_{i=1}^{12} \sigma_i^2} = \sqrt{12 \times 6.25} = \sqrt{75} = 8.66$$

While the initial standard deviation was one month, when the program is broken down into twelve related tasks, the new standard deviation is approximately 8.7 days. In other words, uncertainty in time estimates can be reduced by breaking larger tasks into activities with shorter time durations. The time estimates associated with these tasks are still stochastic, but to a lesser degree.

Use of the Beta Distribution

It is virtually impossible to determine exactly the distribution function and variance of given activities. Even if data were available during the planning stages (an extremely remote likelihood), their validity could be open to question and the cost of attempting to use them wholly impractical during the actual program.

Therefore, two possible alternatives are offered: (1) assume a deterministic (fictitious) case and use a single time estimate; or (2) assume some form of probability distribution function and proceed to establish a range of confidence. The original PERT development team took the latter approach. One of the goals was to estimate time requirements to achieve any given event — that is, to complete all activities ending at a particular point within the total scope of the project — together with a measure of uncertainty. This goal led to the adoption of the so-called beta distribution formula, shown below.

$$t_e = \frac{a + 4m + b}{6} = 1/3 \left(2m + \frac{a+b}{2}\right)$$

The expected time formula is based on the premise that the duration is unimodal (only one mode exists — m) and that the variance of the distribution can be estimated as roughly one-sixth of the range. In this case, the range is the difference between the most pessimistic and optimistic time estimates.

The beta distribution formula is applied under the following assumptions:

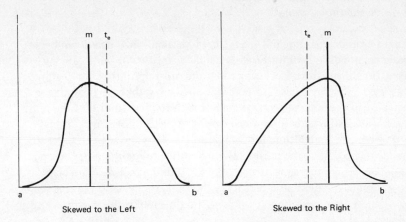

Figure 11-7. Probability Distribution Curves Resulting from Conditions of Uncertainty in Time Estimates (Curve in Figure 11-6 represents "Non-Skewed" Case).

(1) In most cases, the distribution will be asymmetrical, with the expected value falling between the most likely (mode) and the pessimistic time estimates, resulting in a distribution which is skewed to the left (see Figure 11-7).
(2) The expected value is used in its statistical sense; there is a fifty percent probability that the expected value will be exceeded by the actual duration.
(3) The beta distribution function most closely approximates these conditions.

Under the assumptions stated, the expected time can be computed by the beta distribution formula,

$$t_e = \frac{a + 4m + b}{6} .$$

The variance of t_e or $\sigma_{t_e}^2$ is given by:

$$\sigma_{t_e}^2 = \left(\frac{b - a}{6}\right)^2$$

and, therefore, the standard deviation σ_{t_e} is given by:

$$\sigma_{t_e} = \left(\frac{b - a}{6}\right)$$

Three Examples of the Application of the
Beta Distribution Formula

A clearer understanding of how the beta distribution formula can be
applied under conditions of uncertainty can be gained from the following
examples. In the first example, assume that the most optimistic time estimate
for completion of some project or task is twenty days; that the most likely
time estimate in the judgment of the analyst is thirty days; and that the most
pessimistic time estimate is forty days. Applying the formula for t_e, it may
be seen that the estimated time for completion is thirty days (i.e., 20 + 120
+ 40 divided by 6). Thus the most likely time estimate or m and the computed
time estimate, t_e, are the same, which follows from the fact that the distribution
of variance approximates a normal curve. The standard deviation in this
example is 3.33 days (i.e., the most pessimistic time minus the most optimistic
time, divided by six).

In the second example, assume that the most optimistic and most likely
time estimates remain the same (twenty days and thirty days respectively),
but that due to uncertainty surrounding the completion of certain tasks, the
most pessimistic time estimate is extended to fifty-eight days. Since these
conditions result in a distribution which is skewed to the left, the computed time
estimate, t_e, lies to the right of the most likely time (i.e., t_e is larger than m).
Applying the beta distribution formula, t_e equals thirty-three days. The standard
deviation in this case is 6.33 days.

In the final example, the most likely and pessimistic time estimates are the
same as in the first example (thirty and forty days respectively), while the most
optimistic time estimate is reduced to eight days. This results in a distribution
which is skewed to the right, with t_e being smaller than m at twenty-eight days.
The standard deviation of t_e in this case is 5.33 days (i.e., forty minus eight,
divided by six).

Relationship Between Expected Time
and Variance

As may be seen from the above three examples, expected time and variance,
though statistically related, act somewhat independently in real-world situations.
Expected duration or expected time is a statistical term that corresponds to
"average" or "mean" in common language. Variance, on the other hand, is a
measure of uncertainty; if the variance is large, there is greater uncertainty
as to the time at which an activity will be completed. If the variance is small, it
follows that the uncertainty will be small. Thus, although the t_e in the third
example is less than in the first example (twenty-eight days as compared
with thirty days), there is greater uncertainty in the third example as illustrated
by the larger variance ($\sigma^2_{t_e}$).

The variance figures for each activity can be used to develop a probability of completion by some imposed completion date which may serve as an external constraint to any given program or project. The following procedures are applied: (1) use the three time estimates for each activity to determine the single applicable value of t_e for that activity; (2) calculate Earliest Possible Occurrences (EPO) and Latest Possible Occurrences (LPO) for each event and find the critical path; (3) using the concept of variance, evaluate the risk or probability of meeting a specific schedule time, S. To fully understand this notion of risk, particular consideration must be given to the procedures outlined above.

Risk Resulting from Imposed Schedule Requirements

A schedule completion constraint is often imposed to force a solution (if a solution is possible) in order to meet completion requirements for a given project or program. In other words, an attempt is made to achieve 100 percent certainty by taking appropriate action prior to the initiation of the project.

Another school of thought favors the use of activity variance in determining the *risk* of meeting some imposed schedule deadline before any action is taken. This permits the adjustment of a schedule in order to guarantee a level of risk acceptable to management.

Risk is defined in terms of probability. The following formula can be applied to any event to determine the probability of S:

$$F_j = \frac{S_j - E_j}{\sigma E_j}$$

where S is the imposed schedule completion time at event j, E is the earliest time at which all activities are completed at event j (or the earliest possible occurrence of event j), and σ_{E_j} is the standard deviation on E. This latter concept can be expressed as follows:

$$\sigma_{E_j} = \sqrt{\begin{array}{l}\text{sum of } \sigma_{t_e}^2 \text{ values for all activities} \\ \text{from the first event to event } j \\ \text{that affect the calculation of } E \text{ at} \\ \text{event } j.\end{array}}$$

Once the value F_j is found, a table of values for the normal curve can be used to find the probability of meeting S.

Table 11–3
Time Durations for a Seven-Event Network

Event	Optimistic Time	Most Likely Time	Pessimistic Time	t_e
A	2	4	12	5
B	1	4	25	7
C	3	4	17	6
D	3	4	5	4
E	4	4	4	4
F	1	4	13	5
G	1	2	3	2

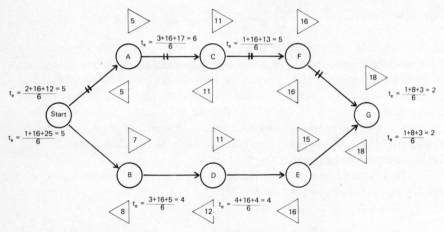

Figure 11–8. Network Diagram for Data in Table 11–3.

This procedure can best be illustrated by an example. Consider the data presented in Table 11–3 and Figure 11–8. These data represent a fairly simple network to which the procedures outlined previously have been applied to calculate the estimated times for each activity, the EPO and LPO for each activity, and the critical path (A, C, F, G).[f]

Assume that a schedule completion constraint of five weeks has been imposed at event C. Therefore, at event C, $S_c = 5$ and $E_c = 11$; that is, the EPO for event C, according to the network diagram in Figure 11–8, is eleven weeks. In order to find the probability of achieving this imposed deadline, it is necessary to find σ_{E_c}. This figure can be derived by the following computations:

---

[f]For purposes of discussion, the event or node and the activity terminating at that node will be referred to by the same alpha character.

(1) For activity A: t_e = 5, therefore σ_{t_e} = $\dfrac{12-2}{6}$ = $\dfrac{10}{6}$

(2) For activity C: t_e = 6, therefore σ_{t_e} = $\dfrac{17-3}{6}$ = $\dfrac{14}{6}$

(3) To this point: $\sigma_{E_c} = \left(\sigma_{t_e}\right)^2$ for activities A & C

$$\sigma_{E_c} = \frac{10^2}{6} + \frac{14^2}{6} = \frac{100+196}{36} = 1/6 \;\; 296 = \frac{17.205}{6} = 2.867.$$

(4) Therefore, $F_c = \dfrac{S_c - E_c}{\sigma_{E_c}} = \dfrac{5-11}{2.867} = -2.093.$

From a table of values for the standard normal distribution function, it can be determined for an entry of –2.09 that the value is 0.0183. In other words, there is less than a two percent chance of event C being completed in five time units (weeks).

Using this same approach, it also is possible to evaluate the probability or risk of missing a schedule date (based on calculations of estimated duration). To illustrate this point, assume that activity C must be completed no later than sixteen time units into the program. In this case, S_c = 16, E_c = 11, and σ_{E_c} = 2,867. Therefore:

$$F_c = \frac{16-11}{2.867} = 1.74.$$

From normal distribution tables it may be determined that a F of 1.74 has a value of 0.9591; i.e., there is a ninety-six percent chance of completing activity C by time 16.

Proceeding the same way, the probability of completing activity C in eleven weeks (i.e., where $S = E = 11$) results in an F equal to zero, which in turn yields a normal distribution value of 0.5000; there is fifty percent chance of completing activity C in eleven time units. Again, it must be reiterated that this approach to estimating probability is based on the PERT procedure, which assumes a beta distribution and an expected value equal to a fifty percent probability. In other words, by splitting the uncertainty, the manager is taking a fifty percent chance of being right; that is using t_e values will result in activity completion times that have a fifty percent probability of being met.

It should be noted that the method outlined above can be applied in reverse to determine an appropriate duration for any element in a project, given an acceptable level of risk. Thus the project manager (or decision-makers) can set an acceptable level of probability (either higher or lower than fifty percent) and can work backward to calculate an acceptable time span.

An Appraisal of the Three Time-Estimate Approach

The controversy has been raging for some time concerning the use of one time estimate or three time estimates. Arguments on both sides are imposing; however, the most important thing is not whether one or three time estimates is better, but rather the objective in using either technique. The circumstances of use are crucial, since there are not exact rules of use as such, only guidelines based primarily on common sense. Consider the possibilities:

(1) In cases where there is no uncertainty, only one time estimate should be used. For most projects and programs, prior experience will provide sufficient basis for adequate certainty in estimating. In cases where there is little or no prior experience, three time estimates may provide the desired improvement. The fundamental question is whether three time estimates will truly improve certainty.
(2) While the use of three estimates results in an apparent improvement in accuracy, the value derived for the expected duration can vary measurably, according to how the manager selects the values of most likely time in the range of optimistic to pessimistic time. Furthermore, the choice of the beta distribution, which leads to the expected duration formula, does not rest on a solid experimental or mathematical basis. Rather, it is based on the assumption that estimated times are exceeded more often than not. It is questionable whether this excess is the result of uncertainty or oversight and poor management.

The concepts of pessimistic and optimistic time are not defined as clearly as that of most likely time. Two technically qualified managers would be apt to give quite similar estimates of the most likely time required to perform an activity. However, they would probably differ considerably in their estimates of the optimistic and pessimistic times. Such differences will not only affect the resulting calculations of expected duration, but also will seriously affect the variance calculation, which leads to a wide spread in the calculated probabilities of achieving an activity completion by some required date.

The effect of using the three time estimates is to give a more pessimistic outlook than would be obtained from using only the most likely duration. In most instances, the project manager should use the best time estimate possible and then control the project in a dynamic fashion. In short, it seems somewhat farfetched to rely on the probability of meeting a certain time estimate when the variances used to calculate the probability are rather nebulously defined. What is sought is one estimate of duration to use in network calculation to find the critical path and activity boundaries. Regardless of how that one number is obtained, the real task lies in the control of the project once it is initiated.

Finding the Critical Path: An Overview as to its Application

In 1959, only a handful of people had ever heard the term "critical path." Today, thousands of people are using PERT and CPM in one way or another to plan and schedule projects and programs. In the intervening years, PERT and CPM have been used for just about every conceivable task of management.

With all the case histories to prove the tremendous power of PERT and CPM, and with all the users who point to its successful application, it is somewhat ironic that very few people really know how to apply the method properly. To most people, PERT and CPM involve nothing more than an arrow diagram and the calculation of a critical path. In truth, this is only the start; and in fact, the critical path is not necessarily the most important product of PERT/CPM analysis.

Planning, Scheduling, and Control: Complementary Phases of Operations Planning

In order to understand the implications of the above statement completely, it should be remembered that the primary purpose of applying PERT or CPM is to create both a plan and a schedule and to provide management with mechanisms for continuous control over the program's operations. In this context, a *plan* is defined as a coordinated model of the order in which all activities must be performed to complete a given program. *Scheduling* is defined as the determination of the calendar dates or times of resource utilization according to the total assigned resource capacity of the program. The scheduling function can be performed properly only after the planning is complete. In order to produce a schedule, resource availability, task or job sequence, resource requirements, and possible starting times for activities (where such a range exists) must be taken into account.

From the time a program is conceived until it is completed or significantly modified to result in a new program, management must be able to maintain control over the entire operation. The function of PERT and CPM is to provide the machinery for systematic control, so that management need be called in only when the program is off schedule or otherwise in trouble — a practice known as *management by exception*.

The concept of program control is based on three premises: (1) management is vitally concerned with coping with change; (2) the future can never be predicted exactly; consequently, estimates will always differ from reality; and (3) it is important to concentrate on responses to a given situation as soon as possible. These premises define dynamic control and further define exceptions by not defining them; that is, exceptions are the deviations or difference between what management anticipates will happen (or what is scheduled to happen) and what actually does happen. Dynamic control, then, is responding with corrective action within the appropriate time necessary to make such action useful and meaningful.

Many factors combine to provide this kind of control, but none is more important than communication. PERT and CPM are excellent tools of communication because they show graphically the interrelationships of all activities in a program and indicate clearly where responsibilities for supervision and management lie. The amount of progress reporting is thereby reduced. When a change in plan or schedule is required, there is no need to inform everyone who is charged with responsibility because the network should show clearly which activities will be affected by any change. This by itself can relieve program supervisors (field staff) of much unnecessary paperwork that only serves to keep them from their more valuable function — the continuous supervision of program activities.

From the Identification of the Critical Path to the Establishment of the Program Schedule

PERT and CPM are not scheduling techniques. While a knowledge of the critical path can be of assistance in producing a schedule, a knowledge of *only* the critical path makes it impossible to arrive at the ultimate schedule. PERT and CPM establish the criteria for scheduling, but the techniques intended for resource allocation and scheduling are MAP (Multiple Allocation Procedures) and heuristic programming.[g] Once the schedule is produced, it can be displayed on a diagram related to a time-scale base. In summary, the steps required to convert an operations plan to a program schedule are displayed in Figure 11–9.

In producing any schedule, the requirement is to level the use of resources. This is accomplished by using total float times to select the "best" starting time for each activity. Thus, in developing a schedule, the longest path in a program or project, i.e., the critical path is determined not so much by the duration of the various activities, but by the segment of resources (men, equipment, funds, etc.) which can be assigned out of the total resource capacity in order to complete each activity. For example, it may be possible to clear and develop

---

[g]For a discussion of heuristic programming see: Catanese and Steiss, *Systemic Planning*, Chapter 7.

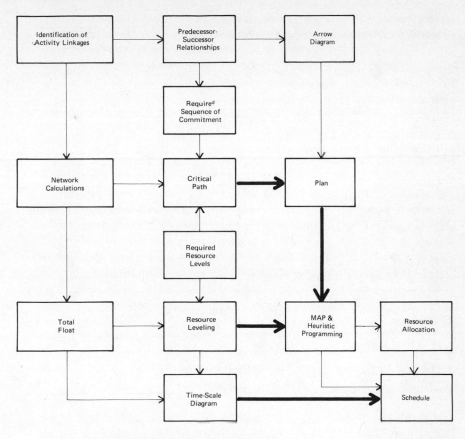

Figure 11-9. Steps in Developing a Schedule.

a park site in five weeks with five men. It also might be possible to clear and develop a park site in one week with 25 men, or in two and a half days with 50 men, or in four hours with 250 men. There is, however, an obvious fallacy in this thinking. As jamming grows, efficiency drops off, and while it may be just as efficient for five men to take five weeks as it is for ten men to take two and a half weeks, it may require fifty men to do the job in one week instead of twenty-five men, due to the drop in efficiency.

The requirement of scheduling, therefore, is to establish a duration for each activity with varying levels of resources to be utilized so that it is still within the limits of peak efficiency. This yields a minimum cost for the activity. It then is possible to take the minimum duration, with a resultant maximum use of resources, and perform the critical path calculations with the estimates of activity duration. This will give a minimum duration for the

Table 11–4
Basic Time Data for a Nine Activity Program

Activity	Duration (in weeks)	Earliest Start	Earliest Finish	Latest Start	Latest Finish	Total Float
(1,2)	2	0	2	0	2	0
(1,3)	1	0	1	5	6	5
(2,3)	4	2	6	2	6	0
(2,4)	2	2	4	8	10	6
(3,5)	5	6	11	6	11	0
(3,4)	3	6	9	7	10	1
(4,5)	1	4	5	9	10	5
(4,6)	2	4	6	10	12	6
(5,6)	3	11	14	11	14	0

Table 11–5
Optimal Schedule for Data in Table 4

Activity	Scheduled Start	Finish
(1,3)	1	2
(2,3)	2	6
(2,4)	6	8
(3,4)	8	11

program; however, it may very well result in personnel and equipment requirements which exceed the capabilities of available resources.

This situation illustrates the essence of the resource allocation problem. A plan shows the proper sequence and optimum utilization of resources for minimum durations. In order to arrive at a schedule (so that the work required to complete the program can be carried out most effectively), it is necessary to allocate available resource capacity according to the priority indicated by the plan.

The distinction between planning and scheduling can be illustrated by a simple example. Consider the program shown in Table 11-4. In order to schedule all the activities in the program, both resource needs and resource availability must be taken into account. If it is assumed that four activities — $(1, 3), (2, 3), (2, 4)$, and $(3, 4)$ — require the same man, then from among the possible schedules, the best one is as shown in Table 11-5. However, by moving the finish time of $(3, 4)$ back by one week in order to accommodate the assignment of this man to that activity, one week must be added to the program completion time and a new critical path emerges. After scheduling, activities $(1, 2), (1, 3), (2, 3), (2, 4), (3, 4), (4, 5)$, and $(5, 6)$ are on the critical path, the program completion time is fifteen weeks, and activity $(3, 5)$ — which was initially on the critical path — now has a total float of one week.

The Application of PERT and CPM: A Total Approach

Failure to proceed beyond the determination of the critical path has prevented many users from realizing the full benefits possible for PERT and CPM. Further, once the predicted schedule is determined, the program must be monitored against actual performance, and management control must be exercised at levels of supervision. Deviations from the predicted schedule should be used to revise the plan, the allocation of resources, and the overall time schedule for the program.

To gain proficiency in the preparation of arrow diagrams takes time and experience. Some proponents of PERT and CPM have suggested that three to six months of experience with such diagrams may be more valuable than intimate knowledge of the program or project to be diagrammed; that an individual with this background in arrow networks is better equipped than the individual who knows the project or program. Complete knowledge of the program may be a liability, since it often results in a tendency to produce an arrow diagram in the order in which things have been done in the past, whereas the true requirement is to find the best sequence of activities.

The objective in applying PERT or CPM to a program is to produce a plan and a schedule and to provide control during program implementation; that is, to serve as a tool in the function of program management. Finding the critical path is the first step — and a vital one — in using PERT and CPM in the management of a program.

Program Management Criteria

The three fundamental elements of a program are:

Operations: the things which must be done (activities or jobs), each with a sequential relation to all other operations; any undertaking that uses resources for some period and involves duration and cost.

Resources: the things utilized in a program, normally reduced to a common standard of cost, but including men, machines, material, money, and time.

Constraints: conditions imposed by outside factors such as completion dates, resource limits, inputs from other sources, and so forth.

If a program is to be controlled, these diverse and often contradictory elements must be coordinated into an operations plan or working model that will permit the program to be completed (or maintained) in the "best" time, at the least cost, and with the smallest degree of risk. In addition to an operations plan, there are certain operational needs to be satisfied. The plan must be dynamic; it must provide the ability to: (1) consider the costs of several alternatives in dollars and time; (2) establish criteria for resource allocation and scheduling; (3) provide criteria for evaluating the accuracy of estimates and assist in refining estimates for later use; (4) understand and evaluate the effect of change without delay; (5) revise and update the plan immediately; and (6) provide a vehicle for communication and assimilation of data. Furthermore, any operations plan which is developed will, of necessity, have certain imposed restraints of a practical nature. For instance, rapid notification of deviations between prediction and actual results must be provided so that the level of management affected may take the necessary action. Also, the available data, however inaccurate they may be, must be made to produce a better result.

Program Management and Control

Program management is best served by a real-time control system — one which makes it possible to respond to situations according to their degree of urgency. If immediate response is required, the control system should give management the means to provide it. If no action is required or if the program is self-correcting, management need not even be informed. This is management by exception as it should operate.

Control encompasses all phases of the project from conception to completion. It is a cycle which begins with setting objectives and terminates only when the last activity has been completed. Throughout each phase of the operation the system must provide management with the capacity to respond to any situation which arises. This dynamic response cycle is illustrated in Figure 11-10.

The first element in the cycle is an arrow diagram or network which shows the interrelationship of all the activities within the program. This diagram provides the base for the overall plan of operations or working model of the program. Estimates of time and cost, derived from the necessary method of operation for each activity, are added to the network. From this information, the start and completion times for activities are calculated, which in turn serve to identify the critical and noncritical activities. A third factor in this phase of the cycle involves the establishment of priorities and the identification of constraints.

Through the mechanism of CPM or PERT, operations and constraints are combined to produce a range of alternative plans reflecting various expenditures

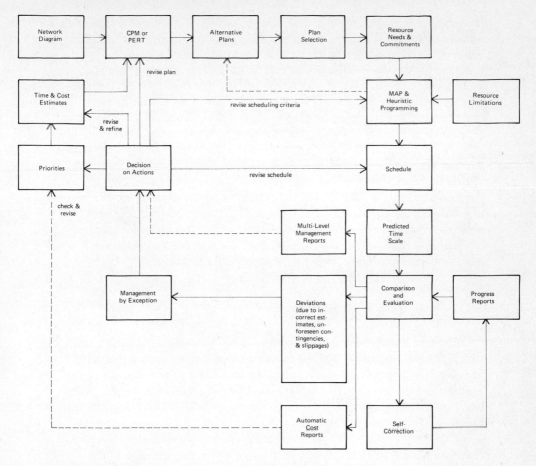

Figure 11-10. The Dynamic Cycle of Program Control: Management by Exception.

of time and resources. Thse plans may be summarized on total program cost curves indicating direct and indirect time and cost factors. When management selects one of these alternatives, resource needs and their order of commitment will be known. At this point, through the application of MAP and heuristic programming techniques, resources can be allocated to the program activities in order to formulate a schedule. If problems arise in the allocation procedure (due to resource limitations), alternative plans must be reexamined by management.

After resource limitations have been examined and MAP and heuristic programming techniques have been applied, it is possible to concentrate on the resources themselves. In fact, the system makes it possible to determine the effects of various resource levels. In a sense, therefore, the dynamic cycle can be used as a simulation device to establish: (1) the best resource level to assign to the program; and (2) the best use of resource levels in scheduling each activity in the program. This has the effect, in both planning (alternatives, logic refinement, and so on) and scheduling (resource levels needed, and the like), of providing a means of simulating the results of a decision before it is made. Hence, all program elements are coordinated into an operations plan aimed at completing the overall program in the best time at the least cost.

Once management has approved a schedule, a time-scale diagram can be produced which provides a visual simulation of the program for all levels of management. Progress reports can be posted on the diagram at regular intervals, and the actual results compared with the estimates or exceptions from the original plan. Management is thus equipped with specific knowledge of the situation and is in a position to act. There will be no need to wade through a sea of irrelevant data and information to find that everything is running smoothly.

The result is a system of planning, scheduling, and dynamic control without equal. But, in the final analysis, it is still a tool that is only as good as the managers who use it. The system cannot make decisions, but it can provide better information on which to base decisions. It does not provide a substitute for effective program supervision, but it will show where responsibilities are not being met. Best of all, it is a relatively simple technique to learn and use, one that will improve communications at all levels of the program.

Summary and Conclusions

CPM, PERT, MAP, and heuristic programming — if used properly — are powerful tools for public management. To be used, they must be understood; after that, as with any other tool, it is a question of effective application. The results, however, usually will more than justify any effort expended.

There are two significant fallacies associated with the application of management science techniques to program planning, management, and control. They are: (1) assuming that these methods will do everything; and (2) assuming that they can be of no help. These techniques, at times, are criticized as being not all that useful because they cannot prevent such problems as missed target dates established for research projects, prevent cost overruns, or avert delays due to bad weather conditions or other natural causes. The fact of the matter is that no method will ever eliminate or prevent these problems of program management. The idea is to attack problems of this sort methodically: this is the essence of good management.

To say that real use cannot be made of these methods is to ignore the many occasions on which they have been of significant assistance in programs both large and small. Any method, if it provides a better answer than another, should be used. The real problem seems to be not whether the method itself can be useful but, rather, whether people will adopt it and apply it.

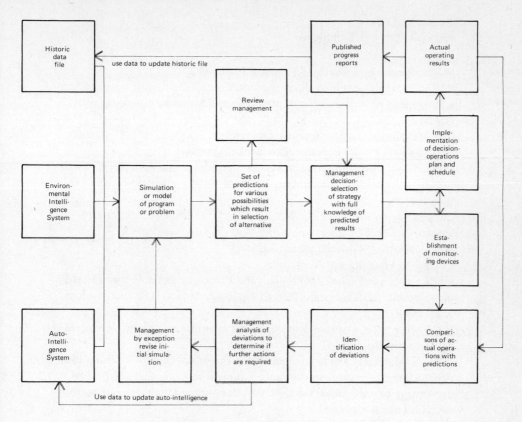

Figure 11-11. The Management System Cycle.

Management, and especially program management, has been defined as the function of judiciously allocating resources to accomplish preselected objectives according to a plan and schedule, and reacting to deviations between predicted and actual results to forestall the development of unfavorable situations. Public management requires a balance between subjective ability and objective (or scientific) method.

The complexities of government and increased demands for more effective utilization of limited public resources give rise to the need for a new breed of public management personnel. This new breed cannot afford to operate on its wits alone, as public management was able to do in the past. Whether he likes it or not, today's public manager must be willing to understand and use all the management techniques at his disposal. A new project cannot be launched, a public facility erected, or any public program successfully initiated unless there is a plan and a schedule of work — one which permits public management to exercise dynamic control throughout the program.

Appendix 11-A
Network Analysis Techniques

1. MAPS: Management Activity Planning System.
2. IMPACT: Implementation, Planning, and Control Technique (used to help management control the cost of preparing and installing computer programs).
3. CRAM: Contractual Requirements Recording, Analysis, and Management System (used for Air Force procurement projects).
4. LESS: Least Cost Estimating and Scheduling Technique (developed by IBM for use in connection with smaller computers and focusing on cost rather than time).
5. COMET: Computer Operated Management Evaluation Technique (a variation of PERT used by the Army Materiel Command).
6. ABLE: Activity Balance Line Evaluation.
7. CPA: Cost Planning and Appraisal.
8. HEPP: Hoffman Evaluation Program and Procedure (an activity-oriented planning and control system tailored especially for research and development work).
9. ICON: Integrated Control (a management information system developed by Sylvania Electronics).
10. MPACS: Management Planning and Control System (involves communication of financial and manpower data — budget versus actual — from the accounting or data collection agency to the program manager and performance functional manager).
11. PEP: Program Evaluation Procedure (the original Air Force version of PERT).
12. PAR: Project Audit Report (a modified version of PERT/Cost).
13. PLANNET: Planning Network (a scheduling technique used in the Guided Missile Range Division of Pan American World Airways).
14. PRISM: Program Reliability Information System for Management (an offshoot of PERT used in the Polaris program).
15. RAMPS: Resource Allocation and Multi-Project Scheduling (an offshoot of CPM and PERT developed by DuPont and CEIR).
16. SPERT: Schedule Performance Evaluation and Review Technique.
17. TOES: Trade-Off Evaluation System (measures cost tradeoffs).
18. TOPS: Operational PERT System.
19. TRACE: Task Reporting and Current Evaluation.
20. SKED: Computer Program for Scheduling Time and Distribution Cost.

12 The Politics of Budgeting

Strategic planning, as described in this book, is a central component in the public policy formulation process. The identification of goals and objectives and the development of alternative programs to achieve those aims are principal contributions of strategic planning in government.[a] Since plans are translated into reality through government spending, there must be a parallel interest in the budget-making process.

Aaron Wildavsky, in his introduction to *The Politics of the Budgetary Process*, has suggested that

a budget . . . may be characterized as a series of goals with price tags attached. Since funds are limited and have to be divided in one way or another, the budget becomes a mechanism for making choices among alternative expenditures. When the choices are coordinated so as to achieve desired goals, a budget may be called a plan.[1]

Having made this statement, Wildavsky attempts, by descriptive analysis, to destroy any notion that the public budget-making process reflects a comprehensive and coordinated approach.

Others have criticized current budgeting procedures as arbitrary and irrational. They have suggested that the specialized, fragmented, and piecemeal aspects of these procedures result in a lack of coordination and a neglect of important consequences. The participants in budgeting have been attacked for their focus on "special" or "vested" interests, rather than on the general public interest.

What makes Wildavsky's book unique, however, is that rather than decrying this lack of comprehensiveness as many of his contemporaries have done he asserts that current budgetary practices serve government and the public fairly well. Wildavsky suggests that those aspects which the critics propose be altered are precisely the political devices that make the public budget process work

---

[a]In discussing the role of strategic planning in public decision-making, a distinction must be made between *program planning* and *policy planning*. The basic objective of program planning is to *effect* policy by determining the specific steps necessary to put into operation and bring to fruition policy decisions that have been formulated. Policy planning, on the other hand, is designed to *affect* policy by providing the decision-makers with a range of alternative courses of action and recommendations concerning the most desirable course(s) to pursue. (See: Steiss, "The State Planning Process – A Framework for Policy Decisions," *State Government* Volume 39 (Fall, 1966), pp. 252–259.)

with an acceptable degree of rationality and self-correcting feedback. He further concludes that the more comprehensive approaches embodied in performance or program budgeting increase the problems of calculations, lead to political conflicts by decreasing agreement among participants, and, in the long run, would result in significant changes in the values realized through the political process.

Little wonder, then, that the writings of Wildavsky, Lindblom, and others, which suggest that public decisions are made incrementally and without the benefits of coordination and strategic planning, and further assert that this situation is in the best interests of the democratic process, have stirred up considerable interest in the public management and planning professions.

The Political Functions of the Budget

The literature on budgeting in the United States has been concerned largely with specific technical matters relating to procedural reforms. Unfortunately, little has been written on the relation of budgeting to the formulation of public policy in a democracy. This concern for technical development — and consequent neglect of political implications — has been due, at least partially, to the relatively short history of responsible budgeting in the United States.

One of the most radical alterations in the American system of public administration, one which has been occurring for the most part since 1920, has been in the field of budget-making, appropriation procedures, and the control of expenditures during the fiscal year. The changes have been not merely in the form of financial transactions, but have penetrated deeply into the relations between the legislative and executive branches and have greatly strengthened the position of the chief executive as the head of the administrative system.

The Historical Background of Budgeting

Ever since the House of Representatives asked Alexander Hamilton to prepare a schedule of proposed expenditures for 1790, Congress has depended on the executive branch for initiative in policy and finance. Almost immediately, Congress began to exhibit jealousy of the initiative and responsibility it had asked Hamilton to assume. One of the most heated controversies between the Federalists and the Jeffersonian Republicans was about whether Congress or the executive branch should take the initial steps in evolving fiscal programs. Time has long since settled this issue; but Congress, and other legislative bodies at lower levels of government, have never ceased to insist on their ultimate and detailed control of expenditure authorization.

Although Hamilton made significant efforts to establish a central executive budget, Jefferson's aversion to strong central government set the tone for many years. In his first Congressional address, President Jefferson supported the reassertion of power by Congress:

In our care, too, of the public contributions entrusted to our direction it would be prudent to multiply barriers against their dissipation by appropriating specific sums to every specific purpose susceptible of definition; by disallowing all applications of money varying from the appropriation or transcending it in amount; by reducing the undefined field of contingencies and thereby circumscribing discretionary powers over money . . . .[2]

In the years of Congressional government following the Civil War, it appeared that the President had little control over either the budget or the conduct of administration. The President had no institutional means of exerting influence on the amount of the budget estimates and, lacking the item veto, had no effective means of controlling the amount of funds voted by Congress. A corresponding situation prevailed in the states and in the large cities.

With only minor exceptions (particularly during wars), national budgeting in the United States from the Jeffersonian era to the early 1920s had the following characteristics:

Federal agencies submitted requests directly to the Congress; no provision was made for presidential authority to review and amend requests before submission.

Appropriations were made in great detail, thus limiting executive flexibility.

As a consequence of the detailed appropriations and a lack of central control authority, departments relied heavily on deficiency appropriations by Congress to bail out their programs from fiscal difficulties; Congress would pass one appropriation act after another, not knowing the total amounts appropriated until they had been summed by the clerks after adjournment.

Congress was interested primarily in controlling the power and discretion of the executive branch; efficiency and performance relative to longer-term objectives were secondary concerns.

In the first decade of the twentieth century, municipal reforms initiated new budget procedures and shifted budget-making responsibilitites to mayors. Shortly after, the city-manager form of government appeared and budgeting became a principal responsibility of the manager. Administrative reforms in the states moved along a similar path, signalized by the Illinois Civil Administrative Code in 1917.

Since the Taft Commission on Economy and Efficiency published its findings in 1912, central management, unification of decisions, and greater comprehensiveness have been principal aspirations in the national budgetary process. As Leonard White has observed, control of budget estimates not only provides executive fiscal coordination, but potentially powerful means for influencing agency programs and coordinating agency activities.[3] Belatedly following the recommendations of the Taft Commission, the Budget and Accounting Act of 1921 established an executive budget for the first time since Hamilton. The Act established the Bureau of the Budget to coordinate and control budget requests and the General Accounting Office to serve as a Congressional watchdog of executive spending.[4] Compared with the almost casual way that federal expenditures had been made and justified before, the 1921 act was a major step in the management and control of federal spending.

The next phase in budgetary reform grew out of the New Deal activities of the National Resources Planning Board and its successor agencies. In 1937, the President's Committee on Administrative Management, headed by Louis Brownlow, sought to integrate administrative and planning functions on a government-wide basis under the Office of the President. Program planning was to be provided through budget and personnel administration, and strategic planning affecting longer-range economic affairs was to be coordinated through the National Resources Planning Board. Unfortunately, the NRPB was allowed to die in 1943 for lack of funds.[5] Three years later, however, Congress created the Council of Economic Advisors to provide this long-range planning capacity in the federal government.

The Employment Act of 1946 (which created the Council of Economic Advisors) was a historic step in American economic and budgetary history, for Congress had realized that the federal government has a major role to play in promoting economic stability and growth. The Act directs the federal government to use "all its plans, functions, and resources . . . to promote maximum employment, production, and purchasing power."[6]

As a result of the Hoover Commission (1949), the Budget and Accounting Procedures Act of 1950 attempted to improve the efficiency with which programs were executed. Performance budgeting and more general appropriations were among the Act's significant contributions. The number and detail of appropriations — a feature of Congressional action since George Washington — were cut from a prewar figure of 2,000 to about 375 by 1955.[7]

The most recent major innovation in budgeting was the introduction of the Planning, Programming, and Budgeting System (PPBS) in the Department of Defense in 1961, and government-wide in 1965. PPBS provides techniques for the entire range of government decision-making. Yet, like most innovative techniques, PPBS has spawned controversy. On one side are pragmatic political types who abhor any attempt to systematize budgeting policy and priority decisions. On the other side are the new technocrats, true believers in the quantificatory powers of electronic data-processing equipment. Somewhere in between these extremes lies the main point: PPBS, as a tool for decision-makers, can provide better inputs to governmental planning and budgeting. This ideal is hardly incompatible with good politics or good technology.

Aspirations, Expectations, Communication, and Precedent

While it is generally recognized that the budget document represents an important executive policy statement as to how public resources are to be allocated to achieve governmental objectives, a number of other important functions served by the budget-making process can be identified. Budgets submitted by administrative agencies may represent their aspirations as well as their expectations. Thus, to the extent that these agencies outline their program objectives beyond the immediate budget period as justification for their requests, the budget and its supporting documentation can provide important insights into the overall direction of governmental activities. One of the primary objectives of program budgeting is to formalize this aspect of budget-making by requiring that definitive statements of long-term goals and objectives accompany budget requests. Anyone who has had experience in attempting to identify agency program goals and objectives can appreciate the value of such requirements, assuming that they can be enforced.

The budget also serves as an important network of communication in which information is continuously generated and fed back to participants. In this respect, the budget serves as one of the key links between the policy-makers, in their interpretation of public demands and supports (to use Easton's terms), and the administrators in carrying out technical programs. Clearly, this communication flow is a two-way street, since agencies in making their budget requests also interpret public demands and supports and so influence the choices made by elected officials.

Finally, the budget, once enacted, becomes a precedent. Once appropriations have been made in support of a particular program, it is likely that this program will continue as a recognized part of the activitites of government. As Wildavsky observes: "Having a project included in the agency's base . . . means more than just getting it in the budget for a particular year. It means establishing the expectation that the expenditure will continue. . . ."[8] New activities not explicitly outlined in an agency's mandate or subsequent executive directives are frequently initiated and "legitimized" through budget appropriations.

Political Budget Techniques

There are three types of budget at the federal level: the administrative (conventional) budget, the consolidated cash budget, and the national income accounts budget. Each of these approaches to budgeting has its strengths and weaknesses and each has potential political implications in application.

The administrative budget is intended to show the administration and control of government spending by the departments of government and the relation of expenditures to receipts. The administrative budget has two main defects: (1) the timing of budgetary transactions does not take into account the substantial time lag by which changes in tax structure or receipts are made known; and (2) it fails to show expenditures and receipts of trust and deposit funds, such as those for Social Security and highway construction.

The cash budget presents information on the flow of money between the federal government and the general public. It includes the activity of the trust funds in addition to those of the administrative budget. The cash budget was first used nationally by the President's Council of Economic Advisors. The national income accounts budget (NIA) goes even farther than the cash budget in considering the total economic picture. Taxes are recorded when they accrue rather than when they are paid.

The importance of the different budget types to the politician are significant. No one budget can give adequate information for national decision-making; equally important, no budget shows the same deficit. During the period 1958–64, for example, the administrative budget showed a total deficit of $38.8 billion, while the cash and NIA budgets showed, respectively, deficits totaling $30.8 and $17.9 billion.

The proposed budget for fiscal 1971 is a good example of political budgeting. The projected total cost was only 1.5 percent higher than the previous fiscal year's budget ($200.8 billion to $197.9 billion). This modest increase was accompanied by a psychologically important 1.3 billion dollar surplus. But both of these politically desirable prospects fade fast when their underlying assumptions are probed.

The anticipated "surplus" was dependent on increases in postal rates, delays in Civil Service pay increases, cuts in space and defense spending entailing base-closings and sizable layoffs, the successful sale of stockpiled materials, and levying of new excise taxes. But in an election year, Congress could not be expected to take full action in all these areas. At the same time, in determining the "surplus," the practice of using cash budgeting was continued as in previous administrations. Excluding the surpluses accrued in the Social Security and highway trust funds, however, resulted in a seven-billion-dollar deficit in the budget as submitted. Thus the choice of budget format has an important bearing on the political acceptance of resulting expenditure and allocation programs.

Approaches to Budgetary Theory

Most students of traditional budgeting and program budgeting would agree that the first method is generally an incremental, current-level base, fragmented approach to budgeting, while the second has the attributes of being more comprehensive and starting from a zero base. These differences between the two approaches to budgeting have been widely discussed in the literature and have

generated a great deal of research into the nature of interactions that lead to
incremental and fragmented, as opposed to comprehensive, centrally-coordinated,
decision-making.[9] Unfortunately, much of the criticism of program budgeting
and comprehensive decision-making has been directed at the political consequences, while most of the defense of these techniques has been in terms of their
economic aspects. Budgeting, of course, is both a political and an economic
mechanism and proposed changes in the budgetary process should be examined
closely for their implied economic and political consequences. At first glance,
it seems that there is no adequate political defense for program budgeting, since
none has yet been offered. The situation, however, is not really that program
budget advocates have defended it economically and are unable to defend it
politically. Rather, advocacy of program budgeting implicitly criticizes traditional
budgeting in terms of economic rationality. Defenders of traditional budgeting,
on the other hand, have been unable to respond adequately in terms of the
economic superiority of incremental budgeting. Therefore, they have shifted the
locus to the realm of politics, using the strategy that the best defense is a good
offense.

The Concept of Marginal Operations

A landmark effort to address the basic issues of politics and economics in a
democratic budget process has been made by Anthony Downs, a consultant
to The RAND Corporation and to a collection of federal commissions, agencies,
and departments. In "Why the Government Budget is Too Small in a Democracy," [10] Downs asserts that public budgets would be higher if they were
"correct." A budget is "correct" when voters have perfect knowledge and make
their decisions accordingly. But information costs (in the form of each individual's opportunity costs for perfect knowledge) are too high. Therefore,
political parties are put into office by voters who have only partial information.

Once in office, an administration tries to give the voters what they want,
according to Downs, and not what they "need" (what they would choose
if perfect knowledge were available). In a bid for economy to satisfy the wants
of the electorate, government budgets are lower than they would be with
"correct" choices by the voters. The resulting budgets are "incorrect" in that
regard.

Downs refines these ideas in his book, *An Economic Theory of Democracy*.
To understand budgeting, Downs suggests that one must first understand
governmental decision-making. Since government wishes to maximize political
support, it carries out those acts of spending which gain the most votes by
means of those acts of financing which lose the fewest votes. Expenditures are
increased until the vote gain of the marginal dollar spent equals the vote loss
of the marginal dollar financed.[11] This concept is called Marginal Operations.

This concept differs radically from the idea of social utility (marginal social returns, social welfare, and so on) as advocated by many economic theorists. Hence, the party in power must take into account not only the utility functions of voters in many resource allocations, but also the proposals of the other party. The opposition, in turn, must wait for the incumbent party to commit itself. The party in power may withhold these commitments until it finds it strategically advantageous to make them, thus denying the opposition a basis for its counter-proposals.

According to Downs, it may be assumed that a new government makes only partial alterations in the scheme of activities inherited from the preceding administration (it cannot perform an entire review of programs, etc.). When voters vote against a party, it is (usually) not a vote against government, but against the marginal actions taken by that party. It is thus a matter of Marginal Alterations which concerns the average voter and politician. No matter how great in actual terms a project or program may be changed (i.e., billions, more or less, for defense), there are rarely any major theoretical or substantive changes in approach by a new government.

Downs' concepts of Marginal Operations and Marginal Alternatives are based on his Majority Principle: government lets each potential decision be subject to a hypothetical poll and *always* chooses the alternative favored the majority. Obviously, this principle assumes that a majority is always readily identifiable.

Budget decisions under the Majority Principle are based on Marginal Alternatives.[12] A new government starts out with a base of programs started by the opposition but never really considers doing away with them. A good example of this happened when the Republicans won the presidency in the early 1950s. Very little of the Democrats' New Deal social legislation was touched by the GOP. Many political scientists maintain that the New Deal was by then "conservative." At the very least, its major elements, such as Social Security, had become popularly accepted.

Not only programs, but revenue-producing measures fit into the concept of marginal alteration of incrementalism. The new government is equally hesitant to tamper with the tax system unless public opinion – in the form of "the majority" – dictates change. Therefore, new expenditures and revenues are weighed most carefully against marginal utility for the majority of voters. Downs summarizes these concepts as follows: "Thus the pressure of competition motivates the government in the same way that it motivates private firms. . . . This pressure even causes parties to innovate so as to meet new social needs and keep technically in step with their competition."[13]

The Strategy of Policy-Matching

The budget theory offered by Downs also considers circumstances when government does not follow the Majority Principle. These circumstances are contingent on action taken by the opposition party. Thus, there are three general postures which the opposition may take on any issue: (1) when there *is* a majority, the opposition normally can best react by agreeing with the party in power (since it always responds favorably to the majority view); (2) it can attempt to form minority coalitions; and (3) when uncertainty is most widespread, the opposition can develop its strategies by "policy-matching" among alternatives to gain the most advantage from voters upset at existing government policy. In other words, *after* the government has made its choice on an issue or budget priority, the opposition attempts to agree with the government party on all other key issues, thus forcing an election campaign to consider only this one issue. Since the government had no clear majority on this issue, the opposition will surely win.

This strategy of "policy-matching" highlights the Arrow Problem (named after Kenneth J. Arrow, who first developed the theory of policy-matching strategies). Since the government cannot adopt any rational policy with such a diversity of voter preferences, the voters cannot make a rational choice either, "in the sense of selecting a stable preferred alternative."[14]

However, this logical stalemate, in the real world, does not destroy governments. Occasionally an election is determined, or at least dominated, by one issue. But the government party has a natural advantage which tends to counteract the Arrow Problem. In cases where the opposition takes position (2) or (3), the government is freed from the necessity of agreeing with the majority on every issue. The government then becomes concerned with the net effect on a voter's utility income of all its actions taken together. A government can offend more than it pleases if it later placates most of the various elements it has offended.[15] It should be obvious, however, that this possibility does not as a rule exist in a parliamentary system.[b]

Challenges to Downs' Theory: The Incrementalist Approach

The rational economic behavior model of Downs and proponents of a rational planning process (along with techniques such as program budgeting, which support the process) have been sharply challenged by public administration theorists as politically simplistic. Lindblom, in "The Science of 'Muddling Through' " [16] and in later articles and books, has developed a general theory of decision-making, including budgetary processes. Lindblom describes public decision-making as a process with little concern for goals or ends; because the objectives of public programs are so difficult to define, and consensus can rarely be achieved on the desirability of general ends/goals, the best course of action is incrementalism. Incrementalism results from competition and

---

[b]Downs is quite specific in stating that his theories apply only to the United States or a similar democratic two-party state.

produces short-range programs rather than rational, long-range policies. In this
sense, ends are quite specific and are a combination of the diverse "goals"
of different political factions. Ends (in the form of programs) serve only as
means to further ends.

Lindblom's concept of incrementalism recognizes two key human traits,
competition and inability to know the future (uncertainty). Democracies are
composed of widely differing factions that compete for the public's interests.
Even if these interests were not contradictory, man's ability to foresee the
full consequences of government action is so limited that objectives must be
approached in small, manageable steps. Lindblom also criticizes any synoptic or
comprehensive approach to decision-making on the grounds that they are not
adapted to: (1) man's limited intellectual capabilities; (2) the inadequacy
of real-world information; (3) the costliness of analysis; (4) failures to construct
a satisfactory set of criteria for evaluation, i.e., a welfare function; (5) the
closeness of fact and value in policy-making; (6) the openness of the systems
with which the decision process must deal; and (7) the diverse forms in which
policy problems arise.[17]

Wildavsky also attacks the concept of comprehensive, "rational" budgeting.
His major criticism is simply that the suggested alternatives to incrementalism
are impossible and utopian. "In appraising the budgetary process," Wildavsky
notes, "we must deal with real men in the real world for whom the best they can
get is to be preferred to the perfection they cannot achieve."[18] While program
budgeting strives to eliminate partisanship, according to Wildavsky it actually
increases conflict by stressing policy differences. When policy is highlighted,
there is ". . . an in-built tendency to an all-or-nothing, 'yes' or 'no' response to
the policy in dispute."[19] The concept suggests that the policy in dispute
". . . is indivisible, that the appropriate response is to be for or against rather
than bargaining for a little more or less."[20]

Neither Lindblom nor Wildavsky is opposed to the use of aids to calculation
in budgeting. They suggest a more scientific approach, but as the means to
"a more thoroughgoing incremental approach rather than a more comprehensive
one."[21]

Former budget director Charles L. Schultze provides a good analysis of the
political/comprehensive debate.

There are enough real value conflicts, institutional rigidities, and scarcities of
information in the way of effective government action. Let us not add a massive
additional obstacle by assuming that complex values can be effectively translated
into necessarily complex programs by nothing more than spirited debate. It may
indeed be necessary to guard against the naivete of the systems analyst who
ignores *political* constraints and believes that efficiency alone produces virtue.
But it is equally necessary to guard against the naivete of the decision maker
who ignores *resource* constraints and believes that virtue alone produces
efficiency.[22]

Basic Elements of the Incremental/Political
Approach to Budgeting

Wildavsky maintains that most practical budgeting takes place ". . . in a twilight zone between politics and efficiency." Taking his lead from the writings of Lindblom, Wildavsky asserts that, although the more comprehensive approaches called for by critics of traditional budgeting can be described, they cannot be put into practice. This is because of the limited abilities of man to make the calculations necessary to comprehend all the implications of governmental activities. As a consequence, it is necessary to rely on a series of devices, or "strategies," to reduce the burden of calculation and to maintain political stability. Principal among these devices are the concepts of "satisficing," task fragmentation and role specialization (division of labor in the separation of powers), partisan mutual adjustment, and disjointed incrementalism. Since these four concepts lie at the heart of Wildavsky's argument against more comprehensive approaches to budgeting, the theoretical origins of each must be explored in some detail in order to evaluate his conclusions.

The Concept of Satisficing

The concept of "satisficing" was first suggested by Herbert Simon in his *Models of Man* and later developed more fully in *Organizations*, with James March. According to Simon, traditional economic theory postulates an "economic man," who in the course of being "economic" is also "rational." Economic man is assumed to possess knowledge of all the relevant alternatives that he needs to make a rational decision; he is able to rank these alternatives so as to reach the highest attainable point on his preference scale. His ranking ability rests on his possession of a "utility function," which can be equated to his value system or goals and objectives. "Satisficing man," on the other hand, is moved by various motivations to search for alternatives. When he finds an alternative that is "good enough" (i.e., one that suffices), he refrains from further search (he is satisfied) and thereby conserves his time, energy, and resources.

Wildavsky applies this concept to the budget-making process by suggesting that agencies simplify their calculations by lowering their sights; instead of trying to maximize their position, budget officials are content to "satisfice." In so doing, Wildavsky contends, public officials ". . . leave the area of intrinsic merits because it does not help them make decisions and turn instead to other criteria which may not be 'rational' but which do help them." Thus, Wildavsky is suggesting that, in the main, these decisions are not made with reference to a basic set of goals.

Since the elementary components of the problem-solving process (the search and screening processes), as Simon has described them, are characterized by a great deal of "randomness," many have interpreted Simon's satisficing model as being without goal identification. According to these interpretations, satisficing man reconciles himself to the fact that his choices are bound to be made intuitively and on extrinsic rather than intrinsic bases, since most of the consequences of any choice are incomparable on any operational scale of values.

In many respects, the above is a misinterpretation of Simon's conceptual framework. Although Simon tends to be relatively indifferent to high-level goal-determining processes, he makes it clear that one can speak of an alternative as being "satisfactory" only if it meets some set of standards established before selection. The notion of formulating standards of adequacy at the outset of the search process is closely related to the concept of means-ends chains as it has been suggested by Simon.

Drawing on the theoretical formulations of Simon, March, and Cyert, Rufus Browning has suggested that a clear distinction must be made between public goals and decision rules.[23] Public goals remain stable for many years, while decision rules used to select specific policies may undergo rapid changes. Advocates of the group basis of politics have suggested that these rules are set by interest groups outside the structure of government. Lathan, for example, suggests that such groups are in a state of constant motion, and it is through this motion and its interaction that these groups generate the rules by which public policy is formulated.[24] While it must be acknowledged that certain organizations outside the framework of government play an important role in establishing public policy, the conclusion that these groups set all or even a major portion of the decision rules is not supported by empirical evidence.

Browning has suggested that the identification of public goals is important because they reveal something about how an agency rationalizes its activities to itself and also how it persuades others to support those activities. Public goals provide the parameters within which decision rules relating to more specific actions must be framed. These decision criteria are expressions of objectives — objectives which are derived from the broader public goals. By the same token, without some form of public goals, it would be difficult if not impossible to achieve interest group or clientele support for an agency's programs. Thus it may be suggested that Wildavsky's interpretation of the satisficing model has overlooked an important set of constraints on the decision-making process. The general discussion of goals and priorities in the budget-making process cannot be dispensed with merely by suggesting that budget officials "satisfice."

Fragmentation and Specialization

A second method of reducing the burden of calculations in budget-making stems from the fact that budgets are made in a piecemeal and fragmented fashion. In Wildavsky's words: "Each subcommittee, and sometimes specialists within these bodies, operates as a largely autonomous unit concerned with a limited area of the budget."[25] Wildavsky further links this concept of task fragmentation and role specialization with the notions of socialization and role expectations. "Sooner or later the participants (in the budgeting process) go through a process of socialization in the kinds of roles they are expected to play."[26] Thus, budgeting proceeds in an "environment of reciprocal expectations" that lead to self-fulfilling prophecies as the actions of each participant generate the reactions that fulfill the original expectations.[27]

This sociological interpretation is well adapted to a description of interaction among participants in any organization or system. It is, of course, inherent in many of the current empirical theories of decision-making. There is, for example, a close parallel between the various roles of the administrative agencies, the Congress, and the Bureau of the Budget, as described by Wildavsky, and the more general concept of "gatekeeping" as postulated in the writings of Easton.[28]

Wildavsky suggests that congressmen, as "guardians of the public purse," are expected to "cast a skeptical eye on the blandishments of a bureaucracy ever anxious to increase its dominion by raising appropriations." The Bureau of the Budget, on the other hand, serves an internal gatekeeping function in seeing that the various administrative agencies carry out the expressed preferences of the President. Since the various administrative agencies strive to develop support from constituent groups, they must also serve in a gatekeeping capacity, screening the demands arising from their clientele and translating these into programs which will ensure the continued support of their constituency, while at the same time keeping their programs within the bounds of established expectations. However, as David Truman has pointed out, attempting to maintain this balance among competing interests makes the gatekeeping function of the administrator most difficult.

Under the circumstances the administrator cannot be guided solely by the formal grant of power in a statute or executive order. Even recourse to legislative debates, hearings, and committee reports may not tell him what he can do, since the crucial relationships may no longer be those that the documents outline. . . . The administrator in such circumstances is in "politics" and cannot help it. Either he will find means of maintaining the strength of supporting groups, or he will have to accept some of the demands of the opposition elements.[29]

If the premise is accepted that in complex problem-solving situations there must be a high degree of role specialization and task fragmentation in order to achieve a solution, does it follow, as Wildavsky has suggested, that this will result in a reduction of central coordination? Most contemporary theorists in the study of formal organizations would agree. Thompson, for example, has noted that a proliferation of specialties results in an undermining of hierarchical authority and consequently a breakdown in centralization of decision-making.[30] Hage, in his axiomatic theory of organizations, has stated that the higher the complexity of an organization, the lower the centralization.[31]

There is some evidence, however, to suggest that while increased complexity leads to a decentralization of decisions of a procedural nature, as a counter-vening force a more highly developed system of organizational controls (formal rules and procedures) evolves, thereby limiting the area of discretion within which procedural decisions can be made. As a result of these limiting factors, it may be suggested that authority for decisions of a policy nature becomes "polycentralized." The concept of polycentralization has been suggested by Charles Perrow. Perrow postulates that in organizations in which there is a high degree of interdependence among technical and supervisory groups, multiple centers of decision-making emerge in which ". . . coordination will be through feedback — that is, considerable mutual adjustment will be made."[32]

Thompson has suggested that innovation and problem-solving is a specialist function, because new programs come from specialist organizations and educational curricula or are suggested by the interpretation of incoming data, an activity which of necessity is specialized. He concludes, however, that: "The right to approve new organizational *goals* as well as programs, is a superordinate right. However, what new goals an organization is able to undertake is a technical or specialist question, as is the question of whether specific alternatives will achieve given goals."[33]

This distinction between procedural decisions and policy decisions is frequently overlooked in studies of decision-making. Snyder has suggested that studies of decision-making should focus their inquiry on a class of actors called decision-makers on the assumption that authoritative action can be decided on and initiated by public officials, who are formally or actually responsible for decisions and who engage in the making of the decisions.[34] However, as Wildavsky has demonstrated in his description of the budget-making process and as Simon has noted in his discussion of the role of expertise, the importance of lower-order decisions cannot be discounted in limiting the range of alternatives and in shaping the contextual framework within which policy decisions are made.

This leads to a further proposition touched upon by Wildavsky, Lindblom, and others, but seldom developed to its full implications. Wildavsky describes a system which lacks overall planning and coordination at the top. He suggests, however, that within the system, at various technical levels, there is considerable mutual dependence and exchange of information. As Blau and Scott, Simpson, and others have noted, problems of coordination in bureaucratic organizations occur primarily between specialized sections whose operations are interdependent. These problems often are solved, not by communicating information up the hierarchy to a common superior and waiting for a decision to be transmitted downward, but through direct contacts among members of the groups affected.[35] It would seem reasonable to postulate, therefore, that much of the coordination lacking at the higher levels of the system may be compensated for at the technical level through contacts and multigroup memberships (i.e., the sharing of common professional affiliations).[c] If this proposition is valid, then the conclusions reached by Wildavsky and others would seem to be oversimplified, resulting from too narrow a focus as to where decisions are made or at least where alternatives are explored and the range of choices narrowed.

Administrative agencies seldom work out their problems in isolation. Legislators, clientele groups, or other organized interest groups, dissatisfied with existing policies and programs, may actively promote new ones. Or technological advances may dictate policy and program innovations. However, as Browning, Thompson, and others have suggested, the main sources of new policies for the rapidly growing administrative agency are neither local clientele demands nor shifting technology. They are the members of several professions working at technical levels within the organizational structure of government. Thus, as Greer has concluded, policy-makers may frequently be called on to legitimize decisions which have been "made" elsewhere in the system.[36]

This may seem to some an overextension of Weber's theories of the role of bureaucracy. However, if we accept Wildavsky's central argument, that some mechanism must be found in complex problem-solving situations to reduce the burden of calculation on the policy makers, then this is perhaps a valid means of achieving the coordination which otherwise must be lacking in the system.

Partisan Mutual Adjustment

This leads to the next point raised in Wildavsky's presentation. The concept of partisan mutual adjustment was formulated by Charles Lindblom after the publication of Wildavsky's study, and although the term does not appear in his work, the concept is quite evident. In undertaking his discussion of decision-making through mutual adjustment, Lindblom suggests that people can coordinate

---

[c]The importance of multiple membership in various groups as a means of achieving coordination has been discussed by a number of writers. As yet, however, a concise and empirically testable hypothesis has not been formulated. (See: Truman, *op. cit.*; Norton Long, "The Local Community as an Ecology of Games," *The American Journal of Sociology*, Volume 64 (November, 1958); William L. C. Wheaton, "Integration at the Urban Level: Political Influence and the Decision Process," in *The Integration of Political Communities*, edited by Philip E. Jacob and James V. Toscano (New York, 1964).

with each other without anyone's coordinating them, without a dominant common purpose, and without rules that fully prescribe their relations to each other. This, then, is partisan mutual adjustment.[d]

Wildavsky approaches the question of partisan mutual adjustment by suggesting that the lack of coordination in the budget-making process is a result of conflicting views about policies held by men and agencies that have independent bases of influence in society and in Congress. He concludes that the only way to secure coordination is for one side to convince, coerce, or bargain with the other. Wildavsky cites several devices or mechanisms within the budgeting process which facilitate this sort of give and take. For example, Wildavsky suggests that an item may be included in an appropriation measure for the sole purpose of providing conferees with something to give in on in the bargaining session.

Wildavsky and Lindblom conclude that partisan mutual adjustment is a plus factor inherent in the current system. Lindblom suggests that by dividing the organizational structure of government into interacting areas, one can rely on competition among agencies to achieve an optimization of decisions and actions.

What Lindblom overlooks, however, is that competing agencies not only come up with different solutions (and thus provide a greater range of alternatives from which the decision-makers can choose), but very often have different viewpoints as to what the problems really are. Rather than simplifying the decision-making process, as its advocates have suggested, the idea of providing a framework which would encourage partisan mutual adjustment, if carried to extremes, might so complicate the process as to make it impossible to arrive at workable coalitions. If these problems can be overcome by striking a balance between these extremes, incentives of competition may result in better solutions to problems since, if nothing else, they will force agencies to expand their information base in order to remain competitive. However, the danger still exists that desirable agency competition will erupt into bureaucratic conflict.

---

[d]The basic concept which Lindblom has identified is not new. Something closely akin to mutual adjustment is recognized as a fundamentally useful feature of social organization in the writings of David Truman, although Truman dismisses it as a basic means of coordination. Simon and March have discussed the role of bargaining to resolve conflict, comparing it with more analytical methods. (Simon and March, *Organizations* (New York, 1958), pp. 129ff.) Other writers in the pluralist tradition (Bentley, Latham, and Herring among others) have dealt with the question of coordination through mutual adjustment, although they have not pursued it very far. Latham, for example, suggests "What may be called public policy is actually the equilibrium reached in the group struggle at any given moment, and it represents a balance which the contending factions of groups constantly strive to weigh in their favor." (Latham, *op. cit.*, p. 48). Although game theory has not come to grips with the possibility of political coordination through mutual adjustment, heightened attention in recent years to bargaining and related phenomena and the work of Thomas Schelling (*The Strategy of Conflict* (Cambridge, Mass., 1960)) and others has increased the feasibility of the fuller exploration of this concept.

Disjointed Incrementalism

It must be concluded that all these aspects of the budget-making process, as described by Wildavsky, hinge on the validity of the concept of disjointed incrementalism. Wildavsky suggests that budgetary calculations are incremental, using a historical basis as the point of departure. Committee members view most of their work as marginal, monetary adjustments to existing programs so that the question of the ultimate desirability of most programs arises only once in a while. Decision-making in budgeting is carried on with the knowledge that few problems have to be "solved" once and for all.

Wildavsky concludes, therefore, that difficulties are overcome not so much by central coordination or planning as by attacking each manifestation in sequence in the different centers of decision-making. He also suggests that the incremental approach is evident in the rules of thumb applied in the Bureau of the Budget to estimate the relative importance of the last proposed increases. The standards of judgment applied by BOB ". . . are not based on intrinsic merit — as an ideal cost-benefit analysis might be — but on 'extrinsic' criteria such as limits beyond which Congress will not go."[37]

The concept of incrementalism has been suggested in the writings of other contemporary observers of the political scene. Simon and March, for example, talk about "programmed decisions," i.e., decisions made many times previously; when the need for a decision arises, the "program" response is applied, perhaps with only slight variations.[38] Simon and March point out, however, that when the choice is one of change versus persistence, a great deal of the process will consist of suggesting alternatives of action where none existed before, either: (1) to solve a problem for which there was no previous programmed solution, or (2) to improve an existing program even if it was satisfactory.

This leads to the question of major changes in policies or major commitments. Are such decisions made incrementally? Lindblom argues that only those policies are considered whose consequences are known incrementally and that those consequences vary only slightly from the status quo. But it must be assumed that programs are brought before decision-makers which have no precedents and which cannot be examined in terms of their incremental differences.

If the preceding discussion as to the role of the professional in narrowing the range of alternatives is valid, then it may be suggested that, while policy alternatives may be evaluated at the higher levels of the decision-making process largely on the basis of immediate consequences, in presenting those alternatives, considerable planning and coordination must go into their development. As Coleman Woodbury has suggested, this is particularly true in the area of major program commitments, such as the decision to build a major capital facility. Unlike day-to-day decisions which can be "corrected" if the

incremental approach proves wrong, investments in capital facilities have a
relatively long life and cannot be easily corrected. Much of Wildavsky's
description focuses on the annual budget-making process — on program allocations. It is, however, in the area of capital facilities programming and long-term
commitments that planning and coordination must be brought into play.

Lindblom has taken cognizance of this argument in his theory of partisan
mutual adjustment by suggesting that there is a series of built-in mechanisms
in the process which screen out undesirable or unwarranted commitments.
However, the notion of checks and balances which Lindblom suggests exist still
beg the central question as to the role of the professional — the strategic
planner in the broadest sense — in providing the alternatives from which the
choice is made.

Increased Burden of Calculations and
Political Trade-Offs

Does the application of program budgeting increase the burden of calculations — of determining both programmatic and political trade-offs — and if
so, is this a sufficient reason for not adopting the techniques of program
budgeting? Lindblom asserts: "If, as is the case, puzzles and mathematical
problems can easily be constructed that outrun human intelligence, we cannot
doubt but that many policy problems will run beyond man's intellectual
capacity, even when he extends these capacities, as he does, with analytical aids
of various kinds ranging from new words or concepts to electronic computation."[38]

Limitations of Intelligence and the Cost of
Comprehensiveness

Lindblom is correct in saying that puzzles can be constructed that outrun
human intelligence; in general, however, aids such as electronic computation
can be used to provide solutions to those puzzles when man alone cannot solve
them. The chess-playing computer that always wins is a good example of this
capacity. The main intellectual limitations of man are the binary nature of
his thought coupled with his limited memory and the slowness of his mental
processes. The computer, while also proceeding in a binary manner, can perform
calculations much faster than man and is capable of a memory many orders
of magnitude greater than man's, which in effect means that it is able to deal
with a much larger amount of information at any one time.

This is not to imply that all problems of resource allocation can be solved
by computer. The particularly complex calculations required by a comprehensive

approach to budgeting, however, need not depend on man's limited mental capacities alone when such electronic aids are available. It is still up to the human participants to determine what questions to ask and what techniques to use and then to put the information obtained by this method to use in an intelligent way. This is a feature of any budgeting process.

Lindblom again is correct about the inadequacy of real-world information, but this is a good reason for using program budgeting. There are two types of ignorance in decision-making: one based on lack of information that is unavailable for making a decision and one based on neglect of or misunderstanding of the information that is available. Program budgeting actually aids in the second process, as it may help define the consequences of certain actions by enabling men to deal with larger amounts of information than currently possible in traditional budgeting. By defining which pieces of information are unavailable, program budgeting can also clarify the degree of uncertainty associated with particular programs (which is in itself a valuable piece of information). Through use of some form of sensitivity analysis, for example, in testing various possible values for a variable on which there is no information for the differing effects on a program, another type of bad decision based on misinformation may be prevented: that of making an arbitrary assumption about or neglecting from analysis entirely a factor about which little is known with certainty. Lack of information limits comprehensiveness but does not necessarily lessen the value of a comprehensive form of analysis.

Lindblom's third point about the costliness of comprehensiveness is also valid. Program budgeting may be very costly to initiate and would perhaps not fully realize its payoffs for a number of years. However, Lindblom does not discuss other cost components in decision-making, nor does he compare them for incremental versus comprehensive budgeting. As Buchanan and Tullock have shown, [40] the total cost of a decision is a function of both the value of the external costs that decision imposes and the cost incurred in actually making the decision. The larger the number of individuals required to make a decision, the greater the decision-making cost. Therefore, it is not inconceivable that, judging by this alone, the partisan mutual adjustment method might be as costly as a comprehensive approach that required fewer decision-makers to reach agreement. Certainly if the comprehensive method better enables one to determine the external costs to be generated by various programs and to minimize those costs, it could easily be a less expensive approach in the long run despite the high cost of analysis.

The Intertwining of Value and Factual Elements

Closely related to the problems of budget calculations and the limitations on information in the resource-allocation process is the issue of the intertwining of factual and value premises in the decision-making process. Clearly this is an issue with which more comprehensive forms of budgeting will have to cope. One possible type of solution is offered by Scherer. [41] The decision-maker, Scherer suggests, should judge alternative programs by paired comparisons when objective measurements of each of their net benefits cannot be made and significant value elements are involved. Programs could be rated on a scale from most valuable to least valuable, and a scaling factor could be determined for each program.[e] The best program (subjectively) would be the one with the highest scaling factor. This method, Scherer suggests, would allow intensities of preference to be taken into account, since if the scaling factor for A minus the scaling factor for B is greater than the scaling factor for B minus the scaling factor for C, one could say that A is preferred to B more than B is preferred to C. In a group sense this is true, but inasmuch as it does not measure intensity in the individual choices, it really is not measuring the intensity with which any program is preferred to any other. If everyone is more or less indifferent as between B and C but all use the same algorithm in making the decision between them (say, alphabetical order) and thus all rank B first, then B would appear to be intensely preferred over C. Scherer says the value of this method could be tested by performing this ranking for programs which can also be measured in cost-benefit terms and testing the agreement between the two methods. This is not offered as a solution to the value-fact problem; however, it might at least be one method of getting at what values were involved in the programs and in what direction decision-makers' value orientations might tend to affect or stack the analysis.

Dealing with Open Systems and Continuous Decision Processes

Critics of program budgeting have suggested that application of this technique results in the establishment of artificial boundaries to an open system. Choosing the correct boundaries for analysis is certainly a crucial factor for a comprehensive method when dealing with open systems. To say, however, that program budgeting handles this problem in an unrealistic or artificial fashion is to condemn all forms of scientific analysis. Obviously, this is an area in which caution must be exercised and difficulties may arise. However, in all forms of analysis, a point must be established beyond which further effects need not be considered. The general magnitude of the effects of changes in

---

[e]Such a "scaling factor" might take the following form:

$$\text{Rank of X} = \frac{\text{Number of times X was chosen over other programs}}{\text{Total number of choices involving X}}$$

various variables on other related programs or environments must be estimated and a cutoff point determined at which the effects tend to be smaller than it is worth determining. This is standard scientific practice. It may, again, be difficult in some cases to determine these limits, but it is ludicrous to imply (as Lindblom does) that, in choosing between various policies for handling racial discrimination in the schools, the comprehensive budgeting process would have to consider effects on the United States' economic rivalry with the Soviet Union. Again, Lindblom is criticizing implications of absolute comprehensiveness, not comprehensive analysis itself.

Lastly, Lindblom criticizes comprehensive decision-making because problem-solving is a continuous, not a one-shot, process. Since a comprehensive systems approach to decision-making emphasizes the ongoing feedback aspects of the process, [42] this criticism is particularly weak. Considering especially the fact that traditional budget preparations are one-shot processes with little emphasis on long-term planning or continuous analysis, this criticism would hardly seem applicable to a program budgeting approach.

The Search for a Welfare Function

The assertion by Lindblom and others, that a comprehensive decision-making process is not politically adapted to construction of a satisfactory set of criteria for evaluation, i.e., a welfare function, has been left for last. Lindblom suggests that there is no way feasible to ascertain preferences on all the public policy decisions that must be taken.[43] Individuals are unable to inform themselves sufficiently on the vast range of questions associated with public decisions. Lindblom implies that this problem is particularly serious for comprehensive decision-making because of its requirement that values be clarified at the outset. He asserts that such clarification will often be impossible.

Lindblom can hardly be blamed for his uncertainty as to how and whence the values will appear for use in a comprehensive analysis. Too often the proponents of such processes have been unclear about or neglectful of this very problem. Thus, Scherer says, in reference to using cost-benefit techniques for a program like the NASA Apollo project: "I am not certain that complex and farsighted decisions of this nature can or should be made through democratic processes."[44] Apparently, such a project is to be paid for by taxes sanctioned by democratic processes, but the initial values are to be determined by some other, unexplained, method.

Two of the earliest and leading proponents of the use of cost-benefit analysis and program budgeting for governmental planning, Charles Hitch and Roland McKean, refer to this issue again and again, but they never really tell the reader how the analysts will determine how much national defense the nation ought to have. The following examples are illustrative:

There is a conflict between defense and other goods in deciding on the size of the military budget. Economizing involves deciding how much of other things to sacrifice in the interests of military strength. . . .

In general the more resources the nation devotes to national security, the less it will have for social security and vice versa. We could (as some economists have done) conceive of a "social welfare function" which we attempt to maximize by an appropriate allocation of the nation's resources among the various activities satisfying these objectives.[45]

But the "correct" combination of defense and nondefense outputs depends greatly upon the unarticulated preferences of Congress and voters.[46]

The right question is, "How much is needed for defense *more than it is needed for other purposes?*[47]

No analysis can yield solutions to the problem of choosing program sizes that would necessarily be valid for all Congressmen and voters.[48]

Hitch and McKean then briefly state that the problem of the proportion of resources to be allocated to the national security is the responsibility of the Bureau of the Budget and the appropriations committees of Congress, without explaining how the analyst obtains the correct input goals to begin with. Little wonder, therefore, that critics of comprehensive decision-making techniques have focused much of their opposition around this point, when vigorous advocates cannot state how social values or goals can be determined for initial input to the analysis. Some proponents of program budgeting tend to ignore this question completely, while others recognize the need for value inputs but take the position that the identification of such inputs is not their responsibility.

It must be acknowledged that societal goals are very elusive. It is very difficult for any group to decide what the goals of a government should be. In fact, it is somewhat undemocratic for a group to make such decisions. But this is the role of the elected officials — the chief executive and the legislators. It is the responsibility of planners and public managers, in turn, to develop sets of goals for the consideration of the decision-makers. Moreover, throughout the public planning process there should be continuous attempts to determine the goals of the society. Without such efforts, public programs may not only lack comprehensiveness, they often may be counterproductive.

Program Budgeting as a Mechanism for Social Choice

What then, if any, are the possible ways in which program budgeting could secure the necessary initial inputs of societal values? Or are Lindblom and the other critics of comprehensive approaches to budgeting correct in their assertion that the "synoptic ideal" is unworkable because too often there is no "formulatable set of governing values" or social welfare function available to the analyst or the decision-maker?

The Calculus of Consent

One approach to the aggregation of individual preferences has been advanced by Buchanan and Tullock, in their model of public choice.[49] This model begins with the individualist, rational economic man approach and is based on the assumption that the individual makes the same choice for a collective decision that he would if he were making the choice for himself alone. It is assumed that the individual always chooses in accord with his individual tastes when he is involved in collective decision-making, without regard for any other consequences. This assumption leads to the conclusion that the only type of decision which is not coercive and which will necessarily be to each individual's benefit would be a unanimous one. Since this would involve extremely high decision-making costs, the next best method for decision-making is vote-selling, since it is assumed that this will lead to projects which have the highest benefit-cost ratios. Vote-trading, e.g., logrolling, is given as the best possible decision-making process given the psychological opposition to direct vote-selling, but again, only if the decision is a unanimous one. This conception assumes, however, that people have complete information and can determine and choose which projects will produce the greatest benefits per given cost. Even in a model based on open vote-selling, one must assume that each individual has perfect information about all possible alternatives in order for the result to be an efficient, universally satisfactory one. This model does not seem to be a truly feasible one for situations in which an extremely large number of decisions of great complexity must be made, involving a high degree of uncertainty and affecting a substantial number of people. In this case, however, there is no need to consider values, since a program budgeting approach could be used to determine the most effective and efficient project or projects, all the national resources could be invested in those projects, and direct payment from the net benefits accrued could be made to obtain unanimous consent for such action. Note that this means that a decision would never be made to invest in a particular program when another program with a higher benefit-cost ratio was available, no matter how different the purposes of the two programs might be.

Arrow's Mechanism for Social Choice

A second method for identifying societal values and determining collective choice is advanced by Arrow, in his well-known mathematical study of social welfare functions.[50] Arrow asserts that an individual makes a collective choice based on his values rather than his tastes (where his values include his tastes, as well as intangibles such as perhaps egalitarian principles, concern for the public good, and so forth). In Arrow's model, the individual chooses or ranks social states in a manner consistent with his values. Of this ranking, Arrow states: "It is the ordering according to values which takes into account all the desires of the individual, including the highly important socializing desires, and which is primarily relevant for the achievement of a social maximum. The market mechanism, however, takes into account only the ordering according to tastes."[51]

A Hypothetical Case Study Applying Collective Choice Mechanisms

To illustrate the difference between the two suggested mechanisms of collective choice — ordering through tastes (Tullock and Buchanan) and ordering through values (Arrow) — the following example might be considered. Assume that a nation discovered, on the basis of a highly sophisticated cost-benefit analysis, that the single most "productive" enterprise, i.e., the one with the highest benefit-cost ratio, was that of continuous war. Using a unanimous decision rule and ordering according to tastes, the individuals who would directly benefit most from this continuous warfare would agree to pay all other individuals in the nation a compensation sum greater than they would receive under any other investment (in the form of higher wages, dividends, and so forth). The unanimous decision is reached to invest all of the nation's resources in war, and each individual uses the compensation payment or benefits they derive to satisfy all of his own personal tastes through private means.

With the value-ranking approach, such a decision would not occur; economically nonoptimal as it might be, pacifists and others would prefer to have less money available for satisfying their tastes rather than agree to such a decision. Therefore, a compromise which is less beneficial economically would have to be reached.

While this example is obviously overdrawn, it seems evident that, in describing man's behavior in the political and economic realm, a social welfare function based on an ordering of choices by values rather than by tastes alone would be a better approximation of real-world phenomena. Work done by Banfield and Wilson, for example, has indicated that upper-middle-class groups will often vote for construction of welfare facilities, such as hospitals, clinics, orphanages, and so forth, even though they will not benefit from such facilities, while bearing the tax burden.[52] Such behavior cannot be explained by ordering by tastes alone.

Ordering Alternative Social States

Arrow chose to take values as inputs to his model, and accordingly was forced to search for some method whereby individual values can be summed and translated into societal values. Of particular concern in his formulation is the question of majority choice.

Arrow defines a function or rule which would aggregate group preferences in a satisfactory, socially maximizing way by the following constraints: (1) a true social ordering can be determined for a wide range of individual orderings; (2) there should be a positive correlation between direction of change in individual and social values; (3) the choices to be made for any given environment should be independent of irrelevant alternatives (i.e., those outside that environment); (4) the choice function should not be imposed; and (5) the choice function should not be dictatorial. Any function or rule satisfying these criteria or constraints Arrow calls a social welfare function, which he defines as "a process or rule which, for each set of individual ordering . . . for alternative social states . . . states a corresponding social ordering of alternative social states."[53] In other words, a social welfare function, in ordering alternative social states, must show correspondence between individual orderings and collective (social) orderings.

Arrow admits that his constraints constitute value judgments; however, conditions (4) and (5) certainly would be acceptable and reasonable within the framework of democratic government. Conditions (1), (2), and (3) essentially require that, for a process to be a social welfare function, it must be rational (where rationality includes the properties of connectedness and transivity). There has been considerable disagreement over Arrow's use of these requirements of rationality in collective decision-making.[54] However, Arrow merely requires consistency as an indicator of rationality. His meaning of rational choice is not to be construed as a psychological attribute possessed by individuals. For collective decision-making to be rational in Arrow's terms it must not lead to a choice of A over B when, if relying on majority rule, a majority favors B over A. This requirement of rationality has been criticized, but as a normative element most individuals would accept it as reasonable. Arrow then demonstrates that if no further assumptions can be made about admissible individual orderings of values, then there is no rule which is independent of irrelevant alternatives which is also not either imposed or dictatorial.

Summary and Conclusions

Perhaps the most significant flaw in the concept of incrementalism, as formulated by Lindblom and illustrated by Wildavsky, is that it fails to consider all of the "incremental" alternatives between the existing system and the strawman extreme of central authority for coordination. For example, Arthur Smithies, whose arguments for comprehensiveness in the budget-making process are attacked by Lindblom and Wildavsky, does *not* equate comprehensiveness and coordination with the concentration of authority in one individual or small group of individuals. In setting this interpretation as the alternative to disjointed incrementalism and partisan mutual adjustment, Lindblom and his followers have oversimplified the problem and have thus stacked the argument in their favor. What remains is to more fully explore the range of alternatives which lie between these two extremes.

In so doing, it will be necessary to take fuller cognizance of the role of the professional in the public decision-making process. If professionals dominate policy initiation by agencies and agency initiatives dominate government policies, as some writers have suggested, then a theory of democratic policy-making, either descriptive or normative, must go beyond an emphasis on elections and the participants in them or the role of interest groups, and at the same time must delve more deeply into the decision-making process beyond the more visible level at which decisions are legitimized.

As a point of departure in the search for a social choice mechanism applicable to the processes of program budgeting, the discussion has focused on the formulations of Kenneth Arrow. Arrow reaches his conclusions through the use of carefully constructed methods of logic; if one accepts his initial criteria for a social welfare function, then his results must be accepted. Thus, it is suggested that Arrow's model of social choice offers a more solid foundation for public decision-making than the incremental model of Lindblom and Wildavsky.

Arrow's conclusions are that the only way to obtain a social welfare function is through the development of further assumptions about individual orderings. Only if the limits of admissible sets of orderings can somehow be defined can one hope to find a function which will satisfy his criteria. As Arrow states the problem:

... it could be held that, since ultimate ends arise out of biological and cultural needs, they are, in part at least, objective. Thus, orderings of social ends, while not identical from individual to individual, are likely to be more similar than individual preference scales for social decisions. It may be that the biological and cultural basis of ultimate ends limits preferences about them sufficiently so that a social welfare function can be formed; then the social ordering of social decisions should be based on the social ordering of social ends plus the use of scientific and statistical methods to limit the amount of ignorance passing from decisions to ends and to limit the effects of the remaining ignorance.[55]

What Arrow has suggested is, that differences in opinion as to which social decisions should be made (i.e., which programs should be followed, to what extent, and so forth) have two components: (1) different orderings of desired social or ultimate ends; and (2) differing opinions about the best way to achieve those ends. If man is limited culturally and biologically in his choice to some definable subset of all possible ultimate ends, and if the effects of disagreement over the best ways to achieve those ends due to ignorance could be eliminated from the social ordering process, then an adequate social welfare function could be found.

An inescapable conclusion, in fact, is that program budgeting can go a long way in providing this second component of a social welfare function. Lindblom's point as to the lack of information available concerning values for distinct social decisions loses its force. If information about orderings of ultimate ends can be obtained, then they can be used again and again in the analysis of each alternative social decision. The social ordering which results would then be compatible with societal goals and the most effective ways of achieving those goals. What would be eliminated by this approach are the false orderings of collective preferences arising from incorrect perceptions of how desired ends can be obtained.

It would now be easy to say that all the analyst must do is conduct a national survey (total or sample) to determine societal values and the ordering of those values (no small task in itself) in order to obtain a social welfare function. If, however, the political structure of our society is examined, a further problem arises.

A comparison of the executive and legislative branches of democratically structured governments at all levels reveals that the people who represent a majority for establishing societal values in one branch do not necessarily represent a majority in the other.[f] Suppose the President were to poll the nation on national values and ordering of goals (in, say, pairwise combinations). In order to obtain an ordering that he would want to use as a planning input for budget decisions, he would want to obtain a clear fifty percent plus one (at least) support for such an ordering. If, however, each Congressman were to conduct such a poll and then the House were to hold a vote by majority rule on a choice of orderings, with every Congressman voting as a majority of his constituents had expressed its choice, an agreement on an ordering could be obtained with only a little over twenty-five percent of the population actually supporting this particular configuration. The voting pattern of the Senate is even less inclusive, since all states have two Senators regardless of population. Thus, as Dahl has shown, [56] in 1950, a measure could have been approved in the Senate by a coalition of Senators from twenty-five states (plus one today)

---

[f]Assume in the following example that the chief executive is elected directly.

containing less than twenty-three percent of the population. That is, slightly more than eleven percent of the population would have been sufficient, theoretically, to ratify a particular ordering of societal values in the Senate with all Senators present and voting. If Congressmen and Senators are most concerned with intense minorities in their constituencies or with the group which can be identi- fied as a majority of the politically active (those who vote, etc.), then values sanctioned by a majority nationally would not necessarily be agreed to by Congress. Actually this problem seems less severe as the society becomes more urbanized and has an increasing uniform mass culture. Recent court decisions removing further inequities in terms of differing worths of a man's vote in rural, suburban, and urban areas will also tend to be a countervailing trend.

Nevertheless, this discrepancy in electorate does pose a problem for those responsible for strategic planning. An ordering of ultimate-ends values could be agreed upon by a majority of the national electorate and used as input to the budgeting process, only to be rejected outright later, when the budget was being reviewed in Congress. If Arrow is correct in his assumptions about cultural and biological limits to admissible orderings, then it is conceivable that this problem might not be as serious as the worst case suggests. However, a wise President might wish to break down any information gathered on value order- ings by districts and by states and then test for agreement with the overall results. If the same ranking of priorities were obtained, he might well want to release those results to increase his chances of securing Congressional approval for his budget. If they did not coincide, or if the Chief Executive had his own ranking which did not agree with any of the others, then an unresolvable problem would exist.

Obviously, this type of value input could be applied to good advantage in smaller communities or regions. The techniques outlined by Arrow in his social choice mechanism would provide a complementary approach to the goals matrix approach discussed in connection with the processes of strategic plan- ning (Chapter 9). At the national level, a determination of social orderings would be a fascinating but extremely complex and expensive undertaking. If performed, however, a program budgeting system could then be used to provide a good approximation to a social welfare function.

In this final chapter, the politics of budgeting has been dealt with in a manner unlike the more traditional discussions of the behind-the-scenes political tradeoffs and compromises which have become an accepted part of budget-making. Such discussions are available in other writings, [57] and have not been repeated here. Some of the preceding discussion may seem somewhat esoteric and not relevant to the practical world of politics. However, taken in the total context of the duties and responsibilities of public manage- ment in the decision-making and resource-allocation processes of government, the significance of these points should become quite obvious. Greater rationality in the processes of government must begin with a direct frontal attack on the problems and issues raised in this final chapter.

Notes

Chapter 1 Systems Techniques in Public Management

1. Olaf Helmer, "Social Technology," RAND Paper P-3063, presented at the Futuribles Conference, Paris (April, 1965).
2. A. D. Hall and R. E. Hagen, "Definition of System," in *Organizations: Systems, Control and Adaptation*, Volume II, edited by Joseph A. Litterer (New York, 1969), p. 31.
3. Litterer, op. cit., pp. 4–6.
4. Ibid., p. xi.
5. Charles J. Hitch, in *Analysis for Military Decisions*, edited E. C. Quade (Chicago, 1964), p. 23.
6. Peter F. Drucker, "The Effective Decision," *Harvard Business Review*, Volume 45, Number 1 (1967), p. 92.
7. Peter F. Drucker, *The Practice of Management* (New York, 1954), p. 353.
8. Anatol Rapoport, "What Is Information?" *ETC: A Review of General Semantics*, Volume 10 (Summer, 1953), p. 252.
9. Robert S. Lynd, *Knowledge for What?* (Princeton, 1967), p. 114.
10. Bernard H. Rudwick, *Systems Analysis for Effective Planning* (New York, 1969), p. 28.
11. Cyril C. Herrmann, "Systems Approach to City Planning," *Harvard Business Review*, Volume 44, Number 1 (1966), p. 73.
12. Henry Maier, "The Troubled City," in *The Challenge to Systems Analysis: Public Policy and Social Change*, edited by Grace J. Kelleher (New York, 1970), p. 57.
13. Simon Ramo, *Cure for Chaos* (New York, 1969), p. 109.
14. Anthony J. Catanese and Alan Walter Steiss, *Systemic Planning: Theory and Application* (Lexington, Mass., 1970).

Chapter 2 The Nature of Decision-Making

1. Robert M. MacIver, *Social Causation* (Boston, 1942), p. 246.
2. Bruno Leoni, "The Meaning of 'Political' in Political Decisions," in *The Making of Decisions*, edited by William J. Gore and J. W. Dyson (New York, 1964), p. 95.
3. Edwin O. Stene, "An Approach to a Science of Administration," *American Political Science Review*, Volume 34 (December, 1940), p. 1120.
4. Robert Tannenbaum, "Managerial Decision-Making," *Journal of Business*, Volume 23 (January, 1950), p. 23.
5. Herbert A. Simon, *Administrative Behavior* (New York, 1947), p. 4.
6. Leoni, op. cit., p. 95.
7. George Katona, *Psychological Analysis of Economic Behavior*, 1st edition (New York, 1951), p. 49.

8. Chester I. Barnard, *The Functions of the Executive* (Cambridge, Mass., 1938), p. 185.
9. For a further discussion of these concepts, see: Adrian M. McDonough, *Information Economics and Management Systems* (New York, 1963).
10. R. H. Coase, "The Nature of the Firm," *Economica*, Volume 4 (1937), pp. 386–405.
11. Herbert A. Simon, "A Behavioral Model of Rational Choice," *Quarterly Journal of Economics*, Volume 69 (1955), pp. 99–118.
12. G. L. S. Shackle, *Expectations in Economics* (Cambridge, Mass., 1949).
13. Herbert A. Simon, *Models of Man* (New York, 1957), chapters 10, 14, 16; Herbert A. Simon and James G. March, *Organizations* (New York, 1958), esp. pp. 140–141, 163, 175; and Herbert A. Simon, "Theories of Decision-Making in Economics and Behavioral Science," *American Economic Review*, Volume 49, Number 2 (June, 1959), pp. 253–283.
14. Aaron Wildavsky, *The Politics of the Budgetary Process* (Boston, 1964), p. 43.
15. Irwin D. J. Bross, *Design for Decision* (New York, 1953), p. 263.
16. James Buchanan, "Individual Choices in Voting and in the Market," *Journal of Political Economics* (1954).
17. Ibid., p. 334.
18. Kenneth Arrow, *Social Choice and Individual Values* (New York, 1951).
19. Leoni, op. cit., pp. 104, 105–106.
20. David Braybrooke and Charles E. Lindblom, *A Strategy of Decision: Policy Evaluation as a Social Process* (New York, 1963); Charles E. Lindblom, *The Intelligence of Democracy: Decision Making Through Mutual Adjustment* (New York, 1965).
21. Harold D. Lasswell, "The Policy Orientation," in *The Policy Sciences: Recent Developments in Scope and Method*, edited by Daniel Lerner and Harold D. Lasswell (Stanford, 1951), p. 5.
22. Ibid., p. 8.
23. Philip E. Jacob and James J. Flink, in "Supplement" to *The American Behavioral Scientist*, Volume 5 (May, 1962), p. 8.
24. Abraham Kaplan, "Some Limitations on Rationality," *Nomos VII: Rational Decision*, edited by Carl J. Friedrich (New York, 1964), pp. 56–57.
25. Robert C. Angell, as cited in Jacob and Flink, op. cit., p. 20.
26. Lasswell, op. cit., pp. 9–10.
27. Harold D. Lasswell and Abraham Kaplan, *Power and Society* (New Haven, 1950), p. 16.
28. Jacob and Flink, op. cit., p. 22.
29. Clyde Kluckholm, "Values and Value-Orientation in Theory of Action," in *Toward a General Theory of Action*, edited by Talcott Parsons and Edward Shils (Cambridge, Mass., 1951). p. 394.
30. See: Edward C. Banfield, "Ends and Means in Planning," in *Concepts and Issues in Administrative Behavior*, edited by Sidney Mailick and Edward H. Van Ness (Englewood Cliffs, 1962), pp. 70–80; Lawrence D. Mann, "Studies in Community Decision-Making," *Journal of the American Institute of Planners*, Volume 30 (February, 1964), pp. 58–65; Alan

Altshuler, *The City Planning Process: A Political Analysis* (Ithaca, 1965); Edward C. Banfield and James Q. Wilson, *City Politics* (Cambridge, Mass., 1965).

31. John Friedmann, "Regional Development in Post-Industrial Society," *Journal of the American Institute of Planners*, Volume 30 (May, 1964), pp. 84–90.

32. Robert T. Daland and John A. Parker, "Roles of the Planner in Urban Development," in *Urban Growth Dynamics in a Regional Cluster of Cities*, edited by F. Stuart Chapin, Jr. and Shirley F. Weiss (New York, 1962), p. 207.

33. Simon and March, op. cit., p. 177.

34. Jay Jackson, "The Normative Regulation of Authoritative Behavior," in *The Making of Decisions: Reader in Administrative Behavior*, edited by William J. Gore and J. W. Dyson (New York, 1964), pp. 213–241.

35. William J. Gore, *Administrative Decision-Making: A Heuristic Model* (New York, 1964), p. 142; emphasis in the original.

36. Simon and March, op. cit., p. 184.

37. W. Ross Ashby, *An Introduction to Cybernetics* (New York: 1963), p. 207.

Chapter 3 Who Makes Public Policies and Decisions?

1. Harold D. Lasswell, *The Decision Process: Seven Categories of Functional Analysis* (College Park, Maryland, 1956).

2. Philip E. Jacob and James J. Flink, in Supplement to *The American Behavioral Scientist*, Volume 5 (May 1962), p. 8.

3. Albert Lepawsky, *Administration: The Art and Science of Organization and Management* (New York, 1949), p. 47.

4. Frank J. Goodnow, *Politics and Administration* (New York, 1914), p. 22.

5. W. F. Willoughby, *Principles of Public Administration* (Washington, D. C., 1927), p. 1.

6. Dwight Waldo, *The Study of Public Administration* (Garden City, 1954), p. 39.

7. Luther Gulick and L. Urwick, editors, *Papers on the Science of Administration* (New York, 1937).

8. See Gulick's essay, "Science, Values and Public Administration," (Gulick and Urwick, op. cit.) for the classic, orthodox statement on the principle of efficiency.

9. Waldo, op. cit., p. 47.

10. F. J. Roethlisberger and W. J. Dickson, *Management and the Worker* (Cambridge, Mass., 1939).

11. Paul H. Appleby, *Policy and Administration* (University, Alabama, 1949), p. 10.

12. Ibid., p. 76.

13. Norton E. Long, *The Polity* (Chicago, 1962), p. 78.

14. Wallace S. Sayre, "Premises of Public Administration," *Public Administration Review*, Volume 17 (Spring, 1958), pp. 102–105.

15. Martin Landau, "The Concept of Decision-making in the 'Field' of Public Administration," in *Concepts and Issues in Administrative Behavior*, edited by Sidney Mailick and Edward H. Van Ness (Englewood Cliffs, 1962), p. 17.

16. Alvin Brown, *Organization* (New York, 1945), p. 88.

17. Wallace S. Sayre, "Trends of a Decade in Administrative Values," *Public Administrative Review*, Volume 11 (Winter, 1951), p. 5.

18. Herbert A. Simon, *Administrative Behavior* (New York, 1957), Chapter 3.

19. Simon, op. cit., p. 53.

20. Robert A. Walker, *The Planning Function in Urban Government* (Chicago, 1941).

21. John C. Dyckman, "What Makes Planners Plan?" *Journal of the American Institute of Planners*, Volume 27 (May, 1961).

22. Francine F. Rabinovitz, "Politics, Personality, and Planning," *Public Administration Review*, Volume 27 (March, 1967), p. 19.

23. Dyckman, op. cit., p. 165.

24. Long, op. cit., p. 193.

25. Ibid., p. 192.

26. Ibid., p. 194.

27. C. Easton Rothwell, "Foreword" to *The Policy Sciences – Recent Developments in Scope and Method*, edited by Daniel Lerner and Harold D. Lasswell (Stanford, 1951), p. ix.

28. Francine F. Rabinovitz and J. Stanley Pottinger, "Organization for Local Planning: The Attitudes of Directors," *Journal of the American Institute of Planners*, Volume 33 (January, 1967), pp. 27–32.

29. James E. Lee, "The Role of the Planner in the Present: A Problem in Identification," *Journal of the American Institute of Planners*, Volume 24 (1958), p. 155.

30. Peter H. Rossi, "Community Decision Making," in *Approaches to the Study of Politics*, edited by Roland Young (Evanston, 1958), p. 364.

31. Lawrence D. Mann, "Studies in Community Decision-Making," *Journal of the American Institute of Planners*, Volume 30, Number 1 (1964), pp. 58–65.

32. Scott Greer, "Mellon Lecture Series," Department of Urban and Regional Planning, The University of Wisconsin, February, 1966.

33. Floyd Hunter, *Community Power Structure* (New York, 1963), p. 63.

34. Robert A. Dahl, *Who Governs? Democracy and Power in an American City*, (New Haven, 1961).

35. Wallace S. Sayre and Herbert Kaufman, *Governing New York City* (New York, 1960).

36. Edward C. Banfield, *Political Influence* (New York, 1961); *Urban Politics* (New York, 1961).

37. Norton E. Long, "The Local Community as an Ecology of Games," *American Journal of Sociology*, Volume 44 (1958), pp. 251–261.

38. William L. C. Wheaton, "Public and Private Agents of Change in Urban Development," in *Urban Expansion: Problems and Needs*, Papers presented at Administrator's Spring Conference, Housing and Home Finance Agency, Washington, D. C., 1963.

39. Roscoe C. Martin, et al., *Decision in Syracuse: Metropolitan Action* (New York, 1961), p. 318.
40. Dahl, op. cit., p. 214; emphasis in the original.

Chapter 4 Authority Relations in the Decision-Making Process

1. John M. Pfiffner and Robert V. Presthus, *Public Administration* (New York, 1953), p. 50.
2. Marshall E. Dimock and Gladys O. Dimock, *Public Administration* (New York, 1964), p. 77.
3. Max Weber, *From Max Weber: Essays in Sociology*, edited by H. H. Gerth and C. Wright Mills (New York, 1958), p. 324.
4. Luther H. Gulick and L. Urwick, editors, *Papers on the Science of Administration* (New York, 1937).
5. Robert V. Presthus, "Authority in Organizations," in *Concepts and Issues in Administrative Behavior*, edited by Sidney Mailick and Edward Van Ness (Englewood Cliffs, 1962), pp. 123–127.
6. Robert L. Peabody, "Perceptions of Organizational Authority," *Administrative Science Quarterly*, Volume 6 (1962), pp. 463–464.
7. For a further discussion of this point, see: Peter Blau and W. Richard Scott, *Formal Organizations: A Comparative Approach* (San Francisco, 1962), p. 36ff.
8. Chester I. Barnard, *The Functions of the Executive* (Cambridge, 1938).
9. Jay Jackson, "The Normative Regulation of Authoritative Behavior," in *The Making of Decisions: A Reader in Administrative Behavior*, edited by William J. Gore and J. W. Dyson (New York, 1964), p. 216.
10. Herbert A. Simon, *Administrative Behavior* (New York, 1957), p. 12.
11. Ibid., p. 12.
12. Herbert A. Simon, "Authority," in *Research in Industrial Human Relations*, edited by C. Arensbery et al. (New York, 1957), pp. 103–118.
13. Richard C. Snyder, H. W. Bruck, and Burton Sapin, *Decision-Making* (Princeton, 1954), p. 57.
14. Peter H. Rossi, "Community Decision Making," *Administrative Science Quarterly*, Volume 1 (March 1957), pp. 415–443.
15. Harold D. Lasswell and Abraham Kaplan, *Power and Society* (New Haven, 1950).
16. Herbert A. Simon, *Administrative Behavior* (New York, 1957), p. xxiv.
17. Victor A. Thompson, *Modern Organizations* (New York, 1963), p. 89.
18. William R. Dill, "Administrative Decision-Making," in *Concepts and Issues in Administrative Behavior*, edited by Sidney Mailick and Edward H. Van Ness (Englewood Cliffs, 1962), pp. 29–48.
19. L. Reissman, "A Study of Role Conceptions in Bureauracy," *Social Forces*, Volume 27 (1949), pp. 305–310.
20. Herbert Gamberg, "The Professional and Policy Choices in Middle-Sized Cities," *Journal of the American Institute of Planners*, Volume 32 (May, 1966), p. 175.

21. For empirical analyses of this mobility, see: George K. Floro, "Continuity in City Managers' Careers," *American Journal of Sociology*, Volume 61 (November, 1955), pp. 240–246; "An Analysis of City Managers," *Public Management* (January, 1954), pp. 5–9; Anthony J. Catanese and Alan Walter Steiss, *Systemic Planning: Theory and Application* (Lexington, Mass., 1970), Chapter 13.

22. Kenneth D. Benne, *A Conception of Authority* (New York, 1943), p. 34.

23. Thompson, op. cit., p. 86.

24. Robert A. Dahl, "Hierarchy, Democracy, and Bargaining in Politics and Economics," *Research Frontiers in Politics and Government* (Washington, D. C., 1955), pp. 45–69.

25. Robert A. Dahl, "The Analysis of Influence in Local Communities," in *Social Science and Community Action*, edited by Charles R. Adrian (East Lansing, 1960), p. 26.

26. Theodore Caplow, *Principles of Organization* (New York, 1964), p. 102.

27. Dorwin Cartwright, editor, *Studies in Social Power* (Ann Arbor, 1959).

28. Weber, op. cit., p. 152. Lasswell and Kaplan (op. cit., p. 77) offer a parallel definition by refering to the power of a person over H with respect to values K if decisions affect the K-policies of H.

29. Jackson, op. cit., pp. 217–218. The problem cited by Jackson is similar to the issue raised in connection with the zero-sum, two-person game in game theory — how to expand the theoretical constructs to make them useful in real social situations.

30. John R. P. French, Jr. and Bertram Raven, "The Bases of Social Power," in Cartwright, op. cit., p. 155ff.

31. Robert Dubin, *The World of Work* (Englewood Cliffs, 1958), p. 48.

32. Ibid., p. 21.

33. Dahl, op. cit. (1957), p. 202.

Chapter 5 Decision-Making and the Communication Process

1. Edward Hodnett, *The Art of Problem Solving* (New York, 1955), pp. 18–19.

2. Jurgen Ruesch and W. Kees, *Nonverbal Communication: Notes on the Visual Perception of Human Relations* (Berkeley, 1956), p. 193.

3. John T. Dorsey, Jr., "A Communication Model for Administration," *Administrative Science Quarterly*, Volume 2 (1957), p. 309.

4. Herbert A. Simon, *Administrative Behavior* (New York, 1957).

5. Alex Bavelas and Dermot Barrett, "An Experimental Approach to Organization Communication," *Personnel*, Volume 27 (1951), p. 368.

6. Chester I. Barnard, *The Functions of the Executive* (Cambridge, Mass., 1938), p. 91.

7. Claude E. Shannon, "A Mathematical Theory of Communication," *Bell Systems Technical Journal*, Volume 27 (July 1948), pp. 623–656.

8. Norbert Wiener, *Cybernetics: Or Control and Communication in the Animal and Machine* (New York, 1948).

9. Claude E. Shannon and Warren Weaver, *The Mathematical Theory of Communication* (Urbana, 1949), pp. 115–116.

10. C. Cherry, *On Human Communication: A Review, A Survey, and A Criticism* (New York, 1957), p. 29.

11. T. Burns, "The Directions of Activity and Communication in a Department Executive Group," *Human Relations* (1954), p. 92.

12. K. Davis, "Management Communication and the Grapevine," *Harvard Business Review*, Volume 31, Number 5 (1953), p. 45.

13. S. Habbe, "Communicating With Employees," *Studies in Personnel Policy*, National Industrial Conference Board Report No. 129 (New York, 1952).

14. M. Dalton, "Unofficial Union-Management Relations," *American Sociological Review*, Volume 15 (1950), pp. 611–619.

15. Jay Jackson, "Reference Group Processes in Formal Organization," *Sociometry*, Volume 22 (1959), pp. 323–324.

16. D. C. Barnlund and C. Harland, "Propinquity and Prestige as Determinants of Communication Networks," *Sociometry*, Volume 26 (1963), p. 468.

17. Alex Bavelas, "Communication Patterns in Task Oriented Groups," in *Group Dynamics*, edited by Dorwin Cartwright and Alvin Zander (Evanston, 1953); Harold H. Leavitt, "Some Effects of Certain Communication Patterns on Group Performance," *Journal of Abnormal and Social Psychology*, Volume 46 (1951); George A. Heise and George A. Miller, "Problem Solving by Small Groups Using Various Communication Nets," *Journal of Abnormal and Social Psychology*, Volume 46 (1951); Harold Guetzkow and Herbert A. Simon, "The Impact of Certain Communication Nets upon Organization and Performance in Task-Oriented Groups," *Management Science*, Volume 1, Numbers 3 & 4 (1955); Harold Guetzkow and William Dill, "Factors in the Organizational Development of Task-Oriented Groups, *Sociometry*, Volume 20 (June 1957); Robert Dubin, "Stability of Human Organization," in *Modern Organization Theory*, edited by Mason Haire (New York, 1959); Mark Mulder, "Communication Structure, Decision Structure, and Group Performance," *Sociometry*, Volume 23 (March, 1960).

18. Gilbert W. King, "Information," *Scientific American*, Volume 187 (1952), p. 132.

19. Karl W. Deutsch, "Communication Theory and Political Integration," in *The Integration of Political Communities*, edited by Philip E. Jacob and James V. Toscano (Philadelphia, 1964), pp. 61–62.

20. Jurgen Ruesch and Gregory Bateson, *Communication: The Social Matrix of Psychiatry* (New York, 1951), pp. 280–281.

21. Barnard, op. cit., p. 225.

22. M. W. Shelly and J. C. Gilcrest, "Some Effects of Communication Requirements in Group Structures," *Journal of Social Psychology*, Volume 48 (1958), p. 43.

23. Dorwin Cartwright, "The Potential Contribution of Graph Theory to

Organization Theory," in *Modern Organization Theory: A Symposium of the Foundation for Research on Human Behavior*, edited by Mason Haire (New York, 1959), p. 261.

24. Herbert A. Simon and James G. March, *Organizations* (1958), p. 166.
25. J. G. Miller, "Information Input Overload," in *Self-Organizing Systems*, edited by M. C. Yovits, G. T. Jacobi, and G. D. Goldstein (Washington, D. C., 1962), p. 64.
26. Richard M. Cyert and James G. March, *A Behavioral Theory of the Firm* (Englewood Cliffs, 1963), pp. 124–125.
27. D. T. Campbell, "Systematic Error on the Part of Human Links in Communication Systems," *Information and Control*, Volume 1 (1958), pp. 334–369. Campbell suggests a number of categories of distortion which arise from the coding of messages.
28. Gordon W. Allport and L. Postman, "The Basic Psychology of Rumor," in *The Process and Effects of Mass Communication*, edited by W. Schramm (Urbana, 1954), pp. 146–148.
29. This discussion of memory as a multistage process has been culled from the writings of Karl W. Deutsch, and in particular, "Communication Theory and Political Integration," in *The Integration of Political Communities*, edited by Philip E. Jacob and James V. Toscano (Philadelphia, 1964); pp. 61–65; *The Nerves of Government*, (New York, 1963), pp. 85–86; "Mechanism, Teleology, and Mind," *Philosophy and Phenomenological Research*, Volume 12 (1951), pp. 185–222.
30. Freud has demonstrated this selective process most convincingly; see: *Psychopathology of Everyday Life* (London, 1928).
31. Deutsch, op. cit. (1964), p. 62.
32. The concept of complementarity of exceptions is more fully developed by Parsons and Shils in "Values, Motives, and Systems of Action," *Toward a General Theory of Action*, edited by Talcott Parsons and Edward T. Shils (Cambridge, Mass., 1952).
33. Dalton, op. cit., p. 233.
34. Theodore Caplow, "Rumor in War," *Social Forces*, Volume 25 (1946–47), pp. 298–302.
35. Norton E. Long, "The Local Community as an Ecology of Games," *The American Journal of Sociology*, Volume 64 (November, 1958), pp. 251–261.
36. H. Menzel, "Innovation, Integration, and Marginality," *American Sociological Review*, Volume 25 (1960), pp. 704–713.
37. Eugene Jacobson and Stanley E. Seashore, "Communication Practices in Complex Organization," *Journal of Social Issues*, Volume 7 (1951), p. 33.
38. Anthony J. Catanese and Alan Walter Steiss, *Systemic Planning: Theory and Application* (Lexington, Mass., 1970), Chapter 14.
39. Long, op. cit., p. 258.
40. Victor A. Thompson, *Modern Organization* (New York, 1963); Jerald Hage, "An Axiomatic Theory of Organization," *Administrative Science Quarterly*, Volume 10 (December, 1965), pp. 289–320; Georges Friedman, *Industrial*

Society (Glencoe, 1955); Wilbert E. Moore, *Industrial Relations and the Social Order* (New York, 1951).

41. "Communication in Administration," A Report prepared for the Forty-first Annual Conference of International City Managers' Association, Bretton Woods, New Hampshire, October, 1955.
42. Simon and March, op. cit., pp. 167–168.
43. Ibid., p. 177ff.

Chapter 6 Decision-Making as a Multistage Process

1. Roscoe C. Martin, Frank Munger, et al., *Decision in Syracuse: A Metro-politician Action Study* (Bloomington, 1961), p. 318.
2. Robert Tannenbaum, "Managerial Decision-Making," *The Journal of Business*, Volume 23 (January 1950), pp. 23–24.
3. Herbert A. Simon and James G. March, *Organizations* (New York, 1958), pp. 178–179.
4. William J. Gore, *Administrative Decision-Making: A Heuristic Model* (New York, 1964), pp. 132–133.
5. Ibid., p. 36.
6. Anthony J. Catanese and Alan Walter Steiss, *Systemic Planning: Theory and Application* (Lexington, Mass., 1970), Chapter 15.
7. Filmer S. C. Northrup, *The Logic of the Sciences and the Humanities* (New York, 1947), p. 1.
8. David A. Easton, *A Systems Analysis of Political Life* (New York, 1965), p. 38.
9. John Dewey, *Logic, The Theory of Inquiry* (New York, 1938), p. 105.
10. Ibid., pp. 105–106.
11. Brand Blanshard, *The Nature of Thought*, Volume II (London, 1939), pp. 63–64.
12. Dewey, op. cit., p. 105.
13. Northrup, op. cit., p. 29.
14. Anatol Rapoport, "What Is Information?" *ETC: A Review of General Semantics*, Volume 10 (Summer, 1953), p. 252.
15. Peter F. Drucker, "The Effective Decision," *Harvard Business Review*, Volume 45 (January-February, 1967), p. 95.
16. Northrup, op. cit., p. 35.
17. Drucker, op. cit., p. 95.
18. Dewey, op. cit., p. 109.
19. Robert W. Morell, *Managerial Decision-Making* (Milwaukee, 1960), p. 22.
20. Dewey, op. cit., p. 111.
21. Peter F. Drucker, *The Practice of Management* (New York, 1954), p. 363.
22. Gore, op. cit., pp. 80–101.
23. Drucker, op. cit. (1967), p. 95.

Chapter 7 The Evolution of Modern
Public Budgeting

1. John F. Cotton and Harry P. Hatry, *Program Planning for State, County, City* (Washington, D.C.: State-Local Finances Project, George Washington University, 1967), p. 3.
2. Committee on Budgeting of the Municipal Finance Officers' Association.
3. Frederick C. Mosher, *Program Budgeting* (Chicago: Public Administration Service, 1954), p. 5.
4. See: Frank J. Goodnow, "The Limit of Budgetary Control," *Proceedings of the American Political Science Association* (Baltimore, 1913), p. 72; William F. Willoughby, "Allotment of Funds by Executive Officials, An Essential Feature of Any Correct Budgetary System," op. cit., pp. 78–87.
5. President's Commission on Economy and Efficiency, *The Need for a National Budget* (Washington, 1912), pp. 210–213.
6. New York Bureau of Municipal Research, "Some Results and Limitations of Central Financial Control in New York City," *Municipal Research*, Volume 81 (1917), p. 67.
7. Allen Schick, "The Road to PPB: The Stages of Budget Reform," in *Planning, Programming Budgeting. A Systems Approach to Management* (Chicago, 1968), p. 34.
8. U.S. Commission on Organization of the Executive Branch of the Government, *Budgeting and Accounting* (Washington, D.C., 1949), p. 8.
9. Mosher, op. cit., p. 79.
10. David A. Page, "The Federal PPBS," *Journal of the American Institute of Planners*, Volume 33 (July 1967), p. 257.
11. David Novick, "Origin and History of Program Budgeting," transcript of talk filmed August 11, 1966 for short course on PPBS sponsored by the U.S. Bureau of the Budget and the U.S. Civil Service Commission.
12. Alan Walter Steiss, *A Framework for Planning in State Government* (Chicago: The Council of State Government, 1968), p. 55.
13. Schick, op. cit., p. 38.
14. Mosher, op. cit., p. 59
15. Anthony J. Catanese and Alan Walter Steiss, *Systemic Planning: Theory and Application* (Lexington, Mass., 1970).
16. Harry J. Hartley, "PPBS: The Emergence of a Systemic Concept for Public Governance," *General Systems*, Volume 21 (1968), p. 152.
17. Ibid., pp. 151–154; see also: Harry J. Hartley, *Educational Planning-Programming-Budgeting: A Systems Approach* (Englewood Cliffs, 1968).
18. David Novick, editor, *Program Budgeting: Program Analysis and the Federal Budget* (Cambridge, Mass., 1967), p. 66; Roland N. McKean, *Efficiency in Government Through Systems Analysis* (New York, 1958), pp. 50–57.
19. Charles J. Hitch and Roland N. McKean, *The Economics of Defense in the Nuclear Age* (Cambridge, Mass., 1963), p. 116; Kenneth E. Boulding, *Economic Analysis* (New York, 1955), p. 741.

20. William J. Baumol, *Economic Theory and Operations Analysis* (Englewood Cliffs, 1961), pp. 192–193.
21. McKean, op. cit., p. 71.

Chapter 8 Effective Preparation of Public Budgets

1. Frederick C. Mosher, *Program Budgeting: Theory and Practice* (Chicago, 1954), p. 7.
2. For a further discussion of the distinction between capital budgeting and capital improvements programming, see: Alan Walter Steiss, *A Framework for Planning in State Government* (Chicago, 1968), pp. 51–56.
3. For a further discussion of the critical distinction between input and output relationships in the process of budgeting, see: Anthony J. Catanese and Alan Walter Steiss, *Systemic Planning: Theory and Application* (Lexington, Mass., 1970), Chapter 5.
4. For a further discussion of these factors, see: International City Managers' Association, *Municipal Finance Administration* (Chicago, 1962), Chapter 6.
5. State of New York, *Guidelines for Integrated Planning Programming Budgeting* (Albany, 1966).
6. For further detail, see: *Municipal Finance Adminstration*, pp. 149–153.
7. Orin K. Cope, "Operation Analysis — The Basis for Performance Budgeting," *Performance Budgeting and Unit Cost Accounting for Governmental Units* (Chicago, 1954).
8. For further detail, see: *Municipal Finance Administration*, pp. 154–158.

Chapter 9 A Framework to Strategic Planning

1. Ingrid Jussil, "Planeringmetodik," *Plan*, Volume 20, Number 1 (Stockholm, 1966), pp. 21–27; Folke Kristensson, *Manniskor, foretage och regioner* (Stockholm: Almquist and Wiksell, 1967); Leo Jakobson, *A Shoreline Policies Plan: Conceptual Framework*, Report No. 1: Muskegon County Shorelands Study (Madison, Wisconsin: University of Wisconsin, 1969); Alan Walter Steiss, *A Framework for Planning in State Government* (Chicago: The Council of State Governments, 1968); Anthony J. Catanese and Alan Walter Steiss, *Systemic Planning: Theory and Application* (Lexington, Mass., 1970).
2. Wesley Bellis, "Increasing City Street Capacity," *Traffic Quarterly*, Volume 13 (January, 1959), pp. 74–89.
3. See: Van Beuren Stanbery, *Some New Techniques for Area Population Projections* (Los Angeles, 1960); Robert C. Schmitt and Albert H. Crosetti, "Accuracy of Ration-Correlation Method for Estimating Post-censal Population," *Land Economics*, 30 (August 1954); Donald J. Bogue

and Beverly Duncan, "A Composite Method for Estimating Postcensal Population of Small Areas by Age, Sex, and Color," Vital Statistics, U.S. Public Health Service (August 1959).

4. Franklyn H. Beal, "Defining Development Objectives," in *Principles and Practices of Urban Planning*, edited by William I. Goodman and Eric C. Freund (Washington, D. C.: International City Managers' Association, 1968).

5. Ibid., p. 338.

Chapter 10 The Use of Effectiveness Measures in Public Decision-Making

1. For a further discussion of this point, see: Don H. Overly, "Decision-Making in City Government," *Urban Affairs Quarterly*, Volume 3, No. 2 December, 1967).

2. A. R. Prest and R. Turvey, "Cost-Benefit Analysis: A Survey," *The Economic Journal*, Volume 75 (December, 1965), p. 683.

3. E. S. Quade, editor, *Analysis for Military Decisions*, The RAND Corporation, R-387-PR (November, 1964), p. 13.

4. Bureau of the Budget Circular 66-3, *Planning-Programming-Budgeting* (October, 1965).

5. C. J. Hitch and R. N. McKean, *The Economics of Defense in the Nuclear Age* (Cambridge, Mass., 1960), pp. 26–28.

6. Prest and Turvey, op. cit., p. 691.

7. Charles Kepner and Benjamin B. Tregoe, *The Rational Manager* (Princeton, 1965).

8. Roland N. McKean, *Efficiency in Government Through Systems Analysis* (New York, 1958).

9. See: Hitch and McKean, op. cit., pp. 209–210, and McKean, op. cit., Chapter 5, for an extensive discussion of time streams and criteria.

Chapter 12 The Politics of Budgeting

1. Aaron Wildavsky, *The Politics of the Budgetary Process* (Boston, 1964), pp. 1–2.

2. Charles L. Schultze, *The Politics and Economics of Public Spending* (Washington, D.C., 1968), p. 7.

3. Leonard D. White, *Introduction to the Study of Public Administration* (New York, 1955), Chapter 17.

4. Schultze, op. cit., p. 8.

5. Marshall E. Dimock and Gladys O. Dimock, *Public Administration* (New York, 1964), p. 301.

6. Walter Heller, *New Dimensions of Political Economy* (Cambridge, Mass., 1966), p. 175.

7. Schultze, op. cit., p. 13.
8. Wildavsky, op. cit.
9. See: Charles E. Lindblom, *The Intelligence of Democracy*, (New York, 1965); David Braybrooke and Charles E. Lindblom, *A Strategy of Decision* (New York, 1963); and Aaron Wildavsky, op. cit.
10. Anthony Downs, in *Private Wants and Public Needs*, edited by Edmund S. Phelps (New York, 1962).
11. Anthony Downs, *An Economic Theory of Democracy* (New York, 1957), p. 52.
12. Ibid., p. 69.
13. Ibid., p. 70.
14. Ibid., p. 61.
15. Ibid., p. 70.
16. Charles E. Lindblom, "The Science of 'Muddling Through'," *Public Administration Review*, Volume 19 (Spring, 1959), pp. 79–88.
17. Lindblom, *The Intelligence of Democracy*, pp. 138–143.
18. Wildavsky, op. cit., p. 178.
19. Ibid., p. 137.
20. Ibid., p. 138.
21. Ibid., p. 179.
22. Schultze, op. cit., pp. 75–76.
23. Rufus P. Browning, "Innovation and Non-Innovation Decision Processes in Government Budgeting," paper presented at the Annual Meeting of the American Political Science Association, New York, September 4–7, 1963.
24. Earl Latham, "The Group Basis of Politics: Notes for a Theory," in *Readings in Political Parties and Pressure Groups*, edited by Frank Munger and Douglas Price (New York, 1964), p. 43.
25. Wildavsky, op. cit., p. 59.
26. Ibid., p. 6.
27. Ibid., p. 23.
28. David A. Easton, *A Systems Analysis of Political Life* (New York, 1965), Chapter 6.
29. David Truman, *The Governmental Process*, pp. 442–443.
30. Victor A. Thompson, *Modern Organizations* (New York, 1961), pp. 83–100. This proposition is in direct confrontation with the ideas expressed in the writings of Max Weber which suggest that technical competence is always found in the authority position or office.
31. Jerald Hage, "An Axiomatic Theory of Organization," *Administrative Science Quarterly*, Volume 10 (December, 1965), pp. 289–320.
32. Charles Perrow, "A Framework for the Comparative Analysis of Organizations," *American Sociological Review*, Volume 32 (1967).
33. Thompson, op. cit., pp. 84–85.
34. Richard C. Snyder, "A Decision-Making Approach to the Study of Political Phenomena," in *Approaches to the Study of Politics*, edited by Roland Young (Evanston, 1958), pp. 15–16.
35. Peter M. Blau and W. Richard Scott, *Formal Organizations: A Comparative Approach* (San Francisco, 1962), pp. 184–185.

36. Scott Greer, *Urban Renewal and American Cities* (Indianapolis, 1965).
37. Wildavsky, op. cit., p. 46.
38. Herbert A. Simon and James G. March, *Organizations* (New York, 1958), Chapters 6 and 7.
39. Lindblom, *The Intelligence of Democracy*, pp. 138–139.
40. James Buchanan and Gordon Tullock, *The Calculus of Consent* (Ann Arbor, 1961).
41. Frederick M. Scherer, in *Measuring the Benefits of Government Investment*, edited by Robert Dorfman (Washington, D.C., 1965), pp. 23ff.
42. Anthony J. Catanese and Alan Walter Steiss, *Systemic Planning: Theory and Application* (Lexington, Mass., 1970), p. 35.
43. Lindblom, op. cit., p. 141.
44. Scherer, op. cit., p. 34.
45. Charles Hitch and Roland McKean, *The Economics of Defense in the Nuclear Age* (Cambridge, Mass., 1960), p. 3.
46. Ibid., p. 20.
47. Ibid., p. 48.
48. Ibid., p. 51.
49. Buchanan and Tullock, op. cit.
50. Kenneth J. Arrow, *Social Choice and Individual Values* (New York, 1951).
51. Ibid., p. 18.
52. Edward C. Banfield and James Q. Wilson, "Public-Regardingness as a Value Premise in Voting Behavior," *The American Political Science Review*, Volume 58 (December, 1964), pp. 876–887.
53. Arrow, op. cit., p. 28.
54. Buchanan and Tullock, op. cit., pp. 331–334.
55. Arrow, op. cit., pp. 87–88.
56. Robert A. Dahl, *A Preface to Democratic Theory* (Chicago, 1956), pp. 116–118.
57. For a particularly lucid discussion of these points, see: Jesse Burkhead, *Government Budgeting* (New York, 1956).

Bibliography

Alchian, Armen. "Cost Effectiveness of Cost Effectiveness," in *Defense Management*. Stephen Enke (ed.). Englewood Cliffs: Prentice-Hall, Inc., 1967.

Allport, Gordon W., and L. Postman. "The Basic Psychology of Rumor," in *The Process and Effects of Mass Communication*. W. Schramm (ed.). Urbana: The University of Illinois Press, 1954.

Altschuler, Alan. *The City Planning Process: A Politcal Analysis*. Ithaca: Cornell University Press, 1965.

"An Analysis of City Managers," *Public Management* (January, 1954), pp. 5–9.

Appleby, Paul H. *Policy and Administration*. Birmingham, Alabama: University of Alabama Press, 1949.

Arrow, Kenneth J. *Social Choice and Individual Values*. New York: John Wiley and Sons, 1951.

Ashby, W. Ross. *An Introduction to Cybernetics*. New York: John Wiley and Sons, Inc., 1963.

Ayres, Robert U. *Technological Forecasting and Long-Range Planning*. New York: McGraw-Hill Book Company, 1969.

Banfield, Edward C. "The Decision-Making Schema," *Public Administration Review*. Volume 17 (1957), pp. 278–284.

Banfield, Edward C. *Political Influence*. New York: The Free Press, 1961.

Banfield, Edward C. (ed.). *Urban Government: A Reader in Politics and Administration*. New York: The Free Press of Glencoe, 1961.

Banfield, Edward C. "Ends and Means in Planning," in *Concepts and Issues in Administrative Behavior*. Sidney Mailick and Edward H. Van Ness (eds.). Englewood Cliffs: Prentice-Hall, Inc., 1962.

Banfield, Edward C., and James Q. Wilson. *City Politics*. Cambridge, Mass.: Harvard University and M.I.T. Presses, 1963.

Barnard, Chester I. *The Functions of the Executive*. Cambridge: Harvard University Press, 1938.

Barnlund, D. C., and C. Harland. "Propinquity and Prestige as Determinants of Communication Networks," *Sociometry*. Volume 26 (1963), pp. 467–479.

Bator, Francis M. *The Question of Government Spending*. New York: Harper, 1960.

Baumol, William J. *Economic Theory and Operations Analysis*. Englewood Cliffs: Prentice-Hall, Inc., 1961.

Bavelas, Alex, and Dermot Barrett. "An Experimental Approach to Organizational Communication," *Personnel*. Volume 27 (1951).

Bavelas, Alex. "Communication Patterns in Task Oriented Groups," in *Group Dynamics*. Dorwin Cartwright and Alvin Zander (eds.). Evanston: Row, Peterson, and Company, 1953.

Beal, Franklyn H. "Defining Development Objectives," in *Principles and Practices of Urban Planning*. William I. Goodman and Eric C. Freund (eds.). Washington, D.C.: ICMA, 1968.

Bellis, Wesley, "Increasing City Street Capacity," *Traffic Quarterly*. Volume 13 (January, 1959), pp. 74–89.

Benne, Kenneth Dean. *A Conception of Authority*. New York: Columbia University, Bureau of Publications, 1943.

Bennis, Warren G. "Leadership Theory and Administrative Behavior: The Problem of Authority," *Administrative Science Quarterly*. Volume 4 (1959), pp. 259–301.

Bierman, Harold, Jr., and Seymour Smidt. *The Capital Budgeting Decision*. New York: Macmillian Company, 1966.

Biren, W. Carl. *Economics and Public Policy*. Columbus, Ohio: Charles E. Merrill Books, Inc., 1966.

Blau, Peter. *The Dynamics of Bureaucracy*. Chicago: University of Chicago Press, 1953.

Blau, Peter, and W. Richard Scott. *Formal Organizations: A Comparative Approach*. San Francisco: Chandler Publishing Company, 1962.

Boulding, Kenneth. "Welfare Economics," in *A Survey of Contemporary Economics*. Bernard F. Haley (ed.). Homewood, Illinois: Richard D. Irwin, 1952.

Boulding, Kenneth E. *Economic Analysis*. New York: McGraw-Hill Book Co., 1955.

Braybrooke, David, and Charles E. Lindblom. *A Strategy of Decision: Policy Evaluation as a Social Process*. New York: The Free Press of Glencoe, 1963.

Bross, Irwin D. J. *Design for Decision*. New York: Macmillan Co., 1953.

Brown, Alvin. *Organization, A Formulation of Principle*. New York: Hibbert Printing Co., 1945.

Browning, Rufus P. "Innovative and Non-Innovative Decision Processes in Government Budgeting," Annual Meeting of the American Political Science Association, New York, September 4–7, 1963.

Buchanan, James. "Individual Choices in Voting and in the Market," *Journal of Political Economics*, 1954.

Buchanan, James, and Gordon Tullock. *The Calculus of Consent*. Ann Arbor: University of Michigan Press, 1961.

Burchard, John E. (ed.) *Mid-Century: The Social Implications of Scientific Progress*. Cambridge-New York: M.I.T. Press-John Wiley, 1950.

Bureau of the Budget Circular 66-3. *Planning-Programming-Budgeting* (October, 1965).

Burkhead, Jesse. *Government Budgeting*. New York: John Wiley and Sons, 1956.

Burns, T. "The Directions of Activity and Communication in a Departmental Executive Group," *Human Relations* (1954).

Campbell, D. T. "Systematic Error on the Part of Human Links in Communication Systems," *Information and Control*. Volume 1 (1958), pp. 334–369.

Caplow, Theodore. "Rumor in War," *Social Forces*. Volume 25 (1946–47), pp. 298–302.

Caplow, Theodore. *Principles of Organization*. New York: Harcourt, Brace & World, Inc., 1964.

Cartwright, Dorwin and Alvin Zander (eds.). *Group Dynamics*. New York: John Wiley and Sons, 1958.

Cartwright, Dorwin (ed.). *Studies in Social Power*. Ann Arbor: Institute for Social Research, 1959.

Carzo, Rocco, Jr., and John Yanouzas. *Formal Organization: A Systems Approach*. Homewood, Ill.: Richard D. Irwin, 1967.

Catanese, Anthony J., and Alan Walter Steiss. *Systemic Planning: Theory and Application*. Lexington, Mass.: D. C. Heath and Company, 1970.

Cherry, E. Colin. *On Human Communication: A Review, A Survey, and A Criticism*. New York: Technical Press of M.I.T. and John Wiley and Sons, 1957.

Coase, R. H. "The Nature of the Firm," *Economica*. Volume 4 (1937), pp. 386–405.

Colms, Gerhard. *Essays in Public Finance and Fiscal Policy*. New York: Oxford University Press, 1955.

Cotton, John F., and Harry P. Hatry. *Program Planning for State, County, City*. Washington, D.C.: State-Local Finances Project, George Washington University, 1967.

Cyert, R. M., W. R. Dill, and J. G. March. "The Role of Expectations in Business Decision-Making," *Administrative Science Quarterly*. Volume 3 (1958), pp. 307–340.

Cyert, Richard M. and James G. March. *A Behavioral Theory of the Firm*. Englewood Cliffs: Prentice-Hall, Inc., 1963.

Dahl, Robert A. and Charles E. Lindblom. *Politics, Economics, and Welfare*. New York: Harper and Brothers, 1953.

Dahl, Robert A. "Hierarchy, Democracy, and Bargaining in Politics and Economics," *Research Frontiers in Politics and Government*. Washington, D.C.: The Brookings Institute, 1955.

Dahl, Robert A. *A Preface to Democratic Theory*. Chicago: University of Chicago Press, 1956.

Dahl, Robert A. "The Concept of Power," *Behavioral Science*. Volume 2 (July, 1957), pp. 201–215.

Dahl, Robert A. "The Analysis of Influence in Local Communities," in *Social Science and Community Action*. Charles R. Adrian (ed.). East Lansing: Michigan State University Press, 1960.

Dahl, Robert A. *Who Governs? Democracy and Power in an American City*. New Haven: Yale University Press, 1961.

Dahl, Robert A. *Modern Political Analysis*. Englewood Cliffs: Prentice-Hall, Inc., 1963.

Daland, Robert T., and John A. Parker. "Roles of the Planner in Urban Development," in *Urban Growth Dynamics in a Regional Cluster of Cities*. F. Stuart Chapin and Shirley F. Weiss (eds.). New York: John Wiley and Sons, 1962.

Dalton, M. "Unofficial Union-Management Relations," *American Sociological Review*. Volume 15 (1950), pp. 611–619.

Davis, Otto A., M. A. H. Dempster, and Aaron Wildavsky. "A Theory of the Budgetary Process," *American Political Science Review*. Volume 60 (September, 1966).

Davis, K. "Management Communication and the Grapevine," *Harvard Business Review*. Volume 31, Number 5 (1953).

Deckert, Charles R. (ed.). *The Social Impact of Cybernetics*. New York: Simon and Schuster, 1966.

Deutsch, Karl W. "Mechanism, Teleology, and Mind," *Philosophy and Phenomenological Research*. Volume 12 (1951), pp. 185–222.

Deutsch, Karl W. *The Nerves of Government*. London: The Free Press of Glencoe, 1963.

Deutsch, Karl W. "Communication Theory and Political Integration," in *The Integration of Political Communities*. Philip E. Jacob and James V. Toscano, (eds.). Philadelphia: J. B. Lippincott Company, 1964.

Dill, William R. "Administrative Decision-Making," in *Concepts and Issues in Administrative Behavior*. Sidney Mailick and Edward H. Van Ness (eds.). Englewood Cliffs: Prentice-Hall, Inc., 1962.

Dimock, Marshall E., and Gladys O. Dimock. *Public Administration*. New York: Holt, Rinehart, and Winston, Inc., 1946.

Dorfman, Robert (ed.). *Measuring the Benefits of Government Investment*. Washington, D.C.: The Brookings Institute, 1965.

Downs, Anthony. "An Economic Theory of Political Choice in a Democracy," *Journal of Political Economy*. Volume 65 (April, 1957), pp. 135–150.

Downs, Anthony. *An Economic Theory of Democracy*. New York: Harper and Row, 1957.

Downs, Anthony. "A Theory of Bureaucracy," *American Economic Review*. Volume 55 (May, 1965), pp. 439–446.

Downs, Anthony. "Why the Government Budget is Too Small in a Democracy," in *Private Wants and Public Needs*, Edmund Phelps (ed.). New York: W. W. Norton and Company, 1965.

Dorsey, John T., Jr. "A Communication Model for Administration," *Administration Science Quarterly*. Volume 2 (1957).

Drucker, Peter F. *The Practice of Management*. New York: Harper and Brothers, 1954.

Drucker, Peter F. "The Effective Decision," *Harvard Business Review*. Volume 45 (Jan.-Feb., 1967), pp. 92–104.

Duberi, Robert. *The World of Work*. Englewood Cliffs: Prentice-Hall, 1958.

Due, John F. *Government Finance: An Economic Analysis*. Homewood, Ill.: Richard D. Irwin, 1963.

Duff, Daniel J. "Authority Considered from an Operational Point of View," *Journal of the Academy of Management*. Volume 2 (Dec. 1959), pp. 167–175.

Dyckman, John C. "What Makes Planners Plan?" *Journal of the American Institute of Planners*. Volume 27 (May, 1961).

Easton, David. "The Perception of Authority and Political Change," in *Authority*. C. J. Friedrick (ed.). Cambridge, Mass.: Harvard University Press, 1958.

Easton, David. *A Systems Analysis of Political Life*. New York: John Wiley and Sons, 1965.

Eckstein, Harry. *Pressure Group Politics*. Stanford: Stanford University Press, 1962.

Emery., F. E. (ed.). *Systems Thinking*. Baltimore: Penguin Books, 1969.

Etzioni, Amitai. "Authority Structure," *Administrative Science Quarterly*. Volume 4 (1959).

Etzioni, Amitai. *Modern Organizations*. Englewood Cliffs: Prentice-Hall, 1964.

Floro, George K. "Continuity in City Managers Careers," *American Journal of Sociology*. Volume 61 (November, 1955), pp. 240–246.

Follett, Mary Parker. *Creative Experience*. New York: Longmans Company, 1924.

Forrester, Jay W. *Urban Dynamics*. Cambridge, Mass.: Massachusetts Institute of Technology Press, 1969.

French, John R. P., Jr., and Bertram Raven. "The Bases of Social Power," in *Studies on Social Power*. Dorwin Cartwright (ed.). Ann Arbor: Institute for Social Research, 1959.

Friedman, Georges. *Industrial Society*. Glencoe: The Free Press, 1955.

Friedmann, John. "Regional Development in Post-Industrial Society," *Journal of the American Institute of Planners*. Volume 30 (May, 1964), pp. 84–90.

Gamberg, Herbert. "The Professional and Policy Choices in Middle-Sized Cities," *Journal of the American Institute of Planners*. Volume 32 (May, 1966).

Given, William B. *Bottom-Up Management: People Working Together*. New York: Harper and Brothers, 1949.

Goodnow, Frank J. "The Limit of Budgetary Control," *Proceedings of the American Political Science Association*. Baltimore, 1913.

Goodnow, Frank J. *Politics and Administration*. New York: The MacMillan Co., 1914.

Gore, W. J. and F. S. Silander. "A Bibliographical Essay on Decision-Making," *Administrative Science Quarterly*. Volume 4 (1959), pp. 97–121.

Gore, William J. *Administrative Decision-Making: A Heuristic Model*. New York: John Wiley & Sons, Inc., 1964.

Gouldner, Alvin W. *Patterns of Industrial Bureaucracy*. New York: The Free Press of Glencoe, 1954.

Guetzkow, Harold, and Herbert A. Simon. "The Impact of Certain Communication Nets Upon Organization and Performance in Task-Oriented Groups," *Management Science*. Volume 1, Numbers 3 & 4 (1955).

Guetzkow, Harold, and William R. Dill. "Factors in the Organization Development of Task-Oriented Groups," *Sociometry*. Volume 20 (June, 1957).

Gulick, Luther, and L. Urwick (eds.). *Papers on the Science of Administration*. New York: Institute of Public Administration, 1937.

Habbe, S. "Communicating with Employees," *Studies in Personnel Policy*, No. 129. New York: National Industrial Conference Board, 1952.

Hage, Jerald. "An Axiomatic Theory of Organizations," *Administrative Science Quarterly*. Volume 10 (December, 1965).

Hall, A. D., and R. W. Hagen. "Definition of System," in *Organizations: Systems, Control and Adaptation*. Volume II. Joseph A. Litterer (ed.). New York: John Wiley and Sons, 1969.

Haire, M. (ed.). *Modern Organization Theory*. New York: John Wiley & Sons, 1959.

Hartley, Harry J. "PPBS: The Emergence of a Systemic Concept for Public
    Governance," *General Systems.* Volume 21 (1968), pp. 149–155.
Hartley, Harry J. *Educational Planning-Programming-Budgeting: A Systems
    Approach.* Englewood Cliffs: Prentice-Hall, Inc., 1968.
Hayes, Frederick O'R. *PPBS in New York.* September 19, 1967.
Heise, George A., and George A. Miller. "Problem Solving by Small Groups
    Using Various Communication Nets," *Journal of Abnormal and Social
    Psychology.* Volume 46 (1951).
Heller, Walter W. *New Dimensions of Political Economy.* Cambridge, Mass.:
    Harvard University Press, 1966.
Helmer, Olaf. "Social Technology," Rand Paper P-3063. Presented at the
    Futuribles Conference. Paris, France. April, 1965.
Herrmann, Cyril C. "Systems Approach to City Planning," *Harvard Business
    Review.* Volume 44, Number 1 (1966).
Hitch, Charles J. "An Appreciation of Systems Analysis," *Journal of the Opera-
    tions Research Society.* Volume 4 (November, 1955), pp. 466–481.
Hitch, Charles J., and Roland N. McKean. *The Economics of Defense in the
    Nuclear Age.* Cambridge, Mass.: Harvard University Press, 1963.
Hodnett, Edward. *The Art of Problem Solving.* New York: Harper and Brothers,
    1955.
Hunter, Floyd. *Community Power Structure.* New York: The Free Press, 1963.
Hyneman, Charles S. *Bureaucracy in a Democracy.* New York: Harper and
    Brothers, 1950.
International City Managers Association. *Municipal Finance Administration.*
    Chicago: Institute for Training in Municipal Administration, 1962.
Isard, Walter, and Robert E. Coughlin. *Municipal Costs and Revenues Resulting
    from Community Growth.* Wellesley, Mass.: Chandler-Davis Publishing
    Company, 1957.
Jackson, Jay. "Reference Group Processes in Formal Organization," *Sociometry.*
    Volume 22 (1959), pp. 307–327.
Jackson, Jay. "The Normative Regulation of Authoritative Behavior," *The
    Making of Decisions: Reader in Administrative Behavior.* William J. Gore
    and J. W. Dyson (eds.). New York: The Free Press, 1964, pp. 213–241.
Jacob, Philip E., and James J. Flink. "Values and Their Function in Decision-
    Making," *The American Behavioral Scientist.* Volume 5, Number 9 (May,
    1962).
Jacobson, Eugene, and S. Seashore. "Communication Practices in Complex
    Organizations," *Journal of Social Issues.* Volume 7 (1951), pp. 28–40.
Jakobson, Leo. *A Shoreline Policies Plan: Conceptual Framework.* Madison,
    Wisc.: The University of Wisconsin, 1969.
Jussil, Ingrid. "Planeringmetodik," *Plan.* Volume 20, Number 1 (Stockholm,
    1966).
Kaplan, Abraham. "Some Limitations on Rationality," in *Nomos VII: Rational
    Decision.* Carl J. Friedrich (ed.). New York: Atherton Press, 1964.
Katona, George. *Psychological Analysis of Economic Behavior.* New York:
    McGraw-Hill, 1951.

Kelleher, Grace J. *The Challenge to Systems Analysis: Public Policy and Social Change*. New York: John Wiley and Sons, 1970.

Kepner, Charles, and Benjamin B. Tregoe. *The Rational Manager*. Princeton: Princeton University Press, 1965.

King, Gilbert W. "Information," *Scientific American*. Volume 187 (1952), pp. 132ff.

Kirschen, E. S. *et al. Economic Policy in Our Times: Volume I, General Theory*. New York: Rand McNally and Company, 1964.

Kluckholm, Clyde. "Values and Value-Orientation in Theory of Action," in *Toward a General Theory of Action*. Talcott Parsons and Edward Shils (eds.). Cambridge, Mass.: Harvard University Press, 1951.

Kristensson, Folke. *Manniskor foretage och regioner*. Stockholm: Almquist and Wiksell, 1967.

Landau, Martin. "The Concept of Decision-Making in the 'Field' of Public Administration," in *Concepts and Issues in Administrative Behavior*. Sidney Mailick and Edward H. Van Ness (eds.). Englewood Cliffs: Prentice-Hall, Inc., 1962.

Lasswell, Harold D., and Abraham Kaplan. *Power and Society*. New Haven: Yale University Press, 1950.

Lasswell, Harold D., and Daniel Lerner (eds.). *The Policy Science: Recent Developments in Scope and Method*. Stanford: Stanford University Press, 1951.

Lasswell, Harold D. *The Decision Process: Seven Categories of Functional Analysis*. College Park: Bureau of Governmental Research, University of Maryland, 1956.

Lasswell, Harold. *Politics: Who Gets What, When, How*. Cleveland: World Publishers, 1958.

Latham, Earl. *The Group Basis of Politics*. Ithaca: Cornell University Press, 1952.

Leavitt, Harold H., "Some Effects of Certain Communication Patterns on Group Performance," *Journal of Abnormal and Social Psychology*. Volume 46 (1951).

Lee, James E. "The Role of the Planner in the Present: A Problem in Identification," *Journal of the American Institute of Planners*. Volume 24 (1958).

Leoni, Bruno. "The Meaning of 'Political' in Political Decisions," in *The Making of Decisions*. William J. Gore and J. W. Dyson (eds.). New York: The Free Press, 1964.

Lepawsky, Albert. *Administration: The Art and Science of Organization and Management*. New York: Alfred A. Knopf, 1949.

Lichfield, Nathan. "Cost-Benefit Analysis in City Planning," *Journal of the American Institute of Planners*. Volume 26 (November, 1960), pp. 273–279.

Lindblom, Charles E. "The Science of 'Muddling Through'," *Public Administration Review*. Volume 19 (1959).

Lindblom, Charles E. *The Intelligence of Democracy: Decision Making Through Mutual Adjustment*. New York: The Free Press, 1965.

Litterer, Joseph A. *Organization: Systems, Control and Adaptation*. New York: John Wiley and Sons, 1969.

Long, Norton E. "The Community as an Ecology of Games," *American Journal of Sociology*. Volume 44 (1958), pp. 251–261.

Long, Norton E. *The Polity*. Chicago: Rand McNally and Company, 1962.

Lyden, Fremont J., and Ernest G. Miller (eds.). *Planning Programming Budgeting: A Systems Approach to Management*. Chicago: Markham, 1968.

Lynd, Robert S. *Knowledge for What?* Princeton: Princeton University Press, 1967.

MacIver, R. M. *Social Causation*. Boston: Ginn and Company, 1942.

McDonough, Adrian M. *Information Economics and Management Systems*. New York: McGraw-Hill Book Co., Inc., 1963.

McKean, Roland N. *Efficiency in Government Through Systems Analysis*. New York: John Wiley and Sons, 1958.

McKean, Roland N. *Public Spending*. New York: McGraw-Hill, Inc., 1968.

Mailick, Sidney and Edward H. Van Ness (eds.). *Concepts and Issues in Administrative Behavior*. Englewood Cliffs: Prentice-Hall, Inc., 1962.

Mann, Lawrence D. "Studies in Community Decision-Making," *Journal of the American Institute of Planners*. Volume 30 (February, 1964), pp. 58–65.

March, James G. and Herbert A. Simon. *Organizations*. New York: John Wiley and Sons, 1958.

March, James G. (ed.). *Handbook of Organizations*. Chicago: Rand McNally Company, 1964.

Martin, Roscoe C., Frank Munger, *et al. Decision in Syracuse: Metropolitan Action Study*. Bloomington, Ind.: Indiana University Press, 1961.

Marx, Fritz Morstein. *The Administrative State — An Introduction to Bureaucracy*. Chicago: The University of Chicago Press, 1957.

Maxwell, James. *Financing State and Local Governments*. Washington, D.C.: The Brookings Institute, 1965.

Menzel, H. "Innovation, Integration, and Marginality," *American Sociological Review*. Volume 25 (1960), pp. 704–713.

Merton, Robert K. *Social Theory and Social Structure*. New York: The Free Press of Glencoe, 1957.

Meyerson, Martin, and Edward C. Banfield. *Politics, Planning and the Public Interest*. Glencoe, Ill.: The Free Press, 1955.

Miller, J. G. "Information Input Overload," in *Self-Organizing Systems*. M. C. Yovits, G. T. Jacobi, and G. D. Goldstein (eds.). Washington, D.C.: Spartan Books, 1962.

Moore, Wilbert E. *Industrial Relations and the Social Order*. New York: Cornell University Press, 1951.

Mosher, Frederick C. *Program Budgeting*. Chicago: Public Administration Service, 1954.

Mulder, Mark. "Communication Structure, Decision Structure, and Group Performance," *Sociometry*. Volume 23 (March, 1960), pp. 1–14.

Munger, Frank, and Douglas Price (eds.). *Readings in Political Parties and Pressure Groups*. New York: Thomas Y. Crowell Company, 1964.

Musgrove, Richard. *The Theory of Public Finance*. New York: McGraw-Hill Book Company, 1959.

New York Bureau of Municipal Research. "Some Results and Limitations of Central Financial Control in New York City," *Municipal Research*. Volume 81 (1917).

State of New York. *Guidelines for Integrated Planning Programming Budgeting*. Albany: State of New York, 1966.

Novick, David. "Origin and History of Program Budgeting," Short Course on P.P.B.S., August, 1966.

Novick, David (ed.). *Program Budgeting: Program Analysis and the Federal Budget*. Cambridge, Mass.: Harvard University Press, 1967.

Optner, Stanford L. *Systems Analysis for Business Management*. Englewood Cliffs: Prentice-Hall, Inc., 1960.

Overly, Don H. "Decision-Making in City Government," *Urban Affairs Quarterly* Volume 3, Number 2 (December, 1967).

Page, David A. "The Federal PPBS," *Journal of the American Institute of Planners*. Volume 33 (July, 1967).

Parsons, Talcott, and Edward T. Shils, *Toward a General Theory of Action*. Cambridge: Harvard University Press, 1952.

Peabody, Robert L. "Perception of Organizational Authority: A Comparative Analysis," *Administrative Science Quarterly*. Volume 6 (1962).

Peabody, Robert L. and Francis E. Rourke. "Public Bureaucracies," in *Handbook of Organizations*. James G. March (ed.). Chicago: Rand McNally Company, 1964.

Perrow, Charles. "A Framework for the Comparative Analysis of Organizations," *American Sociological Review*. Volume 32 (1967) pp. 43–54.

Pfiffner, John M., and R. Vance Presthus. *Public Administration*. New York: The Ronald Press Company, 1953.

Pfiffner, John M., and Frank P. Sherwood. *Administrative Organization*. Englewood Cliffs: Prentice-Hall, Inc., 1960.

Phelps, Edmund S. (ed.). *Private Wants and Public Needs*. New York: W. W. Norton and Company, 1965.

Polsby, Nelson. *Community Power and Political Theory*. New Haven: Yale University Press, 1963.

President's Commission on Economy and Efficiency. *The Need for a National Budget*. Washington, D.C.: 1912.

Prest, A. R., and R. Turvey. "Cost-Benefit Analysis: A Survey," *The Economic Journal*. Volume 75 (December, 1965).

Presthus, Robert V. "Authority in Organizations," in *Concepts and Issues in Administrative Behavior*. Sidney Mailick and Edward Van Ness (eds.). Englewood Cliffs: Prentice-Hall, Inc., 1962.

Quade, E. C. (ed.). *Analysis for Military Decisions*. Chicago: Rand McNally Co., 1964.

Rabinovitz, Francine F., and J. Stanley Pottinger. "Organization for Local Planning: The Attitudes of Directors," *Journal of the American Institute of Planners*. Volume 33 (January, 1967), pp. 27–32.

Rabinovitz, Francine F. "Politics, Personality, and Planning," *Public Administrative Review*. Volume 27 (March, 1967).

Ramo, Simon. *Cure for Chaos*. New York: David McKay Co., 1969.

Rapoport, Anatol. "Information Theory," *ETC: A Review of General Semantics*. Volume 10 (Summer, 1953), pp. 241–320.

Reissman, Leonard. "A Study of Role Conceptions in Bureaucracy," *Social Forces*. Volume 27 (1949), pp. 305–310.

Roethlisberger, F. J., and W. J. Dickson. *Management and the Worker*. Cambridge, Mass.: Harvard University Press, 1939.

Rossi, Peter H. "Community Decision-Making," *Administrative Science Quarterly*. Volume 1 (March, 1957), pp. 415–443.

Rothenberg, Jerome. *The Measurement of Social Welfare*. Englewood Cliffs: Prentice-Hall, Inc., 1961.

Rothwell, C. Easton. In *The Policy Sciencies – Recent Developments in Scope and Method*. Daniel Lerner and Harold D. Lasswell (eds.). Stanford: The Stanford University Press, 1951.

Rudwick, Bernard H. *Systems Analysis for Effective Planning*. New York: John Wiley & Sons, 1969.

Ruesch, Jurgen, and Bateson, Gregory. *Communication: The Social Matrix of Psychiatry*. New York: W. W. Norton Company, 1951.

Ruesch, Jurgen, and W. Kees. *Nonverbal Communication: Notes on the Visual Perception of Human Relations*. Berkeley: University of California Press, 1956.

Sacks, Seymour, and William F. Hellmuth, Jr. *Financing Government in a Metropolitan Area*. New York: Free Press of Glencoe, 1961.

Sayre, Wallace S. "Trends of a Decade in Administration," *Public Administration Review*. Volume 11 (Winter 1951).

Sayre, Wallace S. "Premises of Public Administration," *Public Administration Review*. Volume 17 (Spring 1958), pp. 102–105.

Sayre, Wallace S., and Herbert Kaufman. *Governing New York City*. New York: Russell Sage Foundation, 1960.

Schaller, Howard G. (ed.). *Public Expenditure Decisions in the Urban Community*. Washington, D.C.: Committee on Urban Economics of Resources for the Future, Inc., 1962.

Schelling, Thomas. *The Strategy of Conflict*. Cambridge, Mass.: Harvard University Press, 1960.

Schick, Allen. "The Road to PPS: The Stages of Budget Reform," in *Planning, Programming Budgeting: A Systems Approach to Management*. Chicago: Markham Publishing Company, 1968.

Schultze, Charles L. *The Politics and Economics of Public Spending*. Washington, D.C.: The Brookings Institute, 1968.

Shackle, George L. S. *Expectations in Economics*. Cambridge, England: Cambridge University Press, 1952.

Shannon, Claude E. "A Mathematical Theory of Communication," *Bell System Technical Journal*. Volume 27 (July, 1948), pp. 623–656.

Shannon, Claude, and Warren Weaver. *The Mathematical Theory of Communication*. Urbana: University of Illinois Press, 1949.

Shelly, M. W., and J. C. Gilcrest. "Some Effects of Communication Requirements in Group Structures," *Journal of Social Psychology*. Volume 48 (1958).

Simpson, Richard L. "Vertical and Horizontal Communication in Formal Organizations," *Administrative Science Quarterly*. Volume 4 (1959).

Simon, Herbert A. *Administrative Behavior: A Study of Decision-Making in Administrative Organization*. New York: The Free Press, 1957.

Simon, Herbert A. "A Behavioral Model of Rational Choice," *Quarterly Journal of Economics*. Volume 49 (February, 1955).

Simon, Herbert A. "Authority," in *Research in Industrial Human Relations*. C. Arensberg, *et al.* (eds.). New York: Harper and Brothers, 1957.

Simon, Herbert A. *Models of Man*. New York: John Wiley & Sons, 1957.

Simon, Herbert A. "Theories of Decision-Making in Economics and Behavioral Science," *American Economic Review*. Volume 49, Number 2 (June, 1959), pp. 253–283.

Smithies, Arthur. *The Budgetary Process in the United States*. New York: McGraw-Hill Book Company, 1955.

Snyder, Richard, H. W. Bruck, and Burton Sapin. *Decision-Making*. Princeton: Princeton University Press, 1954.

Steiss, Alan Walter. "The State Planning Process – A Framework for Policy Decisions," *State Government*. Volume 39 (Fall, 1966).

Steiss, Alan Walter. *A Framework for Planning in State Government*. Chicago: The Council of State Government, 1968.

Stene, Edwin O. "An Approach to a Science of Administration," *American Political Science Review*. Volume 34 (December, 1940).

Tannenbaum, Robert. "Managerial Decision-Making," *The Journal of Business*. Volume 23 (January, 1950), pp. 22–39.

Teitz, Michael B. "Cost Effectiveness: A Systems Approach to the Analysis of Urban Services," *Journal of the American Institute of Planners*. Volume 24, Number 5 (September, 1968).

Thompson, Victor A. *Modern Organizations*. New York: Alfred A. Knopf, 1963.

Thompson, Victor A. "Bureaucracy and Innovation," *Administrative Science Quarterly*. Volume 7 (June, 1965).

Truman, David B. *The Governmental Process*. New York: Alfred A. Knopf, 1953.

U. S. Commission on Organization of the Executive Branch of Government. *Budgeting and Accounting*. Washington, D.C.: Government Printing Office, 1949.

U. S. Congress, Senate Committee on Labor and Public Welfare. Subcommittee on Employment, Manpower, and Poverty. *Systems Technology Applied to Social and Community Problems*. Washington, D.C.: Government Printing Office, 1969.

Verba, Sidney. *Small Groups and Political Behavior*. Princeton: Princeton University Press, 1961.

Von Bertalanffy, Ludwig. *General System Theory*. New York: George Braziller, Inc., 1968.

Waldo, Dwight. *Study of Public Administration*. Doubleday Short Studies in Political Science No. 11. Garden City: Doubleday and Company, 1955.

Walker, Robert A. *The Planning Function in Urban Government*. Chicago: The University of Chicago Press, 1941.

Washington Operations Research Council. *Cost-Effectiveness Analysis: New Approaches in Decision-Making*. New York: Frederick A. Praeger, 1969.

Weber, Max. *From Max Weber: Essays in Sociology*. H. H. Gerth and C. Wright Mills (eds.). New York: The Free Press, 1958.

Wheaton, William L. C. "Public and Private Agents of Change in Urban Development," in *Urban Expansion: Problems and Needs*. Washington, D.C.: Housing and Home Finance Agency, 1963.

Wildavsky, Aaron. *The Politics of the Budgetary Process*. Boston: The Little, Brown Company, 1964.

Wiener, Norbert. *Cybernetics: Or Control and Communication in the Animal and Machine*. New York: John Wiley & Sons, 1948.

Willoughby, William F. "Allotment of Funds by Executive Officials, An Essential Feature of Any Correct Budgetary System," *Proceedings of the American Political Science Association*. Baltimore, 1913.

Willoughby, W. F. *Principles of Public Administration*. Washington, D.C.: The Brookings Institute, 1927.

Supplemental Bibliography

Barnaill, Allison J., Francis J. Bridges, and Kenneth W. Olm. *Management Decisions and Organizational Policy*. Boston: Allyn and Bacon, Inc., 1971.

Bass, Bernard M., and Samuel D. Deep. *Current Perspectives for Managing Organizations*. Englewood Cliffs: Prentice-Hall, Inc., 1970.

Beckett, John A. *The Management Dynamics: The New Synthesis*. New York: McGraw-Hill Book Company, 1971.

Beckhard, Richard. *Organization Development: Strategies and Models*. Reading, Mass.: Addison-Wesley Publishing Company, 1969.

Black, Guy. *The Application of Systems Analysis to Government Operations*. New York: Frederick A. Praeger, Inc., 1968.

Blake, Robert, and Jane Mouton. *Building a Dynamic Corporation Through Grid Organization Development*. Reading, Mass.: Addison-Wesley Publishing Company, 1969.

Clark, Terry N. (ed.). *Community Structure and Decision-Making*. San Francisco: Chandler Publishing Company, 1968.

Crecine, John P. (ed.). *Financing the Metropolis: Public Policy in Urban Economics*. Beverly Hills, Calif.: Sage Publications, Inc., 1970.

Dalton, Gene W. *Organization Structure and Design*. Georgetown, Ontario: The Dorsey Press, 1970.

Drucker, Peter F. *The Age of Discontinuity*. New York: Harper and Row, 1969.

Emery, James C. *Organizational Planning and Control Systems*. London: Collier-Macmillan Ltd., 1969.

Ewing, David W. *The Human Side of Planning*. New York: The Macmillan Company, 1969.

Freeman, Howard E., and Clarence C. Sherwood. *Social Research and Social Policy*. Englewood Cliffs: Prentice-Hall, Inc., 1970.

Hampton, David, Charles Summer, and Ross Webber. *Organization Behavior and the Practice of Management*. Glenview, Ill.: Scott, Foresman, and Company, 1968.

Haney, William V. *Communication and Organizational Behavior*. Homewood, Ill.: Richard D. Irwin, Inc., 1967.

Hovey, Harold A. *The Planning-Programming-Budgeting Approach to Government Decision-Making*. New York: Frederick A. Praeger, Inc., 1968.

Kahn, Alfred J. *Theory and Practice of Social Planning*. New York: Russell Sage Foundation, 1969.

Kahn, R. L., and E. Kenneth Boulding (eds.). *Power and Conflict in Organizations*. New York: Basic Books, 1964.

Lawrence, P. R., and J. W. Lorsch. *Organization and Environment*. Boston: Harvard Business School, 1967.

LaBreton, Preston P. *Administrative Intelligence—Information Systems*. Boston: Houghton-Mifflin Company, 1969.

Margolis, Julius (ed.). *The Public Economy of Urban Communities*. Washington, D.C.: Resources for the Future, Inc., 1965.

Michael, Donald N. *The Unprepared Society*. New York: Basic Books, Inc., 1968.

Ranney, David C. *Self Defeating Planning: A Critique of City Planning and Some Proposals for Change*. The Institute of Urban and Regional Research, Working Paper Series 7. Iowa City: The University of Iowa, 1971.

Schick, Allen. *Budget Innovation in the States*. Washington, D.C.: The Brookings Institute, 1971.

Seiler, John A. *Systems Analysis in Organizational Behavior*. Homewood, Ill.: Richard D. Irwin, Inc., 1967.

Sereno, Kenneth K., and C. David Mortensen. *Foundations of Communication Theory*. New York: Harper and Row, 1970

Silverman, David. *The Theory of Organization*. London: Heinmenn Educational Books, Ltd., 1970.

Thayer, Lee O. *Communication and Communication Systems*. Homewood, Ill.: Richard D. Irwin, Inc., 1968.

Torgerson, Paul. *A Concept of Organization*. New York: American Book-Van Nostrand-Reinhold, 1969.

Young, Oran R. *Systems of Political Science*. Englewood Cliffs: Prentice-Hall, Inc., 1968.

Zwick, Charles J. *Systems Analysis and Urban Planning*. Chicago: The Rand Corporation, 1963.

Index

Adaptive decisions, 40–41, 122, 125–126, 128–129, 134
Adaptive planning, 38
A fortiori analysis, 137–138
Analysis
    ambiguity in, 17–18
    defined, 10
    processes of, 13–16
    zero analysis, 17
Appropriation measures, 199
Authority
    Barnard's "bottom-up" model, 74–75
    and communication, 78–79, 91, 96, 99
    and decision-making, 65–66, 76–78
    dyadic formulations of, 84–88
    and influence, 101
    and information access, 79
    legal authority, 71
    polycentralized, 82–84
    and power, 76, 85–86
    structure- versus function-based, 73–74, 78, 82, 159
    and technical competence, 78, 84, 87–88
    and values, 53
    Weberian model, 70–73

Beta distribution, 274–277
Boundary conditions, 130–131, 140, 257
Budgeting
    and accounting, 175
    and appropriations, 151
    budget calendars, 177–180
    budget message, 196–197
    budget presentation, 194–198
    cycles in, 180–182
    defined, 147–148
    expenditure requirements, 173–174, 182, 186–187
    fiscal and management controls, 150–151, 200
    functional accounts in, 150–151
    limitations of, 172–173
    long-range financial plans, 191–193
    management orientation to, 151–153
    performance budgeting, 152–153
    and planning, 148–149
    political budgeting techniques, 295–296
    program budgeting, 154–157
    and programming, 158
    and public policy, 292
    objectives of, 147
    objects of expenditures in, 150–151
    output-orientation, 159, 165, 228–229
    resource requirements in, 190
    and revenue analysis, 173–174, 193–194
    and service standards, 182–184
Bureaucracy, 71–72, 80–82
Bureau of Municipal Research, 151

Capital improvements programming, 148, 173, 175, 180, 191–193
Communications
    barriers to, 104–106
    and budgeting, 148
    feedback in, 111
    programmed and nonprogrammed, 116–118
    queuing of, 108
    storage of, 109
    sensory mechanisms for, 115, 124
    and technical jargon, 107–108
    timing, 104–105
Communication systems
    access to, 78
    basic functions of, 92–93
    and decision clusters, 114
    informal, 96–97
    types of communication flows, 99–101
    types of communication networks, 95–99
Community control systems, 59–60
Community decisions, 58–59
Concept of marginal operations, 297–298
Contingency analysis, 136–137
Control, 2, 9, 83, 148, 151, 200, 282–282, 286
Cost-benefit analysis, 138, 155, 238, 243–244
Cost-effectiveness analysis, 11, 15, 155, 162, 228ff, 241–242, 248–250
    attributes of, 228–231
    and cost-constraint analysis, 242
    and cost-goal analysis, 239–241
    life cycle costs in, 230
    and total systems costs, 231, 244–247
Cost-utility analysis, 163–165
CPM (Critical Path Method), 149, 163–164, 259ff
    and network analysis, 260
    versus PERT, 271

Decisions
    adaptive and innovative, 39–42
    and authority, 76–78
    versus choice, 24
    criteria for selection, 26–27
    individual versus group, 31–34

347

About the Author

Alan Walter Steiss is Assistant Dean of the College of Architecture, Virginia Polytechnic Institute and State University, and Chairman of the Division of Environmental and Urban Systems. A graduate of Bucknell University (A.B. in Psychology and Sociology) and the University of Wisconsin (M.A. and Ph.D. in Urban and Regional Planning), Dr. Steiss has taught at Rider College, New York University, the University of Wisconsin, and the Georgia Institute of Technology. Formerly the head of statewide planning for the State of New Jersey, he has served as a consultant to the states of Wisconsin, New Jersey, Maryland, Virginia, and South Carolina, and the Trust Territory of the Pacific. Dr. Steiss is author of several books (including *Planning Administration; A Framework for Planning in State Government*; *Systemic Planning: Theory and Application* (with Anthony J. Catanese); and *A Public Service Option for Architectural Curricula*) and a contributor to numerous professional journals in the United States and abroad.